THE ILLUSTRATED ENCYCLOPEDIA OF
ANIMALS
BIRDS & FISH
OF NORTH AMERICA

THE ILLUSTRATED ENCYCLOPEDIA OF
ANIMALS
BIRDS & FISH
OF NORTH AMERICA

A NATURAL HISTORY AND IDENTIFICATION GUIDE WITH MORE THAN 420
NATIVE SPECIES FROM THE UNITED STATES OF AMERICA AND CANADA

TOM JACKSON, DAVID ALDERTON,
AMY-JANE BEER, DEREK HALL, AND DANIEL GILPIN

LORENZ BOOKS

This edition is published by Lorenz Books
an imprint of Anness Publishing Ltd
Blaby Road, Wigston
Leicestershire, LE18 4SE
info@anness.com

www.lorenzbooks.com
www.annesspublishing.com

If you like the images in this book and
would like to investigate using them
for publishing, promotions or
advertising, please visit our website
www.practicalpictures.com for more
information.

Publisher: Joanna Lorenz
Editorial Director: Helen Sudell
Project Editor: Melanie Hibbert
Proofreading Manager: Lindsay Zamponi
Desk Editor: Barbara Toft
Production Controller: Wendy Lawson
Book and Jacket Design: Nigel Partridge
Artists: Mike Atkinson, Peter Barret,
Penny Brown, Peter Bull, Vanessa Card,
Jim Channell, Felicity Rose Cole, Julius
Csotonyi, Anthony Duke, John Francis,
Stuart Jackson-Carter, Paul Jones, Martin
Knowelden, Jonathan Latimer, Stephen
Lings, Richard Orr, Denys Ovenden,
Andrew Robinson, Mike Saunders,
Sarah Smith and Studio Galante.

ETHICAL TRADING POLICY
Because of our ongoing ecological
investment programme, you, as our
customer, can have the pleasure and
reassurance of knowing that a tree is being
cultivated on your behalf to naturally
replace the materials used to make the
book you are holding. For further
information about this scheme, go to
ww.annesspublishing.com/trees

© Anness Publishing Ltd 2011

A CIP catalogue record for this book is
available from the British Library.

Previously published as part of four
separate volumes:
*The Illustrated Encyclopedia of Animals of
America*, by Tom Jackson
*The Illustrated Encyclopedia of Birds of
America*, by David Alderton
*The Illustrated World Encyclopedia of
Marine Fish & Sea Creatures*, by
Amy-Jane Beer and Derek Hall
*The Illustrated World Encyclopedia of
Freshwater Fish & River Creatures*,
by David Gilpin

PUBLISHER'S NOTE
Although the information in this book is
believed to be accurate and true at the
time of going to press, neither the authors
nor the publisher can accept any legal
responsibility or liability for any errors
or omissions that may be made.

CONTENTS

INTRODUCTION

The vast continent of North America spans from Mexico in the south, all the way up to the desolate ice fields of the Arctic region, and the geographical range of this continent is reflected in the diversity of its wildlife. Animal evolution, physical characteristics and behavior are partly dictated by the environment in which they live. This book examines the amphibians, reptiles, fish, birds, and mammals that inhabit North America and highlights the extraordinary array of shapes, sizes, and colors in which they appear. Human movement, invasion, and settlement have introduced new species, and threatened or wiped out others.

American wildlife

A huge number of different animals make their home in North America, because of the continent's wide range of habitats, including the icy tundra, oceans, freshwater lakes and rivers, grasslands and prairies, and the barren deserts of Arizona. North America is also inhabited by many of the world's record-breaking animals. The world's largest deer, the moose, is a common resident of the coniferous forests of Canada and the northern United States, and the largest land carnivore, the Kodiak bear, is found on Alaska's Kodiak Island.

Below: The rainbow trout is a native of North America, where it is found in freshwater lakes, rivers, and streams. In some areas, it is migratory, spending part of its adult life at sea, where it loses its pinky-red stripe and becomes silvery in color. This popular game and food fish has been introduced to other parts of the world, including Great Britain.

Above: The national bird of North America, the bald eagle is the only bird that is unique to the continent. Bald eagles are found throughout the area from Alaska and Canada to northern Mexico, with about half of the world's bald eagle population living in Alaska.

The diversity of life is overwhelming. A blue whale can reach lengths of up to 100ft (30m), with weights of up to 352,000lb (160 tonnes), while the smallest salamander is less than 1.25in (3cm) long. The rest appear in every shape and size in between. In North America, noteworthy animals include the emblematic bald eagle, the brown bear, which lives alone but occasionally gathers together in groups to catch schools of salmon beneath waterfalls, and the American alligator, which inhabits freshwater swamps and rivers, and travels long distances to find food, sometimes finding shelter in swimming pools along the way.

About this book

This encyclopedia examines North America's mammals, amphibians, reptiles, birds, and fish, and aims to help you identify and understand the creatures you may see in your garden, the countryside, or even the city streets.

The book opens with the question, "What is an animal?" It identifies the different kingdoms and explains how animal bodies are organized. This is folllowed by a discussion of the principal environments, or "biomes," in which wildlife lives—oceans, fresh water, forests, grasslands, deserts, polar regions, and mountains—and how animals survive.

Above: The American bison, a member of the wild cattle family, was once very common across the grasslands and among the woodlands of North America. Following indiscriminate hunting to clear the prairies for domestic cattle, the bison was pushed to the brink of extinction. It has now recovered thanks to conservation programs.

Above: The American black bear is smaller than the brown and polar bears that also live in North America. This species is found farther south than the other two bears, and unlike them, American black bears can climb trees. Zoologists think that they evolved to do this to avoid being attacked by hungry brown bears.

This volume is divided into three major parts: animals, birds, and freshwater and marine life. Each of these sections begins with a clear overview about biology, behavior, senses and other vital information to help readers understand North American animal life, and the importance of wildlife and habitat conservation. The "Understanding mammals, amphibians, and reptiles" section provides facts about migration, hibernation, and endangered species. "Understanding birds" discusses flight, survival, mating, nesting, and migration, while "Understanding fish" looks at movement, feeding, reproduction, and environments, as well as freshwater and marine conservation issues.

Following these informative chapters, each section then contains a directory. These directories explore in detail the many animals, birds, and fish that populate the varied habitats of North America. Animals are presented in related groups, focusing in turn on mammals, amphibians, and reptiles: there are hoofed animals, cats, dogs, bears, small carnivores, rabbits, raccoons, rodents, armadillos, marsupials, insectivores, bats, salamanders, frogs and toads, turtles and terrapins, lizards, crocodilians, snakes, and dolphins and porpoises. Birds and aquatic wildlife are grouped according to their favored habitats, which are diverse and include: woodland, urban and backyard,

coastal, seashore, estuarine, lakes, shallow seas, open ocean, deep waters, as well as coral reefs.

Each of the directory sections feature at-a-glance fact boxes containing distribution maps and summarized information about an animal's habitat, food, size, maturity, breeding, and lifespan.

Below: Amphibians were the first vertebrate land animals, and have kept their close links to water, where their ancestors originated. Therefore, amphibians such as this bullfrog most commonly inhabit damp places, such as ponds, where they can easily keep their bodies moist.

WHAT IS AN ANIMAL?

More than two million animal species have been described by scientists, and there are probably millions more waiting to be discovered. They live in all corners of the world, and come in a huge array of shapes and sizes. The largest weighs over a hundred tons, and the smallest is just a fraction of an inch long.

The living world is divided into five kingdoms: animals, plants, fungi, protists, and monerans, which include bacteria. The protists and monerans are single-celled microorganisms. Although they do form large masses—for example, yogurt is actually a colony of bacteria—microorganisms do not form bodies. Plants, fungi, and animals do have bodies, which consist of millions of cells. These three types of macroorganism tackle the problems of life in different ways.

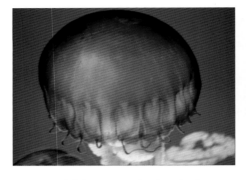

Above: Jellyfish are very simple animals related to corals and sea anemones. They catch food by spearing prey with tiny cells called nematocysts.

Above: Snails belong to a large group of invertebrates called mollusks. Most live in water, but many, such as this giant land snail, survive on land.

The plant kingdom

Plants are the basis of life on Earth and without them, animals could not exist. This is because plants alone can get the energy they need from sunlight. The green pigments in the plants' leaves trap the energy found in light to convert carbon dioxide and water into glucose, a simple sugar, in a process of food production called photosynthesis.

Below: Anemones are members of the group of cnidarians, like jellyfish. Starfish belong to the group of echinoderms.

Above: Crabs, such as this hermit crab, are crustaceans. Other crustaceans include lobsters, shrimp, and krill. Their forelegs are armed with strong pincers.

Above: Spiders, scorpions, and mites are arachnids. Many spiders build a sticky silk web to trap prey; others lie hidden and pounce on passing victims.

The fungi kingdom

Largely invisible organisms, fungi live in large masses of tiny fibers that run through the soil. They only pop up above the surface in the form of mushrooms and toadstools when they are ready to reproduce. Fungi do not photosynthesize, but they are valuable as decomposers. They grow over the dead bodies of other organisms, such as rotting logs, secreting digestive enzymes that break down the dead organism from the outside.

The animal kingdom

Animals, on the other hand, could not be more different from plants and fungi. They are active feeders (called heterotrophs or 'other-eaters'), which

collect food from their surroundings. Unlike plants and fungi, animals have bodies that can swim, walk, burrow, or fly during at least the early part of their lives.

Body organization

With the exception of primitive forms, such as sponges, all animal bodies are organized along the same lines. They process their food in a gut, a tube that passes through the body. In most cases, the food enters the gut through an opening in the head, that is, the mouth. Once inside the body, the food is broken down into its constituent parts. The useful parts, such as proteins, fats, and sugars—made by plants during photosynthesis—are absorbed into the body. The leftover waste material passes out of the gut through the anus, a hole at the other end of the body.

The useful substances absorbed from the food then need to be transported around the body to where they are needed. This job is done by the animal's circulatory system. The insides of many animals are simply bathed in a liquid containing everything required by the body. However, larger animals, including reptiles, amphibians, and mammals, need to pump the useful substances around the body in the blood via the heart.

The blood carries food for the body as well as oxygen, which reacts with the sugar from the food, releasing the energy that is essential for all living things to survive. Animals get their oxygen in a number of ways. Some simply absorb it through their skin, many that live in water extract it using gills, and those that live in air breathe it into their lungs.

Left: Apart from bats, birds, such as this bee-eater, are the only flying vertebrates. Their forelimbs have evolved into wings that allow them to perform amazing feats of flight. Feathers are better than hair for keeping the body streamlined for flight.

Compared with other organisms, animals are more aware of and responsive to their surroundings. This is because they have a nervous system that uses sensors to detect external changes, such as in temperature, sound, or light, and transmit the information, via nerves, to the brain. Mammals, reptiles, and amphibians share a similar body plan, having four limbs. Almost all possess a visible tail. The brain and most of the sensors are positioned at the front of the body in the head. The vital organs, such as the heart and lungs (or gills), are located in the central thorax (chest area), while the gut and sex organs are found mainly in the abdomen at the rear of the body.

Above: Fish live in all corners of the world's oceans. They also live in fresh water, where they are found everywhere from submerged caves to mountain lakes.

Above: Frogs are the most familiar of the amphibians. Others include salamanders and newts. This frog spends its life in trees, using suckers on its feet to cling to the branches.

Above: While a few other lizards can alter the shade of their scales slightly, chameleons can change color completely. This may help them hide from predators or it may reflect their mood.

Above: Mammals, such as this ground squirrel, are the most widespread of vertebrates. Mamma can survive in just about any habitat on Earth.

NORTH AMERICAN HABITATS

The Earth is not a uniform place, but has a complex patchwork of habitats covering its surface from the equator to the poles. Biologists have simplified this patchwork by dividing it into zones called biomes, each of which has a particular climate and a distinct community of animals.

The places where animal communities live can be radically different. Thus, for example, vipers slither along sand dunes in the Mojave Desert and sperm whales live in the ice-cold depths of the ocean. The environmental conditions determine what kind of animals and plants are able to survive there.

The world's habitats are generally divided into 11 biomes: oceans, freshwater rivers or wetlands, tropical forests, temperate forests, boreal forests, tropical grasslands or savannahs, temperate grasslands, tundra, polar ice caps, deserts, and mountains.

The overriding factor that determines whether a piece of land belongs to a particular biome is its climate. Understanding the climate of a place is complicated, because the factors involved—such as temperature, rainfall, and light levels—vary from day to night and all year round. Generally speaking, the regions close to the equator are hot, the coldest places on Earth are the poles, and the territory in between usually cools as you travel to higher latitudes. Other geographical factors—ocean currents, mountains, and depressions in the Earth's surface—also influence climate and biomes.

This section groups the main habitats into the following categories: oceans and fresh water, forests, grasslands, deserts, polar regions, and mountains.

Left: A towering saguaro in Superstition Wilderness, Arizona.

OCEANS AND FRESH WATER

North America is bounded by the Arctic Ocean to the north, the Pacific Ocean to the west, and the Atlantic to the east. These vast waters contain the world's smallest and largest animals. The Great Lakes of North America contain about 84 percent of the country's surface freshwater and a wonderful array of wildlife.

Oceans

The oceans surrounding North America are not a simple biome, because they consist of countless habitats, including everything from colorful coral reefs to mysterious, deep-sea hydrothermal vents.

The depth of the ocean obviously has a marked effect on the conditions. Depth can range from just an inch or so to as much as 6.75 miles (11km). The first 330ft (100m) or so below the surface is called the photic zone, where the water is bathed in sunlight during the day and plant life flourishes. Many ocean animals graze on plants, and so must live in the photic zone. Deeper down, conditions are too dark for plants, but most deep-sea animals get their energy from them indirectly by feeding on marine "snow." This consists of the waste products and dead bodies of the organisms higher up.

These food chains provide the basis of animal life in the ocean, feeding many types of larger vertebrate animals including fish, turtles, and sea mammals.

Fresh water

All the rivers in the world combined contain just a fraction of the Earth's water, though some of them form huge freshwater systems. The Great Lakes of North America form the largest freshwater surface in the world. They all connect with the St. Lawrence River which flows into the Atlantic Ocean.

Freshwater rivers, lakes and wetlands are, in fact, some of the best places in the world to see wildlife, as they teem, with animal and plant life.

While sea water is saltier than the body fluids of animals, fresh water is less salty, which means that water tends to flow into the animal from outside. If the animal does not frequently get rid of some moisture, it will become swollen, and its body fluids will be too diluted to work efficiently.

Freshwater fish and amphibians tackle this problem by excreting all their excess water. Semi-aquatic animals, such as otters and anacondas, rely on their skin to act as a barrier to the influx of water.

FORESTS

Before the rise of agriculture, forests covered most of North America. Today, however, almost all of these wild woodlands have been replaced by meadows and farmland. After tropical forests, temperate forests contain the greatest diversity of animal life.

Temperate Forests

These forests grow in mild regions that receive a lot of rain but do not get too hot or cold. The largest temperate forests are in the Northern Hemisphere, in a belt north of subtropical regions.

Most temperate trees are deciduous. They lose their leaves to save energy during the winter. Because it is rarely very bright over the winter, the leaves would not be able to photosynthesize food from sunlight. As fall progresses, the leaves' valuable green pigments, which trap the sun's energy, withdraw back into the tree and the less important red and brown pigments are revealed, giving the forest its beautiful fall colors.

These forests contain many places for animals to thrive. Tree-dwellers collect seeds and fruit, and snatch insects to eat. On the ground, the forests are populated by larger animals, such as deer, that may migrate to warmer climes in winter. Smaller animals, such as ground squirrels, hibernate to save energy until the spring.

Boreal Forests

Also known as taiga, boreal forests are found in the icy conditions of the far north. This biome is dominated by conifers, which are almost the only trees that can survive the harsh conditions. Boreal forests form the largest swathes of continuous forest and cover about ten percent of the Earth's land. They grow in huge swathes in Canada and Alaska, where the summers are short and the winters are long and cold, with temperatures as low as –13°F (–25°C).

Even the summer is too cold for most cold-blooded animals, such as amphibians and reptiles. Mammals such as marmots and bears, as well as rattlesnakes, hibernate or become inactive during the coldest months. Incredibly, wood frogs endure the winter while frozen inside river ice, becoming active again after the thaw.

Because their growth is so slow, boreal forests are relatively free of animals compared to other forests, but many of the animal inhabitants are much larger than their southern relatives.

GRASSLANDS

The temperate grasslands of North America are called prairies, or plains. The Great Plains of North America span 2,000 miles (3,200 km) north to south and were once home to herds of bison. True grasslands, from prairies to the savannah, have very few trees but contain many creatures.

Grasslands appear in areas where there is some rain, but not enough to support the growth of large numbers of trees. They come in many forms, growing in both tropical and more temperate regions. North America's largest temperate grasslands tend to be located in so-called rain shadows. For example, the North American prairies are in the rain shadow of the Rocky Mountains. A rain shadow is an area that rarely gets rain because the wind bringing it must first travel over mountains. As the wind rises up, it cools and releases the rainwater on the windward side. The wind then whistles down the leeward side, carrying much less water. If the wind is very dry, then that area becomes a desert. However, the wind often carries enough moisture to let grasses grow.

The main plant food in grasslands is, of course, grass. Grass is an unusual type of plant because its growing points are near to the ground rather than at the tip of the stem, as with most other plants. This means that it can keep growing despite having its juicy blades eaten by grazing animals.

Grazing animals are commonly found in grasslands, as are the browsers that pick the leaves and fruit from small shrubs that often grow in the area. With few places to hide in the wide-open spaces, grazing animals group together into herds for safety. Fortunately, grass and other plant foods are virtually omnipresent, which means that members of these herds only need to compete when it comes to choosing a mate. This has led them, especially the males, to evolve elaborate weapons and display structures, such as horns or tusks.

Without trees to hide in, smaller animals, such as ground squirrels and marmots, take refuge under the ground in burrow complexes. Many, such as moles and mole rats, have adapted to a totally subterranean lifestyle.

A large number of the world's temperate grasslands have been transformed into farmland for growing cereal crops and raising livestock. Cereals, such as wheat and rye, are actually domestic breeds of grass that would naturally grow in these regions anyway.

Most of the animals once found on grasslands have suffered because of the rise of agriculture. Prairies formerly contained huge herds of bison, but most were killed off by hunters. Pampas deer were also once common, but were pushed out by cattle and other livestock. Meanwhile, burrowing animals, such as prairie dogs, have been persecuted by cattle ranchers because the holes that they make can injure grazing cattle.

DESERTS

The four major deserts of North America are located to the west. Deserts make up the largest terrestrial biome, covering about one-fifth of the world's dry land. The popular image of a desert is a parched wilderness with no sign of life, but deserts can also be very cold places, and most contain a surprising amount of wildlife.

A desert forms wherever less than 10in (25cm) of rain falls in a year. Areas that get less than about 16in (40cm) of rain per year are semideserts. The largest and hottest desert in the Americas is the Sonoran Desert, which spreads from northern Mexico to Arizona and southern California. The Great Basin Desert around Utah, Nevada, and Idaho is another large American desert. However, although it is dry, this region is also very cold. The driest place in North America is Death Valley in California.

Desert life is tough. The wildlife has to contend with lack of water and also survive extremes of temperature. With little or no cloud cover for most of the year, land temperatures rocket during the day to over 104°F (40°C) but can plunge to near freezing at night. Plants are the basis for all life in this biome, being the food for grazing animals.

Deserts are not completely dry, of course, because rain does eventually arrive. True to the extremes of a desert, rainstorms are so violent that they often cause devastating flash floods that gush down temporary rivers, known as wadis or arroyos. Then, the desert plants bloom and breed for a few short weeks before withering and waiting for the next supply of water.

Many desert animals, such as blind snakes and several types of frog, follow a similar pattern. They only come to the surface during and after the rains, preferring to stay moist underground during the hot and dry parts of the year. Desert frogs prevent themselves from drying out by growing a thin, fluid-filled skin bag around their bodies.

Even the more active desert animals remain hidden during the day, sheltering from the scorching sun among rocks or in burrows. When nightfall comes,

plant-eaters, such as the addax and ass, begin to pick at the dried leaves, fruit, and twigs of scrawny desert plants, as smaller jerboas and ground squirrels collect seeds and insects. Other insect-eaters include geckos and other lizards. Many have wide, webbed feet to help them walk across the loose sand and burrow into it when danger approaches. Larger meat-eaters include vipers, which patrol in search of small rodents, and coyotes, which scavenge for the carcasses of dead animals.

Most of these animals never drink liquid water, getting all the moisture they need from their food. They have to hold on to every last drop, though. In a similar way to how camels store food in their humps, gila monsters and other American lizards store fat in their tails, and many desert rodents build up food stores in their burrows to survive long periods of drought.

POLAR REGIONS

*Despite being freezing cold and largely covered with ice, polar regions can be characterized as deserts.
Although there is solid water almost everywhere, the few plants and animals that do live there often have
great difficulty in obtaining liquid water, just like the wildlife in scorching deserts.*

The polar regions—the Arctic in the north and Antarctic in the south—begin at 66° North and 66° South. These positions on the globe are marked as the Arctic and Antarctic Circles. Within these imaginary circles, something very strange happens on at least one day every summer: the sun does not set. Similarly, for at least a single 24-hour period in the winter, it does not rise. The wildlife of the Arctic is not similar to that around the Antarctic. This is not just because they are at opposite ends of the world, but also because the geography of the two areas is very different. The Antarctic is dominated by Antarctica, a mountainous landmass that is a significantly sized continent, larger than Australia. Meanwhile, the Arctic has the Arctic Ocean—the world's smallest ocean—at its center.

The wildernesses of ice and rock in the Antarctic are the coldest places on Earth, and are too inhospitable for any completely terrestrial animals. Antarctic animals, such as seals, penguins, and whales, rely on the sea for their survival. No reptiles or amphibians survive there, and even warm-blooded animals leave in the winter, with the exception of the hardy emperor penguin.

In the Arctic, seals, whales, and other sea life also thrive, and the lands and islands of the Arctic Ocean provide a home for many animals dependent on land, such as musk ox and reindeer. Animals such as polar bears spend their time on the thick shelves of sea ice that extend from the frozen coastlines for much of the year.

Although Antarctica is almost entirely covered in snow and ice, the ground in lands around the Arctic Circle is mainly ice-free during the summer and so has periods of frenzied growth and breeding. North of the boreal forests it is too cold and dark for trees to grow, and treeless tundra takes over. Plants—mainly tough grass and sedges, mosses, and lichens—must be able to survive long, desolate winters. When the summer—which lasts little more than six weeks—arrives, they must be ready to reproduce.

Although the summer sun thaws the snow and ice, it never heats the soil for more than a few inches below the surface. The deep layer of soil remains frozen and is called permafrost. It forms a solid barrier that prevents the meltwaters from seeping away. The trapped water forms shallow pools and bogs, which are a haven for insects. Billions of insects, which spent the winter underground as inactive pupae, emerge from hiding in the spring. They swarm across the tundra, mating and laying eggs in the water as they race to reproduce before winter arrives again.

MOUNTAINS

The largest mountain ranges in North America, the Rockies and Appalachians, rise out of temperate or boreal biomes. Mountains form an unusual biome because they encapsulate a number of climate zones within a small geographical area. This variation defines the lives of the inhabitants.

A mountainside is like several biomes stacked on top of one another. As the mountain rises out of the surrounding lowlands, the air temperature, wind speed, light levels, water supply, and on the highest peaks, even the amount of oxygen, begin to change. Some animals are highly adapted for mountain life; others have extended their lowland ranges into high altitudes.

The foothills of North American mountain ranges are generally covered in temperate forest or woodland. As the altitude increases, the weather conditions become colder and harsher, and the trees of the temperate forest find it increasingly hard to grow. They eventually become smaller and more gnarled, and then conifer trees take over. Like their relatives in boreal forests, mountain conifers are better at surviving in colder conditions than broad-leaved trees.

Moving further up the mountain, the conditions get worse. Rain that falls on the mountain runs through or over the surface before joining a torrential mountain stream and being carried swiftly down. With all the water sluicing rapidly down the mountain, territory nearer the top has less water for the plants to draw on, and eventually, there is not enough moisture in the soil for trees to grow. The point where conditions become just too tough for even conifer trees to grow is called the treeline or timberline.

Above the timberline, small, hardy alpine plants grow in regions that resemble a cold desert. Alpine plants share features with desert species because they, too, must hang on to any water they can get before it is evaporated by the strong mountain wind. At even higher altitudes, as in the polar regions, plant life eventually

gives way to snow and ice at the snowline. From here upward, very little plant life survives and animals are infrequent visitors, except for the birds of prey soaring on the thermals of warmer air high above the peaks.

North American mountain-dwelling wildlife has adapted well to survive in its rugged environment. For instance, cougars ambush their prey from high vantage points, and shelter in caves and thickets at night. Mountain goats have strong, sturdy legs and hooves to allow them to negotiate steep slopes. Bighorn sheep are excellent climbers and are able to seek refuge in places where predators cannot reach them. Pikas collect piles of grass and leaves, which dry to make alpine hay, and they shelter in areas of scree. Many animals, such as mule deer, spend summer in the mountains and descend to warmer areas during winter.

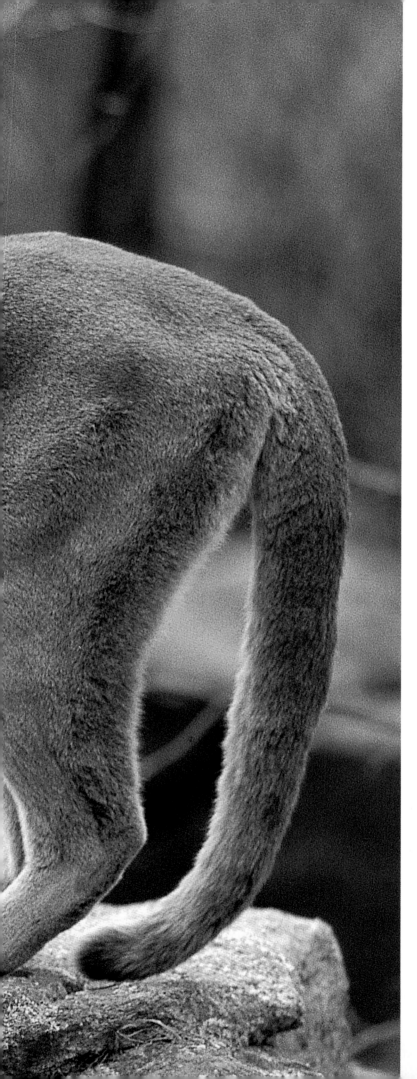

UNDERSTANDING MAMMALS, AMPHIBIANS, AND REPTILES

This book examines mammals, amphibians, and reptiles, but can only scratch the surface of the fantastic range of life forms present on this planet. It concentrates on the vertebrates (the group of animals that have a backbone, which includes the above three groups as well as birds and fish); however, vertebrates form just one of the 31 major animal groups. The huge diversity of life contained in the other groups cannot rival the most familiar vertebrates for size, strength or general popularity. For most people, slugs are not in the same league as tigers, nor can crickets and crabs compete with dolphins and pandas. Yet these relatively unpopular animals are capable of amazing feats. For example, squid travel by jet propulsion, mussels change sex as they get older, and live in harmony in colonies of millions.

Animals can be defined in terms of their body organization, their place in evolution, and their anatomy and key features, and this introductory section about understanding animals examines how they see, hear, smell, and taste; how they find food, how they defend their territories, and how they find mates and care for their offspring. There are also discussions about ecology, migration, and hibernation, as well as introduced and endangered species.

Left: The cougar—also known as the puma, panther, or mountain lion—is the second-largest cat in the Americas, second only to the jaguar. It lives alone, patrolling large territories and hunting mule deer and moose. It is extremely agile, and is able to leap over 16.5ft (5m) into the air. Cougar cubs are able to eat meat at three months old, usually hunting with their mother during their first winter.

EVOLUTION

Animals and other forms of life did not just suddenly appear on the Earth. They evolved over billions of years into countless different forms. The mechanism by which they evolved is called natural selection. The process of natural selection was first proposed by the British naturalist Charles Darwin.

Many biologists estimate that there are approximately 30 million species on Earth, but to date, only two million have been discovered and recorded by scientists. So where are the rest? They live in a staggering array of habitats—from the deep oceans, where sperm whales live, to the deserts of Mexico, inhabited by gila monster lizards. The problems faced by animals in these and other habitats are very different, and so life has evolved in great variety. Each animal needs a body that can cope with its own environment.

Past evidence

At the turn of the 19th century, geologists began to realize that the world was extremely old. They studied animal fossils and measured the age of the exposed layers of rock found in cliffs and canyons. Today, we accept that the Earth is about 4.5 billion years old, but in the early 1800s, the idea that the world was unimaginably old was completely new to most people.

Jumping animals

Most animals can leap into the air, but thanks to natural selection, this simple ability has been harnessed by different animals in different ways. For example, click beetles jump in somersaults to frighten off attackers, while blood-sucking fleas can leap from host to host.

Above: The bobcat is an agile mammal with powerful legs that allow it to leap over 12ft (3.6m) into the air to pounce on its prey, such as hares, birds, and even deer.

In addition, naturalists had always known that there was a fantastic variety of animals, but now they realized that many could be grouped into families, as if they were related. By the middle of the 1800s, two British biologists had independently formulated an idea that would change the way that people saw themselves and the natural world forever. Charles Darwin and Alfred Wallace thought that the world's different animal species had gradually evolved from extinct relatives.

Survival of the fittest

Darwin and Wallace came up with the same idea—natural selection. As breeders had known for generations, animals pass on their characteristics to their young. Darwin and Wallace suggested that wild animal species gradually evolved through natural selection, a system similar to the artificial selection that people were using to breed prize cattle, sheep, and pedigree dogs.

The theory of natural selection is often described as the survival of the fittest because animals must compete with one another for scarce resources, including food and shelter. But they are not all equal or exactly similar, and some members of an animal group will have characteristics that make them "fitter"—better suited to the environment at that time.

The fitter animals will, therefore, be more successful at finding food and avoiding predators. Consequently, they are likely to produce more offspring, and many will have the same attributes as their fit parents. As a result, the next generation will contain more individuals with the "fit" trait. After many generations, it is possible for the whole population to carry the fit characteristic.

Variation and time

The environment is not fixed, and does not stay the same for long. Volcanoes,

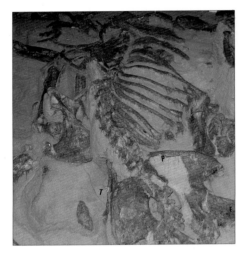

Above: Scientists know about extinct animals from studying fossils such as these mammoth bones. Fossils are the remains of dead plants or animals that have been turned to stone by natural processes over millions of years.

diseases, and gradual climate changes, for example, alter the conditions that animals have to confront. Natural selection relies on the way in which different individual animals cope with these changes. Those individuals that were once fit may later die out, as others that have a different set of characteristics become more successful in the changed environment.

As the process of natural selection continues for millions of years, so groups of animals can change radically, giving rise to a new species. Life is thought to have been evolving for 3.5 billion years.

New species may gradually arise out of a single group of animals. In fact, the original species may eventually be replaced by one or more new species. This can happen when two separate groups of one species are kept apart by an impassable geographical feature and evolve in different ways.

Mammals

Animals of the Mammalia, including whales, carnivores, rodents, bats and primates, are warm-blooded vertebrates with mammary glands, a thoracic diaphragm, and a four-chambered heart. These shared characteristics, however, do not come close to describing the huge diversity within the Mammalia class. For example, the largest animal that has ever existed on Earth, the blue whale, shares several crucial traits with the tiniest shrew. To add to this great diversity, mammals live in more places on Earth than any other animal group, from Arctic icefields to sandy deserts.

Amphibians

Cold-blooded vertebrates, typically living on land but breeding in water, belong to the amphibian class, which includes newts, salamanders, frogs, toads, and caecilians. Although amphibians live on every continent, except for Antarctica, none can survive in saltwater. Being cold-blooded, most amphibians are found in the warmer regions of the world. Unlike other land vertebrates, amphibians spend the early part of their lives in a different form from that of the adults. As they grow, the young gradually metamorphose into the adult body. Having a larval form means that the adults and their offspring live and feed in different places. In general, the larvae are aquatic.

The adults are hunters, feeding on other animals, while the young are generally plant eaters, filtering tiny plants from the water or grazing on aquatic plants which line the bottom of ponds and rivers.

Reptiles

Cold-blooded vertebrates possessing lungs and an outer covering of horny scales are classified as reptiles, a diverse group of animals consisting of about 6,500 species. Many of these look very different from each other and live in a large number of habitats, from the deep ocean to the scorching desert.

Most reptiles lay eggs, but these are different from those of an amphibian because they have a hard, thin shell rather than a soft, jelly-like one. The water-tight shelled egg was an evolutionary breakthrough, because it meant that adult reptiles did not have to return to the water to breed. The eggs could be laid even in the driest places.

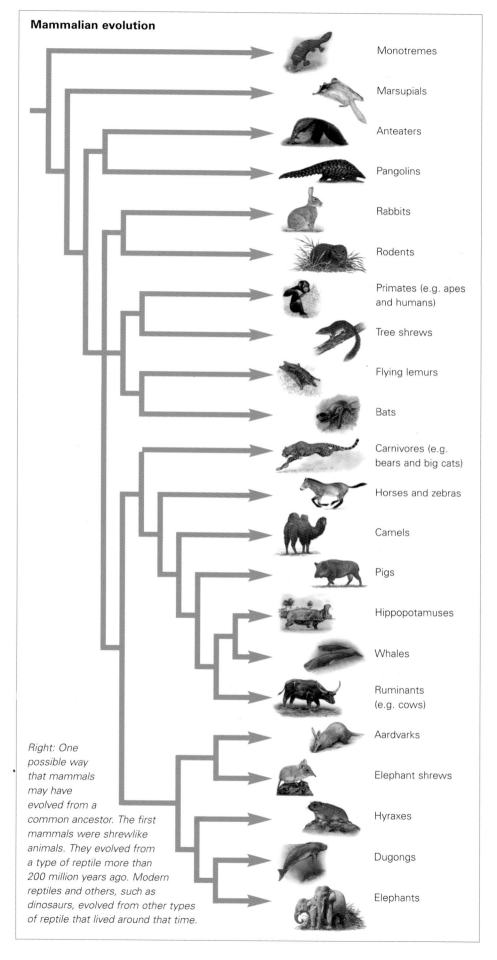

Mammalian evolution

Monotremes
Marsupials
Anteaters
Pangolins
Rabbits
Rodents
Primates (e.g. apes and humans)
Tree shrews
Flying lemurs
Bats
Carnivores (e.g. bears and big cats)
Horses and zebras
Camels
Pigs
Hippopotamuses
Whales
Ruminants (e.g. cows)
Aardvarks
Elephant shrews
Hyraxes
Dugongs
Elephants

Right: One possible way that mammals may have evolved from a common ancestor. The first mammals were shrewlike animals. They evolved from a type of reptile more than 200 million years ago. Modern reptiles and others, such as dinosaurs, evolved from other types of reptile that lived around that time.

CLASSIFICATION

Scientists classify all living things into categories. Members of each category share features with each other—traits that set them apart from other animals. Over the years, a tree of categories and subcategories has been pieced together, showing how all living things seem to be related to each other.

Taxonomy, the scientific discipline of categorizing organisms, aims to classify and order the millions of animals on Earth so that we can better understand them and their relationship to each other. The Greek philosopher Aristotle was among the first people to do this for animals in the fourth century BC. In the eighteenth century, the Swedish naturalist Carolus Linnaeus formulated the system that we use today.

By the end of the seventeenth century, naturalists had noticed that many animals seemed to have several close relatives that resembled one another. For example, lions, lynxes, and domestic cats all seemed more similar to each other than they did to dogs or horses. However, all of these animals shared common features they did not share with frogs, slugs, or wasps.

Linnaeus devised a way of classifying these observations. The system he set up—known as the Linnaean system—orders animals in a hierarchy of divisions. From the largest division to the smallest, this system is as follows: kingdom, phylum, class, order, family, genus, species.

Each species is given a two-word scientific name, derived from Latin and Greek. For example, *Panthera leo* is the scientific name of the lion. The first word is the genus name, and the second is the species name. Therefore *Panthera leo* means the "*leo*" species in the genus "*Panthera*." This system of two-word classification is known as binomial nomenclature.

Lions, lynxes, and other genera of cats belong to the *Felidae* family. The *Felidae* are included in the order *Carnivora*, along with dogs and other

Above: The bats form the order of mammals called the Chiroptera, *which means "hand wings." Vampire bats belong to the major subgroup of bats called microchiropterans, which use sonar to orient themselves in the dark of night. The other subgroup of bats are the megachiropterans, or flying foxes, which fly during the day and orient themselves by sight.*

Below: A young porcupine gazes from a tree in Acadia National Park in Maine, North America. The common porcupine inhabits most of Canada and the western United States, as well as a few states in the eastern United States. Porcupines have black-brown fur and up to 30,000 quills.

similar predators. The *Carnivora*, in turn, belong to the class *Mammalia*, which also includes horses and all other mammals.

Mammals belong to the phylum *Chordata*, the major group that contains all vertebrates, including reptiles, amphibians, birds, fish, and some other small animals called tunicates and lancelets. In turn, *Chordata* belong to the kingdom *Animalia*, comprising around 31 living phyla, including *Mollusca*, which contains the slugs, and *Arthropoda*, which contains wasps and other insects.

Although we still use Linnaean grouping, modern taxonomy is worked out in very different ways from the ones Linnaeus used. Linnaeus and others after him classified animals by their outward appearance. Although they were generally correct when it

Close relations

Cheetahs, caracals, and ocelots all belong to the cat family *Felidae*, which also includes lions, tigers, wildcats, lynxes, and jaguars. Within this family, there are two groups: big and small cats. These can generally be distinguished by their size, with a few exceptions. For example, the cheetah is often classed as a big cat, but is actually smaller than the cougar, a small cat. One of the main differences between the two groups is that big cats can roar but not purr continuously, and small cats can purr but not roar.

Above: The jaguar (Panthera onca) *belongs to the genus* Panthera, *the big cats, to which lions and tigers also belong. All cats are members of the order* Carnivora *(carnivores) within the class of* Mammalia *(mammals).*

Above: The cougar may look like a big cat, being larger than some of the Panthera *genus. However, this hunter belongs to the* Felis *genus, so despite appearances, it is more closely related to small, domestic cats than jaguars.*

Above: The ocelot (Felis pardalis) *is a medium-size member of the* Felis *or small cat genus. Like many cats, this species has evolved a spotted coat to provide camouflage —unfortunately, attractive to fashion designers.*

Distant relations

All vertebrates (backboned animals), including birds, reptiles, and mammals such as seals and dolphins, are thought to have evolved from common fish ancestors that swam in the oceans some 400 million years ago. Later, one group of fish developed limblike organs and came onto the land, where they slowly evolved into amphibians and later reptiles, which in turn gave rise to mammals. Later, seals and dolphins returned to the oceans and their limbs evolved into paddlelike flippers.

Above: Fish are an ancient group of aquatic animals that mainly propel themselves by thrashing their vertically aligned caudal fin, or tail, and steer using their fins.

Above: In seals, the four limbs have evolved into flippers that make highly effective paddles in water, but are less useful on land, where seals are ungainly in their movements.

Above: Whales and dolphins never come on land, and their hind limbs have all but disappeared. They resemble fish but the tail is horizontally—not vertically—aligned.

came to the large divisions, this method was not foolproof. For example, some early scientists believed that whales and dolphins, with their fins and streamlined bodies, were types of fish and not mammals at all. Today, accurate classification of the various genera is achieved through a field of study called cladistics. This uses genetic analysis to check how animals are related by evolutionary change. Thus, animals are grouped according to how they evolved, with each division sharing a common ancestor somewhere in the past. As the classification of living organisms improves, so does our understanding of the evolution of life on Earth and our place within this process.

ANATOMY

*Mammals, reptiles, and amphibians (which are vertebrates, as are fish and birds), come in a
mind-boggling array of shapes and sizes. However, all of them, from whales to bats and frogs
to snakes, share a basic body plan, both inside and out.*

Vertebrates are animals with a spine, generally made of bone. Bone, the hard tissues of which contain chalky substances, is also the main component of the rest of the vertebrate skeleton. The bones of the skeleton link together to form a rigid frame to protect organs and give the body its shape, while also allowing it to move. Cartilage, a softer, more flexible but tough tissue is found, for example, at the ends of bones in mobile joints, in the ears, and the nose (forming the sides and the partition between the two nostrils). Some fish, including sharks and rays, have skeletons that consist entirely of cartilage.

Nerves and muscles

Vertebrates also have a spinal cord, a thick bundle of nerves extending from the brain through the spine, and down into the tail. The nerves in the spinal cord are used to control walking and other reflex movements by coordinating blocks of muscle that work together. A vertebrate's skeleton is on the inside, in contrast to many invertebrates, which have an outer skeleton or exoskeleton. The vertebrate skeleton provides a solid structure that the body's muscles pull against. Muscles are blocks of protein that can contract and relax when they get an electrical impulse from a nerve.

Invertebrates

The majority of animals are invertebrates. They are a much more varied group than the vertebrates and include creatures as varied as shrimp, slugs, butterflies, and starfish. Although some squid are thought to reach the size of a small whale, and although octopuses are at least as intelligent as cats and dogs, most invertebrates are much smaller and simpler animals than the vertebrates.

Below: The most successful invertebrates are the insects, including ants. This soldier army ant is defending workers as they collect food.

Reptile bodies

Reptiles have an internal skeleton made from bone and cartilage. Their skin is covered in scales, which are often toughened by a waxy protein called keratin. Turtles are quite different from other reptiles. They have a simpler skull and a shell that is joined to the animal's internal skeleton.

Below: Crocodiles have a very strong body, designed for life in and around shallow water.

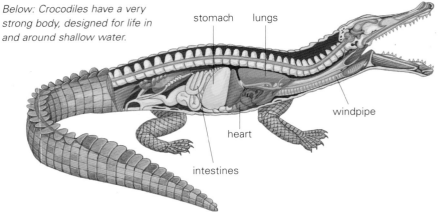

stomach   lungs

windpipe

heart

intestines

Below: Lizards have a similar body plan to crocodiles, although they are actually not very closely related.

Below: Snakes' internal organs are elongated so that they fit into their long, thin body. One of a pair of organs, such as the lungs, is often very small or missing.

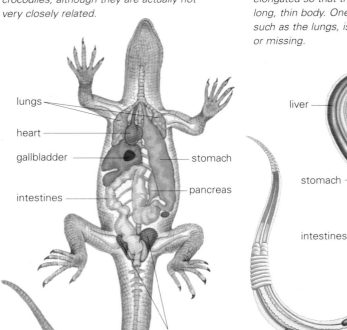

lungs

heart

gallbladder

intestines

stomach

pancreas

kidneys

lung

liver

heart

stomach

intestines

kidneys

When on the move, the vertebrate body works like a system of pulleys, pivots, and levers. The muscles are the engines of the body, and are attached to bones—the levers—by strong cables called tendons. The joint between two bones forms a pivot, and the muscles work in pairs to move a bone. For example, when an arm is bent at the elbow to raise the forearm, the bicep muscle on the front of the upper arm has to contract. This pulls the forearm up, while the tricep muscle attached to the back of the upper arm remains relaxed. To straighten the arm again, the tricep contracts and the bicep relaxes. If both muscles contract at the same time, they pull against each other, and the arm remains locked in whatever position it is in.

Vital organs

Muscles are not only attached to the skeleton. The gut—including the stomach and intestines—is surrounded by muscles. These muscles contract in rhythmic waves to push food and waste products through the body. The heart is a muscular organ made of a very strong muscle that keeps on contracting and relaxing, pumping blood around the body. The heart and other vital organs are found in the thorax, that part of the body which lies between the forelimbs. In reptiles and mammals, the thorax is kept well protected, the rib cage surrounding the heart, lungs, liver, and kidneys.

Vertebrates have a single liver consisting of a number of lobes. The liver has a varied role, making chemicals required by the body and storing food. Most vertebrates also have two kidneys. Their role is to clean the blood of any impurities and toxins, and to remove excess water. The main toxins that must be removed are compounds containing nitrogen, the by-products of eating protein. Mammal and amphibian kidneys dissolve these toxins in water to make urine. However, since many reptiles live in very dry habitats, they cannot afford to use water to remove waste, and they instead get rid of it as a solid waste similar to bird excrement.

Mammalian bodies

Most mammals are four-limbed (exceptions being sea mammals such as whales). All have some hair on their bodies, and females produce milk. They live in a wide range of habitats, and their bodies are adapted to survive. Their internal organs vary, depending on where they live and what they eat.

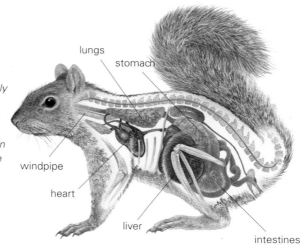

Right: Squirrels have very lightweight bodies, so they are able to climb the thinnest of tree branches. They have a long, slender shape, which ensures that their weight is spread evenly across tree limbs. They extend their tail for balance when jumping, and keep it curved over their back when sitting. Their forelimbs have strong muscles and thick, sharp claws for gripping branches, and their strong leg muscles and large hind feet help to propel them forward when leaping.

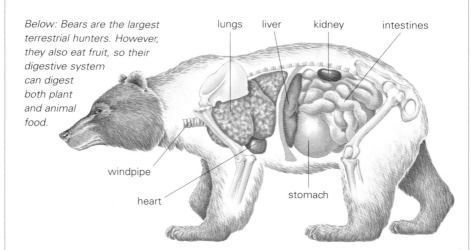

Below: Bears are the largest terrestrial hunters. However, they also eat fruit, so their digestive system can digest both plant and animal food.

Below: River dolphins are streamlined, torpedo-shaped aquatic mammals, and spend their entire lives in water. They breathe air into lungs like other animals, but through a single nostril, or blowhole, on the top of their head. They also have a fatty "melon" inside their domed skull, which is used to focus sonar beams to locate (and possibly stun) their prey. Their muscular tails are used for propulsion.*

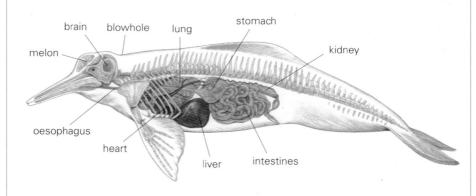

SENSES

To stay alive, animals must find food and shelter, and defend themselves against predators.
To achieve these things, they are equipped with an array of senses for monitoring their surroundings.
Different species have senses adapted to nocturnal or diurnal (day-active) life.

An animal's senses are its early-warning system. They alert it to changes in its surroundings—changes that may signal an opportunity to feed or mate, or the need to escape imminent danger. The ability to act quickly and appropriately is made possible because the senses are linked to the brain by a network of nerves that send messages as electric pulses. When the brain receives the information from the senses, it coordinates its response.

In many cases, generally in response to something touching the body, the signal from the sensor does not reach the brain before defensive action is taken. Instead, it produces a reflex response that is "hardwired" into the nervous system. For example, when you touch a very hot object, your hand automatically recoils; you don't need to think about it.

All animals have to be sensitive to their environment to survive. Even the simplest animals, such as jellyfish and roundworms, react to changes in their surroundings. Simple animals, however, have only a limited ability to move or defend themselves, and therefore, generally have limited senses. Larger animals, such as vertebrates,

have a much more complex array of sense organs. Most vertebrates can hear, see, smell, taste, and touch.

Vision

Invertebrates' eyes are generally designed to detect motion. Vertebrates' eyes, however, are better at forming clear images, often also in color. Vertebrates' eyes are balls of clear jelly that have an inner lining of light-sensitive cells. This lining, called the "retina," is made up of one or two types of cell. The rod cells—named after their shape—are very sensitive to all types of light, but are only capable of forming black and white images. Animals that are active at night generally have (and need) only rods in their eyes.

Color vision is important for just a few animals, such as monkeys, which need, for example, to see the brightest and therefore ripest fruits. Color images are made by the cone cells—so called because of their shape—in the retina. There are three types of cone, each of which is sensitive to a particular wavelength of light. Low wavelengths appear as reds, high wavelengths as blues, with green colors being detected in between.

Below: Like other hunters, a seal has eyes positioned on the front of its head. Forward-looking eyes are useful for judging distances, making it easier to chase down prey.

Above: Frogs have large eyes positioned on the upper side of the head, so that the animals can lie mainly submerged in water with just their eyes poking out.

The light is focused on the retina by a lens to produce a clear image. Muscles change the shape of the lens so that it can focus the light arriving from different distances. While invertebrates may have several eyes, all vertebrates have just two, and they are always positioned on the head. Animals such as rabbits, which are constantly looking out for danger, have eyes on the side of the head to give a wide field of vision. But though they can see in almost all directions, rabbits have difficulty judging distances and speeds. Animals that have eyes pointing forward are better at doing this, because each eye's field of vision overlaps with the other. This binocular vision helps hunting animals and others, such as tree-living primates, to judge distances more accurately.

Eyes can also detect radiation in a small band of wavelengths, and some animals detect radiation that is invisible to our eyes. Flying insects and birds can see ultraviolet light, which extends the range of their color vision. At the other end of the spectrum, many snakes can detect radiation with a lower wavelength. They sense infrared, or heat, through pits on the face that enable them to track their warm-blooded prey in pitch darkness.

Below: The raccoon is a nocturnal animal with excellent night vision, and eyes that glow bright yellow in the dark. These animals have a distinctive black mask across their eyes.

Hearing

An animal's brain interprets waves of pressure traveling through the air, and detected by the ears, as sound. Many animals do not hear these waves with ears but detect them in other ways instead. For example, although snakes can hear, they are much more sensitive to vibrations traveling through the ground, which they detect with their lower jaw. Long facial whiskers sported by many mammals, from cats to dugongs, are very sensitive touch receptors. They can be so sensitive that they will even respond to currents in the air.

In many ways, hearing is a sensitive extension of the sense of touch. The ears of amphibians, lizards, and mammals have an eardrum that is sensitive to tiny changes in pressure. An eardrum is a thin membrane of skin which vibrates as the air waves hit it. A tiny bone (or in the case of mammals, three bones) attached to the drum transmits the vibrations to a shell-shaped structure called a "cochlea." The cochlea is filled with a liquid that picks up the vibrations. As the liquid moves inside the cochlea, tiny, hairlike structures lining it wave back and forth. Nerves stimulated by this wave motion send the information to the brain, which interprets it as sound.

A mammal's ear is divided into three sections. The cochlea forms the inner ear, and the middle ear consists of the bones between the cochlea and eardrum. The outer ear is the tube joining the outside world and the

Below: Hares have very large outer ears, which they use like satellite dishes to pick up sound waves. They can rotate each ear separately to detect sound from all directions.

Above: Snakes have a forked tongue that they use to taste the air. The tips of the fork are slotted into an organ in the roof of the mouth. This organ is linked to the nose, and chemicals picked up by the tongue are identified with great sensitivity.

auricle—the fleshy structure on the side of the head that collects the sound waves—to the middle ear. Amphibians and reptiles do not possess auricles. Instead, their eardrums are either on the side of the head—easily visible on many frogs and lizards—or under the skin, as in snakes.

Smell and taste

Smell and taste are so closely related as to form a single sense. Snakes and lizards, for example, taste the air with their forked tongues. However, it is perhaps the most complex sense. Noses, tongues, and other smelling

organs are lined with sensitive cells, which can analyze a huge range of chemicals that float in the air or exist in food. Animals such as dogs, which rely on their sense of smell, have long noses packed with odor-sensitive cells. Monkeys, on the other hand, are less reliant on a sense of smell, and consequently have short noses capable of detecting only stronger odors.

Below: Lizards do not have outer ears at all. Their hearing organs are contained inside the head and joined to the outside world through an eardrum membrane.

Below: Wolves have an excellent sense of smell and taste. They communicate with pack members and rival packs by smell, as part of a complex set of social behaviors.

SURVIVAL

In order to stay alive, animals must not only find enough food, but also avoid becoming a predator's meal. To achieve this, animals have evolved many strategies to feed on a wide variety of foods, and an array of weapons and defensive tactics to keep safe.

An animal must keep feeding in order to replace the energy used in staying alive. Substances in the food, such as sugars, are burned by the body, and the subsequent release of energy is used to heat the body and power its movements. Food is also essential for growth. Although most growth takes place during the early period of an animal's life, it never really stops because injuries need to heal and worn-out tissues need replacing. Some animals continue growing throughout life. Proteins in the food are the main building blocks of living bodies.

Plant food

Some animals will eat just about anything, while others are much more fussy. As a group, vertebrates get their energy from a wide range of sources—everything from shellfish and wood, to honey and blood. Animals are often classified according to how they feed, forming several large groups filled with many otherwise unrelated animals.

Animals that eat plants are generally grouped together as herbivores. But this term is not very descriptive, because there is such a wide variety of plant foods. Animals that eat grass are known as grazers. However, this term can also apply to any animal that eats

Below: Red foxes are very adaptable animals that have taken to making their homes in the backyards and wasteland of suburban and more built-up areas, where they feed on rubbish.

Above: Bison are grazers. They eat grass and plants that grow close to the ground. Because their food is all around them, grazers spend a long time out in the open. They feed together in large herds, since there is safety in numbers.

any plant that covers the ground in large amounts, such as seaweed or sedge. Typical grazers include bison but some, such as the marine iguana, are not so typical. Animals such as deer, which pick off the tastiest leaves, buds, and fruit from bushes and trees, are called browsers. Other browsing animals include many monkeys, but some monkeys eat only leaves (the folivores) or fruit (the frugivores).

Below: Grizzly bears are omnivores, and eat both vegetation and animals. When salmon are abundant, they congregate in groups to share this protein-rich resource.

Many monkeys have a much broader diet, eating everything from shellfish to the sap that seeps out from the bark of tropical trees. Animals that eat both plant and animal foods are called omnivores. Bears are omnivorous, as are humans, but the most broad of tastes belong to scavenging animals, such as rats and other rodents, which eat anything they can get their teeth into. Omnivores in general, and scavengers in particular, are very curious animals. They will investigate anything that looks or smells like food, and if it also tastes like food, then it probably is.

A taste for flesh

The term "carnivore" is often applied to any animal that eats flesh, but it is more correctly used to refer to an order of mammals that includes cats, dogs, bears, and many smaller animals, such as weasels and racoons. These animals are the kings of killing, armed with razor-sharp claws and powerful jaws crammed full of daggerlike teeth. They use their strength and speed to overpower their prey, either running it down or taking it by surprise with an ambush.

Above: Wolverines are primarily meat-eaters, capable of bringing down prey that are five times bigger than themselves. Their diet includes beavers, squirrels, marmots, rabbits, deer, moose, wild sheep, and carrion.

However, land-dwelling carnivores are not the only expert killers. One of the largest meat-eaters is the orca, or killer whale, which is at least three times the size of the brown bear, the largest killer on land.

Although snakes are much smaller in comparison, they are just as deadly, if not more so. They kill in one of two ways, either suffocating their prey by wrapping their coils tightly around it, or by injecting it with a poison through their fangs.

Arms race

Ironically, the same weapons used by predators are often used by their prey to defend itself. For example, several species of frog, toad, and salamander secrete poisons onto their skin. In some cases, such as the poison dart frog, this poison is enough to kill any predator that tries to eat it, thus making sure that the killer won't repeat its performance. More often, though, a predator finds that its meal tastes horrible, and remembers not to eat the same thing again. To remind the predators to keep away, many poisonous amphibians are brightly colored, which ensures that they are easily recognized.

Many predators rely on stealth to catch their prey, and staying hidden is part of the plan. A camouflaged coat, such as a jaguar's spots, helps animals blend into their surroundings. Many species also use this technique to ensure that they do not get eaten.

Other animals avoid being attacked by advertising their presence. For example, coral snakes let predators know that they will suffer a bite filled with deadly venom by being brightly colored. Many nonvenomous snakes, including harmless milksnakes and corn snakes, have evolved to look the same as venomous snakes so that they, too, are left alone.

Plant-eating animals that live in the open cannot hide from predators that are armed with sharp teeth and claws. Plant-eaters cannot rely on similar weapons to defend themselves. They are outgunned, because they do not possess sharp, pointed teeth, but

Filter-feeders

Some animals filter their food from water. The giant baleen whales do this, sieving tiny, shrimplike animals called krill out of great gulps of sea water. Some tadpoles and larval salamanders filter-feed as well, extracting tiny plantlike animals that float in fresh water. However, after becoming adults, all amphibians become hunters and eat other animals. All snakes and most lizards are meat-eaters, or carnivores, as well.

Below: The largest animals of all, baleen whales, are filter-feeders. They do not have teeth. Instead, their gums are lined with a thick curtain of baleen that filters out tiny shrimplike krill from sea water.

instead have flattened ones to grind up their plant food. The best chance they have of avoiding danger is to run away. Animals such as deer consequently have long, hoofed feet that lengthen their legs considerably; they are, in fact, standing on their toenails. These long legs allow them to run faster and leap high into the air to escape an attacker's jaws.

Animals that do not flee must stand and fight. Most large herbivores are armed with horns or antlers. Although used chiefly for display, the horns are the last line of defense when cornered.

Below: Two male bighorn sheep spar head-to-head in Jasper National Park, Canada.

REPRODUCTION

All animals share the urge to produce offspring that will survive after the parents die. The process of heredity is determined by genes, through which characteristics are passed from parents to offspring. Reproduction presents several problems, and animals have adopted different strategies for tackling them.

Animals have two main goals: to find food and a mate. To achieve these goals, they must survive everything that the environment throws at them, from extremes of the weather, such as floods and droughts, to hungry predators. They have to find sufficient supplies of food, and on top of that, locate a mate before their competitors. If they find sufficient food but fail to produce any offspring, their struggle for survival will have been wasted.

One parent or two?

There are two ways in which an animal can reproduce, asexually or sexually. Animals that are produced by asexual reproduction, or parthenogenesis, have only one parent, a mother. The offspring are identical to their mother and to each other. Sexual reproduction involves two parents of the opposite sex. The offspring are hybrids of the two parents, with a mixture of their parents' characteristics.

The offspring inherit their parents' traits through their genes. Genes can be defined in various ways. One simple definition is that they are the units of inheritance—single inherited

Above: Many male frogs croak by pumping air into an expandable throat sac. The croak is intended to attract females. The deeper the croak, the more attractive it is. However, some males lurk silently and mate with females as they approach the croaking males.

characteristics that cannot be subdivided any further. Genes are also segments of DNA (deoxyribonucleic acid), a complex chemical that forms long chains. It is found at the heart of every living cell. Each link in the DNA chain forms part of a code that controls how an animal's body develops and survives. Every cell in the body contains a full set of DNA, which holds all the genetic information needed for an entire new body.

Animals produced through sexual reproduction receive half their DNA, or half their genes, from each parent. The male parent provides half the supply of genes, contained in a sperm. Each sperm's only role is to find its

Above: In deer and many other grazing animals, the males fight each other for the right to mate with the females in the herd. The deer with the largest antlers often wins without fighting, and real fights only break out if two males appear equally well endowed.

way to, and fertilize, an egg, its female equivalent. Besides containing the other half of the DNA, the egg also holds a supply of food for the offspring as it develops into a new individual. Animals created through parthenogenesis get all their genes from their mother, and all of them are therefore the same sex—female.

Pros and cons

All mammals reproduce sexually, as do most reptiles and amphibians. However, there are a substantial number of reptiles and amphibians, especially lizards, which reproduce by parthenogenesis. There are benefits and disadvantages to both types of reproduction. Parthenogenesis is quick and convenient. The mother does not need to find a mate, and can devote all of her energy to producing huge numbers of young. This strategy is ideal for populating as yet unexploited territory. However, being identical, these animals are very vulnerable to attack. If, for example, one is killed by a disease or outwitted by a predator, it is very likely that they will all suffer the same fate. Consequently, whole communities of animals produced through parthenogenesis can be wiped out.

Below: Crocodiles bury their eggs in a nest. The temperature of the nest determines the sex of the young reptiles. Hot nests produce more males than cool ones. Crocodile mothers are very gentle when it comes to raising young.

Sexual animals, on the other hand, are much more varied. Each one is unique, formed by a mixture of genes from both parents. This variation means that a group of animals produced by sexual reproduction is more likely to triumph over adversity than a group of asexual ones. However, sexual reproduction takes up a great deal of time and effort.

Attracting mates

Since females produce only a limited number of eggs, they are keen to make sure that they are fertilized by a male with good genes. If a male is fit and healthy, this is a sign that he has good genes. Good genes will ensure that the offspring will be able to compete with other animals for food and mates of their own. Because the females have the final say in agreeing to mate, the

Above: Prairie dogs usually have one litter of four to six young per year. The young are born hairless and helpless, with their eyes closed. They remain underground for the first six weeks of life, then emerge from their dens.

Below: An Argentine gray zorro vixen suckles her fox cubs. The milk contains a mixture of fats and proteins, and also includes antibodies, so that they will have resistance to diseases.

males have to put a lot of effort into getting noticed. Many are brightly colored, make loud noises, and they are often larger than the females. In many species, the males even compete with each other for the right to display to the females. Winning that right is a good sign that they have the best genes.

Parental care

The amount of care that the offspring receive from their parents varies considerably. There is a necessary trade-off between the amount of useful care parents can give to each offspring, the number of offspring they can produce, and how regularly they can breed. Mammals invest heavily in parental care, suckling their young after giving birth, while most juvenile amphibians or reptiles never meet their parents at all.

By suckling, mammals ensure that their young grow to a size where they

Above: Grizzly bear cubs are blind and helpless at birth. Their mother's milk is rich in fat and calories, so the cubs develop quickly. Mothers are fiercely protective of their young, defending them against wolves and cougars. Cubs stay with their mothers for up to three years.

can look after themselves. Generally, the young stay with the mother until it is time for her to give birth to the next litter—at least one or two months. However, in many species, including humans, the young stay with their parents for many years.

Other types of animal pursue the opposite strategy, producing large numbers of young that are left to fend for themselves. The vast majority in each batch of eggs—consisting of hundreds or even thousands—die before reaching adulthood, and many never even hatch. The survival rates, of frogs, for instance, are very low.

Animals that live in complicated societies, such as monkeys and humans, tend to produce a single offspring every few years. The parents direct their energies into protecting and rearing the young, giving them a good chance of survival. Animals that live for a only a short time, such as mice, rabbits, and reptiles and amphibians in general, need to reproduce quickly to make the most of their short lives. They produce high numbers of young, and do not waste time on anything more than the bare minimum of parental care. If successful, these animals can reproduce at an alarming pace.

MIGRATION AND HIBERNATION

Everywhere across the Americas, the climate changes throughout the year with the cycle of seasons.
In some places, these changes are hardly noticeable from month to month, but in others, each new season
brings extremes of weather, from blistering summers to freezing winters, or torrential rains followed by drought.

Change of lifestyle

In temperate regions, such as New England, the year is generally divided into four seasons. In contrast, in the far north, the change between the short summer and long winter is so quick that, in effect, there are only two seasons. Other regions experience a different annual cycle of changes. For example, tropical regions do not really have fluctuating temperatures, but many areas do experience periods of relative dryness and at least one period of heavier rains each year.

Animals must, of course, react to these changes if they are to survive the harshest weather and make the most of clement conditions. Monkeys, for example, build up a mental map of their patch of forest so that they know where the fresh leaves will be after the rains, and where to find the hardier forest fruits during a drought. Wolves living in chilly northern forests hunt

Above: Reptiles that live in cooler parts of the world—rattlesnakes, for example—spend a long time lying dormant. They do not hibernate like mammals, but because they are cold-blooded and do not need lots of energy to function, they can go for long periods without food.

together in packs during the cold winter, cooperating to kill animals that are much larger than they are. However, when the summer arrives they tend to forage alone, picking off the many smaller animals, such as rodents and rabbits, which appear when the snow melts.

Hibernation

The reason the wolves find these smaller animals in the summer is that they suddenly emerge having passed the winter in cosy burrows or nests. This behavior is commonly called hibernating, but there is a distinction between true hibernation and simply being inactive over winter.

Animals such as bears and tree squirrels are not true hibernators. Although they generally sleep for long periods during the coldest parts of the winter, hunkered down in a den or drey, they do not enter the deep, unconscious state of hibernation. Unable to feed while they sleep, these animals rely on their bodily reserves of fat to stay alive. However, they often wake up during breaks in the harshest weather and venture outside to urinate

or snatch a meal. Because tree squirrels have smaller fat reserves than bears, they frequently visit caches (stores) of food that they filled up in the fall.

On the other hand, the true hibernators, such as woodchucks, do not stir at all over the winter. They rely completely on their reserves of fat to stay alive, and to save energy, their metabolism slows to a fraction of its normal pace.

Only warm-blooded animals hibernate, because they are the main types of animals that can survive in places where hibernation is necessary. However, rattlesnakes often pass the winter in rocky crevices and burrows in a dormant state. Reptiles and amphibians that live in very hot and dry places have a similar response to inhospitable weather. They become dormant when their habitat becomes too dry. Most bury themselves in moist sand or under rocks, only becoming

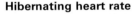

Hibernating heart rate

The hibernating animal's heart rate slows to just a few beats per minute. It breathes more slowly and its body temperature drops to just a few degrees above the surrounding air temperature. The bodies of true hibernators, such as the dormouse, shut down almost completely during hibernation.

Below: Bears may be out of sight for most of the winter, but they do not become completely dormant and their temperature does not fall drastically.

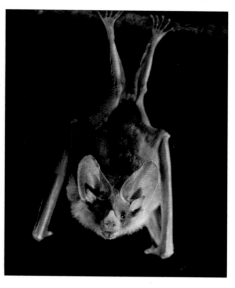

active again when rain brings the habitat back to life. Some estivating frogs (those that are dormant in the summer) even grow a skin cocoon that traps water and keeps their bodies moist while they wait for the rains to return.

Migration

Another way of coping with bad conditions is to migrate. Migrations are not just random wanderings, but involve following a set route each year. In general, they are two-way trips, with animals returning to where they started once conditions back home become favorable again.

All kinds of animals migrate, from insects to whales, and there are many reasons for doing so. Most migrators are looking for supplies of food, or for a safe place to rear their young. For example, when their home territory becomes too crowded, young lemmings stampede over wide areas looking for new places to live, sometimes dying in the process. Herds of caribou leave the barren tundra as winter approaches, and head for the relative warmth of the forest. Mountain goats act in a similar way: having spent the summer grazing in high alpine meadows, they descend below the timberline when winter snow covers their pastures.

Other migrations are on a much grander scale, and in some cases, an animal's whole life can be a continual migration. Among the greatest migrants are the giant whales, which travel thousands of miles from their

Above: Whales make the longest migrations of all mammals. They move from their warm breeding grounds near the equator to feeding areas in cooler waters near the poles.

breeding grounds in the tropics to their feeding grounds near the poles. The cool waters around the poles teem with plankton food, while the warmer tropical waters are a better place for giving birth.

Day length

How do animals know that it is time to hibernate or migrate? The answer lies in the changing number of hours of daylight as the seasons change. All animals are sensitive to daylight, and use it to set their body clocks or circadian rhythms. These rhythms affect all bodily processes, including the buildup to the breeding season. The hibernators begin to put on weight

Above: Bats spend long periods hibernating. They mate before winter, and the females store the sperm inside their body, only releasing it on the eggs as spring approaches.

or store food as the days shorten, and many migrants start to get restless before setting off on their journey. However, not all migrations are controlled by the number of hours of daylight. Some migrators, such as wildebeest and lemmings, move because of other environmental factors, such as the lack of food caused by drought or overcrowding.

Below: Moose move across wide regions of mountains, rivers, and even roads, migrating south each winter. They are known to migrate up to 122 miles (196km) from Alaska to northern Canada. The trigger for this migration is the arrival of large accumulations of snow in their feeding grounds, leading them to search for warmer browsing land.

ECOLOGY

Ecology is the study of how groups of organisms interact with members of their own species, other organisms, and the environment. All types of animals live in a community of interdependent organisms called an ecosystem, in which they have their own particular role.

The natural world is filled with a wealth of opportunities for animals to feed and breed. Every animal species has evolved to take advantage of a certain set of these opportunities, called a niche. A niche is not just a physical place but also a lifestyle exploited by that single species. For example, even though they live in the same rain forest habitat, sloths and tapirs occupy very different niches.

To understand how different organisms interrelate, ecologists combine all the niches in an area into a community, called an "ecosystem." Ecosystems do not really exist, because it is impossible to know where one ends and another begins, but the concept is a useful tool when learning more about the natural world.

Food chains
One way of understanding how an ecosystem works is to follow the food chains within it. A food chain is made up of a series of organisms that prey on each other. Each habitat is filled with them, and since they often merge into and diverge from each other, they are often combined into food webs.

Below: Nature creates some incredible alliances. The American badger, for example, goes on hunting trips with a coyote. The coyote sniffs out the prey, and the badger digs it out of its burrow for both of them to eat.

Ecologists use food chains to see how energy and nutrients flow through natural communities. Food chains always begin with plants. Plants are the only organisms on Earth that do not need to feed. They derive their energy from sunlight, whereas all other organisms, including animals, get theirs from food. At the next level up the food chain come the plant-eaters. They eat the plants, and extract the sugar and other useful substances made by them. And, like the plants, they use these substances to power their bodies and stay alive. The predators occupy the next level up, and they eat the bodies of the plant-eating animals.

At each stage of the food chain, energy is lost, mainly as heat given out by the animals' bodies. Because of this, less energy is available at each level up the food chain. This means that in a healthy ecosystem there are always fewer predators than prey, and always more plants than plant-eaters.

Nutrient cycles
A very simple food chain would be as follows: grass, mule deer, and wolf. However, the reality of most ecosystems is much more complex, with many more layers, including certain animals that eat both plants and animals. Every food chain ends with a top predator, in our example, the wolf. Nothing preys on a wolf, at least when it is alive, but once it dies, the food chain continues as insects, fungi, and other decomposers feed on the carcass. Eventually, nothing is left of the wolf's body. All the energy stored in it is removed by the decomposers, and the chemicals that made up its body return to the environment as carbon dioxide gas, water, and minerals in the soil. These are the very same substances needed by a growing plant. The cycle is complete.

Above: Nothing is wasted in nature. The dung beetle uses the droppings of larger grazing animals as a supply of food for its developing young. Since the beetles clear away all the dung, the soil is not damaged by it, the grass continues to grow, and the grazers have plenty of food.

Living together
As food chains show, the lives of different animals in an ecosystem are closely related. If all the plants died for some reason, it would not just be the plant-eaters that would go hungry. As all of them began to die, the predators would starve, too. Only the decomposers might appear to benefit. Put another way, the other species living alongside an animal are just as integral to that animal's environment as the weather and landscape. This is yet another way of saying that animal species have not evolved isolated from each another.

The result is that as predators have evolved new ways of catching their prey, the prey has had to evolve new ways of escaping. On many occasions, this process of coevolution has created symbiotic relationships between two different species. For example, coyotes guide badgers to ground squirrel burrows.

Some niches are very simple, and the animals that occupy them live simple, solitary lives. Others, especially those occupied by mammals, are much more complex, and require members of a species to live close together. These aggregations of animals may be simple herds or more structured social groups.

Food chain

Food chains show how the energy needed for life passes through an ecosystem. The energy originates in the sun. This makes plants grow, which are then eaten by animals. The plant-eating animals then become meals themselves.

Below: This food chain shows what animals eat in a temperate country, such as Great Britain. Herbivores eat only plants, and carnivores eat mainly other animals. Animals that eat both plants and animals are omnivores—for example, humans.

bird of prey
(carnivore)

human
(omnivore)

fox
(carnivore)

thrush
(omnivore)

hedgehog
(carnivore)

rabbit
(herbivore)

mouse
(herbivore)

grasshopper
(herbivore)

deer
(herbivore)

sheep
(herbivore)

cow
(herbivore)

snail
(herbivore)

Group living

A herd, flock, or school is a group of animals that gather together for safety. Each member operates as an individual, but is physically safest in the center of the group, the danger of attack being greatest on the edge. Herd members do not actively communicate dangers to each other. When one is startled by something and bolts, the rest will probably follow. Members of a social group, on the other hand, work together to find food, raise their young, and defend themselves.

Many mammals, for example monkeys, dogs, and dolphins, form social groups, and these groups exist in many forms. At one end of the spectrum are highly ordered societies, such as wolf packs, which are often controlled by a dominant male-female pair, the other members having their own ranking in a strict, hierarchical structure. At the other end of the

spectrum are leaderless gangs of animals, such as squirrel monkeys, which merge and split with no real guiding purpose.

There are many advantages of living in social groups, with members finding more food and being warned of danger, for example. However, in many societies, only a handful of high-ranking members are allowed to breed. In these cases, the groups are held

together by a complex fusion of family ties in which brothers and sisters help to raise nephews and nieces. Politics also plays its cohesive part, with members forming and breaking alliances in order to rise to the top.

Below: Bison have poor eyesight but good hearing and a good sense of smell. Living in vast herds gives them a better chance of detecting wolves. If attacked, bulls often form a defensive circle around their females and young.

ENDANGERED SPECIES

Many animals are threatened with extinction because they cannot survive in a world that is constantly being changed by human intervention. Many species have already become extinct, and if people do nothing to save them, a great many more will follow.

Surprising though it may sound, there is nothing unusual in extinctions, for they are an important part of the natural world. As the climate and landscape have changed in a given area over millions of years, the animals that live there have also changed. And as a new species evolves, so another is forced out of its habitat and becomes extinct. All that remains, if we are lucky, are a few fossilized bones—a record in stone.

Mass extinction?

Biologists estimate that there are at least several million species alive today, possibly up to 30 million. Whatever the figure, there are probably more species on Earth right now than at any other time. Therefore, because of the habitat destruction caused by people, more species are becoming extinct or are being threatened with extinction than ever before.

Geologists and biologists know that every now and then there are mass extinctions, in which great numbers of the world's animals die out forever. For example, it is widely believed that the dinosaurs and many other reptiles were wiped out after a meteorite smashed into Mexico 65 million years ago. But the questions that geologists and biologists are now asking include: Are we witnessing the natural world's latest mass extinction? Are humans the cause?

Most of the world's animal species are actually insects—especially beetles—and other invertebrates. It is likely that many of these species, especially those that live in tropical forests, are becoming extinct. However, since scientists may never have had a chance to describe many of them, it is difficult to estimate the true numbers of species that are being lost.

Below: The pronghorn is a unique hoofed grazer. Before Europeans arrived, there were 35 million pronghorns in North America. Their numbers plummeted after the prairies were cleared for grazing cattle, and today, only half a million survive in the United States and Canada. They are now extinct in Mexico.

Above: Leatherback turtles are the largest turtles in the world—even larger than the better-known giant tortoises. They are becoming rare because of the decline in untouched beaches on which to lay their eggs. Fewer leatherbacks are being born, and even fewer reach adulthood.

Life list

With vertebrate animals, it is a different story. Because there are only a few thousand species of animals with backbones, most of which have been recognized for hundreds of years, we know a great deal more about the plight of each species. Many species, for example mice, dogs, and horses, thrive in a world dominated by people. However, a great many more species have suffered as people have destroyed their habitats, either deliberately or by upsetting the balance of nature by introducing species from other parts of the world.

The International Union for the Conservation of Nature and Natural Resources (IUCN) produces a Red List of animals that are in danger of extinction. There are currently about 5,500 animals listed in a number of categories, including extinct in the wild, endangered, and vulnerable. Nearly one-quarter of all mammals

are included on the list, and about four percent of reptiles and three of amphibians.

However, although the status of all mammals has been assessed by the IUCN, only a fraction of reptiles and amphibians has been as thoroughly checked, and it is very likely that many more species are much closer to extinction than was previously thought.

Below: The Cuban crocodile is in great danger of extinction. Its habitat is now limited to Cuba, and its main threat is from humans, who have hunted it extensively and invaded its habitats. Today, as few as 3,000 to 6,000 Cuban crocodiles are estimated to live in the wild.

Above: The gray wolf came under threat of extinction because it was considered a pest and therefore heavily hunted. Humans have also encroached on its environment. Almost wiped out as a result, it is now a protected species and thought to be thriving.

Wiped out

People have been clearing forests for thousands of years. Europe and China, for example, were once thickly forested, but were gradually cleared by farmers and turned to the fields and grasslands that we see today. As people migrated to the Americas, a similar process took place, although on a huge scale and at a much faster rate.

Above: Most polar bears live in the Arctic, with over half of the estimated total population of between 22,000 and 40,000 living in Canada. Polar bears are becoming endangered due to global warming and are predicted to become extinct within 100 years.

The major habitat being destroyed was, and still is, the tropical rain forest of South America. The number of species living in this tropical area is much higher than elsewhere, and a large proportion of animals are finding it increasingly difficult to survive while their habitats are shrinking so rapidly.

Although few animals on the Red List have actually become extinct, the situation is becoming graver for most species. The monkeys and apes of the tropical rain forests are among the worst affected, with nearly one in four species being very close to extinction. This is because rain forests are complicated places, and many primate species there have evolved a specialized lifestyle, such as feeding on fruit in the tallest trees. These species are usually very badly affected by sudden changes in their environment, for example, when a logging team cuts down all the tall trees leaving just the shorter ones behind. Without their preferred food, survival is precarious.

DIRECTORY OF MAMMALS, AMPHIBIANS, AND REPTILES

North America, stretching from the top of the Arctic Circle down as far as Panama in the south, is home to an enormous range of animals. This section of the book focuses on the most significant mammals, amphibians, and reptiles that inhabit this continent.

The animal species are organized into a number of related groups: salamanders, frogs and toads, turtles and tortoises, lizards, crocodilians, nonvenomous snakes, venomous snakes, cats, dogs, bears, small carnivores, raccoons, rodents, rabbits, bats, armadillos, marsupials, insectivores, hoofed animals, as well as ocean mammals.

Each entry is accompanied by a fact box containing a map that shows where the animal lives, and details about its distribution, habitat, food, size, maturity, breeding, life span, and conservation status. This last category gives a broad indication of each species' population size, as recorded by the International Union for the Conservation of Nature and Natural Resources (IUCN). At one end of the scale, a species might be described as common or lower risk, then vulnerable, threatened, endangered, or critically endangered. In addition to the main animal entries, the directory also contains lists of related animals, with short summaries indicating their distribution, main characteristics, and behavior.

Left: The caribou—also known as the reindeer—is the only species of deer in which both males and females have antlers. When fighting, they lower their heads, charge, and lock antlers, trying to push each other away. There are over three million caribou living in North America, and each year they migrate very large distances in pursuit of food.

HOOFED ANIMALS

Hoofed animals walk on the tips of their toes. Their hooves are made from the same material as fingernails and claws—keratin. Walking on tiptoes makes their legs very long, and most hoofed animals are fast runners because of this. Hoofed mammals belong to two groups: Perissodactyla, *which includes horses and tapirs, and* Artiodactyla, *which includes pigs, sheep, antelope, deer, and cattle.*

Musk ox

Ovibos moschatus

Distribution: Arctic of Canada and Greenland.
Habitat: Tundra.
Food: Grass, moss, sedge.
Size: 6.25–7.5ft (1.9–2.3m). Height at shoulder: 4–5ft (1.2–1.5m).
Weight: 440–900lb (200–410kg).
Maturity: 2–3 years.
Breeding: 1 young produced every 1–2 years in the spring.
Life span: 18 years.

Although musk oxen look like large, hairy cattle or bison, they are, in fact, relatives of goats and sheep. These animals live on the windswept tundra within the Arctic Circle. This habitat forms in places that are too cold and dry for trees to grow. There is only enough water to sustain grasses and other hardy plants.

Both sexes of this species have large, hooked horns. Male musk oxen are larger than females, because they must fight other males to win and defend a harem of females. They butt each other with their horns in contests of strength. During the mating season, the bulls produce a strong, musky odor. Musk oxen live in herds, usually of 15–20 animals but occasionally up to 100 strong. When predators threaten, the herd crowds together, often in a circle or semicircle, with the calves in the middle. This formation provides a highly effective defense, since adversaries are faced with a wall of horns and risk being gored if they attack.

The musk ox's body is covered in long fur, except the area between lips and nostrils. The fur not only keeps the animal warm, but also protects it against the vast numbers of biting insects that swarm across the tundra during the short summer.

American bison

Bison bison

Distribution: Western Canada and central United States.
Habitat: Prairie and woodland.
Food: Grass.
Size: 7–11.5ft (2.1–3.5m). Height at shoulder 5–6.5ft (1.5–2m).
Weight: 770–2200lb (350–1,000kg).
Maturity: 1–2 years.
Breeding: Single young born in spring every 1 or 2 years.
Life span: 40 years.

American bison are now rare, but are no longer endangered. Once, vast herds of over a million bison grazed the vast prairies of western North America. They were almost wiped out by hunters during the nineteenth century, when the grasslands were cleared to make way for agriculture. Bison were also hunted for their skin and meat. Originally, bison also occurred extensively in mountain areas, and also in open forest and woodland.

These large grazing animals have well-developed senses of smell and hearing. They can run at up to 37mph (60kmh) and are also able to swim well, sometimes crossing rivers as wide as 0.6 mile (1km). Mature bulls either live alone or move in separate groups from the cows. The males join the females to mate in late summer. After mating, a bull guards his mate for several days to protect her from rival males.

Male bison are larger than the females of the species. Both sexes have sharp, curved horns, which stick out from the shaggy, brown hair on their heads.

Mountain goat

Oreamnos americanus

As their name suggests, these goats live on the sides of steep mountains. They prefer broken, rocky slopes to meadows, and they have strong, sturdy legs and hooves to allow them to negotiate such difficult terrain. Mountain goats are native to the mountains of western North America, from southern Alaska to Montana and Idaho. However, they have also been introduced to mountainous regions further south in the United States.

Mountain goats are grazers, feeding on whatever grows in their precipitous habitats—mainly grasses and similar plants. In the winter, when snow covers the higher slopes, mountain goats climb down to lowland feeding grounds. As the snows melt in the spring, the goats return to higher altitudes to feed on the new plant growth. In the winter, mountain goats gather in large herds, but these break up in the summer into smaller groups. During the breeding season, the males fight to form a hierarchy. They do not butt each other head on, like other goats, but stand side by side and jab each other with their short horns.

Distribution: From southern Alaska to Idaho.
Habitat: Steep, rocky slopes.
Food: Grass, mosses, twigs, and lichens.
Size: 4–6ft (1.25–1.8m). Height 3–4ft (0.9–1.2m).
Weight: 100–300lb (46–136kg).
Maturity: 2.5 years.
Breeding: 1–3 kids born in May or June.
Life span: 15 years.

Mountain goats have stout legs with large, oval hooves. The soles of the hooves are very elastic, which helps them to grip surfaces as they climb up rocky slopes.

Bighorn sheep

Ovis canadensis

Bighorns are named after the males' massive spiral horns, which may be up to 3.5ft (1.1m) long. The females have smaller, less curved horns.

Bighorn sheep are the most common wild sheep in North America. They are excellent climbers and are often found on rocky outcrops or high cliffs. They seek refuge in steep areas from cougars and other predators that are not agile enough to keep up with their sure-footed prey.

Flocks of bighorns can contain up to 100 individuals. They head up to high meadows in the summer, then retreat to the valleys when the winter snows come. Male bighorns tend to live in separate groups from the ewes and lambs. The rams have hierarchies based on the size of their horns. Fights are ritualized, with the adversaries butting their horns together. Ewes prefer to mate with rams with large horns and refuse the courtship of others.

Distribution: Southwestern Canada to northern Mexico.
Habitat: Alpine meadows and rocky cliffs.
Food: Grass and sedge.
Size: 4–6ft (1.2–1.8m). Height at shoulder: 2.5–3.5ft (0.8–1.1m).
Weight: 110–275lb (50–125kg).
Maturity: 3 years.
Breeding: 1–3 young born in the spring.
Life span: 20 years.

Moose

Alces alces

Distribution: Alaska, Canada, northern United States, Siberia, and northern Europe. Introduced to New Zealand.
Habitat: Marsh and woodland.
Food: Leaves, twigs, moss, and water plants.
Size: 8–10.25ft (2.4–3.1m). Height at shoulder: 4.5–7.5ft (1.4–2.3m).
Weight: 440–1815lb (200–825kg).
Maturity: 1 year.
Breeding: 1–3 young born in the spring.
Life span: 27 years.

Male moose are almost twice the size of females. The males sport huge antlers—nearly 6.5ft (2m) across—and have flaps of skin hanging below their chins, called dewlaps. In fights over females, male moose clash violently, sometimes goring each other with their antlers.

Moose are the largest deer in the world. They live in the cold conifer forests that cover northern mountains and lowlands. As well as being found in North America, moose live across northern Europe and Siberia, where they are known as elk.

Moose plod through the forests and marshes, browsing on a wide range of leaves, mosses, and lichens. They often feed in the shallows of streams and rivers, nibbling on aquatic vegetation. These large deer have even been seen diving underwater to uproot water plants. In summer, they are most active at dawn and dusk. In winter, they are active throughout the day. They paw the snow to reveal buried plants and twigs.

Although moose may gather together to feed, they spend most of the year alone. In the fall mating season, males fight each other for females. Pregnant females find secluded sites where they can give birth, with thick vegetation to hide the newborn calves. The moose calves are able to stand and walk within two days. They can also swim by the time they are a week old, which is an important survival skill, since taking to water is a good way of escaping some predators. At five weeks, they can outrun slower animals such as bears. Mothers will defend their calves aggressively. The calves become independent when they are about one year old.

White-tailed deer

Odocoileus virginianus

Distribution: North, Central, and South America from southern Canada to Brazil.
Habitat: Shrublands and open woodland.
Food: Grass, shrubs, twigs, mushrooms, lichens, and nuts.
Size: 2.5–7ft (0.8–2.1m). Height, shoulder: 2.5–3.25ft (0.8–1m).
Weight: 110–484lb (50–200kg).
Maturity: 1 year.
Breeding: 1–4 young produced during summer.
Life span: 10 years.

White-tailed deer, or Virginia deer, as they are called in the United States, prefer areas with tall grasses or shrubs to hide in during the day. When the deer spot predators, they raise their white tails to expose the white patches on their rumps. This serves as a visual warning to other deer that danger is near. If pursued, the deer bound away, reaching 37mph (60kmh).

White-tailed deer live in matriarchies, with each small group being controlled by a single adult female, which is the mother of the rest of the group. The adult males live alone or in small bachelor herds. In the fall mating season, males mark plants with scent produced by glands on their faces, and urinate in depressions scraped into the ground. The males fight with their antlers, or "rut," for the right to court females.

White-tailed deer have brown fur on their upper parts and white undersides. The white fur extends under the tail, which gives the species its name. The males shed their antlers in midwinter and grow new ones in the spring.

Mule deer

Odocoileus hemionus

Distribution: Western North America, from northern Canada to central Mexico.
Habitat: Desert, forest and grassland.
Food: Leaves, twigs, grass, moss, fungi and lichen
Size: 4–5.5ft (1.25–1.7m); 95–330lb (43–150kg). Height at shoulder 2.5–3.5ft (0.8–1.1m).
Maturity: 3–4 years.
Breeding: 1–2 fawns born in June or July; gestation is 195–212 days.
Life span: 15 years.

Mule deer are common in the western half of North America. They range from central Mexico all the way to the edge of the Arctic tundra in northern Canada. They occupy all habitats between these points, including desert areas in Nevada, California and Arizona, and around the Great Salt Lake. The deer range eastward to Saskatchewan in the north and Texas in the south. There are also small, isolated populations further east in Iowa and Missouri.

Mule deer are most active at dawn and dusk. They feed mainly on vegetation, plus some fungi and lichens, and they can live almost anywhere where there is sufficient plant growth. Their diet of plant food is relatively poor in nutrients, so it is vital that the deer extract the most from it. To do this, the mule deer ruminate. This involves using stomach bacteria to digest the food for them, and chewing regurgitated food, or cud, to break down as much of the plant fiber as possible.

Each mule deer has a unique set of markings made up of lines along the tail and pale patches on the rump and throat. These patterns stay the same throughout the deer's life. Female mule deer live in small social groups made up of an adult female and a number of her offspring. Males are either solitary or gather in small groups of unrelated individuals.

Caribou

Rangifer tarandus

The caribou, also known as the reindeer in Europe and Asia, is the only deer species in which both males and females possess antlers. American caribou have mainly brown coats with darker legs, while European and Asian animals are more grey.

Caribou herds are organized into hierarchies based on the size of the animals' bodies and antlers. Most herds make seasonal migrations in pursuit of food. Northern populations often make round trips of more than 3,000 miles (5,000km). During the migration, herds congregate into masses up to half a million strong. Caribou have been domesticated for 3,000 years, and there are huge numbers in northern Siberia.

The antlers of male caribou can exceed 3.25ft (1m). Caribou hooves are broad and flat—an adaptation for walking on soft ground and in deep snow.

Distribution: Alaska, Canada, northern USA, Greenland, Scandinavia, Siberia, Mongolia, and north-eastern China.
Habitat: Arctic tundra, boreal forests, mountainous habitats.
Food: Plant material (leaves and twigs; especially new growth in spring) and lichens.
Size: 4–7.25ft (1.2–2.2m); 130–700lb (60–318kg). Height at shoulder 2.5–4ft (0.8–1.2m).
Maturity: 1.5–3.5 years.
Breeding: 1 fawn per year.
Life span: 15 years.

CATS

Cats belong to the Felidae *family of mammals. They fall into two main groups. The* Panthera *genus contains the big cats, such as lions and tigers, and* Felis *comprises the small cats, including the domestic cat. The majority of American cats belong to the second group, with the jaguar being the only big cat found on both continents. Most American cats are rarely seen, and some are threatened with extinction.*

Cougar

Felis concolor

Extremely strong and agile, cougar adults are able to leap more than 16.5ft (5m) into the air. Once they make a kill, their victims are dragged into secluded places and eaten over several days.

Cougars are also known as pumas, panthers, or mountain lions, and have the most widespread distribution of any American species. They live in nearly all habitats, from the mountainsides of the Canadian Rockies, to the jungles of the Amazon and the swamps of Florida.

The cougar is the largest of the small cats in America, with males up to 6.5ft (2m) long. They patrol large territories, moving both in the daytime and at night and taking shelter in caves and thickets. Their preferred food is large deer, such as mule deer or elk. They stalk their prey before bringing it down with a bite to the throat, or ambush it from a high vantage point. Cougars live alone, marking their territories with scent and by scraping visual signals in the soil and on trees.

Distribution: North, Central, and South America from southern Canada to Cape Horn.
Habitat: Any terrain with enough cover.
Food: Deer, beavers, raccoons, and hares.
Size: 3.25–6.5ft (1–2m).
Weight: 132–220lb (60–100kg).
Maturity: 3 years.
Breeding: Every 2 years; litters of 3 or 4 cubs.
Life span: 20 years.

Jaguar

Panthera onca

The jaguar is the only big cat in the Americas. It is smaller in length than the cougar, but much bulkier and heavier. Jaguars are usually a tawny yellow with dark rings, but they can also be black.

Jaguars prefer to live in areas with plenty of water for at least part of the year, although they will stray onto grasslands and into deserts in search of food. They live alone, taking refuge in secluded spots during the day and stalking prey at night. Despite being expert climbers, they hunt on the ground and drag their kills to hideaways before devouring them.

Female jaguars defend smaller territories than males, and a male's territory may overlap those of two or three females. The cats advertise their presence by scenting landmarks with urine or feces and by scraping marks on tree trunks and rocks. When a female is ready to breed, she will leave her home range and be courted by outside males. Litters usually stay with their mother for about two years.

Distribution: Southwestern United States, Mexico, Central and South America, to northern Argentina.
Habitat: Forests and swamps.
Food: Capybaras, peccaries, caimans, and tapirs.
Size: 3.5–6.25ft (1.1–1.9m)
Weight: 80–350lb (36–158kg).
Maturity: 3 years.
Breeding: Litters of 1–4 cubs born every 2 or 3 years.
Life span: 22 years.

Bobcat

Felis rufus

Bobcats are found throughout North America, except its colder northern fringes. They are especially common in the southeastern United States, where there is a population of more than one million. Bobcats survive in a range of habitats including forests, semideserts, mountains, and brush—in fact, anywhere that has plenty of hidden spaces, such as hollow trees, thickets, and crevices, in which the cats can make a den.

Bobcat fur varies from brown to tan, often marked with brown or black stripes and spots. In the past, bobcats were widely hunted for their pelts. Although it is still legal to hunt bobcats in some parts of their range, hunting is strictly controlled.

Bobcats are solitary animals and are most active at night, especially around dawn and dusk. They are good climbers but spend most of their time on the ground, using their exceptional vision, hearing, and sense of smell to locate prey in the gloom. Rabbits and hares are favored prey, but squirrels, chipmunks, rodents, and birds are also eaten. In the winter, when other prey is scarce, bobcats may hunt deer.

Bobcats defend a territory, the size of which depends on the amount of food available in the area. Each cat marks the boundaries of its territory with urine, feces, and oils secreted from an anal gland. A male will control a large territory that overlaps the smaller territories of several females, but he will only interact with them during the mating season, when these normally quiet cats may vocalize with yowling and hissing.

Distribution: From southern Canada to southern Mexico.
Habitat: Forest, semidesert, mountains, and brushland.
Food: Rodents, rabbits, small deer, large ground birds, and reptiles.
Size: 25.5–41.5in (65–105cm).
Weight: 8.75–33lb (4–15 kg).
Maturity: 8 months.
Breeding: Litter of 1–4 babies born once a year.
Life span: 12 years.

Bobcats get their name from their short tails, which are generally only about one-fifth of the animal's overall body length. The tip of the tail and ears are black. Bobcats have hairy tufts on their ears, and tufts like sideburns at the side of the head, which extend from the base of the ears to the jowl.

Jaguarundi

Felis yagouaroundi

Distribution: Texas to southern Argentina.
Habitat: Grassland, shrubland, and tropical forest.
Food: Small mammals, reptiles, birds, frogs, and fish.
Size: 30.5in (77cm).
Weight: 19.75lbs (9kg).
Maturity: 2–3 years.
Breeding: Single litter of 1–4 cubs born in summer.
Life span: 15 years.

Jaguarundis live in a range of habitats, from arid shrublands and exposed grasslands, to steamy jungles and mountain forests up to 10,500ft (3,200m). They are often found near waterways and swamps. With small heads, short legs, and long bodies, jaguarundis most resemble the flat-headed cats of Southeast Asia. Jaguarundis tend to have unspotted fur, either brownish-gray or reddish in color. Cubs are sometimes spotted at birth, but lose these markings in their first two years.

In tropical regions, where food is available all year round, jaguarundis may produce two litters per annum. Elsewhere, breeding is confined to summer. When not breeding, they live a secretive and solitary existence. They hunt by day and return to dens at night.

With their long bodies, dark fur, and rounded ears, jaguarundis have a passing resemblance to small mustelid carnivores, such as weasels and otters. This led early zoologists to name them 'weasel cats.'

DOGS

Domestic dogs belong to the Canidae *family, which includes wolves (from which they are descended), foxes, and jackals. Most types of wild canid live in large family groups called "packs." Dog societies are very complex, because the animals must cooperate to survive, especially during the winter. The dogs hunt together and take turns caring for the young.*

Gray wolf

Canis lupus

Gray wolves howl to communicate with pack members over long distances.

All domestic dogs are descended from gray wolves, which began living alongside humans many thousands of years ago. Gray wolves are the largest dogs in the wild, and they live in packs of about ten individuals. A pack has a strict hierarchy, with a male and female "alpha pair" in charge. The alpha dogs bond for life and are the only members of the pack to breed. The rest of the pack is made up of the alpha pair's offspring. In the summer, pack members often hunt alone for small animals, such as beavers or hares, but in the winter, the pack hunts together for much larger animals. Gray wolves are strong runners and can travel 125 miles (200km) in one night. They generally detect prey by smell and chase them down, taking turns to bite at the faces and flanks of their victims until they collapse from exhaustion.

Distribution: Canada and some locations in the United States and Europe, and across most of Asia.
Habitat: Tundra, pine forest, desert, and grassland.
Food: Moose, elk, musk ox, and reindeer.
Size: 3.25–5.25ft (1–1.6m).
Weight: 66–175lb (30–80kg).
Maturity: 22 months.
Breeding: Once per year.
Life span: 16 years.

Kit fox

Vulpes macrotis

Kit foxes live in the dry desert and scrub areas of the high plateaux and valleys beside the Rocky Mountains in the United States. They generally live in breeding pairs, but social bonds are quite loose and pairs often split. The female does not leave her den—made in a disused burrow—while she is suckling her litter of four or five cubs. During this time, she relies on the male for food, which is generally small rodents and rabbits, insects and fruit.

After three or four months, the young are strong enough to travel with their parents to other dens in their territory. A kit fox family's territory overlaps widely with those of other groups in the area. The size of the territory depends on the climate. Desert territories have to be large to supply enough food for the family. The kit fox is very similar in appearance and behavior to the swift fox (*Vulpes velox*), which lives on the great plains further east. It is possible that hybridization takes place where the ranges of these two dogs overlap.

Distribution: Western United States.
Habitat: Desert and scrub.
Food: Rodents, pikas, insects, and fruit.
Size: 15–19.5in (38–50cm).
Weight: 4.25–4.75lb (1.9–2.2kg).
Maturity: 1 year.
Breeding: Litters of 4–5 cubs.
Life span: 15 years.

The kit fox's large ears are lined with blood vessels that radiate heat to cool the animal down in hot desert climes.

Coyote

Canis latrans

Distribution: From Canada and the United States through Mexico to Panama.
Habitat: Desert, forest, and tundra.
Food: Small mammals, such as rabbits, ground squirrels, and mice; occasionally birds, reptiles, large invertebrates; carrion and some plant matter.
Size: 30–39.5in (76–100cm).
Weight: 17.75–44lb (8–20kg).
Maturity: 1 year.
Breeding: Single litter of 6 pups born in early summer.
Life span: 10–14 years.

Coyotes live throughout North America and Central America, from the humid forests of Panama to the treeless tundra regions of Canada and Alaska. They are most common in the unpopulated desert areas of the southwestern United States and northern Mexico.

These dogs look a little like small gray wolves. They are less likely to form packs than wolves, and are typically found alone, in pairs or in small family groups. Coyotes may dig their own den or enlarge the burrow of another animal. They are primarily nocturnal, being most active around dawn and dusk, but they do sometimes hunt during the day. They can reach speeds of up to 40mph (64kmh) when chasing swift jackrabbits and other prey.

Coyotes are adaptable opportunistic feeders, and they are able to survive in farmland and suburban regions. They are increasingly coming into conflict with human communities expanding into the desert, which see them as pests.

Coyote fur varies from gray to yellow. The head and legs may have reddish hair on them. A black line runs along the back. The bushy tail is about half as long as the rest of the body. Coyotes are much smaller than wolves, but significantly larger than foxes.

Gray fox

Vulpes cinereoargenteus

Distribution: Southern Canada to Venezuela.
Habitat: Woodland.
Food: Rabbits, other small mammals, and birds.
Size: 31.5–44in (80–112cm).
Weight: 8–15lb (3.6–6.8kg).
Maturity: 1–2 years.
Breeding: About 4 pups born in the spring.
Life span: 8 years.

Gray foxes have the bushy tail and large ears that typify foxes. The features that distinguish them from other foxes are the grizzled underparts and black tip to the tail.

Gray foxes are found in woodlands and forests, mostly in the southern half of North America. Their range continues down the western side of Central America to northern Colombia and Venezuela. They are not found in the Rockies and other mountain ranges of the western United States and Canada, nor in the highlands of Central America. They are also absent from the Great Plains region.

Male gray foxes are slightly larger than females. A mature fox has only one sexual partner during each breeding season, the timing of which depends on the location. For example, Canadian gray foxes breed in April, but those in the southern United States mate in February.

The family group usually stays together until the fall, but the young will occasionally stay with their parents until the following breeding season to help raise the next litter. Gray foxes are unusual for dogs, because they climb trees in search of prey such as insects and birds. They also eat fruits.

BEARS

The world's largest land carnivore, the Kodiak bear—a subspecies of brown bear—lives in North America. It is a huge, hairy animal that can grow to 10ft (3m) tall. Despite their immense size and strength, bears are generally not the vicious predators many people think they are. Most eat more plant food than meat, and they are usually shy beasts, preferring to stay away from humans.

Brown bear

Ursus arctos

Brown bears live in many parts of the Northern Hemisphere, and although they belong to a single species, they look somewhat different from place to place. For example, the brown bears in Europe and Asia are smaller and darker than their American cousins. In North America, there are two subspecies of brown bear: Kodiaks and grizzlies.

These bears make their homes in cold places, such as northern forests, mountains, and barren tundra. They feed on a range of fruits, plants, and small animals. Only grizzlies regularly attack large animal prey, which may include deer and even smaller black bears.

Although generally a solitary species, brown bears may gather in groups around large food supplies, such as schools of salmon beneath waterfalls.

As winter approaches, the bears dig themselves dens for semihibernation. Although they sleep during most of the winter, they often come out of the den for short periods between sleeps. Mating takes place in early summer. The female gives birth in the spring, and her cubs stay with her for at least two years.

Brown bears have humps between their powerful shoulders, and longer claws than most other bears.

Distribution: North America, Siberia, Europe, and Caucasus Mountains.
Habitat: Tundra, alpine meadows, and forests.
Food: Salmon, grasses, roots, mosses, bulbs, insects, fungi, rodents, deer, mountain sheep, and black bears.
Size: 5.5–10ft (1.7–3m).
Weight: 220–1,540lb (100–700kg).
Maturity: 6 years.
Breeding: 1–4 cubs born every 3–4 years.
Life span: 25–30 years.

American black bear

Ursus americanus

American black bears vary in coloration from black to dark or reddish-brown and pale tan. They differ from grizzlies in that they have shorter fur and no shoulder hump. They also have shorter legs and claws, which make them much better tree climbers than grizzlies.

American black bears are the smallest bears in North America. They live in the conifer forests of Canada and a few wilderness areas as far south as Mexico. They share these forests with grizzly bears and are sometimes eaten by them. Their main defense against this is to climb trees out of the reach of the less agile grizzly.

Black bears are most active at night. Three-quarters of what they eat is plant matter, with small animals, such as fish and rodents, making up the rest. Like other bears, black bears semihibernate through the winter in dens under fallen trees or in burrows. They often wake through the winter, going on excursions during breaks in the severe winter weather.

Black bears generally forage for food alone, but will congregate around a large source of food. They tend to avoid each other, especially unknown bears. In the middle of summer, males and females come together for short periods. The male leaves soon after mating, and cubs are born at the end of winter. The young stay with their mother until they are two.

Distribution: Alaska and Canada, and patchily throughout parts of the United States, from New England to Tennessee, Florida, Mississippi, and western states. Also in northern Mexico.
Habitat: Forests.
Food: Fruits, nuts, grass, roots, insects, fish, rodents, and carrion.
Size: 4.25–6ft (1.3–1.8m).
Weight: 220–595lb (100–270kg).
Maturity: 6 years.
Breeding: 1–5 cubs born every 2 years.
Life span: 25 years.

SMALL CARNIVORES

Most small carnivores belong to the Mustelidae *family. The mustelids are a diverse group, including otters, martens, and badgers, which are adapted to aquatic, arboreal, and subterranean lifestyles respectively. The world's largest and most successful mustelids live in the Americas, where they are found from the icy north to the humid tropics.*

Striped skunk

Mephitis mephitis

Distribution: North America.
Habitat: Woods, grasslands, and deserts.
Food: Rodents, other small vertebrates, insects, fruits, grains, and leaves.
Size: 11–12in (28–30cm).
Weight: 1.5–5.5lb (0.7–2.5kg).
Maturity: 1 year.
Breeding: 1–10 young born every summer.
Life span: 6 years.

The striped skunk is well known for the foul-smelling spray it produces to ward off attackers. This spray comes out of two tiny apertures inside the anus. The discharge, known as musk, is squirted in spray form or as a directed arc of droplets.

The skunk will only spray when it has exhausted all other defensive tactics. These strategies include arching its back, holding its tail erect, and stamping its feet. If these fail, the skunk will twist its body into a U-shape—so that its head and tail are facing the attacker—and release its musk. The musk, which can be smelled by humans over a mile away, causes discomfort to the eyes of an enemy.

Striped skunks are most active at night, foraging for food under the cover of thick vegetation. They spend the day in sheltered places, such as disused burrows. During the winter, skunks hibernate in their dens, staying underground for between two and three months. Mating takes place in the springtime. Litters of up to ten young are born in the summer.

The striped skunk is characterized by the broad white stripes that extend from the top of its head to the tip of its tail.

American mink

Mustela vison

Distribution: North America. Introduced to northern Europe.
Habitat: Swamps and near streams and lakes.
Food: Small mammals, fish, frogs, and crayfish.
Size: 13–17in (33–43cm).
Weight: 1.5–5lb (0.7–2.3kg).
Maturity: 1–1.5 years.
Breeding: 5 young born in the late spring.
Life span: 10 years.

American mink are small carnivores that live close to water, where they feed on small aquatic animals. They originally came from North America, but were brought to Europe and Asia to be farmed for their fine fur. They have since escaped into the wild and are now a common pest. They are also competition for the similar, but very rare, European mink.

Mink prefer to live in areas with plenty of cover. Their riverbed dens are generally deserted burrows made by other river mammals, but mink will dig their own burrows if necessary.

Mink are active at night and dive into water to snatch their prey. They live alone and will defend their own stretches of riverbank against intruders. Two months after mating, a litter of up to five young is born in a dry underground nest lined with fur, feathers, and leaves. The young begin to fend for themselves in the fall.

Mink are known for their luxurious, fine fur, which is used for clothing. Several domestic varieties of mink have been bred, each with different-colored fur.

Wolverine

Gulo gulo

Wolverines are giant relatives of weasels. As well as being found in the conifer forests of North America, these mustelids occur in northern Europe and Siberia, where they are known as gluttons due to their broad feeding habits.

Wolverines are generally nocturnal, but will forage by day if they need to. Their diet varies throughout the year. In the summer, they feed on small animals, such as rodents and ground-living birds, and readily feast on summer fruits. In the winter, when most other carnivores are hibernating, wolverines may tackle bigger prey, such as deer. The wolverines' wide feet act as snowshoes and allow them to walk in deep snow; deer, in contrast, flounder in the snow and find it difficult to escape from the wolverines. Wolverines mate in the early summer and the young are born in underground dens the following spring. They leave their mothers in the fall.

Wolverines have large heads and heavily built bodies. Their dense coats have hairs of different lengths to prevent winter snow and ice from getting too close to the skin and causing heat loss.

Distribution: Canada, northern United States, Scandinavia, and Siberia.
Habitat: Tundra and conifer forest.
Food: Carrion, eggs, rodents, berries, deer, and sheep.
Size: 25–41in (65–105cm).
Weight: 22–70lb (10–32kg).
Maturity: 2–3 years.
Breeding: Litter of 2–4 born in early spring every 2 years.
Life span: 10 years.

American badger

Taxidea taxus

American badgers are tough animals that live in the open country in the Great Plains region of North America. They are expert burrowers and use this skill to dig out their preferred foods—rodents, such as prairie dogs and ground squirrels. They rest in their own burrows during the day and emerge to feed at night. During the coldest weeks of the year, American badgers do not hibernate, but they sleep underground for several days at a time.

The badgers may bury some of their food so that they can eat it later, or even dig holes big enough for both themselves and their prey to fit into. American badgers and coyotes are known to hunt together in teams. The coyotes sniff out the buried prey and the badgers dig them out. Both parties then share the food.

Mating occurs in the summer and early fall, and births take place in the following spring. The young leave home after two months.

American badgers have a white stripe running from the nose along the back. In northern badgers, the stripe runs to the shoulders, and on those in the south of the range, it runs all the way along the back.

Distribution: Central and southern North America.
Habitat: Dry, open country.
Food: Rodents, birds, reptiles, scorpions, and insects.
Size: 16–28in (40–70cm).
Weight: 9–26.5lb (4–12kg).
Maturity: Females 4 months; males 1.3 years.
Breeding: 1–5 young born in the spring.
Life span: 14 years.

Eastern spotted skunk (*Spilogale putorius*): 11.5in (29cm); 21.25oz (600g)
Eastern spotted skunks live throughout the eastern United States. They range as far west as Minnesota and south into Mexico, and are especially common in the Midwestern states and the Appalachian Mountains. These skunks prefer woodland or other habitats with plenty of cover, such as areas of tall grass and even rocky regions. They dig burrows, possibly expanding a den abandoned by another animal. Several skunks will occupy each burrow. The eastern spotted skunk has short legs, so its body is held close to the ground. The head is small relative to the body size. This skunk is named after the spots on its head and rear.

Pygmy spotted skunk (*Spilogale pygmaea*): 8.5in (22cm); 17.5oz (500g)
The pygmy spotted skunk is restricted to a small area of woodland along Mexico's Pacific coast, where it lives in burrows or in trees. The black coat has white stripes over the back, which break into spots on the rump. Two large scent glands beside the anus spray a cloud of foul-smelling droplets to scare away predators. This is a tactic of last resort: the skunk's initial response to a threat is to lift its tail and make itself appear larger by raising its outer hairs. Then it stands on two legs and marches toward the attacker. Only if this is unsuccessful will it release the spray. Pygmy spotted skunks mate between February and March, and their young are born in May. They hunt at night, preying on smaller mammals, birds, and reptiles. They also eat carrion, insects, and fruits, and may climb trees to reach birds' eggs.

Sea otter

Enhydra lutris

Distribution: Northern Pacific coasts from California and Baja, Mexico, to Japan. Sea ice limits their northern range.
Habitat: Temperate coastal waters up to 60ft (20m) deep and less than 1 mile (1.6km) from shore.
Food: Fish and shellfish, such as sea urchins, abalones, crabs, and mollusks.
Size: 3.25–4ft (1–1.2m).
Weight: 33–99lb (15–45kg).
Maturity: Females 4 years; males 6 years.
Breeding: Single pup every 1–3 years.
Life span: 20 years.

Sea otters live in the cold coastal waters around the northern Pacific Rim. They do not need to come onto land to survive, but often do. Unlike other marine mammals, sea otters do not have thick blubber under their skins for insulation. Instead, they rely on a layer of air trapped by their soft fur to insulate them against the cold. Pollution, such as oil in the water, can reduce the fur's ability to trap air, and otters may die of hypothermia as a result.

The otters spend a minute or two at a time underwater, collecting food such as shellfish and urchins. They then float on their backs to feed. They smash the hard shells against stones to get at the soft meat inside, using their chests as tables.

Sea otters are active during the day. At night, they wrap themselves in kelp before going to sleep to prevent themselves from floating away. They sometimes put their forepaws over their eyes while they are sleeping.

These solitary creatures live alone and only tolerate each other when mating. A male will defend his territory, but fights are unusual, since most disputes are settled by splashing and vocal contests. Breeding occurs all year round. Pups are carried on the female's chest for about two months, when they begin to feed themselves. They are independent by the time they are six months old.

Sea otter fur comprises 100,000 hairs per 0.15sq in (1sq cm), making it the densest fur of any mammal. This keeps the animal warm in the cold ocean. The hind feet are webbed and flipper-shaped.

North American river otter

Lutra canadensis

Distribution: Widespread across most of North America.
Habitat: Rivers and lakes.
Food: Amphibians, fish, crayfish, and aquatic insects.
Size: 23.5–43in (60–110cm).
Weight: 6.5–30lb (3–14kg).
Maturity: 2–3 years.
Breeding: 1–5 young born every year.
Life span: 20 years.

North American river otters rarely stray far from the banks of shallow rivers. They live alone or in pairs, but often play with other individuals in the area. This play strengthens social ties. Each of the otters has an individual scent that it uses to mark its territory. River otters communicate with each other through sounds such as whistles, growls, chuckles, and screams.

North American river otters are known for their boundless energy, and they must eat frequently. They catch fish in their mouths and detect other prey by feeling with their whiskers along the bottoms of streams. Unlike many other otters that chew their food, the river otter's prey is gulped down immediately.

Mating takes place in March and April. The young are born almost a year later. The females give birth in dens close to the water's edge. They drive the males away soon after the birth of their young, but the dog otters return later to help raise the offspring. The young depart at the age of one year.

River otters have streamlined bodies with dark fur, thick tails, and short legs with webbed feet.

Fisher

Martes pennanti

The fisher, or pekan, lives in the thick forests of North America. Despite its name, it feeds on small land animals, such as mice and porcupines. Fishers have no permanent dens, but take shelter in hollow trees, holes in the ground, and even abandoned beaver lodges. They are active during the day and night, and despite being expert climbers, spend most of their foraging time on the ground. When they come across suitable prey animals, they rush forward and kill them with bites to the back of the neck. Larger animals are killed with repeated bites to the face.

Males seek out mates during the spring breeding season and litters are born about ten months later. As with many mustelids, the fertilized eggs do not begin to grow immediately inside the females. Their development is delayed for several months so that they are born at the right time of year. Unusually, births always take place in trees.

Fishers have dark fur that is coarser than that of most mustelids. Nevertheless, they are still hunted by humans for their fur.

Distribution: Canada and northern United States.
Habitat: Conifer forest.
Food: Birds, rodents, carrion.
Size: 19–25in (49–63cm).
Weight: 2.75–7lb (1.3–3.2kg).
Maturity: 1–2 years.
Breeding: 3 young born every spring.
Life span: 10 years.

Black-footed ferret

Mustela nigripes

Before the prairies of the North American West were cultivated for farmland and turned into cattle pasture, black-footed ferrets would have been a common sight. The burrows that they and their prey made in the ground formed dangerous obstacles to grazing cattle and farm machinery, so the animals were methodically exterminated by pioneer farmers. Today, the ferrets—the only species of ferret native to North America—occur wild in just three places in Montana, South Dakota, and Wyoming (all reintroduced populations).

Black-footed ferrets live on and under prairies that have short or medium-length grasses. Each ferret occupies about 100 acres (40ha) of prairie, in which it finds all its food, but a nursing mother needs two or three times this space. Black-footed ferrets take up residence in burrow systems abandoned by prairie dogs, their main food. In places where prairie dogs form large communal "towns," the ferrets may actually live among their prey.

The breeding season is in late spring. The young remain underground for a month after they are born. Mother and young forage together in late summer, generally at night, and by the fall, the young begin to drift away. Males take no part in raising the young.

As well as having black feet, these ferrets have a black "mask" over their eyes. The underside of the body is covered in yellowish fur. Male black-footed ferrets are slightly larger than females.

Distribution: Historically southern Canada to northern Mexico; today, reintroduced populations exist in Montana, South Dakota, and Wyoming.
Habitat: Prairie.
Food: Mainly prairie dogs, along with some mice, ground squirrels, and other small animals.
Size: 15–23.5in (38–60cm).
Weight: 22.75–39.75oz (645–1,125g).
Maturity: 1 year.
Breeding: Single litter of 1–6 young produced in the early summer, after a gestation of 35–45 days.
Life span: 5 years.

Greater grisón

Galictis vittata

Distribution: From Mexico through Central and South America to Brazil and Bolivia.
Habitat: Grasslands and rain forest, often near water.
Food: Small mammals, including chinchillas, viscachas, agoutis, and mice; occasionally reptiles, birds, and some fruits.
Size: 20in (51cm).
Weight: 4.5lb (2kg).
Maturity: 1 year.
Breeding: 2–4 young born between March and October
Life span: 5 years.

The greater grisón's range stretches from southern Mexico to Brazil and Bolivia. These animals are found mainly in lowland areas, rarely ascending to more than 5,000ft (1,500m) above sea level. Within its large range, the greater grisón lives in a variety of habitats, from dry savannahs and grasslands to more verdant areas, including rain forests. The grisón makes its home in secluded spots, such as under tree roots or in rock crevices, and it sometimes takes over the abandoned burrows of armadillos.

Like other small carnivores, the grisón has a long, powerful body, with short legs and a short tail. Although the body form limits the animal to slow running speeds, it does enable it to wriggle into tight spaces, such as the burrows of its prey. The ears are small, so they do not get snagged in tight spots, and the claws are wide and very long for digging and extracting food.

Grisóns have more robust bodies than weasels. The greater grisón's most obvious feature is the white stripe across its face and around its ears. This stripe divides the black face from the gray forehead, giving the animal's face a banded appearance. The rest of the body is grizzled gray and black. Greater grisóns may live alone, in pairs, or in small groups. These agile predators despatch their prey with a bite to the neck.

Long-tailed weasel

Mustela frenata

Distribution: From southern Canada to Bolivia.
Habitat: Grassland, shrubland, and open woodland.
Food: Small rodents, rabbits, birds, and reptiles.
Size: 8–10in (20–26cm);
Weight: 3–12oz (80–350g). Males are larger than females.
Maturity: 6 months.
Breeding: 6 young born in the spring.
Life span: 5 years.

This species has the largest range of any American weasel, from southern Canada through the United States and Central America, to the lower slopes of the Bolivian Andes.

Long-tailed weasels occupy a range of habitats, from farmland and yards to woodland. However, they avoid dense forests and desert areas. The weasels are most easily spotted emerging from their burrows, which tend to be inside tree hollows, under rocks, and in other secluded spots. They often take over the burrow of one of their prey, enlarging the accommodation if necessary. Long-tailed weasels are good climbers and swimmers. They hunt at night, tracking prey by scent.

The fur is reddish-brown, with a yellowish underside. In colder regions, where snowfall is common, the weasel develops a white winter coat.

This weasel's tail is particularly bushy compared with those of other weasels. Apart from this, the form is fairly typical, with short legs, small ears, and a long, flexible body.

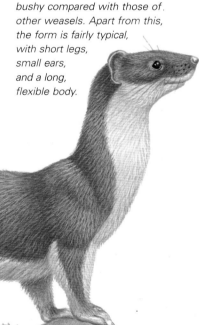

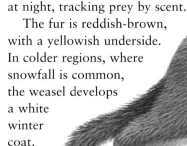

Stoat

Mustela erminea

Although rarely seen, stoats are common in the countryside, where they mainly feed on rodents. The large males will often prey on rabbits, even though rabbits are considerably larger. Stoats are said to mesmerize their prey by dancing around them, before darting in for the kill. This is not just a rural myth. Stoats have been observed leaping around near rabbits in a seemingly deranged fashion. This curious "dance" seems to have the effect of confusing the rabbits, which just watch the stoat draw slowly closer and closer, until it is too late to escape. The stoats then grasp the prey with their sharp teeth.

In mild climates, stoats have chestnut fur all year round. In colder areas, their coats change to pure white by the time the first snows have fallen. White stoats are known as ermines, and their fur was once prized for its pure color and soft feel.

Distribution: Widespread in northern and central Europe, extending into Asia and across northern North America. Introduced to New Zealand.
Habitat: Anywhere with enough cover.
Food: Mammals up to the size of rabbits.
Size: 6.25–12.25in (16–31cm).
Weight: 5–15.75oz (140–445g).
Maturity: 1 year.
Breeding: Single litter of 5–12 young.
Life span: 10 years.

Stoats are distinguished from their smaller cousins, weasels, by having black tips to their tails.

Least weasel

Mustela nivalis

Least weasels are common throughout Canada and Alaska. Their North American range extends to the forests of the Carolinas and the prairies of Wyoming. They are also found throughout much of the Northern Hemisphere, with the exception of most islands and Arabia. They survive in a wide variety of habitats, but they avoid thick forests, sandy deserts, and any exposed spaces.

These creatures have a very long body, with a long neck and flat head. This allows them to move with ease over broken ground and inside burrows. The size of this weasel varies with its distribution across the globe. The largest least weasels are found in North Africa, and those in North America have the smallest bodies.

Least weasels live alone outside of the breeding season. Males occupy territories that are home to two or more females. They forage for food at all times of the day or night. They watch carefully for movements caused by prey, before launching an attack and dispatching their victims with a bite to the neck.

Distribution: Arctic to North Carolina; also found in Northern Asia, Africa, and Europe.
Habitat: Forest, prairie, farmland, and semidesert.
Food: Rodents, eggs, nestlings, and lizards.
Size: 6.25–8in (16–20cm).
Weight: 1–2oz (30–55g).
Maturity: 8 months
Breeding: Two litters of up to 7 young, born in the spring and late summer.
Life span: 7 years.

In the summer, the least weasel's brown fur is about 0.4in (1cm) long, but the winter coat is more than double this length. In the far north, the coat also turns white in winter.

American marten

Martes americana

The American marten lives in the cold northern pine forests of Canada, ranging from Newfoundland in the east to Alaska in the west. Martens also live in the high-altitude mountain areas of the continental United States, where conditions are similar to the cold north. The fur of the American marten is highly valued, and although the species is not endangered, hunting and the destruction of its conifer-forest habitat have caused a severe decline in numbers in many parts of its range.

American martens spend the day in nooks and crannies in the forest, and move through the trees and along the ground in search of food at night. To compensate for the low light levels, martens have large eyes, and large ears (for a mustelid) that resemble those of a cat. They kill their prey with their long, curved claws and sharp teeth. Their diet includes small mammals, carrion, fruits, and insects.

Young martens are born in the spring. Animals of breeding age locate each other by scent, releasing a strong odor from their anal glands. They live alone for the rest of the year.

Distribution: Canada to northern California and Colorado.
Habitat: Pine forests.
Food: Small mammals, carrion, fruits, and insects.
Size: 12.5–18in (32–45cm).
Weight: 0.75–2.75lb (0.3–1.3kg).
Maturity: 2 years.
Breeding: Up to 5 kits produced in March or April.
Life span: 10 years.

The American marten has a long, slender body, and large eyes and ears. The fur on the head is light brown or gray, and the legs, tail, and upper surface of the body are dark brown or black. The underside is pale yellow or cream.

Tayra

Eira barbara

This unusual species is found from central Mexico to northern Argentina, and also on the island of Trinidad. It lives in thick forests, from lowland regions to about 7,900ft (2,400m) above sea level. A few tayras are known to live in areas of tall grass.

Tayras forage for food on the ground and also in the trees, where their long tail helps them to balance as they move through the branches. As well as being nimble climbers and agile on the ground, these weasels can also swim well. Tayras are mainly active during the day. They make their nests in hollow trees or logs, grassy thickets, or in the burrows of other animals. Most tayras live alone or in pairs. Sometimes they form small groups of up to four individuals. Members of the group may work together to prey on animals such as large rodents and small deer. When they are being chased by predators, tayras will evade capture by running up trees and leaping from branch to branch.

Tayras can be tamed, and they are sometimes kept as pets. Indigenous people once used them to control rodent pests in homes.

Distribution: From Central Mexico to Bolivia and Argentina; also found on the island of Trinidad.
Habitat: Tropical deciduous and evergreen forests.
Food: Mainly rodents, but also rabbits, small deer, birds, reptiles, invertebrates, honey, and fruits.
Size: 40in (100cm).
Weight: 8.75–11lb (4–5kg).
Maturity: 2 years.
Breeding: 3 kits born between March and July; however, some authorities claim that breeding is nonseasonal.
Life span: Unknown.

When fully grown, this large weasel is as big as a medium-size dog. The short coat varies from gray to black, and the tail is bushy and long. The tayra has a long, robust body, and large hind feet with long claws.

RABBITS

Rabbits, hares, and pikas belong to the mammal order Lagomorpha. *Most of the lagomorphs that live in the Americas are found north of Mexico. Unlike their cousins in Europe, most American rabbits do not dig burrows. Like hares, they generally shelter above ground. The only rabbit to dig its own burrow is the pygmy rabbit, which is also the smallest rabbit in the world.*

Pika

Ochotona princeps

The pikas of North America live in areas of scree—fragments of eroded rock found beneath cliffs or mountain slopes. They shelter under the rocks and feed on patches of vegetation that grow among the scree. Pikas may forage at all times of the day or night, but most activity takes place in the early mornings or evenings.

During the winter, pikas survive by eating "ladders" of grass and leaves that they have collected during the late summer. These ladders are piles made in sunny places, so that the plants desiccate into alpine hay. Like most of their rabbit relatives, pikas eat their primary droppings so that their tough food is digested twice, in order to extract all of the nutrients.

Adult pikas live alone and defend territories during the winter. In the spring, males expand their territories to include those of neighboring females. Most females produce two litters during each summer. When preparing for winter, the females chase their mates back to their own territories and expel their mature offspring.

Pikas are small relatives of rabbits. They do not have tails, and their rounded bodies are covered in soft red and gray fur. Unlike those of a rabbit, a pika's hind legs are about the same length as its forelegs.

Distribution: Southwestern Canada and western United States.
Habitat: Broken, rocky country, and scree.
Food: Grass, sedge, weeds, and leaves.
Size: 4.75–12in (12–30cm).
Weight: 4–6.25oz (110–180g).
Maturity: 3 months.
Breeding: 2 litters of 2–4 young born during summer.
Life span: 7 years.

Snowshoe hare

Lepus americanus

Like most hares, snowshoe hares do not dig burrows. Instead they shelter in shallow depressions called forms, which they scrape in soil or snow. Snowshoe hares are generally nocturnal, and rest in secluded forms or under logs during the day. When dusk arrives, the hares follow systems of runways through the dense forest undergrowth to feeding sites. They maintain these runways by biting away branches that block the way and compacting the winter snow.

In summer, the hares nibble on grasses and other green plant material. They survive the long winter by supplementing their diet with buds, twigs, and bark. Over several years, the overall population of snowshoe hares can rise and fall dramatically. At the low points, there may be only five animals per square mile. At the peak, there may be as many as 1,300 in the same area.

Snowshoe hares are more social than other hares. During the spring breeding season, the male hares compete with each other to establish hierarchies and gain access to mates. Conflicts often result in boxing fights—hence "mad March hares."

Distribution: Alaska, Canada, and northern United States.
Habitat: Conifer forest.
Food: Grass, leaves, buds, and bark.
Size: 15.5–27.5in (40–70cm).
Weight: 2.75–15.5lb (1.35–7kg).
Maturity: 1 year.
Breeding: 4 litters of 2–4 young produced per year.
Life span: 5 years.

In the summer, the snowshoe hare's fur is a rusty or grayish brown, but in areas with heavy winter snow, the fur is white as a camouflage against predators.

Eastern cottontail

Sylvilagus floridanus

Eastern cottontail rabbits do not dig burrows, although they may shelter in disused ones dug by other animals. Generally, they shelter in thickets or forms—shallow depressions made in tall grass or scraped in the ground. Cottontails forage at night, grazing mainly on grasses, but also nibbling small shrubs. Unlike hares, which rely on their speed to outrun predators, cottontails freeze when under threat, blending into their surroundings. If they have to run, they follow zigzag paths, attempting to shake off their pursuers.

In warmer parts of their range, cottontails breed all year round, but farther north, breeding is restricted to summer. Males fight to establish hierarchies, with top males getting their choice of mates. A pregnant female digs a shallow hole, which is deeper at one end than the other. She lines the nest with grass and fur from her belly. Once she has given birth, she crouches over the shallow end and her young crawl up from the warm deep end to suckle.

Distribution: Eastern Canada and United States to Venezuela.
Habitat: Farmland, forest, desert, swamp, and prairie.
Food: Grass, leaves, twigs, and bark.
Size: 8.5–18.5in (21–47cm).
Weight: 1.75–3.25lb (0.8–1.5kg).
Maturity: 80 days.
Breeding: 3–7 litters per year, each of up to 12 young.
Life span: 5 years.

Female cottontails are larger than the males. The name "cottontail" is derived from their short, rounded tails, which are white on the underside. Their upper bodies are covered in gray, brown, and reddish hairs.

Pygmy rabbit (*Brachylagus idahoensis*): 8.5–10.5in (21–27cm); 7–16oz (200–450g) These rabbits live on an arid plateau in the northwest of the United States. Pygmy rabbits are related to cottontails, but they are about half the size. They dig burrows under thickets of sagebrush—the only North American rabbit to do so—and move through a network of runways above ground. They eat the sagebrush, and are most active at dawn and dusk.

Swamp rabbit (*Sylvilagus aquaticus*): 18–21.5in (45–55cm); 3.25–5.5lb (1.5–2.5kg) Swamp rabbits live in the wetlands around the Mississippi Delta and other rivers in the southern United States. Unlike most rabbits, the males and females of this species are about the same size. Swamp rabbits build nests of dead plants and fur at ground level. They maintain territories by calling to intruders and marking their areas with scent. They breed all year round. Female swamp rabbits may produce up to 40 young per year.

Collared pika (*Ochotona collaris*): 7–8in (18–20cm); 4.5oz (130g) Collared pikas inhabit the cold mountains of central and southern Alaska and northwestern Canada, where they are found in scree and other rocky areas above the timberline. There is a grayish "collar" around the neck and shoulders. These diurnal animals feed on herbs and grasses, and make hay piles to eat during the winter. Collared pikas produce about three young in each litter.

Jackrabbit

Lepus californicus

Jackrabbits are actually a type of hare and so share many of the hare's characteristics, from long ears to large, hairy hind feet. Jackrabbits live in dry areas with only sparse plant cover. This has benefited the species in the past. Overgrazing of the land by cattle in the arid southwest of the United States and Mexico has created an ideal habitat for jackrabbits.

Unlike other hares, jackrabbits make use of burrows. They do not dig their own, but they modify underground shelters made by tortoises. Jackrabbits feed on grasses and herbaceous plants, which also supply them with nearly all the water they need.

Distribution: Southwestern United States to northern Mexico.
Habitat: Dry grasslands.
Food: Grass.
Size: 15.5–27.5in (40–70cm).
Weight: 2.75–15.5lb (1.3–7kg).
Maturity: 1 year.
Breeding: 3–4 litters of 1–6 young each year.
Life span: 5 years.

Female jackrabbits are larger than males. They have gray fur with reddish and brown flecks. Their undersides are paler, and their tails and the tips of their huge ears are black. Like other hares, male jackrabbits indulge in frenzied fights during the breeding season.

RACCOONS AND RELATIVES

Raccoons and their relatives belong to a family of mammals called the Procyonidae. *Procyonids are small, opportunistic feeders and scavenging animals. Many live in trees, but the most successful—the raccoons—live mainly on the ground. Most procyonids live in the Americas, where they range from the cold northern forests of Canada to the humid, tropical swamps of the Amazon.*

Common raccoon

Procyon lotor

Raccoons live in woodland areas and rarely stray far from water. They are more active at night than during the day. Periods of rest are spent in dens in tree hollows or other sheltered places. When on the move, raccoons will readily swim across streams and rivers, and climb into trees in search of food. They use their sensitive forepaws to grab prey and then break it into mouth-sized pieces.

Raccoons do not hibernate in warmer parts of their range, although in cooler northern parts, they may do so. In fact, they only semihibernate, appearing every now and then to feed during breaks in the severest weather.

Males are largely solitary but will tolerate the presence of females living in or near their territories. Mating takes place in the spring, and young are born a couple of months later. The young stay with their mothers until the following spring.

The common raccoon is well known for its black "bandit" mask across the eyes and its tail ringed with black hoops. The animal's footprints look similar to those of a human infant.

Distribution: Southern Canada throughout the United States to Central America.
Habitat: Forests and brushland.
Food: Crayfish, frogs, fish, nuts, seeds, acorns, and berries.
Size: 16–23.5in (41–60cm).
Weight: 4.5–26.5lb (2–12kg).
Maturity: 1 year.
Breeding: 3 or 4 young born in the summer.
Life span: 5 years.

Ringtail

Bassariscus astutus

This species is named after its bushy tail, which is ringed with black and white stripes, much like the tail of a raccoon. However, ringtails have more agile, catlike bodies than raccoons. Both the ringtail and its relative, the cacomistle, are largely solitary, and become aggressive toward intruders into their territory. A ringtail scent-marks its territory by regularly urinating at specific sites.

Ringtails are found from the western United States to southern Mexico. They are most commonly found in highland forests. They prefer rocky areas, such as canyons, but also occupy a range of lowland habitats, including deserts, woodland, and shrubland. Although they prefer dry environments, they are also common near rivers, where food is easier to find.

When ready to give birth, females make a den under a boulder or in a hollow tree. The young are suckled for ten weeks, after which the mother has to hunt for their food. The young disperse after about ten months.

Ringtails are most active at night, spending most of their time foraging. They are excellent climbers, and literally search high and low for rodents, squirrels, insects, and other small animals. When they finish eating, ringtails groom themselves by licking their fur. If threatened, their tail bristles and arches over their head, making them look larger.

Distribution: From southern Oregon and eastern Kansas in the western United States to southern Mexico, including Baja California.
Habitat: Rocky areas, woodland, and shrubland, and montane conifer forest.
Food: Small mammals, insects, birds, lizards, frogs, nuts, and fruits.
Size: 12–16.5in (30–42cm).
Weight: 1.75–3lb (0.8–1.4kg).
Maturity: 10 months.
Breeding: Single litter of 1–4 young born between April and July.
Life span: 7 years.

RODENTS

The Rodentia *order is the largest, most widespread and most diverse mammal group. There are more than 2,000 species of rodent, making up almost half of all mammal species. The secret of the rodents' success is their teeth. Their long, chisel-shaped incisors keep growing throughout their lives. These teeth are self-sharpening, enabling rodents to eat almost any food, from wood to meat and even household trash.*

Gray squirrel

Sciurus carolinensis

Distribution: Eastern North America. Introduced to parts of Europe.
Habitat: Woodlands.
Food: Nuts, flowers, and buds.
Size: 15–20.5in (38–52cm).
Weight: 0.75–1.5lb (0.3–0.7kg).
Maturity: 10 months.
Breeding: 2 litters born each year with 2–4 young per litter.
Life span: 12 years.

Gray squirrels are native to the open woodlands of eastern North America. They have also been introduced into parts of Europe, where they have out-competed the smaller red squirrels for food and breeding sites.

Gray squirrels feed primarily on the nuts and buds of many woodland trees. In the summer, when they are most active just after dawn and before dusk, gray squirrels also eat insects. In the winter, when most animals of their size are hibernating, gray squirrels spend their days eating stores of food that they buried throughout the previous summer. Gray squirrels may make dens in hollow trees, but are more likely to make nests, or dreys, from twigs and leaves in the boughs of trees.

There are two breeding seasons each year: one beginning in midwinter, the other in midsummer. Males begin to chase females through the trees a few days before they are receptive to mating. When females are ready, their vulvas become pink and engorged. Litters of three are born six weeks later.

Gray squirrels have, as their name suggests, grayish fur, although many individuals have reddish patches. Their tails, which have many white hairs, are bushier than those of most other squirrels.

Woodchuck

Marmota monax

Distribution: Southern Canada southward through eastern North America.
Habitat: Woodland or open areas that have plenty of ground cover.
Food: Plant leaves and stems.
Size: 17.5–25.5in (45–65cm).
Weight: 4.5–11lb (2–5kg).
Maturity: 2 years.
Breeding: 3–5 young born in May.
Life span: 6 years.

Woodchucks are also called groundhogs or whistle pigs—the latter because of the shrill alarm call they make when threatened. Unlike most other squirrels, they eat the green parts of plants rather than the seeds and buds. They also eat bark and small twigs. Their natural habitat is the edge of forests or other open areas where there is plenty of cover. With the growth of agriculture, woodchucks have increased in number, making use of hedges beside open fields. They live alone, unlike most other ground squirrels.

Woodchucks hibernate in the winter, living off the fat reserves that they build up over the summer. Their winter sleep is much deeper than that of most squirrels. Mating takes place soon after hibernation ends. Female woodchucks have a single litter every year, and males mate with more than one female. Young woodchucks are thrown out of their mother's burrow after a few months.

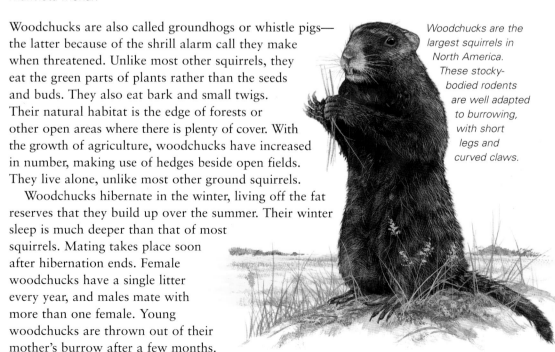

Woodchucks are the largest squirrels in North America. These stocky-bodied rodents are well adapted to burrowing, with short legs and curved claws.

Northern pocket gopher

Thomomys talpoides

Northern pocket gophers have robust, tubular bodies with short legs. Their forefeet have long claws and their tails are naked at the tip. Male gophers are much larger than females.

Pocket gophers spend a great deal of their time burrowing. They feed on the underground parts of plants, such as roots, tubers, and bulbs. The gophers access their food by digging temporary feeding tunnels out and up from deeper and more permanent galleries, located 3.25–10ft (1–3m) underground. Gophers keep their burrow entrances blocked with earth most of the time, and rarely appear above ground during the day. At night, they may move around on the surface. Gophers carry food in pouches inside their cheeks to storage or feeding sites in their burrow systems. They do not drink water, and so get all of their liquid from plant juices.

Only during the mating season will a male be allowed into a female's burrow. Litters are born just 18 days after mating, which generally takes place in summer.

Distribution: Western North America from Canada to Mexico.
Habitat: Burrows under desert, prairie, and forest.
Food: Roots, bulbs, and leaves.
Size: 4.5–12in (11–30cm).
Weight: 1.75–17.75oz (50–500g).
Maturity: 1 year.
Breeding: 1–10 young born in the summer.
Life span: 2 years.

Hoary marmot (*Marmota caligata*): 18–22.5in (45–57cm); 8–20lb (3.6–9.1kg)
This species occurs in the northern Pacific region of North America, from Idaho and Washington to Alaska. It inhabits the pine forests typical of cold climates and high mountains, and also the alpine meadows that bloom above the timberline in the summer. It is called hoary because of the white hairs that grizzle its black fur, giving it a silver-gray appearance. Like other ground squirrels, the hoary marmot is an expert digger, using the long, robust claws on its forefeet for excavation. It hibernates through the winter in large burrows.

Yellow-bellied marmot (*Marmota flaviventris*): 13.5–19in (34.5–48cm); 3.3–11lb (1.5–5kg)
These marmots occur in western North America, from southwestern Canada to the U.S.–Mexico border, typically in meadows, prairies, and around forest edges. Their underside is lined with yellow fur, and there are yellow speckles on the neck. Yellow-bellied marmots live in extensive burrows, in groups comprising an adult male and two or three females. Hibernation burrows are dug several yards down to avoid ground frost. The diet consists of fruits, seeds, and some insects.

Plains pocket gopher (*Geomys bursarius*): 7.5–14in (19–36cm); 10.5–16oz (300–450g)
This brown, burrowing animal lives on the plains between the Mississippi River and the Rocky Mountains, from Texas and northeastern Mexico to the Canadian border. Common in open habitats, it also occurs in sparsely wooded areas where tree roots do not dominate the soil. It prefers deep, sandy soils supporting plants that produce storage tubers and roots—the gopher's main food.

American beaver

Castor canadensis

Beavers are among the largest of all rodents. Family groups of beavers live in large nests, called lodges, in or near forest streams or small lakes. Beavers eat wood and other tough plant foods, which have to be soaked in water before being eaten.

They use their large front teeth to gnaw through the base of small trees. Sections of these logs are transported back to the lodge via a system of canals dug into the forest. If necessary, beavers will also dam a stream with debris to make a pool deep enough to store their food. A beaver colony may maintain a dam for several generations. The lodge has underwater entrances so beavers can swim out to their food supply even when the pool is frozen.

Distribution: North America.
Habitat: Streams and small lakes.
Food: Wood, leaves, roots, and bark.
Size: 23.5–31.5in (60–80cm).
Weight: 26.5–55lb (12–25kg).
Maturity: 1.5–2 years.
Breeding: 2–4 young born each spring.
Life span: 24 years.

A beaver has webbed hind feet, a flattened tail for swimming, and large front teeth for gnawing through wood. Its fur is coated with oil to keep it waterproof.

Alaska marmot

Marmota broweri

Distribution: Brooks Mountains of northern Alaska.
Habitat: Scree, rocky outcrops, and boulder fields.
Food: Grasses, forbs, fruits, seeds, legumes, and occasionally insects.
Size: 21.5–25.5in (54–65cm).
Weight: 5.5–8.75lb (2.5–4kg).
Maturity: 2 years.
Breeding: Single litter of 3–8 young born in the spring, after a gestation period of about 5 weeks.
Life span: 14 years.

Alaska marmots are found only in small areas of the Brooks Mountains in northern Alaska, where they live amid rock slides and on boulder-strewn slopes. The marmots occupy the spaces formed under the rocks, burrowing into the permafrost with their strong foreclaws to make a living area. The plants that grow on the broken, rocky ground resemble those of tundra and alpine areas, and they provide the marmots with most of their food.

Alaska marmots are social animals living in colonies of up to 50 individuals. The colony shares and maintains a tunnel system, although each marmot has its own den. Within a few yards of each den is an observation post, where a marmot can keep a lookout for predators such as wolverines and bears. Members of the colony take turns to keep watch. The larger the colony, the less time each animal has to spend on sentry duty, and the more time it can devote to sunbathing, feeding, and grooming. When danger is spotted, sentries let out a warning call and the colony disappears below ground.

The Alaska marmot has thick, coarse hair, which makes its heavyset body appear even more rounded. It is adapted to a burrowing lifestyle, with powerful legs and strong, sharp claws for digging. Its body weight varies during the year, since it has to build up substantial fat reserves in the summer to see it through hibernation, when it loses one-fifth of its bodyweight.

Southern flying squirrel

Glaucomys volans

Distribution: Southeastern Canada to Central America.
Habitat: Woodland.
Food: Nuts, seeds, fruit, insects, leaf buds, bark, young birds, young mice, and fungi.
Size: 8.25–10.25in (21–26cm).
Weight: 1.75–6.5oz (50–180g).
Maturity: 1 year.
Breeding: 2–3 young born twice a year, in the spring and the fall.
Life span: Up to 10 years.

Southern flying squirrels inhabit woodlands, and their range extends from Quebec in eastern North America to Honduras in Central America. Their bodies resemble those of other squirrels, except that they have loose folds of skin that run along their sides and attach to their elongated arms and legs. When the limbs are outstretched, these skin folds are pulled tight to form winglike membranes. Their eyes are large, as they are nocturnal.

The flying squirrel cannot actually fly, since the lift force created by the flaps of skin is not enough to keep the animal aloft. It can, however, glide down from tall treetops to lower branches or to the ground. The squirrel uses its flattened tail as a rudder during glides. For example, when it is time to land, the tail is lifted, altering the animal's center of gravity and tilting the body upward. This causes the skin membrane to act as a brake, slowing the squirrel for a safe landing. Once on the ground, the squirrel scurries around to the other side of the tree to avoid predators that may have spotted the glide. To get back up the tree, it climbs in conventional squirrel fashion.

The fur-covered flap of skin between a flying squirrel's fore and hind legs is called the gliding membrane. It extends along the side of the body from the ankle to the wrist, and tightens when the animal spreads its limbs during a glide.

Black-tailed prairie dog

Cynomys ludovicianus

Distribution: From southwestern Canada to northeastern Mexico.
Habitat: Grassland.
Food: Grasses and forbs.
Size: 11–13in (28–33cm); 1.5–3lb (0.7–1.4kg).
Maturity: 2 years.
Breeding: 3–6 young born in early spring.
Life span: 5 years.
Status: Low risk.

This species of prairie dog inhabits the great prairies that roll south from southwestern Canada to northeastern Mexico. Black-tailed prairie dogs live in large colonies that excavate extensive communal burrows called "towns." In frontier times, one huge town in western Texas was estimated to contain 400 million prairie dogs. Today, these rodents are much rarer. They have been exterminated in many places, partly because they devour cereal crops, and partly because grazing livestock injure themselves in the prairie dogs' burrow holes.

Prairie dogs are the most social of all ground squirrels. Each town is divided into smaller neighborhoods, or coteries. Females stay in the coterie they were born in, forming a band of sisters and female cousins. However, young males set up home in the surrounding coteries. Generally, there is one adult male per coterie, although brothers sometimes occupy a particularly large coterie.

This rodent is actually a type of ground squirrel, but it is referred to as a prairie "dog" because of its barking call. Black-tailed prairie dogs molt twice a year. After each molt, their hairs are a slightly different mixture of colors, ranging from red and yellow to silver and black. The tail has a black tip.

Olympic marmot (*Marmota olympus*):
18–21in (46–53 cm); 6.5–19.75lb (3–9kg)
Olympic marmots live on the rock-strewn alpine meadows of the Olympic Peninsula, Washington state, in the northwestern United States. They live in groups of about a dozen, made up of an adult male plus two or three females and their offspring. Females produce litters every two years. The marmots forage throughout their territory by day for seeds, fruits, and insects. At dusk, they follow scent trails back to their burrows.

Northern flying squirrel (*Glaucomys sabrinus*):
10.5–13.5in (27–34cm); 2.5–5oz (75–180g)
The northern flying squirrel is smaller than its southern relative, but it has the same gliding membrane for swooping between trees. It occurs from Alaska down North America's Pacific coast to California. Inland it is found in the Rockies, the Appalachians, across the Great Lakes and New England, and as far south as the Sierra Nevada of Mexico. This species inhabits a variety of woodland, from the pine-clad peaks of the sub-Arctic, to the lowland deciduous forests of the Midwest. It eats nuts, fungi, fruits, and lichens.

White-tailed prairie dog (*Cynomys leucurus*):
13.5–14.5in (34–37cm); weight unknown
Slightly larger than the black-tailed prairie dog, this rodent lives in the grasslands of the western United States. It does not live in such large social groups as its black-tailed cousin. White-tailed prairie dogs hibernate from late summer to the spring, and breed as soon as they emerge from their winter burrows.

Mountain beaver

Aplodontia rufa

The main populations of mountain beavers are found in two mountain ranges, one extending from southern British Columbia to northern California, and the other from California to western Nevada. Although these forest-dwelling rodents can be found right up to the timberline at 7,200ft (2,200m), they are more common at lower levels. They prefer to be near a source of water, and they also need areas of deep soil in which they can dig their burrows. The burrows are often located under fallen logs.

Mountain beavers live solitary lives and rarely stray more than a few yards from their burrows. They rely on their senses of smell and touch to orient themselves. Their diet consists of very tough plant food, and they have to digest it twice in order to get all the nutrients out of it. This involves eating pellets of feces.

Despite their name, these animals are not true beavers, and they do not dig canals, fell trees, or build dams.

Distribution: British Columbia to California and Nevada.
Habitat: Forest and alpine meadows.
Food: Forbs, grasses, and ferns.
Size: 12–18in (30–46cm).
Weight: 1.75–3.25lb (0.8–1.5kg).
Maturity: 1 year.
Breeding: 2–3 young born in springtime.
Life span: 5–10 years.

American red squirrel

Tamiasciurus hudsonicus

Distribution: North America, including Canada, New England, the Appalachian Mountains, and the northern Rockies.
Habitat: Forest.
Food: Seeds, fruits, nuts, bark, buds, shed antlers, small animals.
Size: 6.25–9in (16–23cm).
Weight: 5–8.25oz (140–250g).
Maturity: 1 year.
Breeding: Up to 8 young born in late winter. In warmer climates, there are two breeding seasons, in the late winter and midsummer.
Life span: 7 years.

American red squirrels live in a range of forest habitats, from the pine forests of Canada's cold northern regions, to the deciduous woodlands that grow farther south, as far as Arizona. Although the squirrel's name suggests that it has red hairs, in reality, the fur changes color throughout the year, ranging from a dark brown to ginger. The belly is covered in much paler fur. Each eye has a white ring around it.

Red squirrels live alone. They forage for food during the day and do not hibernate, although they become less active in the coldest regions during the winter, when they survive on caches of food. They make their homes in tree hollows and similar small hideaways, including the abandoned holes of woodpeckers. In areas prone to severe frosts, red squirrels make dens in underground burrows to escape from the freezing temperatures.

During the breeding season, females are receptive to males for just one day. After mating, the male and female separate, and the female cares for the young on her own.

Red squirrels eat a wide range of foods. Their diet largely consists of vegetable matter, but they will also feed on eggs, young birds, and small mammals when the opportunity arises.

The tail of the American red squirrel is less bushy than those of related species, and it is more than half the length of the body. The squirrel's coat varies in color, depending on the time of year.

White-tailed antelope squirrel

Ammospermophilus leucurus

Distribution: Southwestern North America, from Oregon to New Mexico and Baja California, Mexico.
Habitat: Deserts, scrublands, and grasslands.
Food: Leaves, seeds, plant stems, roots, and fruits, and some insects and carrion.
Size: 7.4–9.4in (18–24cm).
Weight: 3.4–4oz (96–117g).
Maturity: 1 year.
Breeding: Up to 10 young born in the spring.
Life span: Unknown.

White-tailed antelope squirrels inhabit the deserts of the southwestern United States and Mexico's Baja California peninsula, and the arid scrublands and grasslands of the Great Basin of the northwestern United States. They prefer areas with sandy or gravel soils that can be dug into easily. The squirrels burrow into the loose soil to avoid the most intense heat of the day. They also enlarge the abandoned dens of other burrowing desert rodents, such as those of kangaroo rats.

White-tailed antelope squirrels are solitary for most of the year. They forage at dawn and in the late afternoon to avoid the worst of the heat. They retreat to shaded areas to eat, carrying food in their cheek pouches. At the height of summer, when it is especially hot, the squirrels lie underground, pressing their underside to the cool floor of the burrow. In the northern part of their range, winter temperatures often plummet to below freezing. In these situations, the squirrels huddle together in small groups to conserve their body heat.

The body of the white-tailed antelope squirrel is typical of ground squirrels, although the legs are slightly longer than in most species. The underside of the tail is white. This surface may reflect sunlight when the tail is held over the body.

Cliff chipmunk (*Tamias dorsalis*): 8.5–10in (21–25cm); 2.15–2.6oz (61–74g)
The cliff chipmunk is found in the southwestern United States and northern Mexico. It lives near cliffs in high desert hills covered by scrub, and makes dens under rocks. This solitary species is gray with dark stripes on the back. By day, the cliff chipmunk forages over a wide area, defending a relatively large territory for such a small animal. It searches for seeds, acorns, and juniper berries. Up to six young are produced in spring.

Eastern fox squirrel (*Sciurus niger*): 18–27.5in (45–70cm); 1.5–2.5lb (0.7–1.2kg)
The eastern fox squirrel is an average-sized, tree-dwelling squirrel. Its back is usually covered in yellow-orange fur, but many individuals are completely black. In winter, the squirrel's ears grow tufts. This squirrel ranges from eastern Canada through the eastern and central United States and into northern Mexico. It is found in all forest types, but does best in those with a variety of tree species. This diurnal, largely solitary species eats a range of foods, from nuts, fruits, and buds to insects, young birds, and even dead fish.

Variegated squirrel (*Sciurus variegatoides*): 8.5–13.5in (22–34cm); 15.25–32.75oz (430–900g)
Variegated squirrels range from Chiapas in southern Mexico to Panama. They live in all types of tropical forest, from moist evergreen forests to dryer deciduous or monsoon forests. The coats of variegated squirrels display a variety of bands and other patterns. These solitary animals spend most of their time up in the branches. They eat mainly plant matter such as nuts, fruits, and flowers.

Gray-collared chipmunk

Tamias cinereicollis

Gray-collared chipmunks are not a widespread species, although they are common within their range in the southwestern United States. Their preferred habitat is relatively dry mountain conifer forest, where they are rarely found below 6,400 ft (1,950m). However, gray-colored chipmunks have also adapted to living in suburban areas at lower altitudes, following the recent rapid expansion of human settlements in the region. Here, the chipmunks are often found living under patios and in the foundations of buildings.

Gray-collared chipmunks are diurnal, being most active in the cool of the morning and evening. They live alone in burrows. In winter, they spend long periods underground to avoid the worst of the weather. They mate soon after emerging from their burrows in the spring, and breed again in the fall before preparing for hibernation.

Gray-collared chipmunks, so called because of the distinctive color bands on their body, have dextrous hands and unusually protruding incisors. They hold food in their hands and remove any unwanted material with their teeth, before pushing the food into a cheek pouch.

Distribution: Arizona and New Mexico.
Habitat: Mountain conifer forests.
Food: Nuts, berries, seeds, and insects.
Size: 3.1–6.3in (8–16cm).
Weight: 2–2.5oz (55–70g).
Maturity: 1 year.
Breeding: Litters of 2–5 born in the spring and fall.
Life span: 3 years.

Eastern chipmunk

Tamias striatus

These rodents are found in eastern North America. They live in woodland and bushy habitats, feeding on nuts, seeds, mushrooms, and fruits during the daytime. These solitary animals retire to burrows at night. The burrows are only just below the surface, but their tunnels may extend for several yards. The burrow entrances are hidden (the excavated earth is scattered), and they are often located in secluded areas to avoid discovery by predators such as foxes, snakes, and birds of prey.

Eastern chipmunks forage for food in a small territory around the burrow. They chase away any intruders looking for food in that area. These chipmunks sleep through the winter in their burrows, waking regularly to feed on caches of food made during the fall.

Chipmunks are named after the "chip chip" noises they frequently make, and often gather in groups to "sing" to each other. These noises and other vocalizations are used by chipmunks in communication.

Eastern chipmunks are larger than most chipmunks. Their most obvious feature is the pouched cheeks located inside their mouths. These pouches are used to store food.

Distribution: Eastern North America, from Quebec and Ontario to Iowa and Illinois.
Habitat: Woodland.
Food: Nuts, seeds, mushrooms, and fruits.
Size: 5.25–7.5in (13–19cm).
Weight: 2.5–5oz (70–140g).
Maturity: 1 year.
Breeding: About 4 young are produced in early spring, and again in the summer.
Life span: 1 year.

Pygmy mouse

Baiomys taylori

Distribution: Southwestern United States to central Mexico.
Habitat: Dry scrub.
Food: Stems, leaves, insects, and seeds.
Size: 2–3.25in (5–8cm).
Weight: 0.2–0.3oz (7–8g).
Maturity: Females 28 days; males 80 days.
Breeding: Several litters of 1–5 young each year.
Life span: 2 years.

Pygmy mice are the smallest rodents in the Americas, little more than the size of a person's thumb. They live in areas where plants, logs, and rocks provide them with plenty of cover. The mice create networks of runs through undergrowth and under rocks, leaving piles of droppings at junctions. These may act as signposts or be signals to other mice in their network. Pygmy mice are most active at dawn and dusk, but will also feed throughout the day.

At night, they sleep in nests made from plants and twigs. They do not live in groups as such, but will tolerate the presence of other mice close by. Pygmy mice can breed at a young age. Females can become pregnant after just a month of life. They breed throughout the year, often producing several litters per year. Both parents care for the young, which are born in nests inside shallow dips dug into the ground, or in secluded cavities under logs and rocks.

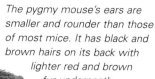
The pygmy mouse's ears are smaller and rounder than those of most mice. It has black and brown hairs on its back with lighter red and brown fur underneath.

Coypu

Myocastor coypus

Distribution: Southern South America, east of the Andes; introduced to the Mississippi Delta.
Habitat: Marshes; river and lake banks.
Food: Water plants and freshwater mollusks.
Size: 18.5–23in (47–58cm).
Weight: 11–22lb (5–10kg).
Maturity: 6 months.
Breeding: Single litter of about 6 young born at any time of year.
Life span: 6 years.

Coypus, or nutrias, live in wetland habitats from southern Brazil and Bolivia, to Tierra del Fuego at the southern tip of South America. They have very large, orange-tinged incisors. These are always visible, since the mouth closes behind them in order to keep out water when the animal is swimming.

These small, largely herbivorous rodents are nocturnal feeders, foraging for food both in and out of the water. They eat aquatic plants, but they will occasionally take freshwater mollusks such as mussels and water snails. They are able to remain submerged for up to 10 minutes. When not feeding, the coypus sunbathe and groom each other on platforms of floating vegetation. They may shelter in the burrow of another animal or dig their own burrow, which can be a simple tunnel or a complex system of chambers and passages.

Coypus live in groups of a single adult male, several females (often related to each other) and up to a dozen of their young. Females may produce their single litter at any time of year, and the males play no part in raising the young. Females tend to stay with their family group, while young males disperse.

Coypus look like large water rats, with soft, thick underfur covered by longer, well-oiled hairs. The hind feet are webbed to help with swimming and moving through boggy ground. The unwebbed forefeet are used for holding food.

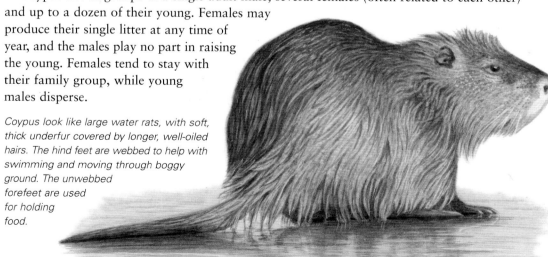

Brown lemming

Lemmus sibiricus

Contrary to popular belief, lemmings do not commit suicide. During favorable years, the lemmings' ability to reproduce very quickly leads to population explosions of amazing proportions. As the population size goes up, space becomes more and more difficult to find, and the young lemmings are pushed away from the best habitat, down the mountains and into the valleys. Lemmings are good swimmers when they have to be, but they have their limits. During dispersal, young lemmings often try to cross large bodies of water that are beyond their swimming capabilities, drowning in the process. It is this behavior that gave rise to the misconception that they kill themselves.

In the summer, lemmings spend much of their time underground in burrows, but when the ground starts to freeze in the fall, they cannot dig through the ground and are forced to forage on the surface. They do not hibernate in the harsh winter, but tunnel under the snow in search of food. Tunnels keep them out of sight from predators such as snowy owls, which are reliant on lemmings as a source of food.

Unlike other lemming species, the brown lemming does not change the color of its winter coat.

Distribution: Arctic mainland and islands of northern Canada, Alaska, and Siberia.
Habitat: Arctic tundra grassland and sub-Arctic tundra above the timberline.
Food: Mosses, grasses, and sedges.
Size: 5–7in (13–18cm).
Weight: 2–4.75oz (50–140g).
Maturity: 5–6 weeks.
Breeding: These prolific breeders may produce as many as 8 litters per year, each of up to 12 young; gestation is about 3 weeks.
Life span: Less than 2 years.

Southern bog lemming

Synaptomys cooperi

With their dark, thick hair, bog lemmings look almost round. However, their bodies are small and they are no more robust than other lemmings or voles. They have powerful jaws and the long, orange-colored incisors typical of rodents, which are kept sharp by frequent gnawing. The fur is gray, grizzled by silver hairs mixed in with the darker ones. Female southern bog lemmings have six nipples, but in northern bog lemmings, their closest relatives, the females have eight.

Southern bog lemmings live in the eastern region of North America, from Labrador to Ontario and Kansas to North Carolina. They are most often found in bogs, generally sphagnum bogs, so called because of the large amounts of thick sphagnum moss that dominate the habitat. However, these lemmings are also found in less water-logged areas, such as pine forests and cultivated fields.

Southern bog lemmings may be active by day or night, but they are largely nocturnal. They eat a wide range of plant foods. By gnawing through the base of the stems, they fell tall plants so that they can eat the tender leaves, shoots, and fruits growing higher up. Bog lemmings construct tunnels and subsurface runways, or utilize those made by other small mammals. They use dried grass and sedge to build concealed nests in clumps of grass, or under tree stumps and sphagnum mounds.

Bog lemmings breed up to three times a year, although in northern areas, more than once is probably unlikely.

Distribution: Eastern North America.
Habitat: Bogs and wet grasslands.
Food: Grasses, moss, sedges, fruits, mushrooms, and roots.
Size: 4.25–5.5in (11–14cm).
Weight: 0.75–1.75oz (20–50g).
Maturity: 5 weeks.
Breeding: Litters of 1–8 young (average 3) are produced 2–3 times a year; most young are born between April and September.
Life span: 2 years.

North American porcupine

Erethizon dorsatum

Distribution: North America, including Alaska and Canada, south to northern Mexico.
Habitat: Forest and brush.
Food: Wood, bark, and needles in the winter; buds, roots, seeds, and leaves in the summer.
Size: 25–31.5in (64–80cm).
Weight: 7.75–15.5lb (3.5–7kg).
Maturity: 2.5 years.
Breeding: Single young born in the summer.
Life span: 18 years.

North American porcupines are nocturnal animals that spend most of the night looking for food on the ground. However, they occasionally climb slowly into trees to find food. They cannot see very well, but have sensitive noses for detecting danger.

During the daytime, porcupines rest in hollow trees, caves, or disused burrows. They regularly move from den to den throughout the year. They do not hibernate and keep feeding throughout the winter, but they will stay in their den during periods of harsh weather.

Porcupines live solitary lives, but do not defend territories, although they may attempt to drive away other porcupines from trees laden with food. When cornered by predators, porcupines turn their backs on their attackers and thrash around with their spiky tails. If the barbed quills penetrate the attacker's skin, they detach from the porcupine and work their way into the assailant's body.

In early winter, males seek out females and shower them with urine before mating. The males are chased away by the females after mating. They give birth to their litters in summer.

Porcupines have sharp, barbed quills (thickened hairs) on their rumps and short tails. North American porcupines have quills that are set individually in the skin; in porcupines from elsewhere, they are grouped into clusters.

Muskrat

Ondatra zibethicus

Distribution: Northern Canada and Alaska to Gulf of Mexico.
Habitat: Swamps and other wetlands.
Food: Water plants.
Size: 8.5–13in (22–33cm).
Weight: 1.5–4lb (0.7–1.8kg).
Maturity: 7 months.
Breeding: 6 young born in the summer.
Life span: 3 years.

Muskrats live in most of the United States and Canada, excluding the high Arctic region. Muskrats were introduced to Eurasia at the beginning of the last century, and they have thrived in parts of Scandinavia and northern Russia, as well as in warmer parts of Siberia.

Muskrats live in large family groups along riverbanks and in marshes, particularly where there is plenty of bankside vegetation to provide shelter. They dig burrows into the banks, which they access through underwater entrances. When living in more open wetlands, they make domed nests from grass. Muskrats are largely nocturnal, but crepuscular (active at dawn and dusk) as well.

In the south of their range, muskrats breed at all times of the year. In the northern areas, the long winters limit the breeding season to the summer.

Muskrats are semiaquatic animals, spending time both in and out of water. Their fur is oily to make it waterproof, and the hind feet are webbed. These rodents use their scaly tails for steering while swimming. Muskrats eat water plants and small aquatic animals, including mussels and crayfish.

ARMADILLOS AND RELATIVES

Armadillos, anteaters, and sloths belong to a group of mammals called the Xenarthra *(formerly named* Edentata, *meaning "toothless"). Most xenarths live in South and Central America. Only one, the long-nosed armadillo, lives as far north as Texas. These animals are taxonomically related to one another but do not share evident common physical characteristics, except for unique bones that strengthen their spines.*

Long-nosed armadillo

Dasypus novemcinctus

Long-nosed armadillos are found in a wide range of habitats, but always require plenty of cover. In the warmer parts of their range, they feed at night. In colder areas, they may be active during the day, especially in the winter. These armadillos build large nests at the ends of their long burrows. The nests are filled with dried grasses. In areas with plenty of plant cover, long-nosed armadillos may also build their nests above ground.

These creatures search for their animal prey by poking their long noses into crevices and under logs. They also eat fallen fruit and roots. When threatened, the animals waddle to their burrows as fast as possible. If cornered, they will curl up.

Although long-nosed armadillos forage alone, they may share their burrows with several other individuals, all of the same sex. The breeding season is in late summer. Litters of identical, same-sex quadruplets are born in the spring.

The long-nosed armadillo is also called the nine-banded armadillo, because it typically has that number of plate bands along its back, although specimens can possess either eight or ten bands.

Distribution: Southern United States to northern Argentina.
Habitat: Shaded areas.
Food: Arthropods, reptiles, amphibians, fruits, and roots.
Size: 9.5–22.5in (24–57cm).
Weight: 2.2–22lb (1–10kg).
Maturity: 1 year.
Breeding: 4 young born in the spring.
Life span: 15 years.

Giant anteater

Myrmecophaga tridactyla

Giant anteaters have powerful digging claws on their forelimbs and incredibly long tongues—often over 24in (60cm)—inside their snouts. They have white stripes along their flanks and a long, bushy tail.

Giant anteaters live wherever there are large ant nests or termite mounds in abundance. They use their powerful claws to rip the colonies apart, then they use their sticky tongues to lick up the insects and their eggs and larvae. A single giant anteater can eat over 30,000 ants or termites in one day.

Despite being powerful diggers, giant anteaters shelter in thickets, not burrows, because of their awkward shape. They spend most of their time alone searching for food, with their long noses close to the ground. While on the move, they curl their forelimbs under their bodies, so that they are actually walking on the backs of their forefeet and their claws do not hinder them.

Females often come into contact with one another, but males keep their distance. Breeding can take place all year.

Distribution: Belize to northern Argentina.
Habitat: Grasslands, forests, and swamps.
Food: Ants, termites, and beetle larvae.
Size: 3.25–4ft (1–1.2m).
Weight: 39.75–86lb (18–39kg).
Maturity: 2.5–4 years.
Breeding: Single young born throughout the year.
Life span: 25 years.

MARSUPIALS

Marsupials are a group of mammals that brood their young in pouches on their bellies, rather than in wombs like placental mammals. The overwhelming majority of marsupials are found in Australia and New Guinea, but several species live in the Americas. However, fossil evidence has led zoologists to conclude that marsupials first evolved in South America, and subsequently spread to Australasia.

Water opossum

Chironectes minimus

Water opossums have short, waterproof coats with a gray and black pattern. Their hind feet are webbed, and both sexes have pouches opening to the rear.

Water opossums, or yapoks, live beside bodies of fresh water in tropical forests. They make dens in burrows in the banks of streams or lakes, with entrances just above water level. Unusually, both sexes have pouches. A female can close her pouch using a ring of muscles to keep her developing young dry while she is underwater. A male's pouch is always open, and he uses it to protect his scrotum while in water or when moving quickly through forest.

Water opossums are superb swimmers, using their hind feet to propel themselves through the water. However, they also forage on land or in trees. They spend the night in their dens, but may rest in bundles of leaves in secluded places on the forest floor between daytime feeding forays. Most births take place between December and January. After their birth, the young opossums spend a few more weeks in the pouch until they are fully developed.

Distribution: Central and South America from southern Mexico to Belize and Argentina.
Habitat: Freshwater streams and lakes.
Food: Crayfish, shrimp, fish, fruit, and water plants.
Size: 10.5–15.5in (27–40cm); 21.25–28.25oz (600–800g).
Maturity: Unknown.
Breeding: 2–5 young born in summer.
Life span: 3 years.

Virginia opossum

Didelphis virginiana

Distribution: United States, Central America, and northern South America.
Habitat: Moist woodlands or thick brush in swamps.
Food: Plants, carrion, small vertebrates, invertebrates.
Size: 13–19.5in (33–50cm).
Weight: 4.5–12.25lb (2–5.5kg).
Maturity: 6–8 months.
Breeding: 2 litters per year.
Life span: 3 years.

Virginia opossums generally live in forested areas that receive plenty of rain. However, the species is very adaptable and is making its home in new places across North America. Many survive in more open country beside streams or in swamps, and others make their homes in people's sheds and barns.

Virginia opossums are most active at night. By day, they rest in nests of leaves and grass, hidden away in crevices, hollow trees, and sometimes in burrows. By night, the marsupials hunt for food. They are good climbers, using their prehensile tails to cling to branches.

Virginia opossums do not hibernate, but they do put on fat as the days shorten with the approach of the fall. They rely on this fat to keep them going during the periods of harshest winter weather, when they cannot get out to feed. In the very coldest parts of their range, these marsupials sometimes suffer frostbite on their naked tails and thin ears.

Mating takes place in both the late winter and spring. The young are only 0.4in (1cm) long and underdeveloped at birth. Over 20 are born, but the mother can only suckle 13 at once, so the weaker offspring die.

Virginia opossums have white faces, often with darker streaks. Their bodies are covered in shaggy coats of long gray and white hairs, but their tails are almost naked.

INSECTIVORES

Insectivores, or insect-eaters, belong to the Insectivora *order of mammals. The first mammals to develop their young in uteruses belonged to this group, and most insectivores still resemble these small, primitive animals. However, insectivores have evolved to live in a wide range of niches, including subterranean, terrestrial, aquatic, and arboreal habitats.*

Giant mole shrew

Blarina brevicauda

Giant mole shrews live in most land habitats within their range, but they are hard to spot. They use their strong forepaws and flexible snouts to dig deep burrows in soft earth, and when they are on the surface, they scurry out of sight beneath mats of leaves or snow. However, they do climb into trees in search of food on occasion.

These small mammals feed at all times of the day and night. They rest in nests of grass and leaves made inside their tunnels or in nooks and crannies on the surface. Giant mole shrews will eat plant food, but they also hunt for small prey, such as snails, mice, and insects. Their saliva contains a venom that paralyzes prey animals. During the mating season, which takes place between the spring and fall, they expand their territories so that they overlap with those of the opposite sex.

Giant mole shrews have stout bodies with long, pointed snouts covered in sensitive whiskers. Their eyes are very small because they spend most of the time underground, and their ears are hidden under thick coats of gray hairs.

Distribution: Central Canada to southeastern United States.
Habitat: All land habitats.
Food: Insects, small vertebrates, seeds, and shoots.
Size: 5–5.5in (12–14cm).
Weight: 0.5–1oz (15–30g).
Maturity: 6 weeks.
Breeding: Litters of 5–7 young born throughout the summer.
Life span: 2 years.

Star-nosed mole

Condylura cristata

Distribution: Eastern Canada to the southeastern United States.
Habitat: Muddy soil near water.
Food: Aquatic insects, fish, worms, and crustaceans.
Size: 4–5in (10–12cm); 1.5–3oz (40–85g).
Maturity: 10 months.
Breeding: 2–7 young born in the summer.
Life span: Unknown.

Star-nosed moles live in waterlogged soil. They dig networks of tunnels in the soil, which generally reach down as far as the water table. They push the mud and soil out of the entrances of the tunnels, making molehills in the process. The moles construct nests at the ends of tunnels, which are lined with dry grass.

Star-nosed moles are expert swimmers. They search for food at the bottom of streams and pools, using their sensitive snouts to feel their way and detect prey. In the winter, star-nosed moles use tunnels with underwater entrances to get into ponds that are iced over. They feed in water both in the daytime and at night, but they are only really active above ground during the hours of darkness.

Most births take place in early summer. The young already have the star of rays on their snouts. Breeding pairs of males and females may stay together throughout the winter and breed again the following year.

Star-nosed moles have unusual fleshy rays that radiate from each nostril. These are sensitive feelers that the moles use in the darkness below ground. The moles' dark, dense fur is coated with water-repelling oils.

Least shrew

Cryptotis parva

Distribution: From eastern United States south to northern Nicaragua in Central America.
Habitat: Grass and brush.
Food: Insects, worms, slugs, and snails, plus some plant matter.
Size: 2–3in (5–8cm).
Weight: 0.1–0.2oz (4–6.5g).
Maturity: 5 weeks.
Breeding: Several litters of about 5 young produced in the summer.
Life span: 1.5 years.

Least shrews live south of the Great Lakes across the eastern United States. They also occur through eastern Mexico to northern Nicaragua in Central America. Within this vast area, the shrews occupy a variety of habitats. In northern parts of the range, least shrews are found in grasslands, meadows, and areas covered in a thick layer of brush. Farther south, where it is generally drier, these shrews are more common in the vegetation that grows along the banks of streams and lakes.

Least shrews move through the plant cover in tunnels called runways, which connect their nests together. The nests are constructed underground in burrows dug by the shrews, and then lined with leaves. Least shrews will also take over and extend burrows made by other animals. Somewhat unusually for shrews, this species is relatively social. The nests are shared, and more than 30 shrews have been found living together in a single nest.

Least shrews are almost exclusively flesh eaters. They have been seen to open up the abdomens of insects such as grasshoppers to eat only the most nutritious internal organs.

The least shrew has black fur on its back and a white underbelly. In summer, the upper fur often pales slightly to brown. The milk teeth of young shrews fall out while the animals are still in the womb.

Desert shrew

Notiosorex crawfordi

Distribution: Southwestern United States, from California to Texas and Colorado; also Baja, California and northern and central Mexico.
Habitat: Deserts, semiarid grasslands, chaparral, woodland, and marshland.
Food: Invetebrates such as insects, spiders, and worms; also lizards, small mammals, and young birds.
Size: 2–2.5in (5–6cm).
Weight: 0.2–0.3oz (4.5–8g).
Maturity: 2 months.
Breeding: 1–2 litters of 3–5 young born each year.
Life span: Unknown.

The desert shrew ranges across the arid southwest of the United States. It is also found in the drier areas parts of Mexico. Although it can survive in desert conditions, this shrew can also be found in a range of other habitats, including marshland.

The desert shrew preys mainly on invertebrates such as worms, spiders, and insects, but it also eats lizards, birds, and small mammals such as mice. The shrew must consume three-quarters of its own body weight in food each day to survive. (This is actually a relatively small amount for a shrew.) In the driest parts of its range, the desert shrew can survive on the water it gets from its food. However, it is most often found close to a supply of drinking water.

Desert shrews hunt at night, restricting themselves to areas with thick brush to avoid owls and other predators. They rest in the burrow of another animal during daylight hours. In the hottest part of the day, the shrews enter a torpor—an inactive state similar to hibernation. In this state, they use only a fraction of the energy that they would when normally active. The female makes a crude nest from hair, grass, and other vegetation. The blind, hairless young develop rapidly and may accompany their mother for a short period before they disperse.

The desert shrew's tail is at least half as long as its small body. Desert shrews are often found living in garbage dumps around human settlements.

Arctic shrew

Sorex arcticus

Distribution: Northern North America.
Habitat: In forests near fresh water.
Food: Invertebrates.
Size: 2.5–2.75in (6–7cm); 0.2–0.5oz (5–13g).
Maturity: 2 years.
Breeding: Up to 9 young born in one litter in April or May.
Life span: Unknown.

This species ranges south from Canada's Northwest and Yukon Territories to Minnesota in the U.S. Midwest and east to Nova Scotia on the Atlantic coast of Canada. It is most often spotted near to supplies of fresh water. Its preferred habitats are forests growing on boggy ground, which are populated with trees such as wet spruce and tamarack. Such marshy woodland is alive with invertebrates, providing the shrew with an excellent supply of food throughout the year.

Like most shrews and other small, warm-blooded animals, the Arctic shrew must eat huge quantities of food to supply its body with the energy it needs to survive. This is especially true in the colder northern parts of this species' range, where it will die if it goes without food for more than two hours. Consequently, Arctic shrews will eat virtually anything. Most of their diet is made up of invertebrates, mainly insects such as beetles and their larvae, but they also eat earthworms, spiders, snails, seeds, and leaves.

The distinctive three-colored fur makes the Arctic shrew easy to identify. There is a black band running along the back from nose to tail. The sides are brown, and the underside is gray.

Giant Mexican shrew (*Megasorex gigas*): 3.25–3.5in (8–9cm); 0.3–0.4oz (10–12g)
Although members of this species are consistently large, they are not by any means the largest of the shrews. They get their "giant" moniker from the fact that they are the last surviving member of the *Megasorex* genus, which once contained truly giant shrews. Giant Mexican shrews live in tropical forests and grasslands in western Mexico. They find worms, grubs, and other invertebrate prey by rooting through loose soil and leaf litter with their pointed snout.

Gaspé shrew (*Sorex gaspensis*): 3.75–5in (9.5–12.5cm); 0.1oz (2.2–4.3g)
This shrew is found on the Gaspé Peninsula of eastern Quebec, and in two small ranges in New Brunswick, and on Cape Breton Island in Nova Scotia. Gaspé shrews live in mountain conifer forests, where they forage among the leaf litter or mosses that grow on the forest floor. They are gray all over, with a very narrow snout. Their diet is mainly grubs, maggots, and spiders, but they also eat worms, snails, slugs, and plant matter.

Masked shrew (*Sorex cinereus*): 2.75in (7cm); 0.1oz (2.5–4g)
This is North America's most widespread shrew, ranging across Canada and Alaska and much of the northern United States. Masked shrews occupy a range of habitats, wherever there is adequate ground cover. They are most commonly found in wet areas, such as near to streams or in marshes. Among American mammals, only the pygmy shrew is smaller than this species.

Long-tailed shrew

Sorex dispar

The long-tailed shrew is found as far north as Nova Scotia in eastern Canada. From there, it ranges south to Tennessee and North Carolina in the southern United States. This shrew can survive in a range of forest types, although most of the forests within its range are cool and damp. The long-tailed shrew is especially abundant in mountain forests, on ranges such as the Appalachians and Adirondacks. It makes its dens in cool rock crevices and under boulders and scree.

Long-tailed shrews forage for food both day and night. They do not hibernate. Like most shrews, they lead a solitary life and chase away any shrew that comes near. A long-tailed shrew must eat twice its body weight in food every day to stay alive. The diet consists of insects, spiders, centipedes, and other invertebrates, as well as plant foods such as seeds.

Distribution: Eastern North America.
Habitat: Damp forest.
Food: Invertebrates and plants.
Size: 1.75–4in (4.6–10cm).
Weight: 0.1–0.2oz (4–6g).
Maturity: 4 months.
Breeding: Several litters of about 5 young produced between April and August.
Life span: 2 years.

Long-tailed shrews are often mistaken for smoky shrews, but long-tailed shrews tend to be more slender and have a longer tail.

Pygmy shrew

Sorex hoyi

Because of its small size, the pygmy shrew is able to occupy a range of microhabitats, such as moss, leaf litter, root systems, rotting stumps, and the burrows of larger animals. It can even travel in the tunnels of large beetles. The coat of the pygmy shrew varies from gray-brown in the winter to gray in summer; the underparts are light gray.

Distribution: From Alaska and eastern Canada to the Rockies and the Appalachian Mountains in the United States.
Habitat: Forest, swamp, and grassland.
Food: Insects.
Size: 2–2.5in (5–6cm).
Weight: 0.1oz (2–4g).
Maturity: 1.5 years.
Breeding: One litter of about 5 young born in the summer, about 18 days after mating.
Life span: Unknown.

Although this is the smallest American mammal, it is by no means the smallest mammal in the world. The white-toothed shrews living in the so-called Old World—Europe, Africa and Asia—are almost half the weight of this species, and the hog-nosed bat of Thailand is equally small, at about half the weight of a penny coin or a dime.

Pygmy shrews occupy a wide range of habitats, but they are sparsely distributed and often hard to locate. They feed on small invertebrates such as ants and spiders, and will also eat carrion if the opportunity arises. These tiny creatures live life at a feverish pace. They forage in short bursts of just a few minutes and then rest for a similar amount of time. They nose through soil and leaf litter in search of prey, and often venture into the tunnels of larger animals to look for food. When threatened, pygmy shrews release a musky odor from glands on their sides. This smell not only deters the attacker, but also alerts any shrews nearby to the potential danger.

Water shrew

Sorex palustris

Distribution: Northern North America.
Habitat: Near streams and other freshwater habitats.
Food: Insects.
Size: 3in (8cm).
Weight: 0.3–0.6oz (8–18g).
Maturity: 1 year.
Breeding: 2–3 litters of 3–10 young produced in the spring and summer.
Life span: 18 months.

One of the most aquatic of all shrews, this species occurs throughout Alaska and Canada. It extends south into high, mountainous regions of the United States, most notably along the Rockies, where climatic conditions are similar to those found farther north. This shrew is often found in or close to water. It also lives in damp conifer forests.

Water shrews live alone and are known to hunt for insects. Most of their prey are the aquatic youngsters of insects such as crane flies and caddis flies. While under water, the shrews detect the movements of prey using whiskers on their snouts. They grab the food with their forefeet or mouth. In captivity, water shrews have been seen feeding once every ten minutes. In the wild, they will die if they go without food for about three hours.

Males of this large shrew species tend to be longer than females. The thick fur traps a layer of air around the body to keep the animal warm while diving in cold water.

Montane shrew (*Sorex monticolus*): 2.5–3in (6–8cm); 0.2–0.25oz (5.9–7.2g)
This solitary species, also called the dusky shrew, occurs from northern Alaska southward to New Mexico, and from the west coast to Manitoba in the east. It occurs in a variety of habitats, including tundra in the far north, prairies in drier parts of the range, and also mountain forests. All these habitats have ground vegetation in which the shrews can hide from predators. Montane shrews feed on insect larvae, spiders, earthworms, and occasionally small salamanders. They also eat nonanimal foods such as seeds and mushrooms.

American shrew mole (*Neurotrichus gibbsii*): 2.75–3.5in (7–9cm); 0.3–0.5oz (8–14.5g)
The smallest American mole, this species is the size of a large shrew. Shrew moles range from northern California to southern British Colombia. They tunnel in soft, deep peaty soils, especially those formed by the highly fertile rain forests of North America's northern Pacific coast. They must eat about one-and-a-half times their body weight in insects and worms each day to survive.

Townsend's mole (*Scapanus townsendii*): 7–9.5in (18–24cm); 3.5–6oz (100–170g)
Confined to a small range between the Cascade Mountains and the Pacific coast of California, Oregon, and Washington, Townsend's mole is the largest mole in North America. This species lives in lowland areas with deep, loamy soil. The mole preys on earthworms and insect larvae by patrolling their territories through a permanent network of tunnels.

BATS

Bats are grouped together in the Chiroptera *order of mammals. They are the only mammals that can truly fly. Their wings are made from thin membranes of skin stretched between elongated arms and legs. Most bats are active at night and "see" the world through sound. They emit high-pitched calls and interpret the echoes that bounce back to build up pictures of their surroundings.*

Western bonneted bat

Eumops perotis

The western bonneted bat, also known as the mastiff bat, occurs in small patches across its range, which stretches from Nevada in the western United Sates and south through Texas and Arizona into central Mexico. The bat is also found on the Caribbean islands of Cuba.

The broken pattern of distribution reflects the bat's need for habitats with steep cliffs, on the side of which the bat roosts. The cliffs must be sheer or overhanging so that, when it is time to hunt, the bat can simply let go of its foothold and drop into the air. It freefalls to gain sufficient airspeed before using its wings. This species is unable to get airborne from the ground.

Beneath the cliffs, western bonneted bats hunt in a variety of open habitats, including desert, scrub, and even dry woodlands. They spend several hours each night foraging for flying insects. Unusually for bats, this species hunts in cold weather, only becoming inactive when temperatures reach 41°F (5°C).

The western bonneted bat has large, linked ears that stand high above the head and project forward beyond the end of the snout. If this species finds itself on the ground, it must climb a tree or other object to gain the 16.5ft (5m) or so in height that it needs to launch itself into the air again.

Distribution: Southern California, Nevada, New Mexico, and Texas; also Mexico and Cuba.
Habitat: Cliffs.
Food: Insects.
Size: 3.25in (8cm).
Weight: 2oz (57g).
Maturity: 1 year.
Breeding: 1 young born in summer.
Life span: Unknown.

Pocketed free-tailed bat

Nyctinomops femorosaccus

Being a free-tailed bat, this species has a tail that extends beyond the skin membrane that forms the wing and other flight surfaces. The "pockets" referred to in the bat's common name are produced by folds in the skin that joins the legs to the arms.

The pocketed free-tailed bat lives in the region on either side of the U.S.–Mexico border. It is most commonly found in desert habitats, where it feeds on flying insects. It eats a range of prey, including moths, crickets, flying ants, and lacewings. Many of its prey are pests that feed on crops, and the bat's presence is encouraged by local farmers.

The pocketed free-tailed bat is a swift, high-flying species that is most active in the hours just after dusk and just before dawn. It uses echolocation to find its way around and locate insect prey. The bat's ears are joined together, so they move as a single unit when detecting echoes. Prey is usually caught on the wing. To drink, pocketed free-tailed bats swoop down on the water's surface and scoop up a mouthful of water.

Small colonies of these bats roost in caves and on rugged cliffs, tall buildings, and rocky outcrops. As well as emitting echolocation calls, they often make high-pitched chattering social calls, especially in the first few minutes of flight and while roosting.

Distribution: Southern California, southeastern New Mexico, western Texas, and Michoacán state, Mexico.
Habitat: Deserts.
Food: Insects.
Size: 4.25in (11cm).
Weight: 0.4oz (12g).
Maturity: 1 year.
Breeding: 1 young born in June or July.
Life span: Unknown.

Red bat

Lasiurus borealis

Distribution: From southern Canada through Central America to Chile and Argentina.
Habitat: Suburban and rural areas.
Food: Insects.
Size: 3.7–4.5in (9.3–11.7cm).
Weight: 0.2–0.5oz (7–13g).
Maturity: 1 year.
Breeding: Mating is in August and September; litter of 2–3 (maximum 4) pups born in summer.
Life span: Unknown.

Red bats range across the Americas, from southern Canada to Chile and Argentina. They are commonly found living alongside humans in rural and suburban areas. Red bats hang in trees during the daytime, often by one foot, and are easily mistaken for dead leaves. In colder parts of their range, they may hibernate in hollow trees or migrate south for the winter.

Red bats are fast flyers, with a medium-size body and long wings. The head is small, and the jaws are equipped with 32 small, sharp teeth. These insect-hunting bats catch their prey on the wing, and they are often seen feeding in brightly lit areas that attract a wide range of insects. The bats fly through the swarming insects, selecting a target 16.5ft (5m) away. They strike every 30 seconds, and catch about half of their intended victims.

The red bat is one of the few bat species that is regularly preyed on in flight. Since red bats often fly around lights, they make easy targets for owls. Opossums, snakes, and racoons also prey on them as they roost in buildings and other structures.

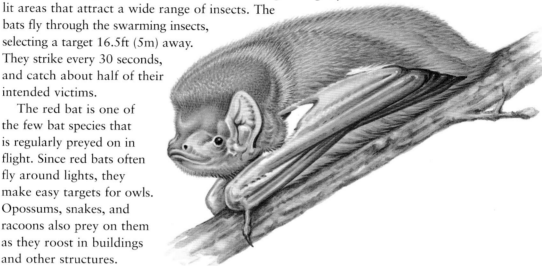

The hairs of this bat's red coat are white at the tips, giving the bat a frosted, grizzled appearance. The coloration of the coat helps to camouflage the bat in sycamore, oak, elm, and box elder trees, which prove popular roosting sites. The rear part of the skin membrane is covered in fur to help keep the bat warm.

Evening bat

Nycticeius humeralis

Distribution: North America, from the Great Lakes Basin south to Texas and Florida.
Habitat: Forest and near rivers.
Food: Insects.
Size: 3.5–4.25in (8.6–10.5cm).
Weight: 0.2–0.5oz (6–14g).
Maturity: 1 year.
Breeding: 2 pups born in the summer.
Life span: 2 years.

The name "evening bat" is given to a great many bats belonging to the *Vespertilionidae* family. Their alternative name of "vesper bats" was acquired because many species would roost in dark church belfries and be seen flying off to hunt while vespers, the evening service, was being conducted. This particular evening bat is found across eastern North America, from the Great Lakes to Texas and Florida. It may live in churches and other buildings, but its natural roosting site is in the hollow of a rotting tree. It forms harems comprising one male roosting with up to 20 females.

This species is medium-size and dark brown. Like all vesper bats, it lacks a nose leaf. Evening bats catch flying insects, such as beetles, flies, and moths. They appear to hunt high up during twilight hours, gradually descending as it gets darker. This may be a defense against owls. In the north of their range, the bats migrate southward in the fall.

These dark brown bats never live in caves, even in winter. Instead, they are found in hollow trees, under loose bark, and in buildings.

Southern long-nosed bat

Leptonycteris curasoae

The southern long-nosed bat lives in the Sonoran desert, which stretches from the southwestern region of the United States to central Mexico. It can also be found in arid areas further south in Mexico. In some parts of its range, the bats inhabit mountain woodlands. By day, the southern long-nosed bat roosts in caves in large numbers, and it occasionally takes up residence in abandoned mines. Roosts may contain tens of thousands of individuals, but despite such vast gatherings, the members of this species do not cooperate with each other.

After dark, the bats can often be seen around flowering cacti, from which they obtain pollen and nectar. They also eat the pulp of cactus fruits. A single bat may visit up to 100 cacti per night, and make a round trip of 18 miles (30km). The cacti tend to flower earlier in the south, so the bats migrate slowly from south to north through their range following blooming patterns. Although cacti are the main food source, the bats will also feed on other plants, including agave and bindweed. Some plants are only pollinated by this species of bat.

This southern long-nosed bat uses its long tongue, which is the same length as its body, to lick nectar and pollen out of large flowers. Unlike most blooms, the flowers on which bats feed are open at night.

Distribution: Southwestern United States and Mexico.
Habitat: Desert, arid grassland, scrubland, tropical dry forest and mountain woodland.
Food: Nectar and pollen.
Size: 3.25in (8cm).
Weight: 0.8oz(23g).
Maturity: 1 year.
Breeding: 1 pup born in December and January; gestation is probably about 5 months.
Life span: Unknown.

Banana bat

Musonycteris harrisoni

These bats are found in banana groves along the Pacific coast of Mexico, west of the Isthmus of Tehuantepec in the south of country. They are found from sea level to 5,600ft (1,700m). Within this small range, banana bats are restricted to dry deciduous forests and thorny shrubland. The species was first described feeding in a banana grove, hence its common name.

Banana bats feed on nectar and pollen, often from banana plants, but not exclusively. Like many flower-feeding bats, they migrate over small distances to find freshly flowering plants. While feeding on nectar at a flower, they may also suck up any insects that they find there. Pollen from the flower clings to the bats' fur, and they swallow this as they lick their fur during grooming.

Young banana bats are cared for by their mothers only. They develop rapidly and are weaned and able to fly within a few weeks. Raccoons, snakes, ringtails, and small cats prey on roosting banana bats, while hawks and owls may catch them when they emerge to feed at dusk.

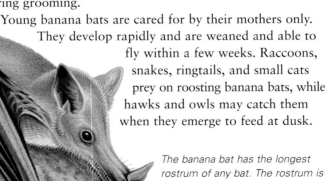

The banana bat has the longest rostrum of any bat. The rostrum is the bone that extends from the skull and forms the bridge of the nose. The banana bat also has a long tongue covered in a ridge of bumps, which helps it to collect pollen from its fur.

Distribution: Pacific coast of Mexico, in the states of Jalisco, Colima, Guerrero, Mexico, Michoacán and Morelos.
Habitat: Thorn scrub and dry forest.
Food: Nectar, pollen and insects.
Size: 2.75–3.25in (7–8cm);
Weight: Unknown.
Maturity: 1 year.
Breeding: 1 pup born in late summer.
Life span: Unknown.

Big brown bat

Eptesicus fuscus

The big brown bat, which hibernates in winter, is one of the largest bats in North America. It is a common resident of artificial structures, and can even be found in the heart of cities. Its natural habitat, however, is heavy forest. The nature of these forests changes considerably across this species' range. In the southern limit, at the northern tip of South America, the forests are dense jungles. Moving north, deciduous forests take over from jungles, especially in the eastern United States. At the northern limit, along the southern fringe of Canada, deciduous trees give way to conifers.

During summer, when the female bats rear their young, the sexes roost separately. This is a common feature of hibernating bat species. The sexes come together to mate at the end of summer, before forming large, mixed-sex winter roosts. The development of the young is delayed over the winter. The embryos begin to grow in spring, and pups are born in summer. The young bats are able to fly within three to four weeks.

Female big brown bats are slightly larger than males. These bats have 32 sharp teeth inside their large, powerful jaws, which can deliver a painful bite when the bats are handled. The teeth are used to crush the tough outer skeletons of the bats' insect prey. Big brown bats can only feed during the warmer months when their insect prey are active. They eat as much as they can to lay down enough fat reserves to see them through the winter, when their body weight can fall by as much as one-third.

Distribution: Southern Canada to Panama and the northern tip of South America; also found in the West Indies.
Habitat: Heavy forest; often found in urban areas.
Food: Insects, especially beetles, plus moths, flies, wasps, flying ants, lacewing flies, and dragonflies.
Size: 4.25–5in (11–13cm).
Weight: 1.75oz (50g).
Maturity: 1 year.
Breeding: 1–2 offspring born in June and July.
Life span: 19 years.

Spotted bat

Euderma maculatum

Distribution: British Columbia to northern Mexico.
Habitat: Dry, open forests and marshlands.
Food: Flying insects, especially large moths.
Size: 5in (12.6cm).
Weight: 0.6–0.7oz (16–20g).
Maturity: 1 year.
Breeding: 1 young born in June.
Life span: Unknown.

Spotted bats occur in small areas of a large range that extends from northern Mexico to British Columbia in southwestern Canada. They live in many habitats, including the marshes of the southern United States and the dry hill forests in the southwest.

These bats use low-frequency echolocation calls, some of which are audible to humans as clicks. The low frequency means that the calls only form clear echoes on bigger objects, and consequently they give a relatively basic representation of the bats' surroundings. Because of this, spotted bats only catch large insects such as moths, and they prefer to occupy open habitats where there is plenty of space between obstacles. In densely forested areas, the bats would have difficulty avoiding branches in their flight path. Spotted bats are still expert hunters in the right environment. They have been recorded catching prey every 45 seconds, and are known to hunt for at least four hours each night.

This species gets its name from the three white spots on its shoulders and rump. The rest of the back is covered by black fur.

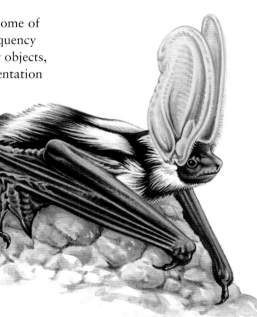

SALAMANDERS

Salamanders and newts are amphibians with tails. All of them have legs, although a few species have lost a pair or have vestigial limbs. Like all amphibians, salamanders need a certain amount of water to reproduce. Some species are completely aquatic, but others live entirely on land. Many species are truly amphibious, spending the early part of their lives in water and living both on land and in water as adults.

Hellbender

Cryptobranchus alleganiensis

Hellbenders are among the largest salamanders in the Americas and one of three giant salamanders in the world. These monstrous and heavy-set amphibians spend their entire lives on the beds of rivers and streams.

These animals are nocturnal and spend the day sheltering under rocks. At night, they become more active, but generally lurk in crevices while waiting for prey. Giant salamanders lose their gills as they change from larvae into adults. They absorb most of their oxygen through their wrinkly skin, but will sometimes rise to the surface to take gulps of air into their small lungs.

Hellbenders breed in late summer. A male digs a hole under a rock and will only allow females that are still carrying eggs into his hole. Several females may lay their eggs in a single male's hole before he fertilizes them with a cloud of sperm. The male guards them for three months until the young hatch.

Hellbenders have a dark, wrinkled skin that secretes toxic slime. These salamanders do not have gills, and the wrinkles in their skin increase the surface area of their bodies so that they can absorb more oxygen directly from the water.

Distribution: Eastern North America.
Habitat: Rivers and streams.
Food: Crayfishes, worms, insects, fish, and snails.
Size: 12–29in (30–74cm).
Weight: 3.3–5.5lb (1.5–2.5kg).
Maturity: 2–3 years.
Breeding: 450 eggs laid in late summer.
Life span: 50 years.

Greater siren

Siren lacertina

The greater siren lives in the mud on the bottom of slow-flowing creeks and in swamps. Most salamanders change considerably as they mature into adults, but the adult body of a siren, with its external gills, long tail, and single pair of legs, is very similar to the larval form. Greater sirens spend the day resting on the bottom. At night, they drag themselves through the mud with their small legs or swim, with an S-shaped motion, through the murky water. These salamanders do not have teeth, but suck their prey through tough, horny lips.

Greater sirens sometimes live in seasonal pools, which dry up in the summer. The salamanders survive these droughts by burying themselves in the moist sediment and coating their bodies with slimy mucus. Breeding takes place at night, under mud. It is thought that females lay single eggs on water plants and males follow the females around, fertilizing each egg soon after it is laid.

The greater siren has a very long body with feathery gills behind its head and a single pair of legs. The body is mottled to help the salamander hide on the river bed. The greater siren propels itself through the water, twisting its body into S-shaped curves.

Distribution: Eastern parts of the United States.
Habitat: Swamps, streams, and lakes.
Food: Crayfishes, worms, and snails.
Size: 19.5–36in (50–90cm).
Weight: 3.8lb (1.7kg).
Maturity: Unknown.
Breeding: Eggs laid in spring.
Life span: 25 years.

Ringed salamander

Ambystoma annulatum

Distribution: Central Missouri to western Arkansas and eastern Oklahoma.
Habitat: Damp forests.
Food: Invertebrates such as insects, worms, and snails.
Size: 5.5–9.25in (14–23.5cm).
Weight: Unknown.
Maturity: 1–2 years.
Breeding: Over 100 eggs laid underwater in clusters of 10–20 during the fall.
Life span: Unknown.

Ringed salamanders live on the Ozark Plateau and in the Ouachita Mountains, the only significant highlands in North America between the Rockies and Appalachians. They are found in the damp forests and clearings of this region. Apart from during the breeding season, ringed salamanders are solitary and rarely seen above ground. They are most active during wet weather. Their diet probably consists of insects and other invertebrates that move through the leaf litter on the forest floor.

Rainfall in the area during fall is high, and numerous temporary pools form in the forests. Ringed salamanders breed in the water, after which the females lay small clusters of eggs on submerged plants. The larvae hatch in October and spend the winter in the water, where they feed on insect larvae and other small invertebrates. They change into the air-breathing form and emerge from the water during the early summer.

This very long mole salamander has a slender body and a small head. It has a brown or black upper body and a gray belly. The body and tail of the salamander are circled by yellow bands— hence its common name.

Pacific giant salamander

Dicamptodon ensatus

Distribution: Coast of southern British Columbia to central California and the Rockies of Idaho and Montana.
Habitat: Rivers, streams, lakes, and ponds, and surrounding forests.
Food: Large insects, mice, amphibians, and small snakes.
Size: 7–12in (18–30cm).
Weight: Unknown.
Maturity: 2–3 years.
Breeding: Both terrestrial and aquatic forms can breed. Females lay 85–200 eggs underwater singly and in clumps.
Life span: Unknown.

The Pacific giant salamander inhabits the many rivers that flow into the Pacific ocean along the U.S. and Canadian coasts. In central California, in the south of its range, the rivers are smaller and more seasonal. Farther north, a wetter climate along the coastal mountains makes the rivers larger. Pacific giant salamanders are found in the lower reaches of the huge Columbia River and its tributaries, including the Willamette of western Oregon. A smaller population survives far from the ocean, in the mountain streams of the Rockies in Idaho.

Giant Pacific salamanders spend more time in water than most mole salamanders. They lay their eggs on submerged wood or rocks. In colder places, the weather may not get warm enough to stimulate the change from aquatic larvae to air-breathing, land-living adults, even though they become sexually mature. Their offspring, however, may transform into land-living adults if the conditions are suitable. Transformed animals forage on the forest floor on rainy nights.

The Pacific giant salamander, one of the world's largest land-living salamanders, has large eyes and a laterally compressed tail. The salamander's coloration typically consists of dark marbling on a brown background. In some parts of this species' range—generally the cooler regions—the salamanders never transform into land-living adults but retain their larval features, including the gills.

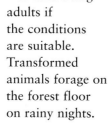

FROGS AND TOADS

Frogs and toads form the largest group of amphibians, called Anura. Toads are better adapted to terrestrial habitats with thicker, warty skin to avoid desiccation, and frogs have thin, smooth skin that needs to be kept moist. Most species follow similar life cycles. Tailed larvae called tadpoles hatch from eggs called spawn and develop in water before sprouting legs, losing their tails, and emerging onto land.

Marine toad

Bufo marinus

Marine toads are the largest toads in the world. They have several other common names, including giant toads and cane toads. Marine toads occur naturally from the southern United States through Mexico to Chile. They were introduced to Queensland, Australia, in the 1930s to help control the pest beetles that were infesting sugar cane crops. However, the toads did not like living among the cane plants and spread out over the countryside, where they ate not pests but small reptiles and mammals, some of which are now rare.

Marine toads are extremely adaptable. They live in a wide range of habitats, eating just about anything they can fit into their mouths, from small rodents, reptiles, and birds to invertebrates such as snails, centipedes, cockroaches, grasshoppers, and beetles. They protect themselves against attack using the toxin glands on their backs, which ooze a fluid that can kill many animals that ingest it. In small amounts, the toxin causes humans to hallucinate.

Female marine toads are larger than the males. Both sexes have warty glands on their backs that squirt a milky toxin when squeezed.

Distribution: Southern North America and Central and South America, from Texas to Chile; now introduced to other areas, including eastern Australia.
Habitat: Most land habitats, often near pools and swamps.
Food: Insects, snakes, lizards, and small mammals.
Size: 2–9in (5–23cm).
Weight: Up to 4lb (2kg).
Maturity: 1 year.
Breeding: 2 clutches of between 8,000 and 35,000 eggs produced each year.
Life span: 40 years.

Red-eyed tree frog

Agalychnis callidryas

Red-eyed tree frogs have long toes with rounded suction disks at their tips. Their bodies have a bright green upper side. These colorful frogs have blue and white stripes on their flanks and yellow and red legs. The family of tree frogs, comprising about 600 species, is found on all the continents except Antarctica.

Red-eyed tree frogs live in the rain forests of Central America. Their long legs allow them to reach for branches and spread their body weight over a wide area when climbing through flimsy foliage. The disks on the tips of each toe act as suction cups, so the frogs can cling to flat surfaces, such as leaves.

Red-eyed tree frogs are nocturnal. Their large eyes gather as much light as possible, so the frogs can see even on the darkest nights. During the day, the frogs rest on leaves. They tuck their brightly colored legs under their bodies so only their camouflaged, leaf-green upper sides are showing.

At breeding time, males gather on a branch above a pond and call to the females with clicking sounds. When a female arrives, a male climbs on her back and she carries him down to the water. She takes in water and climbs back to the branch again, where she lays eggs on a leaf. The male fertilizes the eggs and they are then abandoned. After hatching, the tadpoles fall into the water below.

Distribution: From northeastern Mexico along the Caribbean coast of Central America to Panama.
Habitat: Tropical forests in the vicinity of streams.
Food: Insects, including flies crickets, grasshoppers, and moths; sometimes small frogs.
Size: 1.5–2.75in (4–7cm).
Weight: 0.25–0.5oz (6–15g).
Maturity: Unknown.
Breeding: Eggs laid in summer.
Life span: Unknown.

Tailed frog

Ascaphus truei

Distribution: Pacific coast of North America, from southern British Columbia in Canada to northern California in the United States and the northern Great Basin.
Habitat: Cold mountain streams up to the timberline.
Food: Algae and aquatic invertebrates.
Size: 1.5in (4cm).
Weight: Unknown.
Maturity: 3 years.
Breeding: Strings of eggs laid in fast-flowing streams between May and September.
Life span: Unknown.

Tailed frogs live in the clear mountain streams of the Cascade Range in the northwestern United States and southern Canada. These frogs often stray from the water into damp forests, and are especially common on land during periods of damp weather.

They have a head with a rounded snout. The males have a short, tail-like extension, which is actually a flexible organ used to deliver sperm to a female's eggs while they are still inside her body. This is an adaptation to ensure fertilization, where releasing sperm and eggs into the fast-flowing water would be unlikely to succeed.

After mating, the females lay short strings of eggs on the downstream side of rocks. The tadpoles develop into adults slowly, taking up to four years in colder parts of their range. They use their mouth as a sucker to cling onto rocks so that they are not swept away by the current.

These frogs will attempt to eat anything solid that comes within reach. Their diet generally consists of plant matter and the aquatic larvae of insects and other invertebrates. They will bite into human flesh given the opportunity.

The "tail" seen on the males contains the anus and sexual opening. This is used during mating, which takes place during the summer.

American toad

Bufo americanus

Distribution: United States and eastern Canada.
Habitat: Ponds.
Food: Insects and slugs.
Size: 2–3.5in (5–9cm).
Weight: Unknown.
Maturity: 2 years.
Breeding: Eggs laid in spring.
Life span: 10 years.

This toad has relatively short legs compared to its stout body. Like many toads, it has warts on its head and back. The warts squirt a toxic milky liquid into the mouth of any attacker that tries to bite the toad.

American toads are found in most parts of eastern North America, from Hudson Bay to the Carolinas. Some American toads survive in irrigated areas of the western United States, where it is too dry for them to live naturally. They are also widespread from California to Washington.

This species is similar to its European cousin, the common toad, in that it has a brownish, wart-covered body. American toads are most active at night, especially in warm and humid weather. They eat mainly insects, slugs, and worms. The toads catch their prey by flicking out their sticky tongue, which grabs food and drags it back into the mouth. The tadpoles graze on water plants.

American toads breed in the spring, when the days lengthen and the temperature rises. These normally solitary animals congregate in large numbers to mate. The females lay thousands of eggs in the water, forming a huge string of eggs up to 66ft (20m) long.

Pacific tree frog

Hyla regilla

This variably colored species has a dark stripe that runs from the nostril to the shoulder. The frog's rough skin can change color. Such changes are triggered by the prevailing temperature and humidity, rather than being actively controlled by the frog itself. Female Pacific tree frogs are slightly larger than males.

The Pacific tree frog occurs in the Pacific Northwest region of North America. The northern limit of its range is southern British Columbia and Vancouver Island. From here, the frogs range along the Pacific coast and through the coastal mountains to Mexico's Baja California. They are found inland as far as Montana and Nevada.

Pacific tree frogs usually live on the ground. They occupy a wide variety of habitats, and are most often found near ponds, springs, and streams. They prefer rocky areas, where there are plenty of damp nooks and crannies in which to hide.

Pacific tree frogs are generally solitary, but they may assemble in large numbers during the breeding season. At night, the males repeat their two-toned "kreck-ek" mating call to attract females and tell other males to stay out of their territory. As tadpoles, the frogs eat aquatic plant material such as algae. The adult frogs are carnivores. They catch flying insects with their tongue, which they flick out at high speed. The tongue is coated with a sticky substance that helps the frogs to grab prey.

Distribution: Western North America, from southern Canada and the United States to Baja California, Mexico.
Habitat: Close to water.
Food: Insects.
Size: 0.75–2in (1.9–5cm).
Weight: Unknown.
Maturity: 1 year.
Breeding: Mating season in spring. Female lays a mass of 10–70 eggs, which either floats or is attached to vegetation; eggs hatch within 3–4 weeks.
Life span: Unknown.

Green tree frog

Hyla cinerea

This species has rough, bright green skin and a dark spot under each eye. There are bright yellow patches on the inner thighs. The skin becomes grayer during cold weather, and males turn yellow during the breeding season. The long legs and large, adhesive pads at the end of the toes are adaptations to an arboreal existence. These small frogs can leap about 10ft (3m), and they are able to hang onto leaves and other surfaces with just one toe.

Green tree frogs live along the edges of swampy ponds and in marshes. They are often found at ground level, but also climb into the tall shrubs and trees that grow beside the water. This species is found across southeastern North America, from Delaware to Florida and Texas. The range also extends north up the Mississippi River Valley to the southern tip of Indiana.

Green tree frogs spend the day lurking under the cover of plants. They may give away their presence by their clanking, bell-like calls. During periods of high humidity, many frogs may call together, creating a loud chorus. The rise in humidity is often a prelude to rain, and consequently to mating. The green tree frog is often nicknamed the "rain frog," since it begins to call just before wet weather arrives. However, not all the males call in these mating choruses. Some "satellite" males remain silent and attempt to intercept and mate with females attracted by the bellowing choruses.

By night, the frogs hunt for insects. They are often seen near houses, where they feed on insects attracted by the light.

Distribution: Eastern United States.
Habitat: Swamps and river banks.
Food: Insects.
Size: 1.25–2.5in (3.2–6.4cm).
Weight: Unknown.
Maturity: Unknown.
Breeding: Mating season is between March and September, but later in the Deep South. The female lays up to 400 eggs in small packets or films in shallow water at or near the surface, attached to floating vegetation; hatching occurs within a week.
Life span: Unknown.

North American bullfrog

Rana catesbeiana

Distribution: Atlantic coast of North America west to the Rocky Mountains and south to Mexico.
Habitat: Ponds and lakes.
Food: Snakes, worms, fish, insects, crayfish, tadpoles, turtles, frogs, and small mammals.
Size: 3.5–8in (9–20cm).
Weight: 1.5lb (750g).
Maturity: 3 years.
Breeding: Up to 20,000 eggs laid in early summer; hatching occurs after about 4 days.
Life span: 16 years.

The North American bullfrog is the largest frog in North America. It is found from Nova Scotia on the Atlantic coast of Canada south to central Florida and into Mexico. From the East Coast, it ranges west as far as the Great Plains and Rocky Mountains. It seldom strays far from a pond or other source of water. North American bullfrogs have also been introduced to areas west of the Rockies, such as California and Colorado. Here, they generally survive in cultivated areas that are irrigated by rivers and groundwater.

The North American bullfrog has a reputation for having a large appetite, and will consume almost any animal that it can overpower. It lives in lakes, ponds, and slow-flowing streams. During the summer breeding season, the males defend their territories by wrestling with their rivals. They attract females by voicing deep croaks. The female bullfrog deposits a foaming mass of eggs in water, and the eggs are then fertilized by one or more males.

This large green frog is perhaps most recognizable by the large external eardrums on either side of its head, which in the males are bigger than the eyes. At dusk and during the summer, American bullfrogs give a deep call that sounds like "jugoram."

Mexican burrowing toad

Rhinophrynus dorsalis

Distribution: Extreme southern Texas and Mexico through Central America as far south as Costa Rica.
Habitat: Soil in savannah and seasonally dry forests.
Food: Termites and other insects.
Size: 2.5–3.25in (6–8cm).
Weight: Unknown.
Maturity: 3 months.
Breeding: Several thousand eggs laid in the rainy season, either individually or in small groups; the fertilized eggs sink to the bottom and hatch within a few days.
Life span: Unknown.

Mexican burrowing toads are found from southern Texas to Costa Rica, in areas with soft, sandy soils that are easy to burrow into. The frogs have smooth, moist skin with a red or yellow line running along their back.

Mexican burrowing toads eat insects and other invertebrates. They are especially fond of termites, which they lick up with their tongues. These toads spend most of their time underground to avoid drying out, only coming to the surface after heavy rain. The smooth skin and pointed body makes it easier for the toads to shimmy through the soil, propelled by the powerful rear legs. The hind feet have a thick arc of skin supported by very long toes, making them very effective digging tools.

To deter predators, a threatened toad swells its body by swallowing air. In this inflated state, the toad is difficult to extract from its burrow. These toads breed in the temporary pools that form after heavy rains at the start of the wet season. The tadpoles are filter-feeders, straining tiny, floating plants and animals from the water. They take up to three months to transform into adults.

The Mexican burrowing toad has a unique, egg-shaped body—ideal for wriggling through soft soil—and a small, pointed head with a callused snout. The body is dark brown to near black, with a mid-dorsal red to dark orange stripe and similar-colored patterning on the flanks. Females of this species tend to be substantially larger than males.

TURTLES AND TERRAPINS

Turtles, terrapins, and tortoises have lived on Earth for over 200 million years. They belong to a group of reptiles that have existed since the dinosaurs roamed the Earth. Their soft bodies are protected by shells called carapaces. There is no major difference between turtles and tortoises; however, turtles (and terrapins) live in water, while tortoises tend to live on land.

Alligator snapping turtle

Macroclemys temminckii

The alligator snapping turtle is the largest freshwater turtle. During the day, it is mainly an ambush hunter, lying half-buried in mud on the river bed. While waiting for prey to approach, this turtle holds its large mouth open. The turtle's tongue has a small projection on it, which becomes pink when engorged with blood. The turtle wiggles this fleshy protuberance as a lure to attract prey. Fish and other animals investigate the lure, assuming it is a worm in the mud. As the prey swims into a turtle's mouth, the jaws snap shut. Small prey are swallowed whole, and the sharp, horny beak makes light work of larger prey, which may even be another species of turtle. The largest prey are held in the jaws, while the alligator snapping turtle uses its forefeet to tear the creature apart.

Male alligator snapping turtles spend their whole lives in muddy rivers and lakes. Females, however, climb onto land in spring to lay eggs in holes dug into mud or sand.

Alligator snapping turtles have a tough carapace covered in pointed, triangular knobbles. They have a large head with a sharp, horny beak.

Distribution: Southeastern United States, in the lower Mississippi River Valley.
Habitat: Beds of lakes and slow-flowing rivers.
Food: Fish and turtles.
Size: 15.5–31.5in (40–80cm).
Weight: 175lb (80kg).
Maturity: Unknown.
Breeding: 10–50 eggs buried in mud.
Life span: 70 years.

Stinkpot

Sternotherus odoratus

Stinkpots have smooth, streamlined shells suitable for living in running water. They have sensitive, fleshy projections, called barbels, on their chins.

Stinkpots are so called because they release a nasty smelling musk from glands beneath their shells. This smell is supposed to ward off predators, but the stinkpot will also give a painful bite if the musk does not do its job.

Stinkpots spend their lives in slow-flowing, shallow streams and muddy ponds and lakes. Their shells often have mats of microscopic algae growing on them. Stinkpots feed both during the day and at night. They use the barbels on their chins to sense the movements of prey buried in the muddy stream beds. Like many other musk turtles, stinkpots have a toughened "shelf" attached to their upper jaws. The turtles use this shelf to crush the shells of water snails and other prey.

Female stinkpots leave the water to lay their elongated eggs. They make nests under mats of decaying plant matter or under the stumps of trees. Stinkpots lay the smallest eggs of all turtles—only 0.5 × 1in (1.5 × 2.5cm).

Distribution: Southeastern United States.
Habitat: Shallow, muddy water.
Food: Insects, molluscs, plants and carrion.
Size: 3.25–5in (8–13cm).
Weight: Unknown.
Maturity: Unknown.
Breeding: Eggs laid under tree stumps.
Life span: 54 years.

Snapping turtle

Chelydra serpentina

Distribution: Central and eastern North America, from southern Alberta and Nova Scotia in Canada to Texas and the Gulf of Mexico.
Habitat: Rivers and tidal swamps.
Food: Fish, birds, amphibians, and small mammals.
Size: 7.75–17.75in (20–45cm).
Weight: 10–35lb (4.5–16kg).
Maturity: Unknown.
Breeding: 20–30 eggs laid in a hole in the spring.
Life span: 30 years.

The snapping turtle lives in the rivers and swamps of eastern North America. It prefers fresh-water habitats, but it also occurs in brackish environments, where salt water mixes with fresh water in estuaries and coastal marshes.

Snapping turtles are almost completely aquatic, although they will move across land in search of a new place to live should their home range become too crowded. These highly solitary turtles ensure that no other turtle encroaches into their feeding territory. They ambush their prey, burying themselves in mud on the river bottom and then cutting the heads off their victims using their sharp beaks. They also eat plants and carrion.

The only time a snapper will tolerate another individual's presence is during the mating season, between April and November. The male positions himself on the female's back during mating, clinging to her shell with his claws. Between 20 and 30 eggs are laid in a hole in sandy soil, hatching between 9 and 18 weeks later in the fall or winter.

The shells of snapping turtles range in color from light brown to black. The tail has a serrated keel, and the legs and neck are covered in points called "tubercles."

Painted turtle

Chrysemys picta

Distribution: North America, from southern Canada to Mexico.
Habitat: Muddy fresh water.
Food: Plants, fish, insects, and crustaceans.
Size: 6–9.75in (15–25cm).
Weight: 1.5–3lb (800–1400g).
Maturity: 3–10 years.
Breeding: Eggs laid in the late spring and early summer.
Life span: 40 years.

Painted turtles live in fresh water from British Columbia and much of southern Canada to Georgia and northern Mexico. The turtles sleep on muddy river beds at night, and during the daytime, feed on leaves, fruits, and a range of animal prey. Between feeding periods, large numbers of painted turtles can be seen basking in the sun, often perched on logs. The sun helps to keep parasites, such as leeches, at bay. If disturbed, the turtles dive into the water and hide in the mud or under a submerged object.

Males mature much earlier than female painted turtles. Mating takes place in the late spring and early summer after the turtles emerge from hibernation. Eggs are buried in sandy soil in an open area that is exposed to a lot of sun. Each female lays about ten soft-shelled eggs. The young turtles are independent as soon as they hatch.

Painted turtles are so-called because of their smooth, bright-colored shells. They have black, olive, or brown shells with red, black, and yellow markings along the edges. Female painted turtles tend to be larger than the males.

Wood turtle

Clemmys insculpta

The shells of wood turtles have a low keel along the spine. The scutes, or plates, that make up the shell have well-defined "growth rings."

Wood turtles have a fragmented range across eastern North America. They live in running water, from small streams to the mighty St. Lawrence River. Although they prefer watercourses with rocky bottoms, they are also found in woodlands and meadows far from water. (Females seem to be less water-dependent than males.)

Wood turtles feed both in the water and on land. Being omnivores, they eat a variety of foods, from leaves and fallen fruits to slugs, tadpoles, and fungi. They cannot catch fast-moving, warm-blooded animals, such as small birds and mammals, but they will eat carrion if the chance arises. The turtles drive earthworms, a favorite food, to the surface by thumping their plastron (lower shell) on the ground. Taking the thumping to be vibrations caused by heavy rain, the worms rise to the surface to avoid drowning—only to be eaten by the turtles.

Distribution: From eastern Canada to New England and the Midwest in the United States.
Habitat: Running water.
Food: Plants, fruits, fungi, snails, slugs, tadpoles, and worms.
Size: 5.5–7.5in (14–25cm).
Weight: 1–3lb (0.4–1.5kg).
Maturity: 14–20 years
Breeding: Eggs laid in nests in May and June.
Life span: Unknown.

Bog turtle

Clemmys muhlenbergii

Bog turtles are distributed patchily across the eastern United States. A northern population lives from New York and Massachusetts to northern Maryland, and a southern population can be found in the mountains of Virginia and North Carolina. There are also smaller populations in western Pennsylvania and along the southern shore of Lake Ontario.

The bog turtle's distribution is limited because it is restricted to a very specific habitat—shallow wetlands with water that is slow-flowing yet not choked by aquatic vegetation. Habitats like this tend to support dozens of different water-plant species. Human interference often reduces the number of plants in the habitat, or introduces new species that become rampant and make the area unsuitable for bog turtles. As a result, bog turtles are increasingly endangered. Bog turtles are popular as pets, but collecting wild bog turtles is now banned. Individuals bred in captivity fetch high prices, and this continues to fuel illegal collecting.

Bog turtles are only active during the warmer parts of the day. They emerge from their nocturnal shelters and bask for awhile before foraging. These turtles hibernate through winter, and they may also estivate during the driest months of the year (July and August).

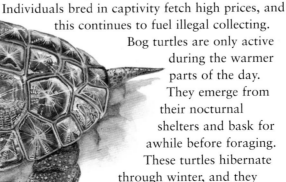

Distribution: Eastern United States.
Habitat: Wetlands.
Food: Invertebrates, seeds, fruits, and leaves.
Size: 3–5in (7.9–11.4cm).
Weight: 4oz (128g)
Maturity: 10 years.
Breeding: Up to 6 eggs laid yearly in shallow nests in June.
Life span: 40 years.

This species is the smallest of the pond turtles. Younger individuals have obvious growth rings, or annuli, on their scutes. By the time a turtle reaches maturity, these marks have been smoothed away.

Diamondback terrapin

Malaclemys terrapin

Distribution: Eastern coast of United States.
Habitat: Estuaries and lagoons.
Food: Snails, crustaceans, fish, and insects.
Size: 5.5–9in (14–23cm).
Weight: 0.5–1.5lb (230–680g).
Maturity: 7 years.
Breeding: About 10 eggs (maximum 18) laid in sand during late spring and early summer.
Life span: Unknown.

Diamondback terrapins range from southern Texas and the Gulf of Mexico, where they are most common, around Florida and up to southern New England. They inhabit the brackish water of the salt marshes, estuaries, and tidal lagoons that form behind barrier islands, being most abundant in heavily reeded areas. While these terrapins can cope with saline conditions, they still need access to fresh drinking water.

Diamondbacks feed on a range of animal life in the tidal zone, including marine snails, clams, and crabs. When not feeding, the terrapins may be seen basking on exposed sandbars or walking across mudflats between feeding sites. They avoid danger by running into water, where they are much more agile and better able to hide than on land.

Diamondback terrapins are named after the pattern of growth rings that appear on the pyramidal scutes (plates) that make up the carapace. They use their ridged, beaklike jaws to crush the bodies of their prey. Males may be only half the size of females.

Eastern box turtle

Terrapene carolina

Distribution: Eastern United States, from Texas in the south to Michigan in the north, and eastward across the Appalachian Mountains to the Atlantic coast.
Habitat: Woodlands, meadows, and marshes.
Food: Snails, insects, worms, roots, amphibians, snakes, birds' eggs, and fruit; turtles become more herbivorous with age.
Size: 4–8.5in (10–21.5cm).
Weight: 1–2lb (0.25–1kg).
Maturity: 5–7 years.
Breeding: Usually 4–5 eggs (maximum 11) laid from May to July in sandy or loamy soil; 2–3 (maximum 6) clutches may be laid per year.
Life span: 100 years.

The Eastern box turtle occurs only in North America, where it ranges from Texas in the south to Michigan in the north, and across the Appalachian Mountains to the Atlantic coast. (A western box turtle species lives in the central United States.)

Eastern box turtles are seldom found far from streams and ponds, but often forage in woodland and damp meadows. The diet of these omnivorous reptiles includes several plants and mushrooms that are poisonous to humans, and many people have died after eating poisoned box turtle meat. The turtles' feeding behavior is influenced by temperature. In midsummer, box turtles are most active in the morning and afternoons. During the hottest part of the day, they crawl under logs or into burrows to keep cool. In the spring and fall, the weather is mild enough for the turtles to feed all day long. In the northern part of their range, box turtles hibernate in burrows in the river bed during the winter.

Many eastern box turtle populations have been reduced by the destruction of their habitat for urban development or agriculture. Collection of wild turtles for the pet trade also threatens their future.

The keeled, high-domed shell of this species has variable markings throughout its range. As in other box turtles, the lower shell (plastron) is hinged, enabling the turtle to close the shell almost completely when its head, tail, and legs are withdrawn inside. Shut in a near-impregnable "box" of horny plates, the turtle is safe from most predators. Male eastern box turtles tend to be slightly larger than the females.

LIZARDS

Lizards are reptiles, belonging to the same group as snakes. They are found all over the world, except for Antarctica, especially in places that are too hot or dry for mammals to thrive. The main group of American lizards are the iguanas, which include the basilisks and anoles. More widespread lizards, such as geckos and skinks, are also found in the Americas, especially South America.

Gila monster

Heloderma suspectum

Gila monsters are one of only two poisonous lizards in the world. They produce venom in salivary glands in their lower jaws. The venom flows by capillary action along grooves in their teeth, giving the lizard a poisonous bite. The venom acts on the prey animal's nervous system, preventing the heart and lungs from working. For a healthy human, a bite from a gila monster will be very painful but not life-threatening.

These lizards are most active at night. They shelter from the heat of the day in rocky crevices or burrows abandoned by mammals. However, in northern parts of their range, the lizards are completely inactive for several months during the winter. Inactive individuals rely on fat stored in their tails to keep them alive when they cannot feed.

Gila monsters mate in the springtime, and their copulation can last for over an hour. The eggs develop inside the females for about ten weeks. They then bury the eggs, which incubate for up to ten months.

Gila monsters have long, robust bodies with short legs. Their bodies are covered in rounded, beadlike scales. Most of them are dark but some have blotches of pink, yellow, or orange.

Distribution: Southwestern United States and northern Mexico.
Habitat: Desert.
Food: Small mammals and eggs.
Size: 14–19.5in (35–50cm).
Weight: 4lb (1.8kg).
Maturity: Unknown.
Breeding: Eggs laid in summer.
Life span: 20 years.

Green anole

Anolis carolinensis

Green anoles live in trees. Their long, thin legs are well adapted for leaping from branch to branch. Thanks to the pads on the tips of their fingers and toes, anoles can grip onto just about any surface, including the fronds of palm trees.

Green anoles rest in dense cover at night. When not foraging in daylight, the lizards bask in the sun, generally on vertical surfaces, such as tree trunks or walls. Anoles are able to darken their normally bright skin when resting in the shade so as not to attract attention.

Although both sexes have dewlaps, only the males use them for communication. They extend them to signal to rival males and mates. A male begins courtship by bobbing his head and displaying his dewlap to a female. He then walks toward her with his legs straightened. If she is receptive to his advances, she allows him to position his body next to hers. He then grasps the back of her neck with his mouth and holds her tail with his hind legs as they copulate. The female lays one egg at a time under moist leaf litter.

Both male and female green anoles have pink dewlaps, which are fans of skin beneath their throats. The lizards have very long tails— nearly twice the length of the rest of their bodies—and their elongated fingers and toes are tipped with pads.

Distribution: Southeastern United States.
Habitat: Woodland and shrubbery.
Food: Insects.
Size: 4.75–8in (12–20cm).
Weight: Under 0.25oz (6g)
Maturity: Unknown.
Breeding: Single eggs laid throughout breeding season.
Life span: Unknown.

Desert horned lizard

Phrynosoma platyrhinos

Distribution: Southwestern United States.
Habitat: Rocky desert.
Food: Ants.
Size: 3–5.25in (7.5–13.5cm).
Weight: Unknown.
Maturity: Unknown.
Breeding: Eggs laid in spring.
Life span: Unknown.

The desert horned lizard has three pointed scales that form horns pointing backward from the rear of its head. There are smaller spikes on its back and along the tail.

These small reptiles are sometimes referred to as horned toads, because of their rounded bodies. Despite living in dry areas, much of the desert horned lizard's range can get cold, especially at night. Its round body helps it to warm up quickly in the morning sunshine. The lizard can eat huge quantities of ants, which it licks up with its long tongue.

The many spikes on this lizard's body serve two functions. They help to break up the profile of the lizard so that it can blend in with the rocky terrain, and if the lizard is spotted by a sharp-eyed predator, the tough spikes make it a difficult and potentially painful meal to swallow. Armed with these weapons, a horned lizard will not run when danger approaches. Instead, it will freeze to avoid giving its position away and rely on its camouflage to hide it. If this defensive strategy fails and it is scooped into the mouth of a predator, such as a coyote, the reptile has one final weapon. The horned lizard can ooze blood from membranes that hemorrhage around its eyeballs. The blood mixes with a foul-tasting chemical, causing the predator to release its grip on the lizard.

Chuckwalla

Sauromalus obesus

Distribution: California, Arizona, and northern Mexico.
Habitat: Desert.
Food: Fruit, leaves, and flowers.
Size: 11–16.5in (28–42cm).
Weight: 2lb (1kg).
Maturity: Unknown.
Breeding: Females breed every 1–2 years.
Life span: Unknown.

Chuckwallas have powerful limbs and thick tails. The males have completely black heads, and the females have yellow and orange patches on black.

Chuckwallas live in the Mojave Desert, one of the driest and hottest places in North America. Like all other living reptiles, chuckwallas are cold-blooded or exothermic. Their bodies do not make any heat of their own apart from that generated by muscle movement. The lizards rely on sunlight and the temperature of the air around them to warm up enough for daily activity. They only become fully active when their body temperature exceeds 100°F (38°C). The temperature of the Mojave Desert is regularly above this, but in other areas of their range, chuckwallas remain inside their rocky dens until the weather gets warm enough.

These lizards are herbivores. They search through the rock-strewn desert for hardy plants that can survive the scorching conditions. With only a limited food supply, female chuckwallas may not be able to reproduce every year. Some females save energy by skipping a breeding season.

Chuckwallas have an unusual defense strategy. When they are under attack by a bird of prey or coyote, they scuttle into a tight crevice between rocks and inflate their lungs. These reptiles have loose folds of skin around their throats and flanks, which allow their bodies to swell up to a considerable size. This makes it difficult for a predator to extract the lizard from its hiding place.

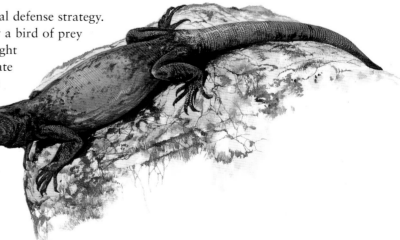

Western banded gecko

Coleonyx variegatus

The western banded gecko is found in southern California, Arizona, and northern Mexico, including half of the Baja peninsula. This slender-limbed, flexible-bodied lizard occupies rocky and sandy habitats such as the walls and beds of canyons. Agile and quick-footed, the Western banded gecko is active at night, when it forages for insects and spiders. Its days are spent sheltering in rocky crevices or rodent burrows.

The western banded gecko holds its tail in the air, a little like a cat, as it stalks insects and spiders. When trapped, this lizard makes high-pitched squeaks, and like many other geckos, it may shed its tail when attacked. There is a constriction at the base of the tail where the break occurs. The tail keeps moving for a short while after separation from the body. This behavior is meant to confuse the predator, which may focus on the tail while the gecko makes its escape. The tail quickly regrows.

As well as the dark brown or black bands across the tan back, Western banded geckos can be identified by their moveable, protruding eyelids. The bands are most prominent in juveniles, and fade as the lizards get older.

Distribution: Southwestern United States to northern Mexico, including California, Arizona, and Baja California.
Habitat: Rocky deserts, also arid grassland and chaparral.
Food: Insects and spiders.
Size: 4.75–6in (12–15cm).
Weight: Unknown.
Maturity: Unknown.
Breeding: 3 clutches of 2 eggs laid in the summer.
Life span: Unknown.

Texas banded gecko

Coleonyx brevis

Texas banded geckos live in Texas, northern Mexico, and parts of New Mexico. They are mainly found west of the Pecos River, in the so-called Trans-Pecos region. These geckos live in dry, rocky areas. They dig burrows in the sandy soil underneath flat rocks.

Texas banded geckos are nocturnal hunters. They feed on insects and spiders, which they stalk on the ground. Being cold-blooded, they have only a short time when their body is sufficiently warm enough to enable them to forage. They begin hunting at dusk, and generally finish about four hours later, by which time it is too cold for them to continue. The geckos find prey by tasting the air and ground to detect chemicals produced by nearby insects. They also locate prey by sight.

If the gecko is threatened by a predator, it turns around and waggles its tail at its attacker. When the predator strikes at the tail, the tail breaks away from the body, enabling the lizard to flee. The tail regrows, as it does in other tail-shedding species.

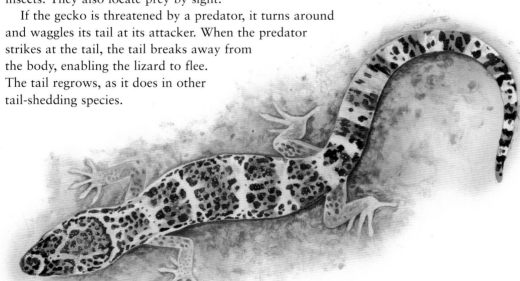

Distribution: Texas, New Mexico, and Mexico.
Habitat: Rocky areas.
Food: Insects.
Size: 4–4.75in (10–12cm).
Weight: Unknown.
Maturity: Unknown.
Breeding: 2 clutches of eggs laid in the late spring and early summer.
Life span: Unknown.

Female Texas banded geckos are larger than males. As the lizards get older, the solid bands across the back break up into spots and blotches. In banded gecko species, the males have a pair of thornlike spurs at the base of the tail.

CROCODILIANS

Crocodilians are an ancient group of reptiles. They include crocodiles, alligators, caimans, and gharials. They all live in or near water. Most crocodilians in North and South America belong to the alligator and caiman group. In fact, only one type of alligator—the Chinese alligator—lives outside of the Americas. American crocodiles tend to be larger than their alligator and caiman cousins, and most are very rare.

American alligator

Alligator mississippiensis

Distribution: Southeastern United States.
Habitat: Swamps and rivers.
Food: Birds, fish, and mammals.
Size: 9.25–16.5ft (2.8–5m).
Weight: 800lb (360kg).
Maturity: 5–10 years.
Breeding: Eggs laid in nest of mud and vegetation in the spring.
Life span: 40 years.

Young American alligators feed on insects, small fish, and frogs. As they get bigger, they begin to take larger prey, such as turtles and water birds. Adults feed on land as well as in water. They are opportunistic feeders, attacking anything that comes within reach. They even leap up to snatch birds perching on low branches.

During cold weather, American alligators become dormant in burrows dug into mud banks. In dry periods, they will travel long distances to find water, sometimes ending up in swimming pools.

After mating, the female makes a mound of vegetation and mud above the high waterline and lays her eggs in a hole in the top. When she hears the hatchlings calling, she breaks open the nest and carries her young to the water. They stay with their mother for about a year.

The American alligator has a broad snout: teeth are not visible when the mouth is closed.

American crocodile

Crocodylus acutus

Distribution: Southern Florida, Mexico, Central America, and northern South America.
Habitat: Rivers and brackish water.
Food: Fish, turtles, and birds.
Size: 13–16.5ft (4–5m).
Weight: Up to 2,000lb (907kg)
Maturity: 5–10 years.
Breeding: Eggs laid in dry season.
Life span: 40 years.

The American crocodile's diet consists mainly of fish and other small aquatic animals. Larger individuals may also eat small mammals, birds, and turtles.

American crocodiles live in fresh water, such as rivers and lakes, but will venture out into coastal waters, especially near estuaries and in lagoons, where the water is brackish. The crocodiles cope with the salty water by taking long drinks of fresh water when possible and removing salt from the body through glands on their faces—secreting "crocodile tears" in the process. Feeding takes place at night, and the crocodiles occasionally come onto land to prey on livestock. They have also been known to attack humans. During periods of drought, the crocodiles burrow into mud and do not feed until the water returns.

Most females lay their eggs in holes dug in the ground, but they may build nest mounds in areas where the soil is likely to become waterlogged and thus chill the incubating eggs. Nesting takes place in the dry season. Between 30 and 60 eggs are laid, which hatch three months later as the rainy season begins. The hatchlings are guarded until they disperse.

SNAKES

Most snakes do not have a venomous bite and are completely harmless to humans. The largest American snakes—the boas—are nonvenomous. They kill by coiling around prey and squeezing until their victims suffocate. However, about 10 percent of snake species use modified fangs to inject prey with venom. The world's most venomous snakes, such as taipans, sea snakes, and cobras, belong to the Elapidae family.

Rubber boa

Charina bottae

This small snake is one of just two boas found in North America, where it lives in damp woodlands and mountain conifer forests in the west of the continent. Rubber boas are burrowers, as well as good swimmers, so they are especially common in sandy areas close to streams. Their small, blunt heads and sturdy bodies help them to force their way through soft soil. Rubber boas are crepuscular, spending the day underground and coming to the surface around dusk or just before dawn.

The prey of rubber boas consists of small mammals, lizards, and birds, which the snakes kill by constriction. These snakes hunt on the ground, but they also use their slender, prehensile tail to climb into shrubs and the lower branches of trees. If danger threatens, a rubber boa will slither under a rock or burrow into sand or leaf litter.

This species does not lay eggs. Instead, the female retains the eggs inside her body until they hatch. When the young emerge, they are miniature versions of the adults. Young rubber boas prey on insects, salamanders, frogs, and other small woodland animals.

Distribution: British Columbia to Utah and southern California.
Habitat: Damp woodland and coniferous forest.
Food: Small mammals, birds, and lizards.
Size: 14–33in (35.5–84cm).
Weight: 3.5–7oz (100–200g).
Maturity: Unknown.
Breeding: 2–8 young born in the late summer.
Life span: 10 years.

With a short, rounded snout and an equally blunt tail, this snake looks as if it has two heads. The dark and matt scales on its body give the snake a rubbery appearance and texture.

Common rat snake

Elaphe obsoleta

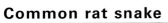

The common rat snake belongs to a group of rat snake species that includes corn snakes and fox snakes. This particular species is found across the eastern, Midwestern, and southeastern United States, from New England to Wisconsin, Texas, and Nebraska. They are most abundant in warmer parts of their range around the Gulf of Mexico and along the Atlantic coast.

The common rat snake lives in a variety of habitats, with each of the many subspecies being adapted to a particular habitat type. For example, black rat snakes are found in highland regions, and yellow rat snakes inhabit oak woodlands and human habitations.

Rat snakes do not inject their prey with venom, but kill by constriction. When threatened, these snakes coil themselves up and rustle dead leaves with their tails to imitate a rattlesnake. They also spread a foul musk with their tail.

The common rat snake occurs in three color forms: almost completely black; yellow with black stripes; and orange with black stripes.

Distribution: Eastern, Midwestern, and southeastern United States.
Habitat: Grassland, forests, and suburban areas.
Food: Small rodents and birds.
Size: 4–6ft (1.2–1.8m).
Weight: Unknown.
Maturity: Unknown.
Breeding: 20 eggs laid in the summer.
Life span: 20 years.

Milksnake

Lampropeltis triangulum

Distribution: Southern Canada and the United States through Central America to Colombia, Ecuador, and Venezuela.
Habitat: Desert, grassland, and forests.
Food: Invertebrates, amphibians, and small rodents.
Size: 2–3ft (0.6–0.9m).
Weight: Unknown.
Maturity: 3–4 years.
Breeding: 15 eggs laid in the summer.
Life span: 21 years.

Milksnakes range from Colombia and other northern parts of South America to southern Canada. They thrive in a wide range of habitats, including semidesert and rain forest. They live high up in the Rockies and are also found in edge habitats, such as where farmland meets woodland. The longest milksnakes live in tropical regions. Those that are found in dry or cold areas to the north are barely half the size of their tropical cousins.

Milksnakes are nocturnal hunters, preying upon small rodents and amphibians. During the day, they hide out in leaf litter or under a rotting log, and sometimes in damp garbage. They live and hunt alone, but gather in large groups to hibernate together. Milksnakes mate while in their winter quarters and the females lay their eggs in the early summer. They construct nests under rocks, in tree stumps, and in other secluded spots.

Milksnakes are very colorful, with at least 25 different color variants described so far. Many milksnakes mimic the bold, banded colors of venomous snakes, such as the coral snake, but others have mostly monochrome bodies, usually in tan, black, or red. Hatchlings are particularly bright-colored, but their markings become duller with age.

Corn snake

Elaphe guttata

Distribution: Eastern United States, from New Jersey to Florida and west into Louisiana and parts of Kentucky.
Habitat: Woodland, rocky areas, and meadows.
Food: Mice, rats, birds, and bats.
Size: 3.25–6ft (1–1.8m).
Weight: Up to 2lb (1kg).
Maturity: 3 years.
Breeding: Between 10 and 30 eggs laid in the summer; incubation takes around 60–65 days.
Life span: 20 years.

Corn snakes range from New Jersey to Florida and across to central Texas. They are most common in the southeastern United States. These snakes live in woodland and meadows, and they are at also home around rural and suburban settlements.

Corn snakes hunt on the ground, up trees, and among rocks. Like other members of the rat snake group to which they belong, corn snakes have a wide underside that helps them grip onto near vertical surfaces such bark, rubble, and even walls. They are not venomous, but when threatened, these rattlesnake mimics will waggle their tail and rise up as if to strike. Corn snakes kill their prey—mainly small rodents—by constriction.

This species mates between March and May. Like other snakes, mating is more or less indiscriminate. The females lay eggs in rotting debris by midsummer. The heat produced by the rotting material incubates the eggs, helping them to hatch more quickly. The young corn snakes eat lizards and tree frogs; adults prey on rodents, bats, and birds.

Corn snakes belong to the rat snake group. Like their relatives, they occur in several color forms. There are four subspecies, which tend to be more colorful in the south of their range.

Rainbow snake

Farancia erytrogramma

The rainbow snake occurs in the southeastern United States, south and east of the Appalachian Mountains. It is most common in South Carolina and Florida. This species lives near to water, especially on the sandy banks of rivers and streams. It is one of the most aquatic snakes in this part of the world, and is often found among floating plant debris.

Female rainbow snakes lay eggs in July. They make a small dip in the sand and deposit up to 50 eggs, each of which is about 1.5in (4cm) long. The snake stays with her eggs and incubates them for awhile before they hatch.

Rainbow snakes are nocturnal hunters that lie in wait in water to ambush their prey. Adult rainbow snakes eat nothing but eels, but younger individuals eat salamanders, small fish, and tadpoles.

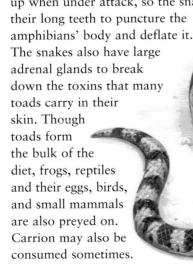

The spine at the end of the tail is used in self-defense. The spine is pressed into an attacker's flesh, provoking a bite to the tail (the least important part of the reptile's anatomy) instead of a lethal strike at the snake's head.

Distribution: Coastal plain of southeastern United States.
Habitat: Sandy areas near water.
Food: Eels.
Size: 35–66in (89–167cm).
Weight: Unknown.
Maturity: Unknown.
Breeding: Eggs laid in July.
Life span: Unknown.

This burrowing snake has a cylindrical body with glossy dark scales. There are yellow or red stripes along the edges of the belly. The underside is generally red. The spine at the tip of the tail is actually a pointed horny scale.

Western hog-nosed snake

Heterodon nasicus

The western hog-nosed snake is found across a swathe of North America, from northern Mexico to southern Canada. It inhabits the Great Plains region between the Mississippi River in the east and the Rocky Mountains in the west. This region is relatively dry, and the hog-nosed snake spends much of its time burrowing through loose, sandy soil, using its snout as a shovel to excavate soil.

Western hog-nosed snakes hibernate between September and March. Mating occurs soon after the snakes emerge in the spring. Females have multiple mates, and initiate the breeding season by molting their skins and releasing an odor that attracts the males. About a dozen eggs are laid in soil in the late summer, and these hatch just before the winter hibernation.

Hog-nosed snakes use their snout to dig up buried toads. Many toads puff themselves up when under attack, so the snakes use their long teeth to puncture the amphibians' body and deflate it. The snakes also have large adrenal glands to break down the toxins that many toads carry in their skin. Though toads form the bulk of the diet, frogs, reptiles and their eggs, birds, and small mammals are also preyed on. Carrion may also be consumed sometimes.

Distribution: Southern Canada to northern Mexico.
Habitat: Dry prairies and rocky areas.
Food: Mainly toads, plus other small vertebrate prey.
Size: 15.5–40in (40–100cm).
Weight: 3–12oz (80–350g).
Maturity: 2 years.
Breeding: Eggs laid in summer.
Life span: 14 years.

The snout of this snake is sharply upturned and pointed, so that it resembles a pig's nose. The western hog-nosed snake has three color forms: brown, gray, and tan. These forms closely resemble the eastern and southern hog-nosed species, which also have red forms.

Sidewinder

Crotalus cerastes

Distribution: Southwestern United States and northwestern Mexico.
Habitat: Desert.
Food: Lizards and rodents.
Size: 18–32in (45–80cm).
Weight: Unknown.
Maturity: Unknown.
Breeding: Live young born in late summer.
Life span: Unknown.

Sidewinders have wide bodies so that they do not sink into sand. Their tails are tipped with rattles that increase in length as the snakes age. Their heads are flattened and triangular.

Sidewinders are named for their unusual method of locomotion, in which they move sideways across loose ground, such as sand. Many snakes that live in similar habitats also "sidewind." This involves a wavelike undulation of the snake's body, so that only two points are in contact with the ground at any given moment. The snake progresses in a sideways direction across the ground (compared to the orientation of the body), leaving parallel S-shaped tracks in the sand.

Sidewinders are desert rattlesnakes that lie under shrubs and ambush small animal prey at night, using sensory pits below their eyes to detect their victims' body heat. They strike with lightning speed, injecting venom from glands in their upper jaws through their hollow fangs. If the prey escapes a short distance before being overcome, the snake soon locates the corpse with its heat-sensitive pits.

Western diamondback rattlesnake

Crotalus atrox

Distribution: Southern United States and northern Mexico.
Habitat: Grassland and rocky country.
Food: Vertebrate prey including small mammals, birds, and lizards.
Size: 6.5ft (2m).
Weight: 13–15lb (6–7kg).
Maturity: 3–4 years.
Breeding: Young born live.
Life span: Unknown.

Diamondbacks are so named because of the brown diamonds, bordered with cream scales, seen along their backs.

Western diamondbacks are the largest and most venomous rattlesnakes in North America. The snake's rattle comprises dried segments, or buttons, of skin attached to the tail. The rattle is used to warn predators that the snake gives a poisonous bite. Although it will readily defend itself when cornered, the diamondback would prefer to conserve venom, and enemies, including humans, soon learn to associate the rattle with danger.

Like all rattlesnakes, diamondbacks are not born with a rattle. Instead, they begin with just a single button, which soon dries into a tough husk. Each time the snake molts its skin, a new button is left behind by the old skin. The rattle grows in this way until it contains around ten buttons that give the characteristic noise when shaken.

Western diamondbacks have a very potent venom. They kill more people each year than any other North American snake, although this number rarely reaches double figures. The venom can kill even large prey, such as hares, in seconds. Like other rattlesnakes, diamondbacks can sense body heat using sensory pits on their faces.

OCEANIC MAMMALS

Dolphins are small members of the mammal order Cetacea, which also includes the whales.
Most dolphins live in the ocean, but a few species are found in the fresh water of large river systems.
Porpoises are similar to dolphins, but tend to be smaller and have rounded snouts, rather than long beaks
like dolphins. All but one species of porpoise inhabit shallow coastal waters, rather than the open ocean.

Vaquita

Phocoena sinus

Most vaquitas have dark gray or black upper bodies, with paler undersides. Like other porpoises, the vaquita has a blunt face. Its triangular dorsal fin is reminiscent of a shark's. Vaquitas live in pods of up to five animals.

Vaquitas live in the upper area of the Gulf of California, near the mouth of the Colorado River. No other marine mammal has such a small range, and consequently vaquitas are extremely rare and may become extinct.

Vaquitas were once able to swim up into the mouth of the Colorado. However, in recent years, so much water has been removed from the river for irrigation and for supplying cities that the Colorado is little more than a trickle where it reaches the ocean. This has probably changed the composition of the Gulf waters, too. The vaquita population was also affected by the fishing industry in the Gulf. Fishermen drowned many vaquitas in their nets by accident, and their activities have also reduced the amount of fish available for the porpoises to eat.

Biologists know little about the lives of these porpoises. Vaquitas probably spend most of their time alone, locating their prey close to the sea floor using echolocation. Births probably take place all year round.

Distribution: Gulf of California in the eastern Pacific.
Habitat: Coastal waters and mouth of the Colorado River.
Food: Fish and squid.
Size: 4–6.5ft (1.2–2m).
Weight: 99–132lb (45–60kg).
Maturity: Unknown.
Breeding: Probably 1 calf.
Life span: Unknown.

Risso's dolphin

Grampus griseus

Risso's dolphins live in small groups, called "pods" or "schools," containing about ten individuals. The pods move to warm tropical waters in the winter, and head toward the poles in summer. The dolphins are often seen leaping out of the water as the pod members play with one another. Risso's dolphins feed in deep water. They dive down to catch fast-swimming squid and fish. Like other dolphins, they probably use echolocation to locate their prey in the dark depths. They produce clicking noises that bounce off objects in the water. The dolphins can hear each other's clicks and echoes, and groups may work together to track down shoals of fish or squid. In areas where there is plenty of food, dolphin pods congregate so that thousands of the leaping mammals may be seen together.

Risso's dolphins have very blunt faces, lacking the beaks of typical dolphins. They have dark gray bodies, which are often scarred by attacks from other dolphins and large squid. Older dolphins may have so many scars that their bodies look almost white.

Distribution: All tropical and temperate seas.
Habitat: Deep ocean water.
Food: Fish and squid.
Size: 11.75–13ft (3.6–4m).
Weight: 880–990lb (400–450kg).
Maturity: Unknown.
Breeding: Single young born once per year.
Life span: 30 years.

White-beaked dolphin

Lagenorhynchus albirostris

Distribution: Ranges widely throughout the North Atlantic and Arctic Oceans.
Habitat: Coastal waters.
Food: Medium-size fish, squid, and crustaceans form the bulk of the diet.
Size: 7.5–9.25ft (2.3–2.8m).
Weight: 397–441lb (180–200kg).
Maturity: Unknown.
Breeding: 1 calf born every year.
Life span: Unknown.

Dolphins are notoriously difficult animals to study because they are very wide-ranging. Consequently, little is known about the habits of this remarkable group compared to most land-living mammals. Like most cetaceans, white-beaked dolphins live in groups known as "pods," or "schools," which have very complex social structures. Pods are usually made up of 2–20 individuals, but occasionally, many pods will come together to form large aggregations containing in excess of 1,000 individuals.

White-beaked dolphins are famed for a behavior known as "breaching," when they leap clear of the water, somersault, and splash back down through the waves. They frequently swim alongside small boats and have also been observed playing games underwater, such as chasing seaweed. White-beaked dolphins undertake annual migrations, moving between temperate and subpolar waters as they track and feed on their favored prey of mackerel and herring.

The white-beaked dolphin's counter-shaded coloration, with a darker upper side and pale belly, helps to camouflage it from both above and below.

Hourglass dolphin
(*Lagenorhynchus cruciger*): 5.25ft (1.6m); 183–220lb (83–100kg)
Hourglass dolphins are found in the colder waters of the Southern Hemisphere. These shy animals live in small groups and travel huge distances in their lifetime. In general, hourglass dolphins keep to the waters around Antarctica, but they occasionally follow cold-water currents moving north, such as the Humboldt Current that flows along the coast of Chile.

Short-finned pilot whale
(*Globicephala macrorhynchus*): 19.75ft (6m); 4,630lb (2.1 metric tons)
Sometimes classed as a separate group of toothed whales, pilot whales (and the closely related orcas) are more usually grouped with the dolphins. This species lives in all tropical waters and is often seen in certain bays and other coastal waters that are used as breeding grounds. The name *pilot whale* refers to the way that pods of up to 20 of these whales follow a single individual, or pilot.

Bottlenosed dolphin

Tursiops truncatus

This is one of the most common and familiar dolphin species. It is found worldwide but often appears along the Atlantic coast of North America, from Cape Hatteras in North Carolina to Argentina, and along the Pacific up to northern California.

Bottlenosed dolphins live in shallow water close to land, and they are generally spotted breaching in large bays. They often enter lagoons and the mouths of large rivers. They do not appear to migrate, but instead make a lifelong journey that may take them to all parts of the world. Since they prefer warmer waters, they tend to move between the Atlantic and Pacific oceans via the Indian ocean.

Bottlenosed dolphins travel at about 12mph (20kmh) and are rarely seen traveling alone. They hunt as a team, rounding up shoals of fish and shrimp. They are also known to herd fish onto mudflats and then slide up the shore to seize their prey. Individuals consume around 15.4lb (7kg) per day.

The bottlenosed is the largest of the beaked dolphins, which are oceanic dolphins with short, stout snouts. Males are much larger than females. This species shows a high degree of intelligence.

Distribution: Tropical and temperate coastal waters worldwide; both Pacific and Atlantic coasts of the Americas and around Hawaii.
Habitat: Warm, shallow water and cooler, deeper waters.
Food: Fish, squid, shrimp, and eels.
Size: 5.7–13ft (1.75–4m); 330–880lb (150–400kg).
Maturity: 5–12 years.
Breeding: Breeding times vary with location. Single calf born every 2–3 years; gestation is about 12 months.
Life span: 40 years.
Status: Unknown.

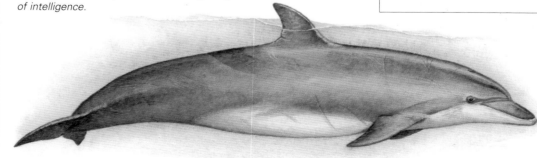

UNDERSTANDING BIRDS

The most obvious thing that distinguishes all birds, from the tiniest hummingbirds (Trochilidae) to the gigantic Californian condor (*Gymnogyps californianus*), is the presence of feathers on their bodies. The need for birds to be lightweight, in order to fly with minimum effort, has led to significant changes within their bodies as well, and yet the basic skeletal structure of all birds is remarkably similar, irrespective of their size. It is instantly clear that even the few groups of flightless birds, such as penguins (Spheniscidae), are descended from ancestors that possessed the power of flight, although these birds have since evolved along different lines to suit their habitat.

The other feature unique to birds is that all species reproduce by means of calcareous eggs. Birds' breeding habits are very diverse, however. Some birds even transfer the task of incubation to other species, by laying eggs in their nests, while others create natural incubators that serve to hatch their chicks and carefully regulate the temperature inside.

There is even greater diversity in the feeding habits of birds, as reflected by differences in their bill structures, and also in their digestive tracts. Birds' dietary preferences play a critical part in the environment as well. For example, in tropical rainforests, many fruit-eating species help to disperse indigestible seeds through the forest, thus helping to ensure the natural regeneration of the vegetation.

The birds of tropical rainforests are often surprisingly hard to observe, betraying their presence more by their calls than by their bright colors. However, birds can be easily observed in many other localities, which has led to birdwatching itself becoming a popular pastime.

Left: Many seabirds, such as these common terns (Sterna hirundo), *are highly social, and form large, open-air colonies in the breeding season.*

EVOLUTION

Vertebrates—first flying reptiles called pterosaurs, and later, birds—took to the air about 190 million years ago. Adapting to an aerial existence marked a very significant step in vertebrate development, because of the need for a new method of locomotion, and a radically different body design.

The age of *Archaeopteryx*

Back in 1861, workers in a limestone quarry in Bavaria, southern Germany, unearthed a strange fossil that resembled a bird in appearance and was about the size of a modern crow, but also had teeth. The idea that the fossil was a bird was confirmed by the clear evidence of feathers impressed into the stone, as the presence of plumage is one of the characteristic distinguishing features of all birds. The 1860s were a time when the debate surrounding evolution was becoming fierce, and the discovery created huge interest, partly because it suggested that birds may have evolved from dinosaurs. It confirmed that birds had lived on Earth for at least 145 million years, existing even before the age of the dinosaurs came to a close in the Cretaceous period, about 65 million years ago. As the oldest-known bird, it became known as *Archaeopteryx*, meaning "ancient wings."

Pterosaurs

A study of the anatomy of *Archaeopteryx*'s wings revealed that these early birds did not just glide but were capable of using their wings for active flight. Yet they were not the first vertebrate creatures to have taken to the skies. The pterosaurs had already successfully developed approximately 190 million years ago, during the Jurassic period, and they even shared the skies with birds for a time. In fact, remains of one of the later pterosaurs, called *Rhamphorhynchus*, have been found in the same limestone deposits in southern Germany where *Archaeopteryx* was discovered. The pterosaur's wings more closely resembled those of a bat than a bird, consisting simply of a membrane supported by a bony framework, rather than feathers overlying the skin.

Some types of pterosaurs developed huge wingspans, in excess of 23ft (7m), which enabled them to glide almost effortlessly over the surface of the world's oceans, much like albatrosses do today. It appears that they fed primarily on fish and other marine life, scooping their food out of the water in flight. Changes in climate probably doomed the pterosaurs, however, since increasingly turbulent weather patterns made gliding difficult, and they could no longer fly with ease.

Avian giants

In the period immediately after the extinction of the dinosaurs, some groups of birds increased rapidly in physical size, and in so doing, lost the ability to fly. Since their increased size meant that they could cover great distances on foot, and as they faced no predators, because large hunting mammals had not yet evolved, these tall birds were relatively safe. In New Zealand, home of the large flightless moas, such giants thrived until the start of human settlement about a millennium ago. The exact date of the final extinction of the moas is not recorded, but the group had probably died out entirely by the middle of the nineteenth century.

Below: The largest species of moa would have dwarfed a man.

Above: An impression of how Archaeopteryx *may have looked. It is impossible to be sure of its coloration from its fossilized remains.*

Below: All pterosaurs had a similar body shape with a narrow head, which may have been embellished with a crest of some sort. This may have been used for display purposes and also to reduce air resistance in flight. The wing structure of pterosaurs was very different from that of birds: their wings basically consisted of skin membranes, stretched out behind the forearms.

It was this large surface area that allowed them to glide easily, but becoming airborne in the first place required great effort. The lack of body covering over the skin also had the effect of causing greater heat loss from the body. In birds, the feathers provide insulation as well as assisting active flight.

Below: Hoatzin chicks (Opisthocomus hoazin) are unique among today's birds in possessing claws on their wing tips, which help them to climb trees. The claws are lost by the time the birds are old enough to fly.

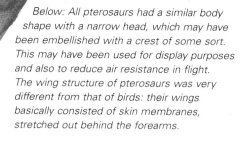

The spread of birds

After the age of *Archaeopteryx,* it is thought that birds continued to radiate out over the globe and became increasingly specialized. Unfortunately, there is very little fossil evidence to help us understand their early history. This lack of fossils is partly due to the fact that the small carcasses of birds would have been eaten whole by scavengers, and partly because their lightweight, fragile skeletons would not have fossilized easily. In addition, most birds would not have been trapped and died under conditions that were favorable for fossilization.

By the end of the age of the dinosaurs, birds had become far more numerous. Many seabirds still possessed teeth in their jaws, reflecting their reptilian origins. These probably assisted them in catching fish and other aquatic creatures. It was at this stage that the ancestors of contemporary bird groups such as waterfowl and gulls started to emerge. Most of the forerunners of today's birds had evolved by the Oligocene epoch, some 38 million years ago.

Some groups of birds that existed in these times have since disappeared, notably the phororhacids, which ranged widely over South America and even into parts of the southern United States. These birds were fearsome predators, capable of growing to nearly 10ft (3m) in height. They were equipped with deadly beaks and talons, and probably hunted together in groups.

Recent finds

During the mid-1990s, the discovery of avian fossils in China that were apparently contemporary with those of *Archaeopteryx* aroused considerable interest. Like its German relative, *Confuciusornis* possessed claws on the tips of its wings, which probably helped it to move around. Similar claws are seen today in hoatzin chicks. *Confuciusornis* resembled modern birds more closely than *Archaeopteryx* in one significant respect: it lacked teeth in its jaws. Further study of the recent fossil finds from this part of the world is required however, as some may not be genuine.

CLASSIFICATION

The presence of feathers is the main distinguishing characteristic that sets birds apart from other groups of creatures on the planet. The number of feathers on a bird's body varies considerably—a swan may have as many as 25,000 feathers, for instance, while a tiny hummingbird has just 1,000 in all.

Birds (class Aves) are winged, bipedal, endothermic (warm-blooded), vertebrate animals that lay eggs. There are around 10,000 living species, making them the most numerous tetrapod vertebrates. They inhabit ecosystems across the globe, from the Arctic to the Antarctic. Bird size ranges from the 2in (5cm) bee hummingbird to the 10ft (3m) ostrich.

Modern birds are characterized by feathers, a beak with no teeth, the laying of hard-shelled

Above: Feathering is highly significant for display purposes in some birds. This male greater prairie chicken (Tympanuchus cupido) shows off the barred plumage that is a feature of many birds found in moors and grasslands.

eggs, a high metabolic rate, a four-chambered heart, and a lightweight but strong skeleton. All birds have forelimbs modified as wings and most can fly, with some exceptions including ratites, penguins, and a number of diverse endemic island species. The presence of feathers are their most important distinguishing feature.

Feathers

Aside from the bill, legs and feet, the entire body of the bird is covered in feathers. The plumage does not grow randomly over the bird's body, but develops along lines of so-called feather tracts, or pterylae. These are separated by bald areas known as "apteria." The apteria are not conspicuous under normal circumstances, because the contour feathers overlap to cover the entire surface of the body. Plumage may also sometimes extend down over the legs and feet as well, in the case of birds from cold climates, providing extra insulation here.

Feathers are made of a tough protein called keratin, which is also found in our hair and nails. Birds have three main types of feathers: the body,

Left: A bird's flight feathers are longer and more rigid than the contour feathers that cover the body, or the fluffy down feathers that lie next to the skin. The longest, or primary, flight feathers, which generate the most thrust, are located along the outer rear edges of the wings. The tail feathers are often similar in shape to the flight feathers, with the longest being found in the center. Splaying the tail feathers increases drag and so slows the bird down.

1 Primaries	9 Auricular region
2 Secondaries	(ear)
3 Axillaries	10 Nape
4 Rump	11 Back
5 Lateral tail feathers	12 Greater under-
6 Central tail feathers	wing coverts
7 Breast	13 Lesser under-
8 Cere	wing coverts

Above: The absence of feathers on the head means that carnivorous birds, such as the turkey vulture (Cathartes aura), *can feed on offal inside large carcasses without staining its plumage with blood.*

or contour, feathers; the strong, elongated flight feathers on the wings, and the warm, wispy down feathers next to their skin.

The functions of feathers

A bird's plumage has a number of functions, not just those relating to flight. It provides a barrier that retains warm air close to the bird's body and helps to maintain body temperature, which is higher in birds than mammals—typically between 106 and 110°F (41 and 43.5°C). The down feathering that lies close to the skin, and the overlying contour plumage, are vital for maintaining body warmth. Most birds have a small volume relative to their surface area, which can leave them vulnerable to hypothermia.

A special oil produced by the preen gland, located at the base of the tail, waterproofs the plumage. This oil, which is spread over the feathers as the bird preens itself, prevents water penetrating the feathers, which would cause the bird to become so water-logged that it could no longer fly. The contour feathers that cover the body are also used for camouflage in many birds. Barring, in particular, breaks up the outline of the bird's

body, helping to conceal it in its natural habitat.

The plumage has become modified in some cases, reflecting the individual lifestyle of the species concerned. Woodpeckers, for example, have tail feathers that are short and rather sharp at their tips, providing additional support for gripping on to the sides of trees. Male ruffs, on the other hand, have elaborate head feathers that they use to impress potential mates.

Social significance of plumage

A bird's plumage can also be important in social interaction. Many species have differences in their feathering that separate males from females, and often juveniles can also be distinguished by their plumage. Cock birds are usually more brightly coloured, which helps them to attract their mates, but this does not apply in every case. The difference between the sexes in terms of their plumage can be quite marked. Cock birds of a number of species have feathers forming crests, and others have magnificent tail plumes, such as the booted racquet-tail hummingbird (*Ocreatus underwoodii*), whose display is one of the most remarkable sights in the avian world.

Recent studies have confirmed that the birds that appear relatively dull in color to our eyes, such as the various species of gull, are seen in a different light by other birds. They are able to perceive the ultraviolet component of light, which is normally invisible to us, making these seemingly dull birds appear much brighter. Ultraviolet coloration may also be significant in helping birds to choose their mates.

Iridescence

Some birds are not brightly colored, but their plumage literally sparkles in the light, thanks to its structure, which creates an iridescent effect. One of the particular features of iridescence is that the color of plumage alters, depending on the angle at which it is viewed, often appearing quite dark, almost black, from a side view. This phenomenon is particularly common in some groups of birds, notably members of the starling family (Sturnidae), and hummingbirds (Trochilidae), which are sometimes described as having metallic feathers because of the shimmering effect they create.

In some cases, the iridescent feathering is localized, while in others, it is widespread over most of the body. Green and blue iridescence is common, with reddish sheens being seen less often. Iridescence is especially common in cock birds, helping them to attract mates. In some cases, therefore, it is seen only in the breeding plumage, notably on the upperparts of the body and the wings rather than the underparts.

Below: A blue-chinned sapphire hummingbird (Chlorestes notatus) *displays its iridescent plumage.*

Right: The feather shaft holds the feather in place in the skin. Barbs run off the shaft at regular intervals, rather like the branches of a tree, and divide into smaller branches called barbules. Tiny hooks are attached to these, that reinforce the structure of each flight feather, making them more rigid.

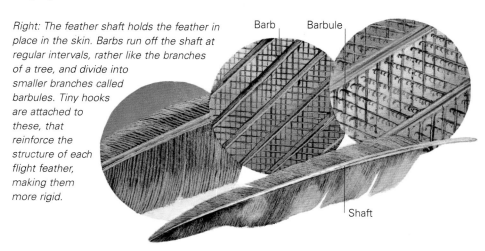

Barb Barbule

Shaft

ANATOMY

The bird's skeleton has evolved to be light yet robust, both characteristics that help with flight. To this end, certain bones, particularly in the skull, have become fused, while others are absent, along with the teeth. The result is that birds' bodies are lightweight compared to those of other vertebrates.

In order to be able to fly, a bird needs a lightweight body so that it can become airborne with minimal difficulty. It is not just teeth that are missing from the bird's skull, but the associated heavy jaw muscles as well. These have been replaced by a light, horn-covered bill that is adapted in shape to the bird's feeding habits. Some of the limb bones, such as the humerus in the shoulder, are hollow, which also cuts down on weight. At the rear of the body, the bones in the vertebral column have become fused, which gives greater stability as well as support for the tail feathers.

The avian skeleton

In birds, the greatest degree of specialization is evident in the legs. Their location is critical to enable a bird to maintain its balance. The legs are found close to the midline, set slightly back near the bird's center of gravity. The legs are powerful, helping to provide lift at take-off and absorb the impact of landing. Strong legs also allow most birds to hop over the ground with relative ease.

There are some differences in the skeleton between different groups of birds. The atlas and axis bones at the start of the vertebral column are fused in the case of hornbills, for example, but in no other family.

Feet and toes

Birds' feet vary in length, and are noticeably extended in waders, which helps them to distribute their weight more evenly. The four toes may be arranged either in a typical 3:1 perching grip, with three toes gripping the front of the perch and one behind, or in a 2:2 configuration, known as zygodactyl, which gives a surer grip. The zygodactyl grip is seen in relatively few groups of birds, notably parrots and toucans. African touracos have flexible toes so they can swap back and forth between these two options.

The zygodactyl arrangement of their toes helps some parrots to use their feet like hands for holding food. Birds generally have claws at the ends of their toes. These have developed into sharp talons in birds of prey, helping them to catch their quarry even in flight. Many birds also use their claws for preening, and they can provide balance for birds that run or climb.

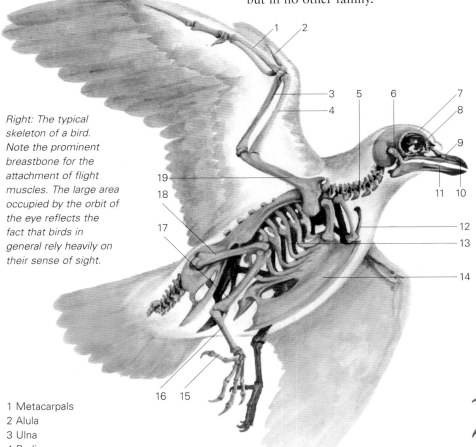

Right: The typical skeleton of a bird. Note the prominent breastbone for the attachment of flight muscles. The large area occupied by the orbit of the eye reflects the fact that birds in general rely heavily on their sense of sight.

Parrot

Above: Parrots use their feet to hold food, in a similar way to human hands.

Bird of prey

Above: In birds of prey, the claws have become talons for grasping prey.

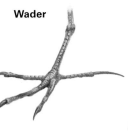

Wader

Above: Long toes make it easier for waders to walk over muddy ground or water plants.

Duck

Above: The webbed feet of ducks provide propulsion in water.

1 Metacarpals
2 Alula
3 Ulna
4 Radius
5 Cervical vertebrae
6 Ear
7 Cranium
8 Eye socket
9 Nostril
10 Bill (upper mandible)
11 Bill (lower mandible)
12 Clavicle (wishbone)
13 Ribs
14 Sternum (breastbone)
15 Metatarsals
16 Tarsus
17 Tibia and Fibula
18 Femur
19 Humerus

Above: The narrow bill of waders such as this whimbrel (Numenius phaeopus) enables these birds to probe for food in sand or mud.

Above: Birds of prey such as the golden eagle (Aquila chrysaetos) rely on a sharp bill with a hooked tip to tear their prey apart.

Above: Cranes (Grus grus) have strong, pointed bills, which they use to seize prey such as frogs between the upper and lower parts.

Above: Flamingos (Phoenicopteridae) have bills that enable them to feed with their heads trailing backward in the water.

Above: The pileated woodpecker (Dryocopus pileatus) uses its sharp bill to strip bark off trees to expose the ants on which they feed.

Above: The curved, twisted bill of the red crossbill (Loxia curvirostra) allows these birds to extract seeds easily from pine cones.

Bills

The bills of birds vary quite widely in shape and size, and reflect their feeding habits. The design of the bill also has an impact on the force that it can generate. The bills of many larger parrots are especially strong, allowing them to crack hard nut shells. In addition, they can move their upper and lower bill independently, which produces a wider gape and, in turn, allows more pressure to be exerted.

Wings

A bird's wing is built around just three digits, which correspond to human fingers. In comparison, bats have five digits supporting their fleshy membranes. The three digits of birds provide a robust structure. The power of the wings is further enhanced by the fusion of the wrist bones and the carpals to create the single bone known as the carpometacarpus, which runs along the rear of the wing.

At the front of the chest, the clavicles are joined together to form what in chickens is called the "wishbone." The large, keel-shaped breastbone, or sternum, runs along the underside of the body. It is bound by the ribs to the backbone, which provides stability, especially during flight. In addition, the major flight muscles are located in the lower body when the bird is airborne.

Darwin's finches

In the 1830s, a voyage to the remote Galapagos Islands, off the northwest coast of South America, helped the British naturalist Charles Darwin to formulate his theory of evolution. The finches present on the Galapagos Islands today are all believed to be descended from a single ancestor, but they have evolved in a number of different ways. The changes are most obvious in their bill shapes. For example, some species have stout, crushing beaks for cracking seeds, while others have long, slender beaks to probe for insects. These adaptations have arisen to take full advantage of the range of edible items available on the islands, where food is generally scarce. Some species have even developed the ability to use cactus spines and similar items as tools to extract seeds and invertebrates. In total, there are now 12 recognized species found on these islands, and nowhere else in the world.

Below: The finches of the Galapagos Islands helped to inspire Charles Darwin's theory of evolution. They are thought to be descended from a common ancestor, and have diverged significantly to avoid competing with each other for food. This is reflected by their bill shapes. The woodpecker finch (Camarhynchus palidus) has even acquired the ability to use a tool, in this case a cactus spine, to winkle out grubs hiding in tree bark.

FLIGHT

Some birds spend much of their lives in the air, whereas others will only fly as a last resort if threatened. A few species are too heavy to take off at all. The mechanics of flight are similar in all birds, but flight patterns vary significantly, which can help to identify the various groups in the air.

In most cases, the whole structure of the bird's body has evolved to facilitate flight. It is important for a bird's body weight to be relatively light, because this lessens the muscular effort required to keep it airborne. The powerful flight muscles, which provide the necessary lift, can account for up to a third of the bird's total body weight. They are attached to the breastbone, or sternum, in the midline of the body, and run along the sides of the body from the clavicle along the breastbone to the top of the legs.

Weight and flight

There is an upper weight limit of just over 40lb (18kg), above which birds would not be able to take off successfully. Some larger birds, notably pelicans and swans, need a run-up in order to gain sufficient momentum to lift off, particularly from water. Smaller birds can dart straight off a perch. Close to the critical weight limit for flight, the male Kori bustard (*Ardeotis kori*) from Asia is the world's heaviest flying bird, although it prefers to run rather than fly because of the effort involved in becoming airborne.

Below: A typical take-off, as shown by a Harris's hawk (Parabuteo unicinctus).

Above: Birds such as the bald eagle (Haliaeetus leucocephalus) can remain airborne with minimal expenditure of energy, by gliding rather than flying.

Wing shape and beat

The shape of the wing is important for a bird's flying ability. Birds that remain airborne for much of their lives, such as albatrosses, have relatively long wings that allow them to glide with little effort. The wandering albatross (*Diomedea exulans*) has the largest wingspan of any bird, measuring about 11ft (3.4m) from one wing tip to the other. Large, heavy birds such as Andean condors (*Vultur gryphus*) may have difficulty in flying early in the day, before the land has warmed up. This is because at this stage, there is insufficient heat coming up from the ground to create the thermal air currents that help to keep them airborne. In common with other large birds of prey, Andean condors seek out these rising columns of air, which provide uplift, and then circle around in them.

The number of wing beats varies dramatically between different species. Hummingbirds, for example, beat their wings more frequently than any other bird as they hover in front of flowers to harvest their nectar. Their wings move so fast—sometimes at over 200 beats per minute—that they appear as a blur to our eyes. At the other extreme, heavy birds such as swans fly with slow, deliberate wing beats.

Lightening the load

It is not just the lightness of the bird's skeleton that helps it to fly. There have been evolutionary changes in the body organs too, most noticeably in the urinary system. Unlike mammals, birds do not have a bladder that fills with urine. Instead, their urine is greatly concentrated, in the form of uric acid, and passes out of the body with their faeces, appearing as a creamy-white, semi-solid component.

1. When resting, a bird typically has a relatively upright stance.

2. As it leans forwards for take-off, it raises its wings and starts to lift its legs.

3. Leaving its perch, the bird pushes off into the air, and opens its wings.

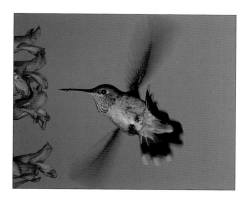

Above: Hummingbirds such as this broadtail (Selasphorus platycercus) have unparalleled aerial maneuverability, thanks to their rapid wing movements.

Below: The black-browed albatross (Diomedea melanophris) and its relatives often skim just above the waves.

The aerofoil principle

Once in flight, the shape of the wing is crucial in keeping the bird airborne. Viewed in cross-section from the side, a bird's wing resembles an airplane's wing, called an "aerofoil," and, in fact, airplanes use the same technique as birds to fly.

The wing is curved across the top, so the movement of air is faster over this part of the wing compared with the lower surface. This produces reduced air pressure on top of the wing, which provides lift and makes it easier for the bird to stay in the air.

The long flight feathers at the rear edge of the wings help to provide the thrust and lift for flight. The tail feathers, too, can help the bird remain airborne. The kestrel (*Falco tinnunculus*), for example, having spotted prey on the ground, spreads its tail feathers to help it remain aloft while it hovers to target its prey.

A bird's wings move in a regular figure-eight movement while it is in flight. During the downstroke, the flight feathers join together to push powerfully against the air. The primary flight feathers bend backward, which propels the bird forward. As the wing moves upward, the longer primary flight feathers move apart, which reduces air resistance. The secondary feathers further along the wing provide some slight propulsion. After that, the cycle simply repeats itself.

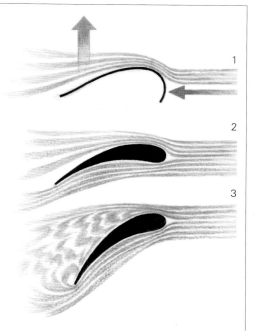

Above: The flow of air over a bird's wing varies according to the wing's position.
1. When the wing is stretched out horizontally, an area of low pressure is created above the wing, causing lift.
2. As the wing is tilted downward, the flow of the air is disrupted, causing turbulence and loss of lift.
3. When the wing is angled downward, lift slows, which results in stalling. The bird's speed slows as a consequence.

Flight patterns and formations

Different species of birds have various ways of flying, which can actually aid the birdwatcher in helping to identify them. For example, small birds such as tits (Paridae) and finches (Fringillidae) alternately flap their wings and fold them at their sides, adopting a streamlined shape, which helps to save energy. This produces a characteristic dipping flight. Large birds such as ducks and geese maintain a straighter course at an even height.

In some cases, it is not just the individual flying skills of a bird that can help it to stay airborne, but those of its fellows nearby. Birds flying in formation create a slipstream, which makes flying less effort for all the birds behind the leader. This is why birds often fly in formation, especially when covering large distances on migration.

4. Powerful upward and downward sweeps of the wings propel the bird forward.

5. When coming in to land, a bird lowers its legs and slows its wing movements.

6. Braking is achieved by a vertical landing posture, with the tail feathers spread.

SENSES

The keen senses of birds are vital to their survival, in particular helping them to find food, escape from enemies and find mates in the breeding season. Sight is the primary sense for most birds, but some species rely heavily on other senses to thrive in particular habitats.

Birds' senses have evolved as a result of their environment, and the shape of their bodies can help to reflect which senses are most significant to them.

Sight and lifestyle

Most birds rely on their sense of sight to avoid danger, hunt for food and locate familiar surroundings. The importance of this sense is reflected by the size of their eyes, with those of

Field of vision

The positioning of a bird's eyes on its head affects its field of vision. The eyes of owls are positioned to face forward, producing an overlapping image of the area in front known as binocular vision. This allows the owl to pinpoint its prey exactly, so that it can strike. In contrast, the eyes of birds that are likely to be preyed upon, such as woodcocks, are positioned on the sides of the head. This eye position gives a greatly reduced area of binocular vision, but it does give these birds practically all-round vision, enabling them to spot danger from all sides.

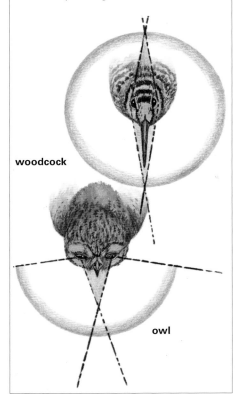

woodcock

owl

starlings (*Sturnus vulgaris*), for example, making up 15 percent of the total head weight. The enlargement of the eyeballs and associated structures, notably the eye sockets in the skull, has altered the shape of the brain. In addition, the optic lobes in the brain, which are concerned with vision, are also enlarged, whereas the olfactory counterparts, responsible for smell, are poorly developed.

The structure of the eye also reveals much about a bird's habits. Birds of prey have large eyes in proportion to the head, and have correspondingly keen eyesight. Species that regularly hunt for prey underwater, such as penguins, can see well in the water. They have a muscle in each eye that reduces the diameter of the lens and increases its thickness on entering water, so that their eyes can adjust easily to seeing underwater. In addition, certain diving birds such as little auks (*Alle alle*) use a lens that forms part of the nictitating membrane, or third eyelid, which is normally hidden from sight. Underwater, when this membrane covers the eye, its convex shape serves as a lens, helping the bird to see in these surroundings.

Eye position

The positioning of the eyes on the head gives important clues to a bird's lifestyle. Most birds' eyes are set on the sides of the head. Owls, however, have flattened faces and forward-facing eyes that are critical to their hunting abilities. These features allow owls to target their prey.

There are disadvantages, though—owls' eyes do not give a rounded view of the world, so they must turn their heads to see around them. It is not just the positioning of owls' eyes that is unusual. They are also able to hunt effectively in almost complete darkness. This is made possible in two

Above: Vultures such as the turkey vulture (Cathartes aura) rely on their keen eyesight and sense of smell to pick up powerful odors arising from carcasses on the ground.

ways. First, their pupils are large, which maximizes the amount of light passing through to the retina behind the lens, where the image is formed. Second, the cells here consist mainly of rods rather than cones. While cones give good color vision, rods function to create images when background illumination is low.

The positioning of the eyes of game birds such as woodcocks (*Scolopax rusticola*) allows them to spot danger from almost any angle. It is even possible for them to see a predator sneaking up from behind. Their only blind spot is just behind the head.

Smell

Very few birds have a sense of smell, but kiwis (Apterygidae) and vultures (forming part of the order Falciformes) are notable exceptions. Birds' nostrils are normally located above the bill, opening directly into the skull, but kiwis' nostrils are positioned right at the end of the long bill. They probably help these New Zealand birds to locate

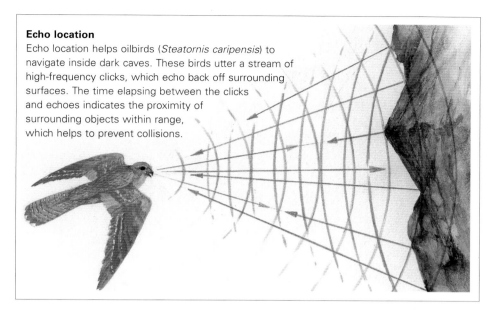

Echo location
Echo location helps oilbirds (*Steatornis caripensis*) to navigate inside dark caves. These birds utter a stream of high-frequency clicks, which echo back off surrounding surfaces. The time elapsing between the clicks and echoes indicates the proximity of surrounding objects within range, which helps to prevent collisions.

earthworms in the soil. Vultures have very keen eyesight, which helps them to spot dead animals on the ground from the air, but they also have a strong sense of smell, which helps when homing in on a distant carcass.

Taste

The senses of smell and taste are linked, and most birds also have correspondingly few taste buds in their mouths. The number of taste buds varies, with significant differences between groups of birds. Pigeons may have as few as 50 taste buds in their mouths, parrots as many as 400.

Birds' taste buds are located all around the mouth, rather than just on the tongue, as in mammals. The close

Below: Birds have good color vision. It is this sense that encourages hummingbirds, such as this long-billed starthroat (Heliomaster longirostris), *to home in on red flowers.*

links between smell and taste can lead vultures, which feed only on fresh carcasses, to reject decomposing meat. They may start to eat it, but then spit it out once it is in their mouths, probably because of a combination of bad odor and taste.

Hearing

Birds generally do not have a highly developed sense of hearing. They lack any external ear flaps that would help to pinpoint sources of sound. The openings to their hearing system are located on the sides of the head, back from the eyes.

Hearing is of particular significance for nocturnal species, such as owls, which find their food in darkness. These birds are highly attuned to the calls made by rodents. The broad shape of their skull has the additional advantage of spacing the ear openings more widely, which helps them to localize the source of the sounds with greater accuracy.

Hearing is also important to birds during the breeding season. Birds show particular sensitivity to sounds falling within the vocal range of their chicks, which helps them to locate their offspring easily in the critical early days after fledging.

The oilbird (*Steatornis caripensis*), which inhabits parts of northern South America, uses echo location to find its way around in the dark, rather like bats do. Unlike the sounds bats make,

however, the clicking sounds of the oilbird's calls—up to 20 a second in darkness—are clearly audible to humans. The bird interprets the echoes of its call to avoid colliding with objects in its path, although it also uses its eyesight when flying. Cave swiftlets (*Aerodramus*) from Asia, which also inhabit a dark environment, use echo location in a similar way to fly.

Touch

The sense of touch is more developed in some birds than others. Those such as snipe (*Gallinago*), which have long bills for seeking food, have sensitive nerve endings called corpuscles in their bills that pick up tiny vibrations caused by their prey. Vibrations that could suggest approaching danger can also register via other corpuscles located particularly in the legs, so that the bird has a sensory awareness even when it is resting on a branch.

Wind-borne sensing

Tubenoses such as albatrosses and petrels (Procellariiformes) have a valve in each nostril that fills with air as the bird flies. These are affected by both the bird's speed and the wind strength. The valves almost certainly act as a type of wind gauge, allowing these birds to detect changes in wind strength and patterns. This information helps to keep them airborne, as they skim over the waves with minimal effort.

Below: A combination of senses, especially touch, helps American oystercatchers (Haematopus palliatus) *to detect their prey, which is normally hidden from view.*

SURVIVAL

The numbers of a particular species of bird can vary significantly over time, affected by factors such as the availability of food, climate, disease and hunting. When the reproductive rate of a species falls below its annual mortality rate, it is in decline, but this does not mean it will inevitably become extinct.

For many birds, life is short and hazardous. Quite apart from the risk of predation, birds can face a whole range of other dangers, from disease and starvation through to human interference or persecution. The reproductive rate is higher and age of maturity is lower in species that have particularly hazardous lifestyles, such as black-capped chickadees (*Poecile atricapilla*), which often breed twice or more a year in quick succession.

Rising and falling numbers
Some birds have a reproductive cycle that allows them to increase their numbers rapidly under favorable conditions. The Galapagos Island penguin (*Spheniscus mendiculus*) is such a species. Fluctuating sea temperatures in the Pacific—part of the El Niño phenomenon—can drive sardines, its principal food source, away from the Galapagos. Very few chicks are reared during the lean years, as the native population faces starvation. During intervening periods,

*Below: A flock of American blackbirds (*Agelaius phoeniceus*). These New World birds have adapted very well to changes in their landscape brought about by agriculture. Although regarded as pests in some areas, they do consume large numbers of harmful invertebrates.*

*Above: Many birds watch over their offspring when they hatch, but are ill-equipped to defend them from predators, as in the case of this male Carolina wood duck (*Aix sponsa*).*

however, the penguin population recovers, as its food source returns. Ultimately, numbers are likely to fall, threatening the species with extinction.

Regular fall-offs in populations can occur on a cyclical basis, as shown by the case of snowy owls (*Nyctea scandiaca*) in North America. As the numbers of lemmings—the main component of the owls' diet—rise, so too does the snowy owl population. This is the result of more chicks per nest being reared successfully, rather than dying of starvation. When the numbers of lemmings fall again, due to a shortage of their food, owls are forced to spread out over a much wider area

than normal in search of food, and their breeding success plummets accordingly. Later they gradually increase again over successive years, as the lemming population recovers.

Group living
Birds that live in flocks find mates more easily than other birds, and group life also offers several other advantages, including the safety of numbers. An aerial predator such as a hawk will find it harder to recognize and target individuals in a flying mass of birds, although stragglers are still likely to be picked off.

Coloration can also increase the safety of birds in flocks. In Florida, U.S.A., there were once feral budgerigar flocks made up of multi-colored individuals. The different colors reflected the diversity of color varieties that were developed through domestication. Today, however, green is by far the predominant color in such flocks, as it is in genuine wild flocks, simply because predators found it much easier to pick off individuals of other colors. Greater numbers of the

Cryptic coloration

Camouflage, also known as "cryptic coloration," enables a bird to hide in its natural surroundings. It offers distinct survival benefits in concealing the bird from would-be predators. Cryptic coloration has the effect of breaking up the bird's outline, allowing it to blend in with the background in its habitat. Posture and, in particular, keeping still can also help, as movement often attracts the attention of would-be predators.

Below: The common or long-tailed potoo (Nyctibius griseus) *is a nocturnal species ranging from Mexico down to Argentina. It relies upon its camouflage to conceal its presence when resting during the day.*

always the case. The expansion of agriculture in countries such as Argentina has resulted in the greater availability of both food and water for birds. This in turn has enabled populations, especially parrots like the Patagonian conure (*Cyanoliseus patagonus*), to grow by alarming degrees in recent years. Shooting and poisoning have been used as methods of population control, but it should be remembered that, overall, these birds have increased in numbers directly as a consequence of changes to the land pioneered by humans.

Other birds have benefited more directly from human intervention, as is the case with the common starling (*Sturnus vulgaris*). These birds have spread across North America, following their introduction from Europe in the late 1800s.

Similarly, the common pheasant (*Phasianus colchicus*) is now found across much of central North America, thanks to human interest in these game birds, which are bred in large numbers for sport shooting. Many more survive than would otherwise be the case, thanks to the attention of gamekeepers who not only provide food, but also help to curb possible predators in areas where the birds are released.

Slow breeders

Birds that reproduce slowly, such as albatrosses (Diomedeidae) and sandhill cranes (*Grus canadensis*), are likely to be highly vulnerable to any changes in

Above: Snowy owls (Nyctea scandiaca) *are often seen near coasts outside the breeding season. They are opportunistic hunters, even catching fish on occasion.*

their surroundings, whether caused by human interference, climate change, disease, or other factors. Great concern has recently been focused on albatross numbers, which are declining wordwide. Many of these birds have been caught and drowned in fishing nets in recent years. Albatrosses are normally very long-lived and breed very slowly. Any sudden decline in their population is therefore likely to have devastating consequences that cannot easily be reversed.

Below: Sandhill crane (Grus canadensis) *with chick. Long-lived, slow-breeding birds such as cranes are the least adaptable when faced with rapid environmental changes of any kind.*

green budgies survived to breed and pass on their genes to their descendants, and so green became the dominant color in the feral flocks.

Group living also means that when the flock is feeding and at its most vulnerable, there are extra eyes to watch out for predators and other threats. Within parrot flocks, birds take it in turns to act as sentinels, and screech loudly at any hint of danger.

Effects of humans

It is generally assumed that human interference in the landscape is likely to have harmful effects on avian populations. However, this is not

MATING

Birds' breeding habits vary greatly. Some birds pair up only fleetingly, while others do so for the whole breeding season, and some species pair for life. For many young cock birds, the priority is to gain a territory as the first step in attracting a partner. Birds use both plumage and their songs to attract a mate.

A number of factors trigger the onset of the breeding period. In temperate areas, as the days start to lengthen in spring, the increase in daylight is detected by the pineal gland in the bird's brain, which starts a complex series of hormonal changes in the body. Most birds form a bond with a single partner during the breeding season, which is often preceded by an elaborate display by the cock bird.

Bird song

Many cock birds announce their presence with their song, which both attracts would-be mates and establishes a claim to a territory. Once pairing has occurred, the male may cease singing, but in some cases he starts to perform a duet with the hen, with each bird singing in turn.

Singing obviously serves to keep members of the pair in touch with each other. In species such as Central and

Below: A cock ruffed grouse (Bonasa umbellus) displaying. The male is using his wings to create a loud drumming sound, uttering a series of quieter calls at the same time, in a bid to attract females. Drumming occurs at dawn and dusk, usually with pauses of about five minutes between displays.

South American wood quails (*Odontophorus*), the pair coordinate their songs so precisely that although the cock bird may sing the first few notes, and then the hen, it sounds as if the song is being sung by just one bird. Other birds may sing in unison. In African gonoleks (*Laniarius*), it may even be possible to tell the length of time that the pair have been together by the degree of harmony in their particular songs.

Studies have revealed that young male birds start warbling quite quietly, and then sing more loudly as they mature. Finally, when their song pattern becomes fixed, it remains constant throughout the bird's life.

It is obviously possible to identify different species by differences in their song patterns. However, there are sometimes marked variations between the songs of individuals of the same species that live in different places. Local dialects have been identified in various parts of a species' distribution, as in the case of gray parrots (*Psittacus erithacus*) from different parts of Africa. In addition, as far as some songbirds are concerned, recent studies

Above: A male ruff (Philomachus pugnax) at a lek, where males compete with each other in displays to attract female partners. Ruffs do not form lasting pair bonds, so the hens nest on their own after mating has occurred.

Below: An American bittern (Botaurus lentiginosus), well disguised in a reed bed. In spite of being solitary by nature, these waders have a remarkable territorial call, which booms out across the marshes, and has led to species becoming known locally as "Thunder-pumpers." The boom is created through the use of the gullet to amplify sound, rather like a voice box.

Above: Tundra swans (Cygnus columbianus) *normally mate for life. A highly migratory species, they breed across the extreme northern coast of North America. Pairs usually breed on their own, but once the nesting period is over, large numbers form into great flocks and head south for the winter.*

have shown that over the course of several generations, the pattern of song can alter markedly.

Birds produce their sounds—even those species capable of mimicking human speech—without the benefit of a larynx and vocal cords like humans. The song is created in a voice organ called the syrinx, which is located in the bird's throat, at the bottom of the windpipe, or trachea.

The structure of the syrinx is very variable, being at its most highly developed in the case of songbirds, which possess as many as nine pairs of separate muscles to control the vocal output. As in the human larynx, it is the movement of air through the syrinx that enables the membranes here to vibrate, creating sound. An organ called the interclavicular air sac also plays an important role in sound production, and birds cannot sing without it. The distance over which bird calls can travel is remarkable— up to 3 miles (5km) in the case of some species, such as bellbirds (*Procnias*) and the American bittern (*Botaurus lentiginosus*), which has a particularly deep, penetrating song.

Breeding behavior

Many birds rely on their breeding finery to attract their mates. Some groups assemble in communal display areas known as "leks," where hens witness the males' displays and select a mate. A number of species, ranging from cocks of the rock (*Rupicola*) to birds of paradise (Paradisaeidae), establish leks.

In other species, such as the satin bowerbird (*Ptilonorhynchus violaceus*), the male constructs elaborate bowers of grass, twigs and similar vegetation, which he then decorates with items of a particular color, such as blue, varying from flowers to pieces of glass. Male bowerbirds are often polygamous,

meaning that they mate with more than one female. African weaver birds, such as the orange bishop (*Euplectes orix*), demonstrate the same behavior. The males molt to display brightly colored plumage at the onset of the breeding season, and construct nests that are inspected by the females. Hens are often drawn to the older cocks, whose nest-building abilities are likely to be more sophisticated.

Pair bonding

Many male and female birds form no lasting relationship, although the pair bond may be strong during the nesting period. It is usually only in potentially long-lived species, such as the larger parrots and macaws, or waterfowl such as swans, that a life-long pair bond is formed.

Pair bonding in long-lived species has certain advantages. The young of such birds are slow to mature, and are often unlikely to nest for five years or more. By remaining for a time in a family group, therefore, adults can improve the long-term survival prospects of their offspring.

Below: Two greater male sage grouse (Centrocercus urophasianus) *circle each other at a lek. These prominent displays help watching hens to choose a partner. There are usually just one or two dominant males with whom the hens mate: younger males—also present—are likely to be ignored. Lekking takes place from early dawn to late morning.*

NESTING

All birds reproduce by laying eggs, which are covered with a hard, calcareous shell. The number of eggs laid at a time—known as the clutch size—varies significantly between species, as does egg coloration. Nesting habits also vary, with some birds constructing very elaborate nests.

The coloration and markings of a bird's eggs are directly linked to the nesting site. Birds that usually breed in hollow trees produce white eggs, because these are normally hidden from predators and so do not need to be camouflaged. The pale coloration may also help the adult birds to locate the eggs as they return to the nest, thus lessening the chances of damaging them. Birds that build open, cup-shaped nests tend to lay colored and often mottled eggs that are camouflaged and so less obvious to potential nest thieves.

Nesting holes

Many birds use tree holes for nesting. Woodpeckers (Picidae) are particularly well equipped to create nesting chambers, using their powerful bills to enlarge holes in dead trees. The diameter of the entry hole thus created

Below: African ostriches lay the largest eggs in the world, which can weigh up to 3.3lb (1.5kg). In comparison, a chicken's egg, shown in front of the ostrich egg, looks tiny. The egg nearest to the viewer is a hummingbird egg. These tiny birds lay the smallest eggs in the avian world, weighing only about 0.01oz (0.35g).

Above: A northern flicker (Colaptes auratus)—a member of the woodpecker family—returns to its nest hole. Tree holes offer relatively safe nesting retreats, although predators such as snakes may sometimes be able to reach them.

is just wide enough to allow the birds to enter easily, which helps to prevent the nest being robbed. Old World hornbills (Bucorvidae) go one stage further—the cock bird walls the hen up inside the nest. He plasters the hole over with mud, leaving just a small gap through which he can feed the female. The barrier helps to protect the nest from attacks by snakes and lizards. The female remains entombed inside until her young are well grown. At this stage she breaks out and then helps her mate to rear the chicks, having walled them back up again.

Nest-building

Some birds return to the same nest site each year, but many birds simply abandon their old nest and build another. This may seem a waste of effort, but it actually helps to protect the birds from parasites such as blood-sucking mites, which can otherwise multiply in the confines of the nest. Most birds construct their nests from vegetation, depending on which

The reproductive systems

The cock bird has two testes located within his body. Spermatozoa pass down the vas deferens, into the cloaca and then out of the body. Insemination occurs when the vent areas of the male and female bird are in direct contact during mating. Cock birds do not have a penis for penetration, although certain groups, such as waterfowl, may have a primitive organ that is used to assist in the transference of semen in a similar way.

Normally only the left ovary and oviduct of the hen bird are functional. Eggs pass down through the reproductive tract from the ovary. Spermatozoa swim up the hen's reproductive tract, and fertilize the ova at an early stage in the process. Generally, only one mating is required to fertilize a clutch of eggs. Spermatozoa may sometimes remain viable in the hen's body for up to three weeks following mating.

1 Testes	7 Magnum
2 Kidneys	8 Isthmus
3 Vas deferens	9 Egg with shell
4 Cloaca	contained in
	the hen's
5 Ova	reproductive tract
6 Infundibulum	10 Cloaca

Male   **Female**

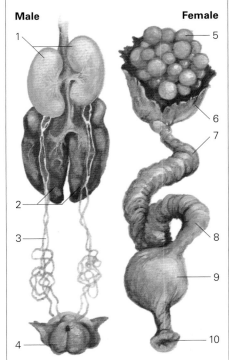

materials are locally available. In coastal areas, some seabirds use pieces of seaweed to build theirs. Artificial materials such as plastic wrappers or polystyrene may be used by some birds.

Nest styles

Different types of birds build nests of various shapes and sizes, which are characteristic of their species. Groups such as finches build nests in the form of an open cup, often concealed in vegetation. Most pigeons and doves construct a loose platform of twigs. Swallows are among the birds that use mud to construct their nests. They scoop muddy water up from the surface of a pond or puddle, mold it into shape on a suitable wall, and then allow it to dry and harden like cement.

The simplest nests are composed of little more than a pad of material, resting in the fork of a tree or on a building. The effort entailed in nest construction may reflect how often the birds are likely to nest. The platforms of pigeons and doves can disintegrate quite easily, resulting in the loss of eggs or chicks. However, if disaster does befall the nest, the pair will often breed again within a few weeks. At the other end of the scale, albatrosses expend considerable effort on nesting, because if failure occurs, the pair may not breed again for two years or so.

Cup-shaped nests are more elaborate than platform nests, being usually made by weaving grasses and twigs together. The inside is often lined with soft feathers. The raised sides of the cup nest lessen the likelihood of losing eggs and chicks, and also offer greater security to the adults during incubation. The hollow in the nest's center is created by the birds compressing the material here before egg-laying begins.

Suspended nests enclosed by a domed roof offer even greater security. They are less accessible to predators because of their design and also their position, often hanging from slender branches. Some African waxbills (*Estrilda*) build a particularly elaborate nest, comprising two chambers. There is an obvious upper opening, which is

Above: The piping plover (Charadrius melodus) from North America breeds in the open and so must also rely on camouflage to hide its presence when sitting on the nest.

always empty, suggesting to would-be predators that the nest is unoccupied. The birds occupy the chamber beneath, which has a separate opening.

Nest protection

Some birds rely on the safety of numbers to deter would-be predators, building vast communal nests that are occupied by successive generations and added to regularly. Monk parakeets (*Myiopsitta monarchus*) from South America breed in this way. Their nests may weigh over 4cwt (200kg) or more.

Other birds have evolved more sophisticated methods not only of protecting their nests, but also of minimizing the time that they spend

incubating their eggs. Various parrots, such as the red-faced lovebird (*Agapornis pullaria*) from Africa, lay their eggs in termite mounds. The insects tolerate this intrusion, while the heat of the mound keeps the eggs warm. Mallee fowl (*Leipoa ocellata*) from Australia create a natural incubator for their eggs by burying them in a mound where the natural warmth and heat from decaying vegetation means that the chicks eventually hatch on their own and dig themselves out.

Other birds, such as the cowbirds (*Molothrus*) of North America, simply lay and abandon their eggs in the nests of other species. The foster parents-to-be do not seem able to detect the difference between their own eggs and that of the intruder, so they do not reject the cowbird egg. They incubate it along with their own brood, and feed the foster chick when it hatches out.

Birds that nest on the ground, such as the long-billed curlew (*Numenius americanus*), are especially vulnerable to predators and rely heavily on their fairly drab plumage as camouflage. Skylarks (*Alauda arvensis*) have another means of protecting their nest site—they hold one wing down and pretend to be injured to draw a predator away.

Below: Most eggs have a generally rounded shape, but seabirds such as guillemots (Uria aalge), breeding on exposed rocky outcrops by the ocean, lay eggs that are more pointed. This shape helps to prevent the eggs from rolling over the cliff.

BEHAVIOR

Bird behavior, or avian ethology as it is known, is a very broad field. Some patterns of behavior are common to all birds, whereas other actions are very specific, just to a single species or even to an individual population. Interpreting behavior is easier in some cases than in others.

All bird behavior essentially relates to various aspects of survival, such as avoiding predators, obtaining food, finding a mate and breeding successfully. Some behavior patterns are instinctive, while others develop in certain populations of birds as a response to certain conditions. Thus, the way in which birds behave is partly influenced by their environment as well as being largely instinctual.

Age also plays a part in determining behavior, since young birds often behave in a very different way from

Above: An albatross (Diomedeidae) preens the downy plumage of its chick. This helps to cement the bond between them, as well as ensuring that the plumage around the bill does not become matted with food.

adults. Some forms of bird behavior are relatively easy to interpret, while others are a great deal more difficult to explain.

Garden birds

One of the first studies documenting birds' ability to adapt their behavior in response to changes in their environment involved blue tits (*Parus caeruleus*) in Great Britain. The study showed that certain individuals learned to use their bills to tap through the shiny metallic foil covers on milk bottles to reach the milk. Other blue tits followed their example, and in certain areas householders with milk deliveries had to protect their bottle tops from the birds.

The way in which birds have learned to use various types of garden feeders also demonstrates their ability to modify their existing behavior in response to new conditions when it benefits them. A number of new feeders on the market, designed to thwart squirrels from stealing the food,

exploit birds' ability to adapt in this way. The birds have to squeeze through a small gap to reach the food, just as they might enter the nest. Once one bird has been bold enough to enter in this fashion, others observe and soon follow suit.

Preening

Although preening serves a variety of functions, the most important aspect is keeping the feathers in good condition. It helps to dislodge parasites and removes loose feathers, particularly during molting. It also ensures that the plumage is kept waterproof by spreading oil from the preen gland at the base of the tail.

Preening can be a social activity too. It may be carried out by pairs of males and females during the breeding season, or among a family group.

Aggression

Birds can be surprisingly aggressive toward each other, even to the point of sometimes inflicting fatal injuries. Usually, however, only a few feathers are shed before the weaker individual backs away, without sustaining serious injury. Conflicts of this type can break out over feeding sites or territorial disputes. The risk of aggressive outbreaks is greatest at the start of the breeding season, as this is when the territorial instincts of cock birds are most aroused. Size is no indicator of the potential level of aggression, since some of the smallest birds, such as hummingbirds (Trochilidae) can be ferociously aggressive.

Below: A dispute breaks out between a pair of great-tailed grackles (Quiscalus mexicanus). Such encounters rarely result in serious injury, as the weaker individual usually flies away to escape its rival.

This behavior is seen in a variety of birds, ranging from parrots to finches. Some parrots perform mutual preening throughout the year, which reinforces the pair bond. In some of the Asiatic psittaculid parakeets, however, such as the Alexandrine (*Psittacula eupatria*), the dominant hen allows her mate to preen her only when she is in breeding condition, in which case preening may be seen as a prelude to mating.

Bathing

Preening is not the only way in which birds keep their plumage in good condition. Birds often bathe to remove dirt and debris from their plumage. Small birds wet their feathers by lying on a damp leaf during a shower of rain, in an activity known as "leaf-bathing." Other birds immerse themselves in a pool of water, splashing around and ruffling their feathers.

Some birds, especially those found in drier areas of the world, prefer to dust-bathe, lying down in a dusty hollow known as a scrape and using fine earth thrown up by their wings to absorb excess oil from their plumage. Then, by shaking themselves thoroughly, followed by a period of preening, the excess oil is removed.

Sunbathing

Sunbathing may be important in allowing birds to synthesize Vitamin D3 from the ultraviolet rays in sunlight, which is vital for a healthy skeleton. This process can be achieved only by light falling on the bird's skin, which explains why birds ruffle their plumage at this time. Some birds habitually stretch out while sunbathing, while others, such as many pigeons, prefer to rest with one wing

Right: The natural waterproofing present on the plumage ensures that birds do not become saturated when swimming or caught in a shower of rain. This would destroy the warm layer of air surrounding the body created by the down feathering, and leave them vulnerable to hypothermia. Nevertheless birds do need to dry their plumage, which is what this American anhinga (Anhinga anhinga) *is doing, with its wings outstretched.*

raised, leaning over at a strange angle on the perch. Vasa parrots (*Coracopsis*), found on the island of Madagascar, frequently behave in this fashion, although sunbathing is generally not common in this group of birds.

Maintaining health

Some people believe that when birds are ill, they eat particular plants that have medicinal properties, but this theory is very difficult to prove. One form of behavior that does confer health benefits has been documented, however: it involves the use of ants. Instead of eating these insects, some birds occasionally rub them in among their feathers. This causes the ants to release formic acid, which acts as a potent insecticide, killing off lurking parasites such as mites and lice. Blue jays (*Cyanocitta cristata*) and also starlings (Sturnidae) and Eurasian blackbirds (*Turdus merula*) are among the species that have been observed using insects in this way. Members of the crow family have also been seen perching on smoking chimney pots or above bonfires, ruffling their feathers and allowing the smoke to penetrate their plumage. The smoke is thought to kill off parasites in a process that confers the same benefits as anting.

Above: Birds such as the cattle egret (Bubulcus ibis) *form unusual associations with large mammals. They will mingle among herds as they feed, keeping a sharp watch for potential prey such as invertebrates, or other creatures, that may be flushed from the grass by the mammals as they move.*

Below: A Gila woodpecker (Melanerpes uropygialis) *feeding on cactus fruit. These desert-dwelling woodpeckers will also bore into larger cacti to create their nest site.*

MIGRATION

Some birds live in a particular place all year round, but many are only temporary visitors. Typically, species fly north into temperate latitudes in spring, and return south at the end of summer. They have a wide distribution, but are seen only in specific parts of their range at certain times of the year.

Many species of birds regularly take long seasonal journeys. The birds that regularly undertake such seasonal movements on specific routes are known as "migrants," and the journeys themselves are known as "migrations." Many birds migrating from North to South America prefer to fly across Central America rather than the Caribbean. Birds migrate to seek shelter from the elements, to find safe areas to rear their young and, in particular, to seek places where food is plentiful. Birds such as waxwings (Bombycillidae) irrupt to a new location to find food when supplies become scarce in their habitat, but such journeys are less frequent and are irregular. The instinct to migrate dates back millions of years, to a period

Right: This diagram illustrates the main migratory routes in the Americas, where birds fly either down the Central American isthmus, or across the Caribbean via the local islands. In following these traditional routes over or close to land, the birds avoid long and potentially hazardous sea crossings.

Below: The routes taken by birds migrating back and forth to Africa from parts of Europe and western Asia are shown here. Again, crossings are not always made by the most direct route, if this would entail a long and possibly dangerous sea journey.

when the seasons were often much more extreme, which meant that it was difficult to obtain food in a locality throughout the year. This forced birds to move in search of food. Even today, the majority of migratory species live within the world's temperate zones, particularly in the Northern Hemisphere, where seasonal changes remain pronounced.

Migratory routes

The routes that the birds follow on their journeys are often well defined. Land birds try to avoid flying over large stretches of water, preferring instead to follow coastal routes and crossing the sea at the shortest point. For instance, many birds migrating from Europe to Africa prefer to fly over the Straits of Gibraltar. Frequently

Banding birds

Much of what we know about migration and the lifespan of birds comes from banding studies carried out by ornithologists. Lightweight aluminum bands placed on the birds' legs allow experts to track their movements when the ringed birds are recovered again. Unfortunately, only a very small proportion of ringed birds are ever recovered, so the data gathered is incomplete, but now other methods of tracking, such as radar, are also used to follow the routes taken by flocks of birds, which supplements the information from banding studies.

Below: Banding and collection of "biometric" data from shorebirds in New Jersey. By taking careful measurements of various parts of the body, and weighing the bird as well, scientists are able to build up a physical portrait of various bird populations.

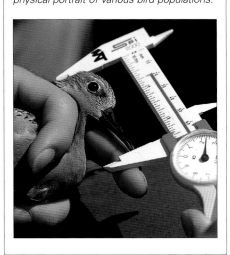

birds fly at much greater altitudes when migrating. Cranes (Gruidae) have been recorded flying at 16,400ft (5,000m) when crossing the mountainous areas in France, and geese (*Anser*) have been observed crossing the Himalayas at altitudes of more than 29,500ft (9,000m). Even if the migratory routes are known, it is often difficult to spot migrating birds because they fly so high.

Speed and distance

Migrating birds also fly at greater speeds than usual, which helps to make their journey time as short as possible. The difference can be significant—migrating swallows (*Hirundo rustica*) travel at speeds of 1.8–8.7mph (3–14km/h) faster than usual, helped by the greater altitude, where the air is thinner and resistance is less.

Some birds travel huge distances on migration. Arctic terns (*Sterna paradisea*), for example, cover distances of more than 9,300 miles (15,000km) in total, as they shuttle between the Arctic and Antarctic. They fly an average distance of 100 miles (160km) every day. Size does not preclude birds from migrating long distances, either. The tiny ruby-throated hummingbird (*Archilochus colubris*) flies over the Gulf of Mexico from the eastern USA every year, a distance of more than 500 miles (800km).

Preparing for migration

The migratory habits of birds have long been the subject of scientific curiosity. As late as the 1800s, it was thought that swallows hibernated at the bottom of ponds because they were seen skimming over the pond surface in groups before disappearing until the following spring. Now we know that they were probably feeding on insects to build up energy supplies for their long journey ahead.

Even today, the precise mechanisms involved in migratory behavior are not fully understood. We do know that birds feed up before setting out on migration, and that various hormonal changes enable them to store more fat

Above: Many birds, like this scarlet tanager (Piranga olivacea), migrate after molting. Damaged plumage can make the task of flying harder and more hazardous.

in their bodies to sustain them on their journey. Feeding opportunities are likely to be more limited than usual when birds are migrating, while their energy requirements are, of course, higher. In addition, birds usually molt just before migrating, so that their plumage is in the best condition to withstand the inevitable buffeting that lies ahead.

Navigation

Birds use both learned and visual cues to orient themselves when migrating. Young birds of many species, such as swans, learn the route by flying in the company of their elders. However, some young birds set out on their own and reach their destinations successfully without the benefit of experienced companions, navigating by instinct alone. Birds such as swifts (Apopidae) fly mainly during daytime, whereas others, including ducks (Anatidae), migrate at night. Many birds fly direct to their destination, but some may detour and break their journey to obtain food and water before setting out again.

Experiments have shown that birds orient themselves using the position of the sun and stars, as well as by following familiar landmarks. They also use the Earth's magnetic field to find their position, and thus do not get lost in cloudy or foggy weather, when the sky is obscured. The way in which these various factors come together, however, is not yet fully understood.

ENDANGERED SPECIES AND CONSERVATION

It has been estimated that three-quarters of the world's birds may come under threat in the 21st century. Habitat destruction poses the most serious danger, so conservationists are striving to preserve bird habitats worldwide. Direct intervention of various kinds is also used to ensure the survival of particular species.

Around the world, threats to birds are varied and complex, but most are linked to human interference in the ecosystem, and will thus continue to grow as human populations increase.

Habitat destruction

Habitat destruction includes the deforestation of the world's tropical rainforests, which host a wide variety of birds, and also the conversion of many grassland areas into crop fields or livestock pasture. The first casualties of habitat destruction are often species with specialized feeding or nesting requirements, which cannot easily adapt to change.

In recent years, there have been a number of instances of opportunistic species adapting and thriving in altered habitats. One example is the common mynah (*Acridotheres tristis*), whose natural distribution is centered on India but has been introduced to other locations worldwide, often to control locust numbers. Such success stories are the exception rather than the rule,

Below: The woodstork (Mycteria americana), one of the largest North American wading birds, is endangered because of a loss of its wetland habitat, due to human encroachment.

Above: The northern spotted owl (Strix occidentalis caurina) is currently threatened by the rapid felling of the ancient forests on the west coast of California.

however. Generally, the diversity of bird life in an area declines drastically when the land is modified or cleared.

Hunting and pollution

Unregulated hunting of adult birds, eggs or young threatens a variety of species worldwide. The birds may be killed for their meat or feathers, or captured live and sold through the pet trade. In many countries, laws are now in place to protect rare species, but hunting and trading still go on illegally.

Overfishing is a related hazard facing seabirds, especially now that trawling methods have become so efficient. Global shortages of fish stocks are forcing fishermen to target fish that had previously been of little commercial value, but that are an important part of seabirds' diets.

In agricultural areas, pesticides and herbicides sprayed on farmers' fields decimate bird populations by eliminating their plant or animal food supplies. The deliberate or accidental release of industrial chemicals into the air, water or soil is another hazard, while in the oceans, seabirds are killed by dumped toxins and oil spills. Disease is another major threat that may increase.

Climate change

In the near future, global warming caused by increased emissions of carbon dioxide and other gases is likely to impact on many bird habitats, and will almost certainly adversely affect birds' food supplies. If plants or other foods become unavailable in an area, birds must adapt their feeding habits or face extinction. As temperatures rise, the melting of the polar ice caps will threaten seabird populations by destroying their traditional nesting areas. Rising sea levels will also threaten low-lying wetlands favored by wading birds.

Threats to island birds

Some of the world's most distinctive birds have evolved in relative isolation on islands. Unfortunately, these species are also extremely vulnerable to changes in their environment, partly because their populations are small. One of the greatest threats comes from

Above: This guillemot (Uria aalge), *which died in polluted waters, is just one of the countless avian victims claimed by oil spillages each year. Large spills of oil can have devastating effects on whole populations.*

introduced predators, particularly domestic cats. Cats have been responsible for wiping out a host of island species, including the flightless Stephen Island wren (*Xenicus lyalli*) of New Zealand waters, which became extinct in 1894, thanks to the lighthouse-keeper's cat.

Cats are not the only introduced predators that can cause serious harm to avian populations. Grazing animals such as goats, introduced to islands by passing ships to provide future crews with fresh meat, have frequently destroyed the native vegetation, so reducing the birds' food supply.

Today, control of harmful introduced species is helping to save surviving populations of endangered birds on islands such as the Galapagos off Ecuador, home to the flightless cormorant (*Phalacrocorax harrisi*) and other rare birds.

Conservation and captive-breeding

Preserving habitat is the best and most cost-effective way to ensure the survival of all the birds that frequent a particular ecosystem. A worldwide network of national parks and reserves now helps to protect at least part of many birds' habitats. In addition,

conservationists may take a variety of direct measures to safeguard the future of particular species, such as launching a captive-breeding program. This approach has proven effective in increasing numbers of various critically endangered species, from the Californian condor (*Gymnogyps californianus*) of the U.S.A., to the echo parakeet (*Psittacula echo*) of Mauritius. In some cases, the technique of artificial insemination has been used to fertilize the eggs.

Artificially or naturally fertilized eggs can be transferred to incubators to be hatched, effectively doubling the number of chicks that can be reared. This is because removing the eggs often stimulates the hen to lay again more quickly than usual. Hand-rearing chicks on formulated diets helps to ensure the survival of the young once hatched. When hand-reared chicks are later released into the wild, it is vital that they bond with their own species and retain their natural fear of people, so glove puppets shaped like the parent birds are often used to feed the chicks.

Reintroduction programs

Breeding endangered species is relatively easy compared with the difficulties of reintroducing a species to an area of its former habitat. The cost of such reintroduction programs is

Above: Glove puppets resembling the parent bird's head are often used when hand-rearing chicks, such as this peregrine falcon (Falco peregrinus), *to encourage the birds to bond with their own kind when eventually released.*

often very high. Staff are needed not only to look after the aviary stock and rear the chicks, but also to carry out habitat studies. These assess the dangers that the birds will face after release and pinpoint release sites. The newly released birds must then be monitored, which may include fitting them with radio transmitters.

Ecotourism

Working with local people and winning their support is often essential to the long-term success of conservation programs. This approach has been used successfully on some of the Caribbean islands, such as St Vincent, home to various indigenous Amazon parrots (*Amazona*). Increasing clearance of the islands' forests, a growing human population and hunting all threatened these birds.

Effective publicity about these rare parrots, including portrayals of them on currency and postage stamps, helped to raise local people's awareness of the birds as part of their islands' heritage. A publicity campaign brought the parrots' plight to international attention and attracted visitors to the region, which brought in much-needed foreign currency. Thus, so-called "ecotourism" both helped the local economy and enlisted the islanders' support to conserve the parrots.

Left: The rapid destruction of the world's rainforests, seen here in Costa Rica, is the single most important threat facing tropical birds.

DIRECTORY OF BIRDS

Recognizing birds is not always easy, particularly if you have only a relatively brief sighting. However, armed with the information in this comprehensive directory, you'll soon learn how to easily recognize and identify the colorful array of species that inhabit the vast land that is North America.

Distribution maps accompanying all the illustrated entries provide a visual guide as to where bird species are to be found within these regions, while the text provides information on the time of year and locations where the birds are most likely to be seen, in the case of migratory species.

Fact boxes contain information about habitat, feeding and breeding habits. A bird's general shape, and the characteristic way in which it moves and behaves, all add up to what birdwatchers call its "jizz," which can help to identify birds even from a tiny speck in the sky or a dark shape scuttling behind a hedge.

Not every North American species is covered, but the representative sample featured in the following pages should help you to identify the type of bird you spotted. Browsing through these pages also affords an opportunity to learn more about the varying lifestyles of the birds, from puffins on the bitterly cold breeding grounds of the Alaskan peninsula, to the various woodpeckers and predatory birds that inhabit cities.

Note: Where an (E) appears after the scientific name of a bird, this indicates that it is an endangered species.

Left: The majestic bald eagle (Haliaetus leucocephalus), *the national symbol of the United States of America, often inhabits harsh environments, from the freezing tundra in the north to the scorching deserts in the south.*

ALBATROSSES

These birds often have a wide distribution, roaming far out from the shore over the oceans. They will only return to land in order to nest, frequently choosing remote islands for this purpose, so they are unlikely to be seen by the casual observer. However, they may be attracted to passing ships, particularly trawlers, in search of offerings of food.

Laysan albatross

Diomedea immutabilis

The Laysan is the most common albatross of the northern Pacific region. According to reports of sightings, especially from the larger islands, these birds now appear to be venturing closer to the shoreline of the Hawaiian islands. Unlike many albatrosses, the Laysan rarely follows ships, and comes to land only during the breeding season. It is thought that pairs remain together for life, and albatrosses rank among the longest-lived of all birds, having a life expectancy often exceeding half a century. These birds face few natural enemies, but, sadly, a number are dying prematurely after seizing baited hooks intended for fish left on long lines by fishing boats. Albatrosses usually feed by scooping up prey from the surface of the ocean while in flight.

Identification: Relatively small. Predominantly white with a sooty-brown back, upperwings, and tail, and dark feathering around the eyes. In flight, the largish, pinkish feet extend beyond the tail. Yellow curved bill has a black tip. Sexes are alike.

Distribution: Extends from the northern Pacific Ocean to the western coast of North America. Especially common on Midway and Laysan Islands, Hawaii.
Habitat: Open ocean.
Food: Fish and other aquatic creatures.
Size: 36in (91cm), wingspan 77–80in (195–203cm).
Nest: Area of ground.
Eggs: 1, white, may be blotched.

Short-tailed albatross

Diomedea albatrus (E)

Distribution: Occurs off the west coast of North America, up to the Gulf of Alaska.
Habitat: Open ocean.
Food: Mainly fish and squid.
Size: 37in (94cm), wingspan 85–91in (215–230cm).
Nest: Earth mound incorporating plant matter.
Eggs: 1, white.

Short-tailed albatrosses breed mainly on Torishima Island, which is part of the Izu group lying off the southeast of Japan. They return every second year, with the nesting season starting in October. However, Torishima has an active volcano at its core, which has led to a dramatic decline in their numbers, as repeated eruptions have decimated the breeding population. In addition to this, they were also once hunted for their plumage. These long-lived ocean wanderers were thought to have become extinct during the 1940s, but some of them had survived, and now about 70 chicks are reared annually on Torishima, where they are protected. Another breeding population is established on Minami-kojima, in the nearby South Ryukyu Islands, where the albatrosses use cliffs for nesting. Out at sea, birds may scavenge scraps thrown overboard from trawlers, and hunt squid at night.

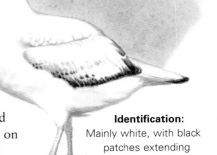

Identification: Mainly white, with black patches extending from tips of wings and on tip of tail. Yellowish-orange on the head. Pinkish bill with pale blue tip. Sexes alike. Young have dark-brown plumage.

PETRELS

Many of the seabirds found in American waters have a wide distribution, which can be pan-global, often extending around the southern oceans and sometimes even further afield. Petrels are well adapted to spending virtually their entire lives over these waters, even to the extent of being able to scoop up their food directly from the surface of the ocean and sleeping on the wing as they glide.

Hawaiian petrel

Dark-rumped petrel *Pterodroma phaeopygia* (E)

Distribution: Pacific Ocean, Hawaiian and Galapagos Islands.
Habitat: Open ocean.
Food: Fish and other aquatic creatures.
Size: 17in (43cm), wingspan 36in (91cm).
Nest: Sited in underground burrows.
Eggs: 1, white.

The alternative name, "dark-rumped petrel," is not a clear guide to its identification, since various petrels display this feature. The Hawaiian petrel appears to be quite rare compared to other species and is thought to be declining in numbers. It spends its time at sea, coming onto land to breed. The largest colony is found around the Haleakala Crater on Maui. These petrels nest in underground burrows, remaining there during the day and emerging to search for food at night. Outside the breeding period, Hawaiian petrels are most likely to be sighted to the southeast of the Hawaiian islands.

Identification: Black upperparts, with white plumage just above the bill and extending right across the underparts. The undersides of the wings are also mainly white, with a black area evident on each of the leading edges when seen from below. There is usually a white, V-shaped marking present at the base of the uppertail coverts, above the tail. Sexes are alike.

Mottled petrel

Pterodroma inexpectata

Distribution: Wide-ranging, occurring in the Pacific Ocean from the Gulf of Alaska southward down the west coast of North America, and has been recorded off the southern tip of South America.
Habitat: Lives at sea, only comes on land to nest.
Food: Fish, squid, and crustaceans.
Size: 14in (35cm), wingspan 29–32in (74–82cm).
Nest: Rocky crevices or underground, in colonies on remote islands and outcrops.
Eggs: 1, white.

These petrels spend most of their lives flying across the oceans. They range over a very wide area along the Antarctic coastline, with their distribution extending as far south as the pack ice. In the north, they occur throughout the central Pacific area but are rarely sighted close to land. Mottled petrels migrate south across the equator before the nesting period, which begins in October. Only at this stage do they come to land, nesting colonially on small rocky outcrops and remote islands. The incubation period is lengthy, lasting approximately 50 days. After hatching, nestlings may spend up to three and a half months in the nest. By the time the petrels are ready to head north again, the dark days of the southern winter are descending. Mottled petrels have disappeared from some parts of their former breeding range, notably New Zealand and nearby islands, where the introduction of land predators such as cats has greatly reduced their success rate.

Identification: Upperparts are dark. A black stripe on the underside of each wing joins to form a characteristic M-shape when viewed from below. The sides of the head are grayish, with a black stripe through the eyes. The underparts are white, aside from a distinctive gray patch running across the center of the body. Sexes are similar in appearance.

AUKLETS

This group of seabirds found around the shores of North America are much more at home on the sea surface than in the air. They often struggle to take off, paddling to raise their body up before they can use their wings to get clear of the water. Once in the air, a group will often fly behind each other in a straight line, rather than opting for a V-shaped formation.

Crested auklet

Aethia cristatella

Crested auklets spend much of the winter period at sea, before returning to their breeding islands in the spring after the snow has melted. Huge numbers, sometimes as many as 100,000 birds, may congregate at these colonies. Dominant individuals with the tallest crests are favored breeding partners, though members of an existing pair will return to breed together every year. Unusually, while males are responsible for brooding the young, it is the females who provide the majority of food for the chicks, frequently traveling distances of 31 miles (50km) or more from the nest site, carrying the food back in their throat pouches. Egg-laying occurs at roughly the same time in a colony, which means that most of the young will fledge together within a short period. This brings survival advantages by increasing the percentage of young that are likely to escape waiting predators. Once at sea, crested auklets remain in large groups.

Identification: Dark gray underparts, blacker head, back and wings, with a white stripe behind the eyes. There is a forward-pointing, semicircular crest of feathers on the head. Breeding adults develop orange plates on the face. Sexes alike. Young have a tuft of feathers instead of a crest.

Distribution: Extreme northern Pacific, extending from Alaska across to Asia, through the Gulf of Alaska, especially near Kodiak Island.
Habitat: Ocean and shore.
Food: Mainly crustaceans, plus fish.
Size: 8in (20cm), wingspan 16–19.5in (40–50cm).
Nest: Rocky crevices and crags.
Eggs: 1, white.

Parakeet auklet

Aethia psittacula

Distribution: Occurs in northern Pacific Ocean, extending between north-eastern Asia and the far northwest of North America, and southward down as far as California.
Habitat: Ocean and shore.
Food: Crustaceans and fish.
Size: 10in (25cm), wingspan 18in (45cm).
Nest: Underground holes.
Eggs: 1, white.

These auklets breed along the western coast of North America, as well as in the Aleutians and other islands. Large colonies may be formed in areas where nesting sites are available. Breeding underground offers a degree of security from larger predators, but the eggs and young chicks are still vulnerable to attack by voles. It takes approximately five weeks for the chicks to reach fledging size, at which stage they will emerge from the nest under cover of darkness and head directly to the sea. The young are unlikely to breed until they are three years old. Parakeet auklets have been known to dive as deep as 100ft (30m) in search of food, and they are capable of remaining underwater for at least a minute. They spend much of their winter at sea, typically heading south, away from the Gulf of Alaska, and are commonly seen in the vicinity of Washington and California.

Identification: Dark upperparts, with white underparts and an intervening mottled gray area. A thin white streak extends back from the eye on each side of the head. Bill reddish outside the breeding season, brighter in breeding adults. Sexes alike. Young birds are duller, with light blue rather than white eyes.

PUFFINS AND AUKS

Although seabirds generally have a reputation for being quite dull in terms of coloration, members of this group often undergo a striking transformation in appearance at the onset of the breeding period. In flight or at a distance, puffins can generally be distinguished from other alcids since they tend to fly relatively high above the water, rather than skimming low over the waves.

Puffin

Fratercula arctica

These auks have unmistakable bills, said to resemble those of parrots. Young puffins have much narrower and less brightly colored bills than the adults. Puffins come ashore to nest in colonies on cliffs and in coastal areas where they can breed largely hidden from predators. Sand eels figure prominently in their diet at this time, and adult birds often fly quite long distances to obtain food. When underwater, puffins use their wings like flippers, which enables them to swim faster. Adult birds fly back to their young with eels arranged in a row, hanging down each side of their bills. They can carry as many as ten fish at a time in this way.

Above: The appearance of the puffin's bill varies, depending on the bird's age and the time of year.

Identification: Distinctive whitish sides to the face, with black extending back over the crown. Black neck, back and wings; underparts white, with a gray area on the flanks. Broad, flattened bill has a red area running down its length and across the tip, and a grayish base with a yellow area intervening. During the winter, the bill is less brightly colored, and the sides of the face turn grayish. Sexes are alike.

Distribution: From the far north of eastern Canada to the south, occasionally as far down as Long Island.
Habitat: Ocean and coastal.
Food: Fish.
Size: 13in (32cm), wingspan 21–24in (55–61cm).
Nest: Underground burrows.
Eggs: 1, white.

Right: Puffins excavate nesting tunnels underground or use existing holes.

Tufted puffin

Fratercula cirrhata

After nesting at high densities, both on the coast of North America and on islands, including the Aleutians, tufted puffins disperse widely through their extensive range. These puffins prefer to nest in burrows, which they dig in grassy areas. The single egg is laid at the end of the burrow on the bare soil, or sometimes on a bed of feathers. Puffins react badly to human disturbance when nesting, a likely reason why the small southerly breeding population in California has declined over the past century. Further north, in the breeding grounds on the Alaskan peninsula, predators such as Arctic foxes take their toll, while gulls are a hazard on the Aleutians. Young puffins leave the nest after dark and head out to sea.

Identification: Breeding plumage is mostly blackish, with prominent white areas on the face and long, straw-colored tufts of feathers that extend over the back. The large bill is red, with a prominent horn-colored area at its upper base. Entire body is grayish-black in winter, the bill being red with a brownish base (those of young birds are completely brown).

Distribution: Ranges right up into the polar region and throughout the northern Pacific, occurring as far south as the Farallon Islands off central California.
Habitat: Ocean and shore.
Food: Fish and squid form the bulk of the diet.
Size: 16in (41cm), wingspan 15in (38cm).
Nest: Burrows, sometimes rocky crevices.
Eggs: 1, white, often spotted.

SOCIAL SEABIRDS

Although seabirds generally feed on fish, their bills can differ significantly in shape, as revealed by a comparison between the pointed bill of the guillemots, the relatively stumpy bill of the murrelets and the uniquely broad shape of the razorbill's beak. These differences can be very helpful when trying to identify birds such as these from their silhouettes.

Ancient murrelet

Gray-headed murrelet *Synthliboramphus antiquus*

The unusual name of these members of the auk family comes from the white streaks in the plumage of breeding adults, which suggest an old appearance. Though occurring right across the Pacific to the eastern coast of Asia, the ancient murrelet can sometimes be found on inland waters in North America, and may even extend as far south as northern Baja California. It is possible to distinguish between these and other murrelets thanks to their flight pattern, since they keep their head in a more upright position rather than extending it horizontally. Ancient murrelets prefer to nest in burrows that they excavate themselves. Weaning takes place rapidly, with the adult pair simply abandoning their young, forcing them to emerge. The family group then flies off, usually at night, and will travel a long distance, typically up to 30 miles (50km), within a day of leaving the nesting grounds.

Identification: White underparts and sides of the neck, with gray on the back and wings. Black bib and head, which is variably streaked with white. Black barring on the sides of the body too, usually concealed by the wings. Sexes are alike, and the throat region of young birds is mainly white.

Distribution: Represented through the Aleutian chain and southern Alaska southward along the North American coast to northern California.
Habitat: Ocean and shore.
Food: Crustaceans and fish.
Size: 11in (27cm), wingspan 18in (45cm).
Nest: Burrows and crevices.
Eggs: 2, brownish-green with darker spots.

Razorbill

Alca torda

The distinctive broad, flattened shape of the bill, resembling a cut-throat razor, explains the common name of these auks. They are often observed swimming with their tails held vertically, rather than flat, enabling them to be distinguished from seabirds of similar size and coloration. Razorbills are adaptable in their feeding habits, with a diet varying according to locality. Pairs display a strong bond, and return to their traditional breeding sites, which may sometimes be no more than steep, inaccessible rocky stacks located off the coast. They show no tendency to construct a nest of any kind, with hens sometimes laying their single egg on a narrow ledge directly above the ocean. The pearlike shape of the razorbill's egg helps to prevent it rolling over the edge if accidentally dislodged. Even so, losses of eggs are fairly high, with predators such as gulls swooping down on unguarded sites.

Identification: Black upperparts, with white edging along the back of the wings, and a vertical white stripe across the bill. Black coloration more strongly defined in breeding birds, with a white horizontal stripe reaching from the eyes to the bill. Sexes are alike. Young birds have smaller bills with no white markings.

Distribution: Spans the North Atlantic, occurring on the eastern side of North America, from northern Canada south to Long Island, New York.
Habitat: Ocean and shore.
Food: Fish and crustaceans.
Size: 15in (39cm), wingspan 25–27in (63–68cm).
Nest: Cliff face crevices.
Eggs: 1, whitish with brown spots.

Pigeon guillemot

Cepphus columba

These guillemots are most conspicuous during the early summer when they come ashore to breed, with pairs returning to the same site throughout their lives. Southerly populations are likely to be seen around six weeks before egg-laying commences in April, returning about a month later further north. The adults are determined hunters, submerging to catch fish and other prey for up to 2¹/₂ minutes. They comb the seabed for fish, invertebrates, crabs, other crustaceans, and mollusks. Chicks are normally fed on fish such as sand eels. The young are independent once they leave the nest at just over five weeks old, although this period may be longer if food is scarce. They are unlikely to breed until at least three years old.

Identification: Relatively long neck and pointed bill. Adult breeding birds are black with a white area on the wings, and have a mottled back, whitish neck and white underparts in the winter. The area around the eyes remains dark, as does the bill. Sexes are alike. Young birds display more pronounced, grayer mottling on the neck than the adults.

Distribution: Northern Pacific region, on both the east coast of Asia and the west coast of North America, reaching as far south as southern California.
Habitat: Ocean and shore.
Food: Fish and marine invertebrates.
Size: 14.5in (37cm), wingspan 23in (60cm).
Nest: Rock crevices, burrows.
Eggs: 2, whitish with dark spots.

Thick-billed murre (*Uria lomvia*): 17in (43cm), wingspan 25–30in (64–75cm).
Murres are members of the auk family. This species occurs right around the northern part of North America. It is occasionally recorded as far south as California, and is a regular sight around the Aleutian Islands. This murre has a broad, relatively short bill, with an arched tip and a white line along the lower mandible. Black head, back and wings, with a white area across the underwing coverts. Sexes are alike.

Black guillemot (*Cepphus grylle*): 13in (33cm), wingspan 19–23in (49–58cm).
Black guillemots occur on the northern shore of Alaska and more widely in the northeast, southward along the Atlantic coast as far as Maine. These seabirds are jet black in color, with a vivid white wing patch and red feet in summer. They are predominantly white in the winter, with mottling evident on the head and over the back, but with the back of the wings remaining blackish. Young black guillemots display more mottling on the head.

Xantus' murrelet (*Synthliboramphus hypoleucus*): 10in (25cm), wingspan 16in (40cm). This species is present off the coast of western North America, breeding on islands off southern California and Baja California. The southern Californian race (*S. h. scrippsi*) is very similar to Craveri's murrelet but lacks the black collar across the breast, with white rather than gray plumage under the wings. The subspecies occurring in Baja Californian waters (*S. h. hypoleucus*) has more extensive white markings on the sides of the face.

Common murre

Guillemot *Uria aalge*

The upright resting stance of the common murre and its ability to hop, combined with its black and white coloration and fish-eating habits, have led to these birds being described as the penguins of the north. However, unlike penguins, they can fly. This enables them to reach their rocky and inhospitable nesting sites, where large numbers pack onto ledges. The sheer density of numbers there offers protection against raiding gulls, since there is little space for the predators to land, and they will be met with a fearsome barrier of sharp, pointed bills if they swoop down. As many as 20 breeding pairs can crowd every 11 square feet (1 square meter). Fall-offs in fish stocks can have an adverse effect on numbers, as will oil pollution.

Identification: Black head, neck and upperparts, aside from a white area at the edge of the wing coverts. Slight mottling on the flanks, otherwise underparts completely white. Outside the breeding season the entire throat and sides of the neck are white. Sexes are alike. Dark plumage extends up the sides of the neck in young birds.

Distribution: Northern waters across the Atlantic and Pacific oceans, from Alaska to California in the west down to the Gulf of Maine on the east.
Habitat: Ocean and shore.
Food: Fish and marine invertebrates.
Size: 17in (43cm), wingspan 24–29in (61–74cm).
Nest: Cliff ledges and crevices.
Eggs: 1, bluish-green, dark spots.

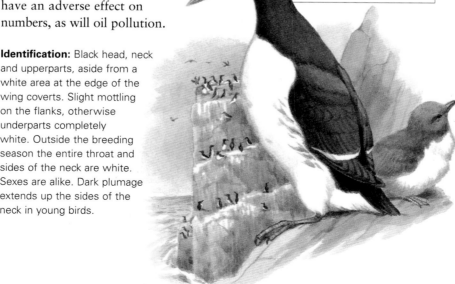

PELICANS AND BOOBIES

These large birds, which belong to the same family, both hunt fish, but whereas pelicans are well-equipped to trawl for fish by virtue of their pouches, boobies are more opportunistic, relying sometimes on their size to harry and dispossess other birds of their catches. Both groups possess webbed feet, which are ideally suited to swimming in watery habitats.

American white pelican

Rough-billed pelican *Pelecanus erythrorhynchos*

These pelicans are found mainly on stretches of fresh water, sometimes hunting in groups for fish and other creatures such as crayfish. They are also seen in saltwater habitats but do not venture far from coasts. Occasionally, they may fly long distances to obtain food if the waters that they inhabit have a low fish population. On migration, American white pelicans fly over land rather than the ocean, although populations in the southern part of their range will remain in the same region throughout the year. These birds breed communally, usually on quite inaccessible islands. Their chicks associate together in groups, known as "pods," before they are fully fledged.

Identification: Predominantly white plumage with contrasting black primary flight feathers. The large yellow bill develops a distinctive raised area on the ridge toward the tip from late winter through the breeding season. Sexes are alike, but the female is smaller.

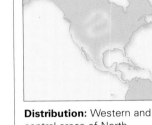

Distribution: Western and central areas of North America, down as far as Guatemala and Costa Rica.
Habitat: Both freshwater and saltwater areas, not ranging far out to sea.
Food: Fish and other aquatic creatures.
Size: 70in (178cm), wingspan 95–120in (240–300 cm).
Nest: On the ground.
Eggs: 2–3, whitish with darker markings.

Left: The pelican's pouch is used to trawl for food.

Brown pelican

Pelecanus occidentalis

Distribution: Ranges down the Pacific coast of America, from California to Chile, and on the Galapagos Islands. Another population is centered on the Caribbean.
Habitat: Ocean and shore.
Food: Mainly fish.
Size: 60in (152cm), wingspan 90in (230cm).
Nest: On the ground or in trees.
Eggs: 2–3, white.

Brown pelicans trawl for fish at the surface, but also dive to depths of 30ft (10m), where small fish are numerous, returning to the surface to swallow their catch. They also fly in formation close to the surface and spot fish below with their good eyesight. Brown pelicans frequent ports in search of fish leftovers, but retreat to islands and other remote locations to breed. They usually nest on the ground, but build more substantial platform nests in mangrove swamps, with chicks taking longer to fledge there.

Identification: Golden-yellow area on head, grayish-brown body and white neck, with the white becoming browner in the breeding season. The top of the head becomes speckled when adults are rearing young. Sexes are alike.

Double-crested cormorant

Phalacrocorax auritus

Distribution: Much of the U.S.A., south to parts of Central America in the winter. Also from Florida to Cuba.
Habitat: Areas of fresh water and sea water.
Food: Fish and other aquatic creatures.
Size: 36in (91cm), wingspan 45–52in (115–132cm).
Nest: Built of sticks and often seaweed.
Eggs: 3–4, pale blue.

These cormorants are found mainly in coastal waters, sometimes using unorthodox sites such as wrecked ships as perches. They also venture to inland areas, where they are found on suitable stretches of water. They can form large flocks, often hunting together for fish, which form the main ingredient of their diet. In the past, double-crested cormorant numbers have plummeted in some parts of their range due to DDT entering the food chain. This pesticide has had a harmful effect on eggshell thickness, and, as a result, has significantly reduced the number of chicks that hatch. The ban on DDT has seen their numbers rise again. These cormorants have also benefited from the increasing number of freshwater reservoirs in various parts of their range, providing them with additional areas of habitat.

Identification: Adults are entirely black. Immatures show a whitish hue to their underparts. A double crest of feathers is evident on the back of the head during the breeding period, with a variable amount of white coloration. Has bare yellowish-orange skin around the face, with a powerful hooked bill. Females are smaller in size. Several different races are recognized through their range, differing in the extent of the white feathering forming the crest as well as in the depth of coloration.

Great cormorant
(*Phalacrocorax carbo*): 40in (102cm), wingspan 48–63in (122–160cm). Great cormorants breed from Newfoundland and around the Gulf of St. Lawrence southward as far as Maine. Different races occur elsewhere in the world. Nominate North American race is blackish overall, with purplish hue on the wings and white patches in the throat region and near the top of the legs when in breeding condition. Bluish skin around the eyes, and horn-colored bill with a darker tip.

Red-faced cormorant
(*Phalacrocorax urile*): 35in (89cm), wingspan 48in (122cm). This species occurs on southern coasts of Alaska extending via the Aleutian Islands to Asia. Blackish overall, with white plumage at the top of the legs. Slight crest on the top of the head and another behind. Red areas of bare skin encircle the eyes. Pale bill. Hens are smaller in size.

Brandt's cormorant

Phalacrocorax pencilliatus

The social behavior of these cormorants is fascinating to observe, as they sometimes join together in their hundreds to head out over the sea in search of fish. When a school is discovered the cormorants dive down, collectively harrying the fish and working together to maximize their catch. These birds also breed colonially, and, although males return to the same nest site each year, they may choose a new partner. The nest is sited on the ground on a larger area than the cliff nests of pelagic cormorants. Breeding success is influenced greatly by the availability of a plentiful supply of food, and in years when the El Niño effect alters the pattern of ocean currents off the coast, and thus the distribution of anchovies and other fish, success may plummet accordingly. This generally has no lasting effect on the cormorant population, however, because they are long-lived birds with a potential life expectancy of more than a decade.

Distribution: Restricted to the western coast of North America, from southern British Columbia down to Baja California in Mexico.
Habitat: Ocean and shore.
Food: Mainly fish.
Size: 35in (89cm), wingspan 50in (127cm).
Nest: Gently sloping cliffs.
Eggs: 3–6, whitish-blue.

Identification: Relatively large. Buff feathers across throat, pouch bright blue at outset of breeding. Plumage generally blackish, aside from a few white feathers on the head at this time. Sexes alike. Young birds brown.

GULLS

Gulls are linked in many people's minds with the seaside, but some species have proved very adept at adjusting to living closely alongside humans, and generally profiting from this association. A number of different gulls have now spread to various inland locations as a result. Shades of white and gray generally predominate in the plumage of these birds, making them quite easy to recognize.

Heermann's gull

Larus heermanni

Distribution: Occurs along much of the Pacific coastline of North America, being recorded from Vancouver Island down as far south as Panama.
Habitat: Ocean and shore.
Food: Fish and various invertebrates.
Size: 21in (53cm), wingspan 41–45in (104–115cm).
Nest: Scrape on the ground.
Eggs: 2–3, buff-colored.

Like most of its kind, Heermann's gull is very adaptable, ever ready to obtain food opportunistically. These gulls may harry pelicans, persuading them to disgorge their catches, or dart in among feeding sea lions to grab food. They often follow fishing boats too, swooping on waste thrown overboard, and will scavenge on the shoreline for edible items. When Heermann's gulls obtain their own food they usually do so inland, seizing lizards and invertebrates, although they are able to catch fish in the ocean also. While most migrants head south for the winter, these gulls will often move further north. Some prefer to head to warmer climates further south of their breeding grounds, which are centered on Isla Raza and other neighboring islands in the Golfo de California, as well as the San Benito Islands, lying off western Baja California.

Identification: Dark gray back and wings, with the body being lighter in color and the tail edged with white. Head whitish, becoming streaked in winter. Bill bright red with a dark tip. Sexes alike. Young birds are dark brownish-black, lightening over successive molts and gaining a buff tail tip in their second year.

Black-headed gull

Larus ridibundus

These gulls are a common sight not only in coastal areas but also in town parks with lakes. They move inland during the winter and are often seen following tractors plowing at this time of year, seeking worms and grubs in the soil. Black-headed gulls nest close to water in what can be quite large colonies. Like many gulls, they are noisy birds, even calling at night. On warm, summer evenings, they can sometimes be seen hawking flying ants and similar insects in flight, demonstrating their airborne agility.

Identification: These gulls have their distinctive black heads only during the summer, with a white collar beneath and white underparts. Wings are gray, and the flight feathers mainly black. In the winter, the head is mainly white, aside from black ear coverts, and a black smudge above each eye. In the winter, the bill is red at the base and dark at the tip.

Above: The black feathering on the head is a transient characteristic, appearing only in the summer (above right).

Distribution: On the tip of Greenland and along the coast of Newfoundland south to New England.
Habitat: Coastal areas.
Food: Typically mollusks, crustaceans, and other small aquatic creatures.
Size: 15in (39cm), wingspan 39.5–43in (100–110cm).
Nest: Scrape lined with plant matter.
Eggs: 2–3, pale blue to brown with darker markings.

Black-legged kittiwake

Rissa tridactyla

Identification: Head usually whitish with a black marking on the back. Back and wings grayish. Flight feathers black, white spots on tips. Bill yellow, legs black. Sexes alike. Young birds have a black bill, plus a black band across the neck, wings, and on tail tip.

The largest breeding colonies of black-legged kittiwakes in the Arctic comprise literally hundreds of thousands of birds. They seek out high, steep-sided cliffs, with so many birds packing onto these ledges that both adults may encounter difficulty in landing at the same time. These sites are defended from takeover most of the year, not just during the nesting period. The nest is made using scraps of vegetation, especially seaweed, combined with feathers and bound together with mud. The narrow, shelf-like nature of the site may make it difficult for aerial predators to attack the kittiwakes, but in some parts of their range, such as Newfoundland, it also reduces breeding success. Away from the nest, these birds remain largely on the wing, swooping down to gather food from the ocean surface.

Distribution: Circumpolar, from the far north of Alaska down to Mexico. Occurs down to northeastern U.S.A. in the north Atlantic. Also on Greenland. The commonest gull in the Arctic region.
Habitat: Ocean and shore.
Food: Fish and marine invertebrates.
Size: 16in (40cm), wingspan 35.5–39.5in (90–100cm).
Nest: Cliff ledge.
Eggs: 2, buff-olive and blotched.

Iceland gull (*Larus glaucoides*): 25in (64cm), wingspan 54in (137cm).
Iceland gulls occur in the north Atlantic, being present in Iceland, Greenland and northeastern Canada. They overwinter south from Labrador down to Virginia and inland to the Great Lakes. This species has a relatively pale gray area on the back and wings, with the head and underparts being white. The bill is yellowish, with a red spot on the lower mandible. Legs and feet are pink.

Red-legged kittiwake (*Rissa brevirostris*): 15in (38cm), wingspan 33–35.5in (84–90cm). Red-legged kittiwakes are found in the northern Pacific, occurring off the southwest coast of Alaska and through the Aleutian Islands. Their head and underparts are white. The wings are relatively dark gray, with white edging on the longer feathers. The flight feathers are black with white markings. These birds have a white tail and yellowish bill. Their reddish legs and feet help to distinguish them from other species.

Northern gannet

Sula bassana

This species is the largest of all gannets and can weigh up to 8lb (3.6kg). It is the only member of this group found around the North Atlantic. These gannets are powerful in the air. Their keen eyesight allows them to detect schools of fish such as herring and mackerel in the ocean below. When feeding, gannets dive down into a school, often from a considerable height, seizing fish from under the water. Their streamlined shape also enables them to swim. Breeding occurs in the spring when the birds form large colonies in which there is often a lot of squabbling. The young mature slowly, and are unlikely to breed until they are at least four years of age.

Distribution: Occurs on both sides of the Atlantic, in North America ranging down most of the eastern coastline via the Gulf coast to Central America.
Size: 35–39in (88–100cm).
Habitat: Ocean.
Nest: Usually on cliffs, built from seaweed and other marine debris held together by droppings.
Eggs: 1, whitish.
Food: Fish.

Identification: Mainly white, aside from pale creamy yellow plumage on the head extending down the neck, and black flight feathers. Tail feathers are white, and the feet are dark gray. Sexes are alike. Young birds are dark brown in color.

TERNS

Terns as a group can usually be distinguished quite easily, even from gulls, by their relatively elongated shape. Their long, pointed wings are an indication of their aerial ability, and some terns regularly fly longer distances than other migrants. Not surprisingly, their flight appears to be almost effortless. When breeding, terns generally nest in colonies.

Black skimmer

Rynchops niger

Distribution: Southern North America, from California and North Carolina on the Atlantic coast south through Central and South America to Chile and northern parts of Brazil.
Habitat: Coastal areas and rivers.
Food: Mainly fish.
Size: 18in (46cm), wingspan 44in (117cm).
Nest: Depression in the sand.
Eggs: 2–6, bluish with dark spots.

As their name suggests, these narrow-bodied birds with long wings have a distinctive way of feeding, skimming over the surface of the water with their mouth open and lower bill beneath the water level. Contact with a fish will result in the skimmer snapping its bill shut, with its head briefly disappearing under its body before it moves forward and takes off. The catch is consumed either in flight or once it has landed. This fairly specialized method of fishing is most suited to the shallows, so when hunting inshore in rivers these birds favor areas near sandbars, becoming most active in tidal rivers at low water. Black skimmers breed colonially, with up to 1,000 pairs nesting on beaches in remote localities. The North American population overwinters in Central America. Those breeding in South America also head south, while pairs nesting along rivers in eastern Brazil move to coasts.

Identification: Recognizable by uniquely longer lower bill, red with a black tip. Top of head and wings black, white collar evident in winter. Face and underparts white. Females smaller. Young have brown mottled backs.

Sandwich tern

Cabot's tern *Sterna sandvicensis*

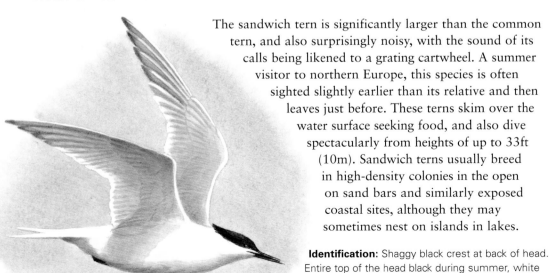

The sandwich tern is significantly larger than the common tern, and also surprisingly noisy, with the sound of its calls being likened to a grating cartwheel. A summer visitor to northern Europe, this species is often sighted slightly earlier than its relative and then leaves just before. These terns skim over the water surface seeking food, and also dive spectacularly from heights of up to 33ft (10m). Sandwich terns usually breed in high-density colonies in the open on sand bars and similarly exposed coastal sites, although they may sometimes nest on islands in lakes.

Identification: Shaggy black crest at back of head. Entire top of the head black during summer, white forehead evident in winter. The bill is long and black with a yellow tip. Rest of the head and underparts white, wings gray. Sexes are alike.

Distribution: Eastern North America, from Virginia southward through the Caribbean and down the Pacific coast of South America to Peru and Uruguay.
Habitat: Coastal areas.
Food: Fish, especially sand eels.
Size: 17in (43cm), wingspan 34–38.5in (85–97cm).
Nest: Scrape on the ground.
Eggs: 1–2, brownish white with darker markings.

SANDPIPERS

This group of waders tend to have a fairly compact body shape, and are not especially brightly colored. They have thin, narrow bills that are used for probing, although they also provide a very efficient means of grabbing the invertebrates that feature in their diets. The way in which they feed and move on the ground can aid identification.

Spotted sandpiper

Actitis macularia

Distribution: Northern Alaska through most of Canada and the U.S.A. Moves south in winter, down to South America.
Habitat: Shores and waterways.
Food: Invertebrates and fish.
Size: 8in (20cm), wingspan 37–40cm (14.5–16in).
Nest: Scrape in the ground.
Eggs: 4, greenish buff with brown spots.

In spotted sandpipers, some aspects of the traditional breeding roles of male and female are reversed. It is the female that returns first to the breeding grounds in the far north and establishes the breeding territory, driving off would-be rivals. During the breeding season she is likely to mate with a number of males, producing several clutches of eggs in succession. These are incubated and hatched by the male on his own, although occasionally the bond is strong enough for the female to stay and assist him. Spotted sandpipers start to leave the breeding grounds in June, heading south. Although some birds may only travel as far as British Columbia, the majority fly much closer to the equator, overwintering in the Caribbean and as far south as northern parts of Chile and Argentina. They are also not uncommon on the Galapagos Islands at this time.

Identification: Dark upperparts with darker brown speckling, white stripe above each eye and a long red bill with a dark tip. Underparts are white with dark spotting, with streaking on the sides of the face. Outside the breeding period the underparts are white, with speckling also absent from the wings, and the bill is yellowish-brown. Sexes are alike. Young birds resemble adults not in breeding plumage.

Dunlin

Red-breasted sandpiper *Calidris alpina*

Identification: The Alaskan (*C. a. pacifica*) and Canadian (*C. a. hudsonia*) races are the largest. Coloration is quite variable. Generally grayish head and wings in winter, with streaking on the breast. Underparts white. In summer, underparts display black streaking, with brown and black on wings. Center of abdomen black, flanks white. Sexes alike.

Dunlin favor muddy estuaries rather than sandy coasts, and outside the breeding season may be seen in large flocks numbering hundreds of birds. They feed by probing repeatedly in one area, then dart off and begin probing again nearby, a distinctive feeding method that enables them to be identified from a distance. Flocks invariably head north early in the year to nest, but if the winter is more prolonged than normal the pools and marshland where they feed will still be frozen over. This forces the dunlin to return south for a further period, before they venture north once again to begin breeding. They build a simple nest using grass and other vegetation, which helps to conceal their eggs from would-be predators. Both members of the pair are involved in caring for the brood.

Distribution: Circumpolar, breeding along the coast of Alaska and through northern Canada around to the western shore of Hudson Bay. Winters south down the Pacific coast of North America, along the Atlantic coast too.
Habitat: Frequents tundra and beaches.
Food: Invertebrates are the main constituent of diet.
Size: 8in (20cm), wingspan 13–14.25in (32–36cm).
Nest: Cup on the ground.
Eggs: 4, greenish brown with dark spotting.

PLOVERS AND DOWITCHERS

Many shorebirds occur over a wide area, but on occasion they may additionally be sighted in areas well outside their natural range. The young birds especially can become disorientated and end up in the wrong location, sometimes after being blown off course by gales and storms, which may force them to travel further inland than normal.

Ringed plover

Charadrius hiaticula

Distribution: Far northeast of North America, in Canada and also present on Greenland.
Habitat: Coastal and tundra.
Food: Freshwater and marine invertebrates.
Size: 7.5in (19cm), wingspan 14–16in (35–41cm).
Nest: Bare scrape on ground.
Eggs: 4, stone-buff with black markings.

Ringed plovers are relatively small in size. These waders have strong migratory instincts. They breed mainly in the far north, migrating to Canada via Iceland and Greenland from more southerly areas in Europe. This is quite different from the more standard migratory patterns among shorebirds, which generally move in a north-south direction through America. Ringed plovers typically breed on beaches and on the tundra. They can be seen in reasonably large flocks outside the nesting season, when they often seek food in tidal areas. If a nesting bird is disturbed, it will try to lure the would-be predator away from the vicinity of its nest site by feigning a wing injury. The mottled appearance of the eggs and the absence of an elaborate nest provide camouflage.

Identification: Black mask extends over the forehead and across the eyes. There is a white patch above the bill and just behind the eyes. A broad black band extends across the chest, forming a bib. The underparts are otherwise white. Wings are grayish-brown, and the bill is orange with a black tip. In winter plumage the black areas are reduced, apart from the bill which becomes entirely blackish. White areas extend from the forehead above the eyes. Cheek patches are grayish-brown with a grayish-brown band on the upper breast. Hens have less black on their heads.

Wilson's plover

Thick-billed plover *Charadrius wilsonia*

Wilson's plovers, also known as thick-billed plovers, are widely distributed in North America. They frequent sandy coasts and mud flats, where they use their relatively large bill to feed on crabs and other invertebrates. They tend to avoid hunting directly on the shoreline, preferring the upper areas of the beach instead. Wilson's plovers nest on sandy beaches, sometimes close to coastal lagoons, but they do not usually venture far inland.

Distribution: Breeding range from southern New Jersey south to Texas and Florida. Winters mainly in Florida, along the Gulf coast.
Habitat: Sandy beaches and mud flats.
Food: Invertebrates.
Size: 8in (20cm), wingspan 19in (48cm).
Nest: Scrape in sand.
Eggs: 3–4, buff with dark markings.

In winter the northern population heads south as far as Brazil, leaving just a remnant overwintering population in southern Florida. On the Pacific coast, many of the Wilson's plovers that spend the summer there retreat as far south as central Peru for the duration of the winter. The young birds molt rapidly, and are indiscernible from the adults within months of fledging. It is not uncommon to see Wilson's plovers in the company of similar species.

Identification: In breeding plumage males have a black area on the center of the crown and a broad black chest bar, with brown areas on the head and extending down over the wings. The underparts are white. Hens lack the male's black areas, which are replaced by brown feathering; this also applies to cock birds outside the breeding period. Young birds have scaly areas on the head, chest, back, and wings.

Short-billed dowitcher

Limnodromus griseus

Breeds in northern areas, typically the marshy and sparsely wooded muskegs of Canada. The short-billed dowitcher is one of the first shorebirds that nest in this region to head back south again, with females leaving in late June. The young will follow slightly behind the adults, seeking out their coastal wintering grounds. These dowitchers can be encountered on both Atlantic and Pacific coasts, as well as through the Caribbean region, though some travel down to South America. The three distinctive races all follow separate routes as they leave the Arctic. Short-billed dowitchers form large flocks in their wintering grounds. They feed by probing with their bills for edible items underwater, often submerging their heads while doing so. On the return journey, southerly populations start to pass through the U.S.A. from March onward.

Distribution: Breeding range from southern Alaska across central Canada to Hudson Bay and northern Quebec. Overwinters on coasts south from California in the west and Virginia in the east as far as tip of South America.
Habitat: Tundra, tidal marshes.
Food: Invertebrates.
Size: 11in (28cm), wingspan 18–22in (45–56cm).
Nest: Scrape on the ground.
Eggs: 4–5, white.

Identification: Crown of breeding birds dark, with pale orange area on underparts broken by blackish speckling. Wings are black and gray with pale edging, although races differ. Sexes are similar. Silvery-gray winter plumage, becoming paler on the underparts. Young birds resemble breeding adults, but underparts are much whiter.

Black-bellied plover (*Pluvialis squatarola*): 12in (30cm), wingspan 29–32in (74–82cm). Breeds from northern Alaska eastward to the vicinity of Hudson's Bay. Migrates south for the winter to the Pacific coast of North America and via Florida through the Caribbean. Prominent black area on the face and belly, with white patches on the sides of the body. Mottled black and white plumage over the wings and white undertail coverts. Hens are similar, but black on the underparts has white barring. During the winter upperparts are silvery-gray, with similar streaking on the white underparts.

Pacific golden plover (*Pluvialis fulva*): 10in (25cm), wingspan 24in (61cm). Breeds in western Alaska, overwintering mainly in Asia, though some remain in North America. Black areas on sides of face extend over chest and underparts, which are bordered by white feathering and barring. Coarse mottled pattern of brown, black and white plumage on the wings. In winter plumage underparts are mottled with black and white feathering too. Sexes alike.

Long-billed dowitcher (*Limnodromus scolopaceus*): 12in (30cm), wingspan 18–20in (45–52cm). Breeds on the north Alaskan coast and offshore islands, migrating south to the Pacific coast and across the southern U.S.A. into Central America. Only the hen has a longer bill than the short-billed dowitcher. In breeding plumage all of the underparts are orangish, with a white stripe above the eyes. In winter, these birds become silvery-gray with whiter underparts.

American oystercatcher

Haematopus palliatus

This wader's large size and noisy nature make it quite conspicuous. The powerful bill is an adaptable tool, used to force mussel shells apart, hammer limpets off breakwaters, prey on crabs and even catch worms in the sand. Individuals will defend favored feeding sites such as mussel beds from others of their kind. They are not likely to be observed in large groups, and tend to be quite sedentary. It takes young birds two years to gain their full adult coloration.

Identification: Black head, white underparts, brown back and wings. White wing bar. Large reddish-orange bill, reddish eye ring, legs and feet pink. Sexes alike. Young birds have brown head with speckled wings.

Distribution: Breeding range from Baja California in the west to Massachusetts in the east. Winters along the Gulf coast from North Carolina, and into South America.
Habitat: Tidal mud flats.
Food: Various invertebrates.
Size: 18.5in (47cm), wingspan 32in (82cm).
Nest: Scrape on the ground.
Eggs: 2–4, light buff with blackish-brown markings.

LOONS AND GREBES

Most wetland birds that breed in the far north during the summer cannot stay there throughout the year because the winter conditions are too harsh. While some head to warmer climates further south, others may seek sanctuary along the coast, where the ocean is unlikely to freeze even in winter. This shift usually brings a dramatic change in both the bird's lifestyle and diet.

Red-throated loon

Red-throated diver *Gavia stellata*

Distribution: Throughout far north of North America and in parts of Greenland when breeding. Overwinters farther south, from the Aleutians down to California in the west and down to Florida.
Habitat: Pools, open country.
Food: Mainly fish.
Size: 25in (64cm), wingspan 42–45in (106–116cm).
Nest: Pile of vegetation.
Eggs: 1–3, olive-brown with dark spots.

Red-throated loons pair up for life and stay together throughout the year. In May they return to their northern nesting grounds, revisiting the same location each year. Their nest, usually located among vegetation and surrounded by water, is simply a loose pile of plant matter. This is added to during the incubation period, potentially developing into a large mound. Both parents share incubation duties, although the female normally sits for longer than the male. Young red-throated loons can take to the water almost immediately after hatching, but usually remain at the nest for the first few days. Even once the chicks have entered the water they may still occasionally be carried on their parents' backs. Survival rates can be low, but if they make it through the critical early months of life, these divers may live for up to 23 years.

Identification: Distinctive red throat patch present in adults of both sexes during the breeding period. The head is gray, and the back of the neck is streaked black and white. Upperparts are brown, underparts white. During winter it has a pale gray crown, with speckling extending down the back of the neck and white spotting on the back, while remaining underparts are white. Yellowish-gray bill. Young birds can be identified by their grayish-brown heads.

Horned grebe

Podiceps auritus

Horned grebes return to their freshwater breeding grounds in spring, after overwintering in bays and other sheltered locations along the coast. The nest consists of a mass of floating aquatic plants, although it is sometimes built on rocks. The young, which hatch covered in striped down, can take to the water almost immediately, but prefer to be carried on their parents' backs. Horned grebes obtain much of their food by diving rather than feeding at the surface. Their natural underwater agility enables them to catch fish with ease. Diet varies according to season and location. At sea during winter they eat mostly fish, while brine shrimps are important when passing the Great Salt Lakes on migration. Diet is more varied on the breeding grounds.

Distribution: Breeds in much of Alaska and southeast across Canada to the shores of the Great Lakes. Overwinters through the Aleutians and down the west coast of Canada to mainland U.S.A., and down the eastern seaboard to Florida and Texas on the Gulf coast.
Habitat: Marshland, ponds and lakes.
Food: Fish and invertebrates.
Size: 13.5in (34cm), wingspan 18.5–21.5in (46-55cm).
Nest: Pile of vegetation.
Eggs: 1–7, bluish-white.

Identification: Distinctive golden horns created by raised feathers on each side toward rear of head. A red-brown area extends from bill to eyes, with others on the neck and flanks. Remainder of head black, as are wings. Much duller plumage in winter, when black on top of head extends down back of the neck to the wings. Throat and area below eyes remain white. Iris is reddish, bill black. Sexes alike.

Western grebe

Aechmophorus occidentalis

Identification: Black head, encompassing the eyes when breeding, with a narrow white stripe running to the bill. Black plumage extends down back of neck over back and wings, with some mottling on flanks. Iris reddish, bill black in center, with yellowish sides. Area around eyes mottled in winter. Sexes are alike.

Western grebes hunt fish by diving, becoming most active when the sun is high in the sky, illuminating the water and improving visibility. Their habitat alters significantly through the year, as they range between the coast and their freshwater breeding haunts in the north. Western grebes begin nesting during May, often forming large groups comprised of thousands of birds. It is not uncommon for hens to lay in nests other than their own, which can result in some nests containing ten or more eggs. Once the chicks have fledged, typically about ten weeks after hatching, the grebes head south to their wintering grounds, migrating over land during the hours of darkness.

The habits of the Mexican population are rather different, as they have a more extended nesting season, with egg-laying continuing until October. Mexican birds are also more sedentary by nature, and significantly smaller in size than their northern cousins.

Distribution: Breeds in south-central and south-western parts of Canada, and in western and central parts of the U.S.A. Overwinters down the Pacific coast to Baja California, with a separate Mexican population. Also present on the Gulf coast in winter.
Habitat: Lakes and reservoirs, overwinters on coasts.
Food: Fish form the bulk of the diet.
Size: 25in (64cm), wingspan 31–40in (78–101cm).
Nest: Pile of vegetation.
Eggs: 3–4, bluish-white with buff markings.

Common loon (great northern loon, *Gavia immer*): 35in (86cm), wingspan 58in (148cm). Breeds on Greenland and from Alaska through Canada. Winters farther south on both Pacific and Atlantic coasts and inland, notably south-eastern U.S.A. Black head, with barring on throat and neck. The back is patterned black and white, with white spots. Underparts white. Less contrast in winter, when white extends from lower bill and throat down over underparts. In winter eyes are dark rather than red. Sexes alike.

Least grebe (*Tachybaptus dominicus*): 10in (25cm), wingspan unknown. Southern Texas and Baja California to northern Argentina and southern Brazil, also Caribbean. Grayish head and neck, darker crown, browner on chest, with dark flanks. Chin and throat are white, and flanks pale, outside the breeding season. Iris is yellowish. Sexes are alike. Young resemble non-breeding adults, except for stripes on sides of the head.

White-tufted grebe (*Rollandia rolland*): 14in (36cm), wingspan unknown. Found in central Peru and southeastern Brazil down to tip of South America; also Falklands. Has a unique black and white tuft of feathers on head, with black crown, neck, chest, and wings. Red-brown barring on flanks and red-brown underparts. Browner overall when not breeding, with a white throat and underparts. Sexes alike. Young birds similar to adults out of breeding color, but with black striping across the cheeks.

Sungrebe

Heliornis fulica

The sungrebe is the smallest member of the finfoot family. Shy by nature, its habits have proved hard to determine, partly because it prefers wooded areas with dense vegetation by waterways. Sungrebes usually feed on the water, but may also venture onto land. They feed on insects such as dragonflies and their larvae, also hunting crayfish and amphibians. When breeding, males choose a nest site overhanging the water, typically only 3ft (1m) from the surface. The incubation period is short, lasting just ten days. The male sungrebe then carries the helpless chicks in a special pocket created by a skin fold under each wing, and can even fly with them in there. This method of care is completely unique.

Identification: Black and white stripes on top of head, running through eyes. White throat and underparts, yellowish hue on upper breast. Back and wings are brownish. Legs and especially feet banded gray and yellow. White tail tip. Breeding hens have chestnut area on sides of the head and red upper bill, plus scarlet eyelids.

Distribution: Extends from southeastern Mexico through Central America down to Peru in the west, and across much of northern South America east of the Andes down as far as northern Argentina.
Habitat: Streams, rivers and lakes.
Food: Mainly aquatic invertebrates.
Size: 13in (33cm), wingspan 15in (38cm).
Nest: Platform of twigs.
Eggs: 2–3, buff with darker markings.

FLAMINGOS AND CRANES

A number of relatively large birds, including flamingos and cranes, have evolved to live in wetland areas, where their height can be an advantage in finding food and wading through the water. Unfortunately, some have become so specialized in their habits that changes in their environment, such as pollution of waterways or clearing of land, could have serious consequences.

American flamingo

Phoenicopterus ruber

The distinctive coloration of these birds comes from their diet of algae or small creatures that have eaten the microscopic plants. They feed in a unique fashion by walking along with their head submerged, their long neck allowing them to filter relatively large quantities of water by sweeping their unusually shaped bill from side to side. As a result of their highly specific feeding requirements, American flamingos are vulnerable to habitat loss or pollution of the shallow coastal lagoons that they inhabit. Young are reared on nests of mud raised above the water level, and are covered in a whitish-gray down at first. At a month old, they molt into a brownish down. Their bills are short and straight at this stage. American flamingos are known to live for more than 30 years in the wild.

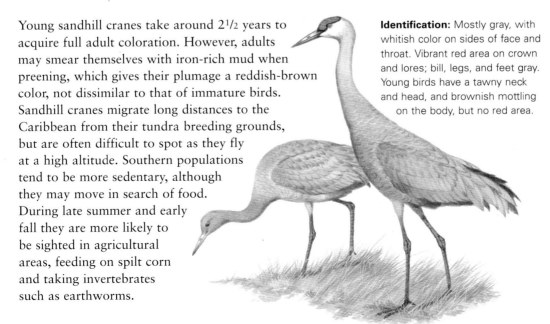

Distribution: The Caribbean Islands, Mexico, north coast of South America and the Galapagos Islands. Subspecies found in parts of southern Europe and Africa.
Habitat: Shallow saline lagoons.
Food: Small mollusks, crustaceans, and plant matter.
Size: 57in (145cm) tall, wingspan 60in (152cm).
Nest: Mud.
Eggs: 1, white.

Identification: Bright, almost reddish plumage on the neck, with a paler pink body. Bill also has a pink hue behind the black tip. Outstretched wings in flight show black areas. Sexes alike.

Sandhill crane

Grus canadensis

Young sandhill cranes take around 2½ years to acquire full adult coloration. However, adults may smear themselves with iron-rich mud when preening, which gives their plumage a reddish-brown color, not dissimilar to that of immature birds. Sandhill cranes migrate long distances to the Caribbean from their tundra breeding grounds, but are often difficult to spot as they fly at a high altitude. Southern populations tend to be more sedentary, although they may move in search of food. During late summer and early fall they are more likely to be sighted in agricultural areas, feeding on spilt corn and taking invertebrates such as earthworms.

Identification: Mostly gray, with whitish color on sides of face and throat. Vibrant red area on crown and lores; bill, legs, and feet gray. Young birds have a tawny neck and head, and brownish mottling on the body, but no red area.

Distribution: Breeds along the Arctic coast of North America, and at Great Lakes. Winters in southern U.S.A. and Mexico.
Habitat: Wetland areas.
Food: Omnivorous.
Size: 48in (122cm), wingspan 79in (200cm).
Nest: Mound of vegetation.
Eggs: 2, buff with brown markings.

WATERFOWL

This group of birds has diversified to occupy a wide range of habitats, and has adopted a correspondingly broad range of lifestyles, ranging from grazing in wetland areas through to hunting for fish. Breeding habits vary significantly too, with some members of the group choosing to breed on the ground, while others prefer the relative safety afforded by tree hollows.

Carolina wood duck

American wood duck *Aix sponsa*

Although these ducks have been seen as far north as Alaska, they move south to warmer climates for the winter months. In some areas their numbers have benefited from the provision of artificial nesting boxes, so that today they rank among the most common water-fowl in the United States. Carolina wood ducks are likely to be seen dabbling for food in open stretches of water, dipping their heads under the surface, but they also come ashore to nibble at vegetation. Although vagrants sometimes appear in the Caribbean, Carolina wood ducks observed in other parts of the world will be descendants of escapees from waterfowl collections.

Identification: Crest with glossy green and purple tones in breeding plumage. The lower neck and breast are chestnut with white speckling, while the abdomen is buff with barring on the flanks. Cock in eclipse plumage resembles the hen, but with a more brightly colored bill. The hen is duller in overall coloration, with dark brown underparts.

Distribution: Occurs widely over much of North America and south to Mexico, being present in western, central and southeastern parts of the continent, as well as on western Cuba.
Habitat: Wooded stretches of fresh water.
Food: Mainly vegetable matter, from acorns to aquatic plants.
Size: 20in (51cm), wingspan 25.5–29.5in (65–75cm).
Nest: In tree holes.
Eggs: 5–9, buff.

Muscovy duck

Cairina moschata

These dull-colored waterfowl are far removed in appearance from their more brightly colored domesticated counterparts. They prefer freshwater areas but sometimes move into saltwater lagoons during the dry season. Muscovies live in groups and are arboreal by nature, with powerful claws that help them to climb trees and roost easily on branches. They generally prefer to nest off the ground, but in areas where they are not commonly hunted, hens may lay eggs on the ground in spots that are well camouflaged by surrounding vegetation. The young develop the white wing patches at one year of age.

Identification: Mainly black but with white patches on the wings and glossy greenish suffusion on the surrounding plumage. Has a prominent, dull reddish-purple bill knob. Hens are smaller and lack the knob on the bill. Young birds can be distinguished by their lack of white plumage.

Distribution: From Mexico south to parts of Argentina and Uruguay.
Habitat: Forested lakes and marshes.
Food: Omnivorous.
Size: 33in (84cm), wingspan 118in (300cm).
Nest: Usually in a tree hollow.
Eggs: 8–15, white with greenish suffusion.

MORE WATERFOWL

Waterfowl are generally conspicuous birds on water, but their appearance and distribution can differ markedly through the year. Drakes often resemble hens outside the breeding season, when their plumage becomes much plainer. Some species are migratory, heading to warmer climates to escape freezing conditions, although others may fly to coastal areas, seeking out estuaries and sheltered bays.

American wigeon

Anas americana

These wigeon are sometimes seen well outside their normal range, with reports of sightings in locations as far apart as Hawaii, the Komandorskie islands off Siberia, and Europe. Almost every year a few vagrant American wigeon are recorded by birdwatchers in the British Isles. The ability of these ducks to cross the Atlantic Ocean is all the more surprising because they are essentially vegetarian in their feeding habits, browsing on plants in and out of the water. A number of American wigeon also migrate south each year to South America, and are observed here in larger numbers outside the breeding season.

Identification: In breeding condition, a prominent white stripe extends back over the top of the head, with a broad dark green area incorporating the eyes, and speckling beneath. The remainder of the plumage is brownish with a white belly and broader white area on the lower body close to the tail. Ducks have completely speckled heads and lack the drake's white forewing, which is retained in the eclipse plumage. The duck has paler chestnut coloration than the drake in eclipse plumage.

Distribution: Much of North America. Often moves southward in winter.
Habitat: Freshwater marshland.
Food: Aquatic vegetation, small aquatic invertebrates.
Size: 22in (56cm), wingspan 33in (84cm).
Nest: In a hollow often hidden in grass, lined with down feathers.
Eggs: 6–12, creamy white.

Hawaiian duck

Koloa *Anas wyvilliana*

Considered a smaller relative of the mallard, Hawaiian ducks have declined over recent years. This is due to a combination of hunting pressures, drainage schemes and predation by introduced species such as cats and mongooses. However, it has proved possible to breed these waterfowl successfully in captivity, and this has provided the nucleus of stock for release schemes in areas where they formerly occurred. Already there are indications that they may be re-establishing themselves on Oahu. Hawaiian ducks are shy. Where they do occur in the company of mallards, the populations tend not to mix, although hybridization is a possibility, confirming their close relationship. Hawaiian ducks usually breed between March and June, choosing a well-hidden site for their nest. Although often feeding by dabbling in the water, these ducks may sometimes feed on land, especially in agricultural areas.

Identification: Some variation in appearance. Drakes have a dark greenish top to their heads, with a fine brown speckled area on the cheeks and neck. Chestnut markings with black scalloping on the chest, and brownish underparts. Darker over the back and wings. Drakes have an olive-green bill. Ducks similar, but of a lighter shade overall, with a dull orange or sometimes grayish bill.

Distribution: Restricted to the Hawaiian Islands, mainly on Kauai but reintroduced to both Oahu and Hawaii.
Habitat: Freshwater areas.
Food: Plant matter and invertebrates.
Size: 19in (49cm), wingspan 30in (76cm).
Nest: Scrape on the ground.
Eggs: 7–16, grayish-green.

GAMEBIRDS

A variety of gamebirds are found in the woodlands of North America, extending southward. The most significant is undoubtedly the wild turkey, the original ancestor of all modern domestic strains worldwide. Grouse also occur in this region. All are shy and wary by nature, relying on cover to elude detection, and seeking their food at ground level. A number migrate.

American woodcock

Scolopax minor

The mottled appearance of the American woodcock provides exceptional camouflage when on the ground in forests, where these birds blend in with the leaf litter. They tend to rely on camouflage to escape danger, but if flushed will take off with a noisy flapping of their wings, flying not in a straight line but swerving from side to side. The courtship display of these woodcocks is spectacular, with males taking off and flying almost vertically before circling and plunging down again. The nest is sited in a secluded spot, and even the eggs blend in with the leaves, which are used to line the nest scrape. American woodcocks have relatively large eyes, which help them see well in the gloom of the forest. The position of the eyes high on the head also gives them excellent vision, so it is difficult for predators to creep up on them. The long bill is used to extract worms from muddy ground and catch insects.

Identification: Pale buff sides to the face, a barred crown, and gray above the bill and around the throat. A gray stripe extends down the edge of the wings, with a broader gray area across the wings. The rest of the back is mottled. Pale rufous-brown underparts, with the undersides of flight feathers gray, and a black band across a very short tail. Long, tapering bill. Sexes alike.

Distribution: Ranges from Newfoundland and southern Manitoba in Canada down through eastern parts of the U.S.A. as far as Texas, Florida and the Gulf coast. Overwinters in these southerly areas.
Habitat: Wet woodland.
Food: Invertebrates including earthworms and insects.
Size: 11in (28cm), wingspan 18in (45cm).
Nest: On the ground.
Eggs: 4, buff with brown spots.

Wilson's snipe

Gallinago delicata

Not easy to observe, Wilson's snipe tends to feed either at sunrise or toward dusk, probing the ground with jerky movements of its stocky bill. It remains out of sight for most of the day. If surprised in the open, these birds will sometimes freeze in the hope of avoiding detection, relying on their cryptic plumage to provide camouflage. More commonly they take off in a zigzag fashion, flying quite low and fast before plunging back down into suitable cover. Cocks perch and call loudly on their display grounds in the far north. When plummeting down as part of their display flight, the movement of air through their tail feathers creates a distinctive hooting sound, which has been likened to the call of the boreal owl. They migrate south in the fall, flying in flocks under cover of darkness. Subsequently they split up and forage separately, which helps to conceal their presence.

Identification: Pale buff stripe runs down the center of the crown, with pale stripes above and below the eyes. Dark mottled plumage on chest and wings. Blackish stripes on sides of the body, with white underparts. Wings have white stripes, tail is rufous. Long, pointed bill. Sexes alike.

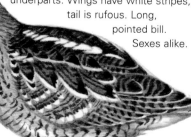

Distribution: Breeds right across northern Alaska and Canada, southward to New Jersey in the east and California in the west. Wintering grounds extend up to British Columbia, to western and southeastern U.S.A., and the Gulf coast.
Habitat: Lightly wooded areas, and fields offering plenty of concealment.
Food: Mainly invertebrates.
Size: 11in (28cm), wingspan 18in (45cm).
Nest: Hidden in grass.
Eggs: 4, olive-brown with black spots.

Wild turkey

Meleagris gallopavo

These large members of the fowl family are difficult to spot in their natural woodland habitat because the barring on their plumage breaks up their outline very effectively to create good camouflage. Shafts of sunlight filtering through the trees highlight the natural iridescence in the plumage, with shades of green appearing on the feathering from some angles. The wild turkey is unmistakable, especially when the male erects his tail feathers into a fan-shape as part of his courtship display. The color of his bare skin intensifies during the breeding season, and he often utters a loud gobbling call. Males, called "stags," frequently live in the company of several females. It is only these wild turkeys that have rusty brown tips to their tail feathers, those of domestic turkeys being white.

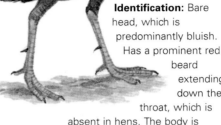

Identification: Bare head, which is predominantly bluish. Has a prominent red beard extending down the throat, which is absent in hens. The body is bronzy brown in color, with black barring on the wings and tail.

Distribution: Southern U.S.A. south into Mexico. It has a very patchy distribution that has given rise to numerous localized subspecies, especially in western parts of the range. **Habitat:** Wooded areas, including swampland. **Food:** Berries, seeds, and nuts, also invertebrates. **Size:** 48in (120cm) cock; 36in (91cm) hen, wingspan 49–57in (124–145cm). **Nest:** Scrape on the ground. **Eggs:** 8–15, buff with dark brown spots.

Ocellated turkey

Meleagris ocellata

Ocellated turkeys are shy, and despite their relatively large size are not easy to spot in the wild. However, the species has been domesticated in some parts, where birds are seen near settlements. They naturally live in groups, comprised of a single stag and several hens, and may emerge from wooded areas into clearings in search of food on the ground. If disturbed, they often run off rather than fly, as they are fairly clumsy in the air. When displaying, the stag inflates his wattle, which otherwise hangs down over his bill, and utters a call that has been likened to a motor being started. The nest is hidden in vegetation. The young grow rapidly but develop slowly, only gaining adult plumage at around three years old.

Distribution: Restricted to specific areas of Central America, such as the Yucatan Peninsula in Mexico, Belize and Guatemala. **Habitat:** Deciduous woodland. **Food:** Seeds, berries, and invertebrates. **Size:** 40in (102cm) cock; 33in (84cm) hen, wingspan 59–71in (150–180cm). **Nest:** Scrape on the ground. **Eggs:** 8–15, buff with brown markings.

Identification: Male has greenish-blue neck, underparts, and back, merging with brown. Prominent copper wing patch. Whitish flight feathers. Broad tail with blue and coppery patches like ocelli. Pale blue skin on the head has warty areas. Female much smaller, with a pinkish bill. Young birds have grayish-brown feathers.

Spruce grouse (*Dendragapus canadensis*): 16in (41cm), wingspan 22in (56cm). From Alaska south to northern parts of the neighboring U.S.A. Prominent red area above the eye. Forehead down to the throat and upper breast are black with a white border. White barring on the flanks. Grayish upperparts. Hens are much duller, lacking the red and black areas, and are significantly smaller in size.

Ruffed grouse (*Bonasa umbellus*): 18in (46cm), wingspan 20in (52cm). Alaska and northwestern Canada to central U.S.A. Distinguishable by the slight crest and ruff of black or reddish-brown feathering on the neck. There are two color phases; the reddish-brown rather than gray phase predominates in south-western British Columbia. Hens have a shorter ruff and an incomplete tail band.

Blue grouse (*Dendragapus obscurus*): 20in (50cm), wingspan 26in (68cm). Western North America, from southeastern Alaska down to San Francisco Bay. Also further inland in the Sierra Nevada and the Rocky Mountains. Cock has sooty-gray plumage from the back of the neck to the yellow-orange comb on the head. Mottled brown markings with an inflatable neck sac apparent on the sides of the head, and surrounding plumage is white with brown edging. Brown plumage on the legs extends to the toes. Broad fan-shaped tail with whitish plumage around the vent. Hens much plainer, with mottled brown plumage edged with white.

NORTHERN VISITORS

Woodland areas are rich in invertebrate life, so it is not surprising that a variety of birds seek their food there. Some have a highly specialized style of feeding, while others are opportunistic, which has helped them to spread over a wide area. Insectivorous species occurring particularly in northern areas of North America are forced to head south in the fall, in order to maintain their food supply.

Black and white warbler

Mniotilta varia

Distribution: From Canada (through central Manitoba to Newfoundland) to much of southern U.S.A. east of the Rockies. Overwinters along the Gulf coast and down through Central America into northern South America.
Habitat: Woodland.
Food: Invertebrates.
Size: 5in (13cm), wingspan 8.5in (22cm).
Nest: Cup-shaped.
Eggs: 4–5, white with purple spots.

With its bold patterning and a call that has been likened to a noisy wheelbarrow, the black and white warbler is relatively conspicuous. These birds arrive back in their breeding grounds during April, although they may head north before then, sometimes being spotted in more open country as well as in backyards and parks. These warblers are often better known by their traditional name of black and white creepers, due to their habit of foraging on tree trunks, probing for insects in the bark. They are surprisingly agile, being able to move both up and down the trunk. In their breeding territories, black and white warblers prefer stretches of deciduous woodland where good cover is available, since they breed on the ground. Here the pair will construct a well-disguised nest, usually close to a tree. They start to head south again from July onward. Like other wood warblers, these birds often forage as part of mixed species flocks, especially over winter.

Identification: In breeding plumage males have black feathering on the cheeks and in the vicinity of the throat, with the lower throat area becoming white over the winter. A prominent white stripe is evident above the eyes, with black and white streaking on the flanks. The lower underparts are white. Hens recognizable by their whitish cheeks, with a slight buff suffusion on the flanks. This is more apparent in young birds.

Worm-eating warbler

Helmitheros vermivorus

These warblers are difficult to observe since they frequent areas of dense undergrowth, their small size and coloration helping them to blend into their environment. Although their distribution is centered on the eastern U.S.A., they have on rare occasions been recorded in more westerly areas, even in California. Worm-eating warblers seek their food close to the ground, often on their own, though they can sometimes be found in the company of other warblers. This species is so called not because they favor earthworms, but rather because they seek out caterpillars of various moths, which at this stage in their life-cycle resemble worms. Pairs return to their breeding grounds during April, and the males sing as they establish their breeding territories, often perching on a high branch, although even here they can be hard to observe. The nest is built on the ground, and is comprised mainly of dry leaves, with moss and feathers used to create a softer lining.

Identification: A black stripe extends up the sides of the crown down over the neck, with another black stripe passing through the eyes. Rest of upperparts are buff-colored. Back and wings brownish-olive. Narrow light-colored bill with pink legs and feet. Sexes alike.

Distribution: Breeds in the eastern U.S.A., from south-east Iowa to New York and eastern parts of North Carolina, down as far as the central Gulf coast. Overwinters from south-eastern parts of Mexico down into South America.
Habitat: Dry woodland.
Size: 5.5in (14cm),. wingspan 8.5in (22cm).
Food: Invertebrates.
Nest: Cup-shaped.
Eggs: 4–5, white with brown spots.

HAWAIIAN FOREST-DWELLERS

In appearance and lifestyle, native birds occurring on the Hawaiian Islands are among the most unusual to be found anywhere in the world, having developed in complete isolation from mainland species until relatively recently. However, a number of these species have, sadly, become extinct over recent years, largely as a direct result of human interference in their environment.

I'iwi

Vestiaria coccinea

Distribution: Confined to the Hawaiian Islands; now extinct on Lanai, so occurs only on Hawaii itself, Kauai, Maui, Oahu, and Molokai.
Size: 6in (15cm), wingspan unknown.
Habitat: Woodland.
Nest: Cup-shaped, made of vegetation.
Eggs: 1–3, white with brown markings.
Food: Nectar and invertebrates.

As with many of Hawaii's birds, the common name of this honeycreeper is derived from its native name. It is most likely to be spotted around flowering plants, both native and introduced. In spite of their vivid coloration I'iwis are not easy to observe; like other red forest birds, they blend very effectively with the background. Even if only briefly glimpsed, however, their downward-curving bill sets them apart from other Hawaiian birds of similar color and size. I'iwis' calls are surprisingly varied, ranging from whistles to gurgles, their most distinctive vocalizations being likened to the sound of a rusty hinge creaking open. They are also talented mimics, replicating the calls of other species such as the elepaio (*Chasiempis sandwichensis*). I'iwis are most commonly found above 2,000ft (600m), being less common on Oahu and Molokai.

Identification: Brilliant red coloration over much of the body. Wings and tail are black, with a small area of white plumage at the top of the wings. Legs and bill, which is narrow and down-curved, are also red. Young birds much duller in coloration, being yellowish-green with dark barring over their body. The plumage on the back is darker than on the underparts. Wings are black, with paler edging on some of the feathers, with the tail also black. Bills of young birds are less brightly colored than those of adults, lightening toward the tip.

Akohekohe

Crested honeycreeper *Palmeria dolei* (E)

Identification: Highly distinctive loose, bushy crest extends up between the eyes, with buff above each eye and blue beneath on the cheeks. Remainder of the head is dark, with a reddish nape. Bluish markings on the throat, with blue and brownish patterning on the underparts. Wings similarly colored on the top, with a blue band running across and blue edging to the flight feathers. Fan-shaped tail is black with a white tip, undercoverts grayish. Sexes alike. Young birds have a much shorter crest and are much duller.

Another honeycreeper that is not always easy to spot. Its rather dark overall coloration and relatively small size help to conceal its presence in the treetops where it feeds. However, the akohekohe has a very lively nature and is highly vocal, uttering a series of buzzing and whistling sounds, some not unlike a person whistling. Unfortunately this species has seriously declined in numbers. It has already vanished from Molokai, although it is not uncommon on the eastern side of East Maui, where it inhabits the upland forest areas, frequenting ohia-lehua trees in particular. Here it can sometimes be seen in flight, although sightings are made difficult by the frequent misty weather that obscures visibility in this area. From a distance, the akohekohe may be confused with the smaller apapane (*Himatione sanguinea*).

Distribution: Hawaiian Islands; believed to be extinct on Molokai, but survives on Maui.
Habitat: Flowering trees.
Food: Nectar and invertebrates.
Size: 7in (18cm), wingspan unknown.
Nest: Cup-shaped, made of vegetation.
Eggs: 2, white with brown markings.

Nukupuu

Hemignathus lucidus (E)

The nukupuu occurs in thick ohia forest, using its strong legs to clamber up the bark of trees. Its slender bill is used to probe for invertebrates among the moss and crevices in the bark, and it may often be seen hanging upside down looking under leaves as well. The nukupuu is already extinct on Oahu, and localized in its surviving haunts elsewhere. The Kauai race (*H. l. hanapepe*), with its distinctive white undertail coverts, is restricted to the Alakai swamp, while on Maui most sightings are likely to be on Haleakala's upper slopes. The nukupuu's presence on Hawaii itself was not confirmed until 1982. Much of the confusion surrounding its distribution there arose from its close likeness to the akiapolaau (*H. munroi*), which occurs on Hawaii too. A very detailed comparison will reveal that the akiapolaau's straight rather than slightly curved lower mandible sets it apart.

Distribution: Now restricted to Kauai, Maui, and Hawaii.
Habitat: Forest.
Food: Mainly invertebrates.
Size: 5.5in (14cm), wingspan unknown.
Nest: Apparently unrecorded.
Eggs: Believed to be 2, white with brown markings.

Identification: Cock bird has a yellow head and underparts, with paler undertail coverts. The plumage on the back of the head is relatively long. Back and wings are dark olive-green. Small black area of plumage around the eyes, with the legs black too. Narrow bill is dark, with the upper part being curved and much longer than the short lower part. Hens easily distinguished by their dull olive-green plumage. Young birds resemble hens.

Ou (*Psittirostra psittacea*, E): 6.5in (17cm), wingspan unknown.
Hawaiian Islands, being found only in small numbers in the Alakai swamp on Kauai, and on Hawaii itself, between the Volcanoes National Park and Hamakua. Male is predominantly green with a yellow head. Bill is salmon-pink and hooked at its tip. Legs are pink. Hens can be distinguished by their green heads.

Palila (*Loxioides bailleui*, E): 7.5in (19cm), wingspan unknown.
Occurs only on the island of Hawaii, notably near Mauna Kea. Cock bird has a yellowish head and breast, with a narrow black area around the eyes. Rest of underparts are white. Back and rump slaty-blue, with dark yellowish-green on the wings. Bill and legs black. Hens duller, with gray merging with the yellow on the hindneck.

Maui parrotbill (*Pseudonestor xanthophrys*, E): 5.5in (14cm), wingspan unknown.
Restricted to Maui, on the eastern side of Haleakala. The massive, dark-colored and downward-curving upper bill of this species resembles that of a parrot. It has a bright yellow stripe above each eye. A dark olive stripe through the eyes separates the duller yellow cheeks and underparts. Dark olive-green area extends from the top of the bill over the wings.

Akikiki (Kauai creeper, *Oreomystis bairdi*): 4.5in (11cm), wingspan unknown.
Occurs only on Hawaii itself. Dark gray above, with grayish-whitish underparts and darker gray flanks. Short tail feathers and short, pointed, slightly down-curving pink bill.

Bishop's oo

Moho bishopi (E)

This relatively large nectar-feeder has very distinctive, flute-like tones in its song. The bishop's oo is exceedingly difficult to spot, however, as it inhabits dense areas of rainforest and prefers the upper level of the canopy. For a period it was even considered to be extinct, having vanished from both of the islands where it was sighted at the start of the 20th century. Then, remarkably, about 80 years after it was last recorded, the bishop's oo was rediscovered on Maui in 1981. It still survives there today, notably on the northeastern slope of Haleakala, but sadly there have been no sightings of the Molokai population since 1904. Like other honeyeaters, bishop's oos have tiny swellings on their tongue, called papillae, which act as brushes, helping them to collect flower pollen. Not surprisingly, honeyeaters are important pollinators of forest trees.

Distribution: Restricted to the Hawaiian Islands, being recorded only from Molokai and Maui.
Habitat: Dense forest.
Food: Mainly nectar.
Size: 12in (30cm), wingspan unkown.
Nest: Cup-shaped.
Eggs: 2, pinkish with dark spotting.

Identification: Predominantly blackish, with faint yellow streaking on the body and more prominent yellow areas behind the eyes and at the bend of the wing. Yellow undertail coverts. Long tail feathers, tapering to a point. Slightly down-curving bill, also tapering to a point, and black legs. Sexes are alike.

THE WOODLAND CHORUS

It is not always easy to identify birds with certainty, especially in the case of immatures coming into their adult plumage, a process that can involve several molts. There can also be regional variations in the appearance of some birds, particularly those that are widely distributed. Furthermore, distinctive color forms can crop up among normally-colored individuals. These are described as color morphs.

Mexican jay

Gray-breasted jay *Aphelocoma ultramarina*

Identification: Predominantly bluish-gray overall, differing in the depth of color through its range. Bluish-gray plumage on the head and neck, extending over the wings, with the tail also bluish. Grayish-white underparts, becoming white around the vent and on the undertail coverts. Northern birds are paler than their southerly relatives. Sexes alike. Young birds duller, typically displaying a yellowish area at the base of the bill.

Seven different races of the Mexican jay have been identified, though it is not always easy to distinguish them in the field, especially since juvenile coloration is a key factor. The length of time taken for the bills of young birds to change color varies greatly, sometimes taking up to two years. Differences in vocalizations and lifestyle have also been identified. The race *A. u. couchii*, found in southern Texas and south across the border, has a harsher call and has adopted a more territorial lifestyle than the Arizona race (*A. u. arizonae*), which lives in flocks of up to 20 birds. These flocks are usually made up of an adult pair and their young from previous years that are not yet breeding, and so are able to help the parents rear the new brood.

Distribution: From Texas, Arizona, and New Mexico in southwestern U.S.A., down through much of Mexico.
Habitat: Arid woodland.
Food: Omnivorous.
Size: 13in (33cm), wingspan 6.5in (17cm).
Nest: Cup-shaped platform of sticks.
Eggs: 4–7, blue to greenish-blue.

Clark's nutcracker

Nucifraga columbiana

These members of the corvid family are relatively conspicuous, often approaching campsites in search of food. Clark's nutcrackers have a varied diet, hunting small vertebrates and preying on the eggs and chicks of other birds, as well as searching rotting wood for invertebrates such as beetles. Pine nuts are also significant in their diet. They use their narrow, curved bill to prize out the seeds, sometimes wedging the pine cone in a rock crevice, which acts like a vice. Clark's nutcrackers are territorial by nature. In late summer a pair will begin to create stores of nuts and seeds. Although some of this food is consumed over winter, most of it is used to rear the chicks the following spring. If the pine crop fails, the birds are forced to abandon their territories and head elsewhere in search of food. This happens once every 15 years, on average.

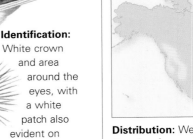

Identification: White crown and area around the eyes, with a white patch also evident on each wing and on the undertail coverts. Underside of the tail is also white. Wings and tail otherwise black, with the remainder of the body gray. Powerful, pointed black bill, with black legs and feet. Sexes alike. Young birds duller, with a more brownish tone to their gray plumage.

Distribution: Western North America, from southwestern Canada and western U.S.A. south to northern parts of Mexico. Sometimes irrupts into other areas from central Alaska to Texas, but uncommon in the Midwest.
Habitat: Typically montane coniferous forests.
Food: Omnivorous.
Size: 12in (30cm), wingspan 18in (45cm).
Nest: Twigs and sticks.
Eggs: 2–6, green with dark brown markings.

Unicolored jay (*Aphelocoma unicolor*):
14in (35.5cm), wingspan unknown.
Parts of Mexico south to northern El Salvador and western Honduras, being found in cloud forest. Blue overall, with a darker blue area on sides of the head, extending below and behind the eyes. Some races are a more purplish-blue shade. Bill, legs, and feet blackish. Sexes alike. Young birds duller, with yellowish bills.

Pinyon jay (*Gymnorhinus cyanocephalus*):
11in (28cm), wingspan 18in (45cm).
Western U.S.A. south to northern Baja California. Dull blue, with whitish streaking around throat. Relatively narrow, pointed black bill. Sexes alike.

Brown jay (*Cyanocorax morio*; previously *Psilorhinus morio*): 17in (44cm),
wingspan 26in (67cm).
Southeastern Texas via Mexico and much of Central America to northwestern Panama. Grayish-brown head, chest, and upperparts. Grayish-white underparts. Bill, legs, and feet are black. Southern individuals have white tips on inner tail feathers. Sexes alike. Young have yellowish bills.

Northern waterthrush (*Seiurus noveboracensis*):
6in (15cm), wingspan 8–9in (20–23cm).
Breeds from Alaska right across Canada except the far north, also northern U.S.A. Winters in Mexico, Ecuador and Peru. Brown upperparts, with a fawn streak from the upper bill behind each eye. Spotted throat. Underparts lemon-yellow, with darker streaking toward the vent. Undertail coverts white. Bill dark, legs and feet pinkish, bobbing as it walks. Sexes alike.

Varied thrush

Ixoreus naevius

This migratory member of the thrush family is sometimes placed within the genus *Zoothera*. It is inconspicuous, often hard to observe in the dark woods and areas near water it frequents. Varied thrushes are not shy birds, however, and have a powerful song with buzzing tones which is most often uttered in the rain. They sing most at the start of the breeding period in March, from upper branches in the forest. Varied thrushes normally feed close to the ground, foraging for invertebrates as well as eating berries. They normally nest around 15ft (4.5m) off the ground. The bulky nest often includes moss. After the breeding period the thrushes leave Alaska, with many overwintering in British Columbia, while others head farther south, where they may be seen in open woodland.

Identification: Bluish-gray upperparts, with a broad black stripe on the sides of the head and a prominent black band across the chest. Bright orange areas above the eyes and on the throat, upper chest, and lower underparts, the latter being mottled with gray. Orange bars also on the wings. Hens browner, with duller orange and an indistinct breastband. Young birds much duller, with brownish mottling on the throat and chest.

Distribution: Western North America, ranging from Alaska southward as far as northern parts of California.
Habitat: Coniferous forest.
Food: Invertebrates, some berries.
Size: 10in (25cm), wingspan 15in (38cm).
Nest: Bulky and cup-shaped.
Eggs: 3–5, pale blue with dark spots.

American redstart

Setophaga ruticilla

Belonging to the wood warbler rather than the thrush family, American redstarts are naturally very lively and active, almost constantly on the move seeking food, fanning open their tails and lowering their wings. Invertebrates may be hawked in flight or grabbed off bark. In parts of Latin America, where they overwinter, they are known locally as "candelita," since their jaunty nature and the coloration of cock birds combine to resemble the movements of a candle flame. Male American redstarts will sing loudly even before they gain adult plumage, which is not attained until they are over a year old. The song is most evident in spring at the start of the breeding season. The nest is built at a variable height in a suitable bush or tree, up to 75ft (23m) above the ground, and the hen incubates alone, with the eggs hatching after approximately 12 days. The young birds are reared almost entirely on invertebrates, and fledge about three weeks later.

Identification: Cock birds are very colorful, with orange patches on the wings and tail contrasting with the white plumage on the underparts and black elsewhere. Hens are a dull shade of olive-brown, with yellow rather than orange markings. Young birds resemble hens.

Distribution: Southeastern Alaska to Newfoundland, south to California in the west and South Carolina in the east. Overwinters in extreme south of the U.S.A. and via Mexico to northern South America.
Habitat: Deciduous woodland.
Food: Invertebrates and berries.
Size: 6in (15cm), wingspan 8in (20cm).
Nest: Cup-shaped.
Eggs: 3–5, white to bluish, with brownish spots.

OWLS

Owls rank among the most distinctive of all birds, thanks partly to their facial shape. Representatives of this group are very widespread in America, ranging from the coniferous forests of the far north, through the Amazon rainforest and right down to Tierra del Fuego at the southern tip of South America. Although the majority are nocturnal by nature, some will actively hunt during the daytime.

Northern saw-whet owl

Aegolius acadicus

Despite their distinctive calls, which resemble the sound of a saw being sharpened, northern saw-whet owls are hard to observe due to their small size and nocturnal nature. They are also able to fly very quietly to escape detection. This is strictly a woodland species, not found in northern coniferous areas. In southern areas it can be seen in more open, drier deciduous forest. During the day the owls rest on a branch close to a tree trunk, where their color and size make them hard to locate. They eat a variety of prey, especially rodents but also birds, invertebrates, and frogs. Pairs only come together for breeding, with the male seeking a mate by singing close to his nest hole. The young remain in the nest for a month.

Identification: Brown and white area on the face above the eyes, with white spotted area on the nape. Brown markings on the sides of the face. Underparts are white with rufous-brown markings. Wings and tail brownish with white spotting. Bill is black, irides yellow. Young birds have white eyebrows and lores, while the rest of the face is brown. Their underparts are tawny brown in color.

Distribution: Range extends across North America from British Columbia to Newfoundland, and south as far as Mexico. The race *A. a. brooksi* occurs on the Queen Charlotte Islands and *A. a. brodkorbi* in southwestern Mexico.
Habitat: Mainly coniferous forest.
Food: Mainly small vertebrates.
Size: 7.5in (19cm), wingspan 19in (48cm).
Nest: Tree hole.
Eggs: 3–7, white.

Northern hawk owl

Surnia ulula

These owls, occurring in the far north where day length varies significantly through the year, can be encountered at any time. Northern hawk owls are solitary by nature outside the breeding season. In late spring the male calls to attract a mate. The pair may choose from a variety of nesting sites, making use of a hole created by a woodpecker, taking over an abandoned stick nest, or simply choosing a site on top of a tree whose crown has snapped off, creating a depression. They make no attempt at nest-building themselves. The eggs are laid at two-day intervals, with the hen sitting alone and the male bringing food for her. Lemmings usually predominate in their diet, but in years when the lemming population plummets other prey, even small fish, may be caught. Breeding success is directly related to the availability of food. The young fledge at four weeks old, but it will be a further two weeks before they can fly, and they remain dependent on their parents for food for a further month.

Distribution: Range is circumpolar, right across North America in the boreal region from southern Alaska east to Labrador. Also present in Newfoundland.
Habitat: Coniferous forest.
Food: Small mammals.
Size: 16in (40cm), wingspan 17in (43cm).
Nest: Tree holes.
Eggs: 5–13, white.

Identification: Prominent white eyebrows and white cheeks, with whitish spotting on the dark head and wings. Broad black bars on each side of the neck. More brownish on the underparts and tail, with the underparts barred too. Eyes and bill pale yellow. Sexes are alike.

QUAILS

It is no coincidence that many of these birds have mottled upperparts, since they face danger from above, in the form of avian predators swooping overhead. This characteristic patterning serves to break up their outline, making them hard to spot among the vegetation. They move largely on foot, which also helps to conceal their presence, and often fly only if they detect danger nearby.

Common bobwhite

Northern bobwhite *Colinus virginianus*

Taxonomists have recognized at least 22 different races of these quail, and color variation is quite marked in some cases. Differences in size are also apparent, with individuals found in southern parts of their range being smaller than those occurring in northern regions. Common bobwhites live in groups, typically numbering around a dozen birds or so. They will invade agricultural areas to forage for food, especially when crops are ripening. These birds generally prefer to seek cover on the ground, where their cryptic coloration helps to conceal them from predators, but they will fly if threatened. Populations of these quail have also been introduced well outside their normal range, not only in other parts of the U.S.A., including the northwest and on Hawaii, but also further afield in New Zealand.

Identification: There is considerable variation through the birds' wide range. Most races have a black stripe running from the bill through the eyes, with a white stripe above and a broader white area on the throat. Chestnut underparts, usually speckled with white. Wings are brownish. Hens are duller, having buff rather than white patches on the head.

Distribution: Northeastern USA southward through Mexico into western Guatemala.
Habitat: Woodland and farmland.
Food: Seeds and invertebrates.
Size: 10in (25cm), wingspan 14–16in (35–40cm).
Nest: Scrape on the ground lined with vegetation.
Eggs: 10–15, dull white, often with blotches.

Californian quail

Callipepla californica

Californian quail are highly adaptable through their range, and this characteristic has enabled breeding populations of these popular game birds to be established in locations as far apart as Hawaii, Chile, and King Island, Australia. Nesting on the ground makes Californian quail vulnerable to predators, and although the young are able to move freely as soon as they have hatched, relatively few are likely to survive long enough to breed themselves the following year. Overgrazing by farm animals can adversely affect their numbers, presumably because this reduces the food that is available to the birds. However, these quail also forage in crop-growing areas, and sometimes associate in groups of up to a thousand individuals where food is plentiful.

Identification: Prominent, raised black crest that slopes forward over the bill. Top of the head is chestnut, with a white band beneath and another bordering the black area of the face. Chest is grayish, flanks are speckled. Hens lack the black and white areas, with grayish faces and smaller crests.

Distribution: Native to western North America, ranging from British Columbia in Canada southward to California and Mexico.
Habitat: Semi-desert to woodland.
Food: Seeds, vegetation, and invertebrates.
Size: 11in (27cm), wingspan 13–14.5in (32–37cm).
Nest: Grass-lined scraping on the ground.
Eggs: About 15, creamy white with brownish patches.

GROUSE

These gamebirds rely on their appearance to blend in with the background. The distribution of grouse extends to the frozen wastelands of the tundra zone in the far north. They are adapted to living on the ground there, molting their plumage to match the seasons. They also have feathering that extends right down over the toes to restrict heat loss and guard against frostbite.

Rock ptarmigan

Lagopus mutus

These grouse live in a region where natural cover is very scarce, and undergo a stunning transformation in appearance through the year. Their summer plumage is mottled brown, and their winter plumage is white, enabling them to merge into the snowy landscape. When snow is on the ground, they feed on buds and twigs of shrubs such as willow, which manage to grow in this treeless region. Pairs nest in the brief Arctic summer, often choosing a site protected by shrubs. The cock stays nearby while the hen incubates alone. The chicks are covered in down when they hatch and can move easily, but are not able to fly until their flight feathers have emerged fully, at about ten days old.

Identification: Mottled, brownish head with red above the eyes. Similar patterning across the body in summer, becoming white in winter. Blackish stripes on the face, lacking in hens.

Distribution: Circumpolar, extending across the far north of North America; also present on Greenland. Similar distribution in Europe and Asia.
Habitat: Tundra.
Food: Buds, leaves, berries and other plant matter.
Size: 15in (38cm), wingspan up to 22in (56cm).
Nest: Scrape on the ground lined with vegetation.
Eggs: 6–9, creamy buff, heavily blotched and spotted with blackish-brown.

Willow ptarmigan

Willow grouse *Lagopus lagopus*

Identification: In summer plumage, cock has brownish head and upperparts, white wings and underparts, and black tail feathers. Hens can be distinguished by the speckled appearance of their underparts. During the winter, both sexes become white overall.

Living in a very inhospitable part of the world, where the earth is permanently frozen even in the summer, these grouse rely on meagre plant growth to sustain themselves. Willow (*Salix*) is vital as a food source over winter, when the ground is blanketed with snow, while in summer, berries and even invertebrates are sought. Breeding occurs during May and June, with the eggs being laid in a scrape on the ground. Both pairs share the task of incubation, with the young hatching after about three weeks. At this stage they are especially vulnerable to predators such as the Arctic fox, and studies suggest their lifespan is unlikely to exceed two years. Their transformation into white plumage helps them to merge with the background in winter. Sometimes, if conditions get very harsh, these grouse will move much farther south, having been recorded in southern Ontario and northern Minnesota.

Distribution: Range is circumpolar, extending from the Aleutian Islands, Alaska, and northwestern British Columbia right across northern Canada, including Arctic islands such as Victoria, down as far as Newfoundland on the east coast.
Habitat: Arctic tundra.
Food: Willow buds and twigs.
Size: 17in (43cm), winspan 22in (56 cm).
Nest: Scrape on the ground.
Eggs: 2–15, yellowish with brown blotches.

SONGBIRDS OF THE PLAINS

Some birds of the open country draw attention to themselves with their song, particularly at the start of the nesting period, as is the case with thrashers. Others with a relatively dull appearance, such as some of the New World blackbirds found here, may also undergo something of a metamorphosis, with the plumage of the males becoming more brightly colored.

Western meadowlark

Sturnella neglecta

Distribution: Breeds from British Columbia and Manitoba to parts of Texas and into northern Mexico. Northern populations move slightly southward in winter.
Habitat: Meadows and grassland.
Food: Invertebrates.
Size: 10in (25cm), wingspan 14–16in (35–40cm).
Nest: Domed cup.
Eggs: 3–7, white with darker markings.

Male western meadowlarks are very vocal, especially at the start of the nesting season when they are laying claim to their territories. They will choose a conspicuous site, such as a fence post, and seek not only to attract females but also to drive away rival males. In areas where their distribution overlaps with eastern meadowlarks, even eastern males are perceived as a threat and chased off, since hybridization between these two forms is not unknown. Meadowlarks, which are actually icterids or New World blackbirds, are polygamous in their breeding habits, with a single male mating with several females. Each female constructs a separate and fairly elaborate dome-shaped nest, which takes about a week, before starting to lay. The male plays no part in nest building, but will help to provide food for the young once the eggs have hatched. Western meadowlarks become more social in winter, when they may be observed in small flocks.

Identification: Brown crown extends back over the top of the head, with a brown stripe running behind the eyes. Pale brown cheeks. Back and wings brown with darker barring. A black band runs across the chest, with lores, throat, and central underparts yellow. Flanks whitish with darker spotting. Sexes alike. Young birds paler with barring rather than a band across the chest.

Bobolink

Dolichonyx oryzivorus

The bobolink's unusual name originates from the sound of the male's song, which is audible through the breeding period. Like many birds found in open country, these icterids often sing in flight. They are known locally in South America as ricebirds, due to the way they have adapted to feeding on this crop. Though found in open country in North America, bobolinks are more likely to be observed in reedy areas of marshland during their winter migration. Remarkably, despite flying such long distances, these birds travel back to the same familiar breeding grounds every spring, with the mature males arriving first. Studies of their unique song patterns have revealed not only local dialects but also that the males use different call notes to communicate with each other, compared with those that are intended to attract females. Although the majority pair individually with a female, some males have more than one partner.

Identification: Cock in breeding condition is primarily black, with pale buff on the hind neck. Prominent white wing bar, with the lower back and rump also white. Hens have a dark crown with a streak down the center, and a dark streak behind each eye. Their underparts are yellowish, with streaking on the flanks. Young birds have spotting on the throat and upper breast, with no streaking on their underparts.

Distribution: Breeds from British Columbia to Newfoundland south to northern California, Colorado, and Pennsylvania. Winters in southern South America, reaching Argentina and southern Brazil.
Habitat: Prairies and open areas.
Food: Seeds and invertebrates.
Size: 7in (18cm), wingspan 10–12.5in (24–31cm).
Nest: Cup-shaped.
Eggs: 4–7, gray with reddish-brown spotting.

Red-winged blackbird

Agelaius phoeniceus

Distribution: Occurs across North America, breeding as far north as Alaska, and south into Central America.
Habitat: Relatively open country.
Food: Seeds and invertebrates.
Size: 9.5in (24cm), wingspan 12–16in (30–40cm).
Nest: Cup-shaped.
Eggs: 3, pale greenish blue with dark spots.

Unrelated to the European blackbird, the red-winged blackbird is a member of the icterid family. It frequents marshland areas when nesting, but is seen in a much wider range of habitats during winter. In North America, red-winged blackbirds move southward for the winter period, typically traveling distances of about 440 miles (700km). Populations in Central America tend to be sedentary throughout the year, however. There is a quite marked variation in the appearance of these birds through their wide range, and it is also not uncommon for individuals to display pied markings. Both sexes sing, particularly at the start of the nesting period,and some of their call notes are different, so it is possible to tell them apart.

Identification: Only the mature male in breeding plumage displays the typical glossy black feathering and red shoulder patches with a paler buff border. Females have dark streaks running down their bodies, with more solid brownish coloration on the head, sides of the face, and over the wings.

Eastern meadowlark (*Sturnella magna*): 10in (25cm), wingspan 14–16in (35–40cm). Southeastern Canada across eastern U.S.A. (resident through much of this area) and west to Nebraska, Arizona and Texas. Also in Mexico, ranging to northern South America. Similar to western meadowlark, with a brownish crown and a lighter central stripe, and a further stripe behind the eyes. Black band across the chest, with yellow central underparts. Flanks are whitish with dark speckling, back and wings are brownish with black barring. Yellow on face varies. Sexes are alike. Young birds are paler.

Brewer's blackbird (*Euphagus cyanocephalus*): 9in (23cm), wingspan 14–16in (35–40cm). Southern British Columbia east to the Great Lakes and down to Baja California and western Texas. Winters south to Central Mexico, sometimes to Guatemala. Cock in breeding color is iridescent blue with a purplish hue on the head and a greenish suffusion over rest of body and wings. Eyes yellow, pointed bill black. When not breeding, may display darker brownish plumage with black barring, and blackish wings. Hens and young birds grayish-brown, with slight mottling on the back. Black wings, dark eyes.

Bendire's thrasher (*Toxostoma bendirei*): 10in (25cm), wingspan 13–15in (33–38cm). Southwestern U.S.A. and northwestern Mexico. Mainly brown, with mottling on the breast. White tips to the long tail feathers. Undertail coverts are lighter brown. Yellow irides. Relatively long, slightly down-curved beak, with a paler lower bill. Sexes are alike.

Le Conte's thrasher

Toxostoma lecontei

Thrashers are members of the mockingbird family, and as such are talented songsters, even capable of mimicking the songs of other birds. The powerful, melodious song of these particular thrashers is most likely to be heard either at dusk or dawn, when it is most active. At this stage of the day it is easier for the birds to catch the invertebrates that form their diet. Le Conte's thrasher does not appear to be common in any part of its range. Its coloration provides effective camouflage in the sandy desert terrain, and its habits also make it inconspicuous. If disturbed, these mockingbirds generally seek to slip away undetected through the scrub, running with their long tail held upright. During the hottest parts of the day, they hide away in the shade. Their bulky nests consist mainly of twigs and are sited near to the ground, well hidden, in a cactus or shrub.

Distribution: Southwestern U.S.A. (California, Arizona, Nevada, and Utah), adjacent parts of Mexico, as well as Baja California and Sonora.
Habitat: Arid, open country.
Food: Invertebrates.
Size: 11in (28cm), wingspan 12.5in (31cm).
Nest: Made of twigs.
Eggs: 2–4, light blue-green with brown speckling.

Identification: Distinguished from other related species by its very pale coloration, having a grayish-brown body and darker tail, with tawny undertail coverts. Dark, strongly down-curved bill, with slight streaking on the throat. Sexes alike.

INSECT-HUNTING MIGRANTS

Many New World species undertake marked seasonal movements in the course of a year. Though the focus is often on birds from inhospitable northern latitudes flying south for the winter, others in the Southern Hemisphere also move north toward the equator before the southern winter. Birds found close to or in the Tropics, where the food supply is unaffected by the climate, remain as residents.

Groove-billed ani

Crotophaga sulcirostris

Distribution: Southwestern U.S.A. south through Central America and Colombia, Venezuela, and French Guiana as far as northern Chile and Argentina; also on Caribbean islands from Aruba to Trinidad.
Habitat: Scrub and pastureland.
Food: Mainly invertebrates.
Size: 12in (30cm), wingspan 17in (43cm).
Nest: Bowl-shaped, made of vegetation.
Eggs: 4, blue-green with chalky glaze.

These unusual members of the cuckoo clan have a relatively slim body shape and are highly social by nature, living in groups. They even sometimes associate with the slightly larger smooth-billed ani, although they can be distinguished in flight by their more languid flight pattern, as they flap their wings and glide. Neither species is a powerful flier. Groove-billed anis have unusual breeding behavior. A number of females will lay their eggs in the same location, reflecting their highly social nature. Up to 18 eggs have therefore been recorded in a single nest. Although these birds sometimes take over open nests abandoned by other birds, they may also construct a suitably large receptacle for their eggs from sticks and other vegetation. Groups of groove-billed anis typically feed on the ground by walking along and seizing any prey that comes within reach, which may include lizards.

Identification: Dull black in color, with a distinctively shaped bill. The culmen (central ridge of the bill) is in the form of a smooth curve from the tip to the forehead. Grooves in the bill leading to the nostrils are apparent on the sides. Iris is blackish. Tail is long, with a rounded tip. Sexes similar, although hens may be slightly smaller in size.

Smooth-billed ani

Crotophaga ani

Distribution: Southern Florida through Central America west to Ecuador and east into northern Argentina. Also present in the Caribbean.
Habitat: Brushland and open areas of country.
Food: Invertebrates.
Size: 13in (33cm), wingspan 18in (45cm).
Nest: Large cup of vegetation.
Eggs: 4, bluish green, with chalk-like glaze.

This species tends to occur in more humid areas than the groove-billed type, although they are similar in their habits. They are a common sight, partly as a result of their size and also because of their habit of perching in the open, even on fences. In cattle-ranching areas in Colombia, the anis' habit of following the herds has led to them being nicknamed *garrapateros*, meaning "tick eaters," and they are welcomed by ranchers for removing these parasites from their animals. Smooth-billed anis breed communally, like their groove-billed cousins, and can produce many eggs: 29 have been recorded in a single nest.

Identification: Dull, black plumage, with a decidedly rounded shape to the tail. Bill is black, with a distinctive smooth, raised area on the top of the upper bill close to the eyes. Sexes are similar, but hens are smaller in size. Recently fledged young of this species lack the raised area on the bill, resembling groove-billed anis at this stage, although the sides of their bills are smooth.

Purple martin (*Progne subis*): 8.5in (22cm), wingspan 15.5–16.25in (39–41 cm).
North America and parts of the Caribbean, notably the Cayman Islands and Cuba, to northern South America. Cock bird is an unmistakable shade of bluish-purple overall, with black flight and tail feathers. Hens are duller, with a bluish area confined to the top of the head and the wings. Throat, breast, and flanks are brownish, as are the sides of the neck, with the lower underparts being white.

Cave swallow (*Petrochelidon fulva*): 5.5in (14cm), wingspan 12in (30cm).
South-central parts of the U.S.A. down through Mexico and across many islands in the Caribbean, being permanently resident on Puerto Rico, Hispaniola, and Jamaica. Forehead reddish-brown, dark blue behind with a reddish-brown collar. Reddish brown underparts too. Wings are blackish. The back is bluish with prominent white streaking, while the rump is a deep reddish-brown.

Tawny-headed swallow (*Stelgidopteryx fucata*; previously *Alopochelidon fucata*): 4.5in (12.5cm), wingspan unknown.
Isolated populations in northern South America, notably in Venezuela and northern Brazil. Occurs widely in central South America to parts of Argentina and Uruguay. Distinctive tawny-rufous head, becoming buff on the sides of the head, extending down to the breast. Back, wings, and rump are brownish, often with paler edging. Sexes are alike. Young birds are yellowish and fawn rather than tawny.

Bank swallow

Sand martin; African sand martin; *Riparia riparia*

In the summer months, sand martins are usually observed relatively close to lakes and other stretches of water, often swooping down to catch invertebrates near the surface. They are likely to be nesting in colonies nearby, in tunnels that they excavate on suitable sandy banks. These can extend back for up to 3ft (1m), with the nesting chamber lined with grass, seaweed, or similar material. The eggs are laid on top of a soft bed of feathers. When the young birds leave the nest, they stay in groups with other chicks until their parents return to feed them, typically bringing about 60 invertebrates back on each visit. Parents recognize their offspring by their distinctive calls. If danger threatens, the repetitive alarm calls of the adult sand martins cause the young to rush back to the protection of the nest.

Identification: Predominantly brown, with white plumage on the throat, separated from the white underparts by a brown band across the breast. Long flight feathers. Small black bill. Sexes alike. Immature sand martins have shorter flight feathers and are browner than the adults.

Distribution: Throughout North America, except in the more arid regions of southwestern U.S.A. Winters in South America.
Habitat: Open country, close to water.
Food: Flying invertebrates.
Size: 4in (11cm), wingspan 11in (28cm).
Nest: Holes in sandbanks.
Eggs: 3–4, white.

Northern rough-winged swallow

Stelgidopteryx serripennis

Distribution: Breeds from southern Alaska down through British Columbia, the southern prairies of Canada and across virtually the entire U.S.A. Migrates to Central America, down as far as Panama.
Habitat: Open country.
Food: Invertebrates.
Size: 5in (13cm), wingspan 13in (32cm).
Nest: In burrows.
Eggs: 4–8, white.

These swallows take their name from the tiny hooks on the feather vane of the outermost primary feather on each wing, near the shaft. These can only be seen with magnification; their purpose is unknown. Although they range over a wide area, these swallows are likely to be seen close to water, where they hawk insects such as midges on the wing. They also hunt prey such as caterpillars and spiders near the ground. Often seen in groups, they sometimes roost communally in holes to conserve warmth in cold weather. Pairs start to nest in May and adopt a variety of nest sites, rarely excavating their own burrows. The nest chamber is lined with available materials, from seaweed to pine needles.

Identification: Mainly brown, darker on head and wings, with long, broad flight feathers. Tail brown, underparts whitish. Thin, narrow bill. Sexes are alike. Young birds have a cinnamon tone to the upperparts.

LONG-DISTANCE TRAVELERS

A number of small birds undertake two remarkable journeys each year, flying thousands of miles up to the Arctic to breed, and then moving south again for winter. Their nesting cycle has to coincide with the brief Arctic summer, otherwise there will be no food for the young, and the adults too could starve. In summer, however, this area literally teems with insect life, providing vital food for the young.

American pipit

Anthus rubescens

Distribution: Arctic North America and western U.S.A., in parts of northern New Hampshire, California and New Mexico. Winters across southern U.S.A., and up to British Columbia in the west and New England in the east.
Habitat: Tundra, grassland, and fields.
Food: Seeds and invertebrates.
Size: 6.5in (17cm), wingspan 10.5in (25cm).
Nest: Cup-shaped.
Eggs: 4–5, gray with dark spots and streaks.

Identification: Grayish upperparts, with an indistinct whitish stripe passing through each eye, becoming more brownish-gray over the back. Wings blackish. Streaking on the reddish-buff underparts, varying according to race. Rump brown, with the tail being black above. Has darker, more brownish upperparts outside the breeding period, and is more heavily streaked overall. Sexes are alike.

American pipits are active birds by nature, tending to walk rather than hop across the ground, bobbing their tails up and down regularly. Their range does not extend to northeastern parts of the U.S.A., probably because until quite recently this area was heavily forested. The males establish their territories once they reach their breeding grounds in the Arctic tundra. The nest site is carefully chosen to reduce the risk of the eggs becoming chilled: it may be partly buried, or sheltered by a rock, often apparently orientated to catch the warm rays of the sun. It is not uncommon for hens to reuse a nest which has been built previously. The hen sits alone, and the eggs hatch after about 14 days. The chicks fledge after a similar period, and are reared on invertebrates. American pipits leave their breeding grounds in early September, and head south for the winter.

Savannah sparrow

Passerculus sandwichensis

Distribution: Breeds across Alaska and Canada, extending south across much of the U.S.A. (except for part of the southwest) and into northern Mexico.
Habitat: Grassland and open terrain.
Food: Seeds and invertebrates.
Size: 5.5in (14cm), wingspan 8–9.5in (20–24cm).
Nest: Cup-shaped.
Eggs: 4–6, blue-green with dark speckling.

These widely distributed birds are as adept at running as they are flying. It is not unusual for them to escape danger by dropping down into vegetation and scampering away. Savannah sparrows can be found in a wide range of habitats, from the tundra of the far north to the grassy sand dunes of Mexico. They breed on the ground, with spiders usually featuring in the diet of the young. Various distinctive races of these sparrows are recognized; some have very limited distributions, none more so than the so-called Ipswich sparrow (*P. s. princeps*), which breeds on a tiny area of land just 20 miles (32km) long on Sable Island, Nova Scotia. It winters more widely along the east coast, including around Ipswich, Massachusetts. Another localized and distinctive form is *P. s. rostratus* from the western side of the U.S.A., which has not only developed a much broader bill but also has a quite different song pattern from all other savannah sparrows.

Identification: Varies through its range, with those from the west coast being darker than those found farther east or in Alaska. Streaked appearance, with dark markings running down over the head and on the flanks. Brownish-gray to brownish-black upperparts. Underparts grayish-white. Often a yellow or whitish streak above or through the eyes, with a paler stripe on the center of the crown. Sexes are alike.

BIRDS OF PREY

Agile, aerial predators, falcons are opportunistic hunters, relying on strength and speed to overcome their prey, which frequently includes smaller birds. Caracaras, on the other hand, prefer to seek their quarry on the ground, and have benefited to a certain extent from road-building, which has provided carrion in the guise of animals and birds killed by vehicles.

Crested caracara

Common caracara *Caracara plancus*

This predatory species has a wingspan approaching 4ft (1.2m) but tends not to fly, preferring to spend its time on the ground. Crested caracaras can move quickly on their relatively long legs, running through open country in pursuit of prey such as small rodents. They often seek out carrion in the form of road kills along highways, and when feasting on larger casualties even take precedence over vultures. However, their diet does vary according to habitat, and sometimes they will eat invertebrates. On the Falkland Islands they are considered to be a threat to newborn lambs, while in coastal areas they have learned to harry returning seabirds into dropping their catches. Crested caracaras usually build their nests off the ground, using an untidy framework of twigs with fresh vegetation added to it. The young hatch after an incubation period of around 30 days.

Identification: Blackish cap and crest on the head, with whitish area beneath becoming barred on the back and chest. Wings and abdomen are more blackish. Bare reddish skin on the face. Neck and throat white. Dark band at the tip of the tail. Sexes alike, but hens are slightly larger in size. Young birds have brown rather than black plumage.

Distribution: Occurs in southern U.S.A., south through Central America and across South America to Tierra del Fuego and the Falkland Islands.
Habitat: Prairies, arid areas.
Food: Meat-eater.
Size: 23in (59cm), wingspan 48in (122cm).
Nest: Platform of twigs.
Eggs: 2–3, white with brown markings.

Prairie falcon

Falco mexicanus

It has been estimated that the breeding range of these falcons covers about 1.4 million square miles (3.6 million square km), but as with other predatory species the density of the birds in this area varies. Prairie falcons are opportunistic hunters, a key factor in their spread across much of North America. They prey heavily on small birds such as lark buntings, and also rodents. In arid areas greater numbers of reptiles, including lizards, snakes, and tortoises, are caught. Prairie falcons prefer to catch their prey at or just above ground level, but also harry other birds in flight. Breeding occurs from March to July, depending on latitude. With woodland becoming scarce, these falcons have adapted to using cliff faces, laying on the rock rather than building a nest, though pairs may take over nests abandoned by other large birds.

Identification: Brown crown, with white streaking running round each side of the head above the eyes. White area behind each eye, and a dark streak running from below each eye onto the cheeks. Dark brown ear coverts, with a brown and white spotted neck and underparts. Bill pale yellow, darker at its tip. Legs and feet yellow. Sexes alike. Young birds have grayish legs and feet, with long flight feathers extending back almost as far as the tail feathers.

Distribution: British Columbia eastward through Canada around the southern part of Hudson's Bay to Newfoundland, and through western U.S.A. to northern Mexico and east via Texas along the Gulf coast to Florida.
Habitat: Prairies and plains.
Food: Meat-eater.
Size: 20in (51cm), wingspan 30–40in (76–101cm).
Nest: Often lays on a cliff ledge.
Eggs: 4–5, whitish with brownish blotches.

Bald eagle

Haliaeetus leucocephalus

Distribution: From the Aleutian Islands and Alaska east across Canada and south across the U.S.A. into northern Mexico.
Habitat: Areas where there are large stretches of water.
Food: Vertebrates and some carrion, especially in the winter when hunting is more difficult.
Size: 38in (96cm), wingspan up to 96in (244cm).
Nest: Often huge, located in a tree or even on the ground.
Eggs: 1–3, white.

The national symbol of the U.S.A., the bald eagle is a highly adaptable species, and is encountered as far north as the freezing tundra of Canada and south to Mexico. Its feeding habits are diverse; these eagles tend to catch fish during the summer months, switching at other times of the year to birds as large as geese, which are seized in flight. They hunt both by sight and sound, and are drawn to areas where sea otters are feeding by recognizing their calls. The species remains far more common in the northern part of its range, where it has been subject to less habitat disturbance.

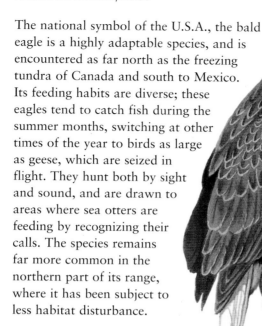

Identification: Distinctive white head and tail, yellow bill and talons. Remainder of the plumage is predominantly brown, with lighter edging to some of the feathers on the back and wings. Female is larger, and young birds have dark bills.

Above: Bald eagles may migrate more than 1,250 miles (2,000km).

Turkey vulture (*Cathartes aura*): 32in (81cm), wingspan 68–72in (173–183cm).
Ranges across much of the U.S.A. south via Central America to much of South America; also on islands including the Greater Antilles and the Falklands. North American population moves south in winter. Can find carcasses by scent, and feeds mainly on mammals. Bare, reddish-pink head and brownish-black plumage. Varies in size through its range. Sexes are alike.

Swainson's hawk (*Buteo swainsoni*): 22in (56cm), wingspan 49in (124cm).
From Alaska southward, mainly in the central U.S.A. Usually migrates south for the winter to southern Brazil, Argentina, and Paraguay via Central America, although some may remain in the southern U.S.A. White area from above the bill to the throat. Chest is brown and underparts are whitish with brown barring. Head and upperparts are dark. Tail is barred. Rarer reddish and black morphs occur, with these colors predominating on the underparts. Hens are larger.

Swallow-tailed kite (*Elanoides forficatus*): 22in (62cm), wingspan 48in (122cm).
Southeastern U.S.A., notably Florida, and into Mexico, extending to northeastern Argentina and Uruguay in South America. Head and underparts are whitish. Black on the back, with purplish and metallic green hues evident on the wings. Long flight feathers and a distinctive V-shaped tail, most apparent in flight. The bill is blackish, the eyes reddish. Sexes are alike. Young birds have shorter tails and sometimes dusky markings on their head.

Golden eagle

Aquila chrysaetos

These eagles generally inhabit remote areas away from people, where they are likely to be left undisturbed. When seen in flight, the golden eagle's head looks relatively small compared to its broad tail and large, square-ended wings. Although it has some yapping call notes similar to those of a dog, calls are generally quite shrill. Its hunting skills are well adapted to its environment. In some areas, for instance, golden eagles take tortoises, dropping the reptiles from a great height in order to smash their shells before eating them; in other areas, they may prey on cats. They prefer to capture their quarry at ground level, swooping down low, rather than catching birds in the air.

Distribution: Occurs widely across the far north of North America, and also in western areas down into Mexico.
Habitat: Mountainous areas.
Food: Mainly birds and mammals.
Size: 35in (90cm), wingspan 60–96in (152–244cm).
Nest: Massive cliff nest made of sticks.
Eggs: 2, white with dark markings.

Identification: Brown overall, with yellowish-brown plumage on the back of the head, extending down the nape. Eagles inhabiting desert areas, such as the Middle East, tend to be slightly paler overall. Bill is yellow with a dark tip. Feet are yellow with black talons. Hens are bigger than cocks.

WOODPECKERS

This group of birds is at home in areas close to woodland, which is where the invertebrates that feature prominently in their diets are likely to be numerous. Though woodpeckers are traditionally regarded as bark hunters, they will also descend to the ground to seek their prey. Woodpeckers possess distinctive calls.

Red-bellied woodpecker

Melanerpes carolinus

Red-bellied woodpeckers have a variable diet that changes through the year. Over the summer, invertebrates are plentiful and form a high percentage of their food intake. They will also prey on vertebrates, including the nestlings of other species. In the fall, fruits of various kinds start to figure more prominently. During the winter period they sustain themselves largely on nuts and seeds, which have a high energy content, though cock birds will still spend time foraging for insects in the branches of trees (hens less so). Red-bellied woodpeckers prefer to feed off the ground, and are most likely to be sighted in deciduous trees, particularly oaks. Pairs will nest through much of the summer, often raising two or occasionally three broods of chicks. The breeding chamber is usually larger than that used for roosting.

Distribution: Eastern North America, southward from Ontario via South Dakota and southern Minnesota as far as central Texas and Florida.
Habitat: Open woodland, parks and suburban areas.
Food: Omnivorous.
Size: 9.5in (24cm), wingspan 16–18in (40–45cm).
Nest: Tree hollows.
Eggs: 3–8, white.

Identification: Cocks have a red top to the head, extending to the back of the neck, whereas only the nape is red in hens. Black and white barring extends over the back and wings, and to central tail feathers. Underparts grayish-white, with reddish suffusion to center of abdomen.

Gila woodpecker

Melanerpes uropygialis

Gila woodpeckers are noisy, conspicuous and also quite aggressive by nature, particularly when close to the nest site, which may be located in a tree. Alternatively, since they occur in arid areas, it may be sited in the less conventional surroundings of a tall cactus, as high as 23ft (7m) off the ground. This affords good protection from would-be predators, but can only be occupied once the hole has dried up thoroughly and is not leaking sap. Other creatures, including small mammals and even reptiles, may subsequently take over such chambers once they have been vacated by the birds. The breeding period is usually between April and June, although a pair may sometimes nest again in July. Once fledged, the young remain with their parents until the adults begin nesting again. Their bold nature means that gila woodpeckers will readily feed on backyard bird tables, driving off other species such as European starlings (*Sturnus vulgaris*) which may otherwise seek to monopolize this food supply.

Distribution: Ranges from southwestern U.S.A. to Sonora. Other races occur in Baja California.
Habitat: Scrubland and woods, extending into urban areas.
Food: Invertebrates, seeds, and fruits.
Size: 9.5in (24cm), wingspan 15–18in (38–45cm).
Nest: Tree hollow.
Eggs: 3–6, white.

Identification: Pale grayish head and underparts, with a slightly whiter area above the bill and barring on the flanks. Black and white barring also extends down over the back and wings, and onto the tail feathers too. Cocks can be distinguished by the small red cap of plumage on the top of the head.

URBAN INSECT-HUNTERS

A number of birds such as swifts and swallows have developed the ability to prey on insects in flight. Their acrobatic agility makes them exciting to observe as they twist and turn. Other insect hunters are more opportunistic, like the cowbirds, whose lifestyles have changed significantly in North America in the course of little more than a century.

Chimney swift

Chaetura pelagica

Distribution: Eastern North America. Migrates through Central America to its South American winter quarters in Peru and northern Chile.
Habitat: Urban and agricultural areas.
Food: Flying insects.
Size: 5in (13cm), wingspan 11in (28cm).
Nest: Twigs held together with saliva.
Eggs: 2–7, white.

It is not always easy to identify swifts with certainty as they wheel far overhead in the sky, but the small and quite stocky appearance of this species can help. Chimney swifts have long wings and actively fly rather than glide, flapping their wings fast to stay airborne. When seen at close quarters their square-shaped tails have obvious spines at their tips. Being dependent on flying insects for food, the swifts are forced to head south for the winter, returning north to their breeding grounds in March and April. Just prior to migration, literally thousands of chimney swifts may congregate at favored roosts. Their habits have changed significantly due to the spread of cities in North America. Instead of the hollow trees that they would formerly have inhabited for roosting, they have switched to using chimneys, barns, and similar sites, even breeding in these surroundings.

Identification: Dark brown overall, with a paler area around the throat. Body slightly box-like in bulk, with short tail feathers and long wings. Usually seen in flight from beneath, often at a great height as they soar high. Sexes are similar.

Cliff swallow

Petrochelidon pyrrhonota

Distribution: North America and Mexico, except northern Alaska and the far northeast. Migrates via Central America to southern Brazil, Paraguay, parts of Argentina, and Chile.
Habitat: Open areas near buildings.
Food: Invertebrates.
Size: 5.5in (14cm), wingspan 10.5–12in (25–30cm).
Nest: Gourd-shaped structure of mud.
Eggs: 3–6, whitish with brown speckling.

The cliff swallow has adjusted its habits to benefit from the spread of urbanization in its North American breeding grounds. In the past, these swallows built their nests on cliff faces, as their name suggests, but now pairs will breed in barns, bridges and similar structures. They may even decide to use dry, hollowed gourds placed in suitable sites as artificial nests. These swallows may also nest in large colonies. The mud that forms the nest is scooped up in the swallow's bill, and, unlike in related species, is the only building material. The interior is lined with vegetation. Pairs typically take five days to build the nest. In fall the swallows head south for winter, although a few fly no further than Panama. Their return is greeted as a sign of spring.

Identification: Pale forehead, with a blue top to the head, which is encircled with chestnut plumage. Blackish area at the base of the throat. Upper chest and rump are orangish-brown, underparts otherwise whitish, with dark edging to undertail coverts. Back and wings are dark and streaked with white. Young birds have blackish heads.

HUMMINGBIRDS AND JAYS

Hummingbirds feeding in backyards, either from flowers or special feeders, are one of the unique sights of America. These birds are a source of fascination as they hover in flight and feed, demonstrating their remarkable aerial agility. However, they may not always be resident throughout the year, with some species moving to warmer climes for the winter.

Ruby-throated hummingbird

Archilochus colubris

Distribution: Breeds in eastern North America, moves south to Florida and south-west to Texas through Central America to Panama for the winter. Sometimes seen in the adjoining Caribbean region.
Habitat: Lightly wooded areas with flowering plants.
Food: Nectar, pollen, sap and invertebrates.
Size: 3.5in (9cm), wingspan 11–12in (28–30cm).
Nest: Cup built in trees bound with spiders' silk.
Eggs: 2, white.

The small size of these hummingbirds is no barrier to flying long distances, which they do back and forth to their wintering grounds each year. Cock birds usually arrive back in their breeding areas about a week before the hens are seen in May. Staying in temperate areas would mean that these birds would have difficulty finding sufficient plant nectar to sustain them through the winter. In fact, ruby-throated hummingbirds are far less specialized in their feeding habits than some members of this family, and have been recorded feeding on more than 31 different types of plant, although they display a preference for red flowers. Hens build their nest alone, binding it with the silk threads of spiders' webs, and are responsible for rearing the chicks on their own. Tiny invertebrates feature prominently in their diet at this stage.

Identification: Metallic, greenish-bronze upperparts. Has a large glossy red area of plumage under the throat. The remainder of the underparts are whitish. Hens are similar in appearance, but they have a dusky white area on their throat instead of the glossy red patch of the cocks.

Anna's hummingbird

Calypte anna

These hummingbirds are sometimes seen feeding at the holes in tree bark drilled by sapsuckers (*Sphyrapicus* species), which results in the plant's sap oozing, providing an accessible source of nutrients. At the outset of the breeding season, males become very territorial. Soon afterward, hens begin to seek out suitable nest sites, which can include human-made structures, such as electric wires. They gather small lengths of plant fibers and bind them together with silk from spiders' webs. Lichens are used to fill in gaps between the stems, and the cup is lined with feathers. The chicks leave the nest for the first time when only 18 days old.

Identification: Mostly rose-colored head, with a bronzy-green area behind the eyes and a small white spot evident there as well. Upperparts are a shade of metallic, bronzy green, and underparts are green and whitish. Hens lack the rose-colored plumage on the head, and have a brownish throat.

Distribution: Western U.S.A., from California and offshore islands southeast to Arizona; may move to southern Oregon during the winter. Sometimes even recorded in Alaska.
Habitat: Generally woodland areas with flowers.
Food: Nectar, pollen, sap and invertebrates.
Size: 4in (10cm), wingspan 5in (13cm).
Nest: Cup-shaped.
Eggs: 2, white.

Steller's jay

Cyanocitta stelleri

Ranging over a vast area, Steller's jay has proved to be a highly adaptable species. In some areas, such as at picnic sites in the Rocky Mountains in Colorado, these jays have become very tame, accepting food from people. Elsewhere, they are much shyer. They eat a varied diet; where food is likely to be hard to find because of snow in winter, they forage for acorns in the fall, which are then stored for later use. Family groups may remain together over the winter in northern areas, and the young leave in the spring when the adult pair start to nest again. Mud is often used like cement to anchor the bulky nest of twigs together.

Identification: Dark, grayish-blue head and back, with blue underparts. Tail and wings are blue with black barring. North American variety have darker coloration and more prominent crests than those occurring further south, which have a much bluer appearance. Sexes alike.

Distribution: The largest distribution of all North American jays, extending from Alaska south through Central America to Nicaragua.
Habitat: Woodland and forest.
Food: Omnivorous.
Size: 12.5in (32cm), wingspan 17in (43cm).
Nest: Mound of twigs.
Eggs: 2–6, greenish or bluish with brown spotting.

Black-chinned hummingbird (purple-throated hummingbird, *Archilochus alexandri*): 4in (10cm), wingspan 4.25in (12cm).
Breeding range extends from southwestern British Columbia across southern U.S.A. into Mexico. Moves further south over the winter. Black area merging into broader purple area on the sides of the face and throat. Underparts are buff-brown, and upperparts are dull bronzy green. Hen is similar, also with a white stripe behind the eyes, and buff-brown on the sides of the face and throat.

Broad-tailed hummingbird (*Selasphorus platycercus*): 4.5in (11cm), wingspan 5in (13cm). Breeding ranges from California through Texas into southern Mexico and Guatemala. Winters entirely in Central America. Wide tail feathers. Metallic, deep reddish-purple throat and sides of the face, with buffy-brown underparts and metallic green upperparts. Hens are duller, with brown speckling on the buff throat plumage.

Rivoli's hummingbird (magnificent hummingbird, *Eugenes fulgens*): 5in (13cm), wingspan 7in (18cm). Breeding ranges from southern Arizona and New Mexico in the U.S.A., with these birds wintering in Mexico. A separate population in Central America ranges as far south as western Panama. Deep purple coloration on the head, becoming blackish with a white spot behind the eyes, and a brilliant green throat. Hens have lighter brown underparts.

Blue jay (*Cyanocitta cristata*): 12in (30cm), wingspan 16in (40cm).
Found extensively in Eastern North America, down to Florida, although southerly populations tend to be smaller. Blue crest, white area on the face, edged by black feathering. Wings are blue with distinctive white markings. Black barring extends from the flight feathers to the tail. Underparts are white.

Green jay

Inca jay *Cyanocorax yncas*

These woodland birds are found in two distinct populations. Birds forming the northern population are better known as green jays, while the southerly and more social Andean races are usually described as Inca jays. One of the most unusual features of these jays is their habit of seeking out smoking areas of woodland, not only in search of small creatures that may be escaping the flames, but also to hold their wings out, allowing the smoke to permeate their plumage. This action is believed to kill off parasites such as lice that may be lurking on their bodies. Young green jays may remain with their parents and help to rear the new chicks before establishing their own territories.

Identification:
Green plumage is characteristic. The northern race has a combination of blue and black plumage on the head, being green elsewhere, and underparts, including the underside of the tail, are yellowish. Iris is black. South American race has a pronounced blue crest above the bill, and pale green plumage extending right over the forehead. Iris is yellow. Sexes are alike.

Distribution: Northern population extends from Texas to Honduras. The separate South American form ranges from Colombia to Ecuador.
Habitat: Woodland and forest.
Food: Omnivorous.
Size: 10.5in (27cm), wingspan 15in (38cm).
Nest: Platform of twigs and similar material.
Eggs: 3–5, grayish-lilac with dark speckling.

BACKYARD HUNTERS

Predators are not always welcomed in the backyard, but these birds at the top of the avian food chain are quite remarkable in the way they hunt and, in many cases, communicate with each other. Their generally bold nature helps them to thrive in the human environment, while their intelligence allows them to profit from environmental changes.

Black-billed magpie

Pica hudsonia

Distinguishable from its European relative by its calls rather than its appearance, the black-billed magpie is a common sight through much of its range. These members of the crow family are quite agile on the ground, holding their tail feathers up as they hop along. They are often blamed for the decline of songbirds because of their habit of raiding nests, taking both eggs and young chicks. These magpies also sometimes chase other birds, particularly gulls, to make them drop their food. They also eat invertebrates and fruit. Bold and garrulous by nature, a pair of black-billed magpies will not hesitate to create a commotion if their nest is threatened by a predator such as a cat. Their calls draw other magpies to the area, who then join in harrying the unfortunate feline. Their nest is a stout and usually large structure, with a protective dome of twigs.

Identification: Black head, upper breast, back, rump and tail, with a broad white patch around the abdomen. When folded, wings have a broad white stripe and dark blue areas below. Black plumage may have a green gloss. Sexes alike, but cock may have a longer tail.

Distribution: Western North America, extending from Alaska eastward to Ontario down to northeastern parts of California and northern New Mexico.
Habitat: Trees with surrounding open areas.
Food: Omnivorous.
Size: 19in (48cm), winspan 24in (61cm).
Nest: Dome-shaped stick pile.
Eggs: 2–8, bluish-green with darker markings.

American crow

Common crow *Corvus brachyrhynchos*

Few birds have more highly developed communication skills than these crows. It is almost impossible to approach them without being noticed, since even when feeding they have sentinels keeping a look-out for danger. They are heavily persecuted in farming areas, due to the damage that they can inflict on crops; however the benefits that they bring in foraging for potentially harmful invertebrates are frequently overlooked. American crows are highly adaptable birds, just as likely to be encountered in towns and cities as in open countryside. Noisy by nature, they tend to be much less vocal in the vicinity of their nests, which are sited in tall trees, often in public parks. The height at which they build—60ft (20m) or more off the ground—keeps them safe from most predators.

Identification: Jet-black plumage, with dark eyes and a large black bill. Sexes are alike. Calls help to distinguish this species from other crows, while the fan-shaped appearance of the tail in flight distinguishes these corvids from ravens.

Distribution: Across much of North America, from British Columbia to New Foundland and south to Baja California, Colorado and central Texas.
Habitat: Ranges widely, including into suburban areas.
Food: Omnivorous.
Size: 17.5in (45cm), wingspan 17–20in (43–52cm).
Nest: Platform of sticks.
Eggs: 3–7, greenish with brown blotches.

American kestrel

Falco sparverius

The smallest of the North American falcons, the American kestrel can easily be overlooked unless it is hovering conspicuously along a roadside. Their remarkably keen eyesight allows these birds to spot a mouse or similar prey from as far as 90ft (30m) away. They dive down quickly to seize the unsuspecting quarry, their sharp talons ensuring a secure grip on their prey. After making a kill, the kestrel will fly up to a convenient perch with its meal, or back to the nest site if it has young. Insects such as grasshoppers are also likely to fall victim to these falcons, particularly during the summer months when they are generally more plentiful and can play a vital part in nourishing a growing brood. The vast range of these kestrels means that they need to be adaptable feeders. They have been documented in Peru as preying on both lizards and scorpions, while amphibians will also be caught on occasion.

Distribution: Extends over virtually all of America, from Alaska to Tierra del Fuego at the tip of South America.
Habitat: Open countryside and urban areas.
Food: Insects and small vertebrates.
Size: 10.5in (27cm), wingspan 21–24in (52.5–61cm).
Nest: Typically in a hollow tree.
Eggs: 3–7, white with brown blotching.

Identification: Cock has russet back barred with black, and a russet tail with a broad black subterminal bar and whitish feather tips. Top of the head is russet with adjacent grayish-blue area. Wings grayish-blue above, with black barring but much paler below, and white circular spots along the rear edge. Two distinctive vertical black stripes on the sides of the face, with an intervening whitish area and chin. Underparts paler. Hens have chestnut wings and a barred tail.

Yellow-billed magpie (*Pica nuttalli*): 16.5in (42cm), wingspan 24in (61cm). Occasionally seen as far north as Oregon, but more typically resides in the Central Valley area of California and in coastal valleys as far south as Santa Barbara County. Similar to the black-billed magpie, with a black head, back and breast. Wings and underparts have white patches. Bill is yellow, with a variable yellow patch of bare skin adjacent to the eyes. Sexes are alike.

Black-shouldered kite (*Elanus caeruleus*): 16in (41cm), wingspan 3.5–34in (80–85cm). Mainly occurs through Central and South America. In North America, is sometimes seen as far north as British Columbia, hunting along highways. Grayish crown, back and wings, with prominent black patches at the shoulders. Underparts are white, enabling it to be distinguished from the Mississippi kite (*Ictinia mississippiensis*). Sexes alike. Young birds have reddish-brownish striations on their underparts, with similar suffusion on the head and neck.

Western screech owl (*Otus kennicotti*): 8.5in (22cm), wingspan 21in (54cm). Western side of North America, from northern Canada down to Mexico. Also occurs in two color morphs, although reddish individuals are decidedly uncommon outside the humid coastal northwest. The pattern of cross-barring on the plumage of this species is denser, creating an overall impression of a darker-colored bird, although depth of gray coloration varies.

Eastern screech owl

Otus asio

The red and gray morphs of these owls are equally common, sometimes even cropping up in the same nest. Habitat appears to play no part in determining coloration. Lightly wooded areas, including backyards, are favored by these birds of prey. In true owl fashion, eastern screech owls hunt at night and, despite their size, are able to take relatively large quarry, including adult rats. They are opportunists, catching anything from worms to snakes and even moths, which can be seized in flight. In urban areas these owls are even known to plunge into backyard ponds at night, seizing unwary fish near the surface. The shape of their wings means that virtually no sound betrays their presence until after they have launched their deadly strike. As with other owls, the study of the pellets regurgitated after meals has allowed ornithologists to confirm their feeding habits.

Distribution: Eastern North America, from eastern Montana and the Great Lakes down via the Gulf states to northeastern Mexico.
Habitat: Variable, from forests to suburban areas and parks.
Food: Small mammals and invertebrates.
Size: 8.5in (22cm), wingspan 20in (52cm).
Nest: In a hollow tree.
Eggs: 2–8, white.

Identification: Red and gray color morphs. Widely spaced cross-barring on the underparts matches spacing of vertical stripes on a whitish ground. Yellowish-green base to the bill. Ear tufts may be raised or lowered. Lines of white spots with black edging extend diagonally across top of wings. Sexes are alike.

INVADERS

The present-day distribution of some birds is the direct result of past human interference. The effects of this can be clearly seen in North America, where some introduced European species have now become established across virtually the entire continent. Mimics such as the native catbird may even pick up the songs of these feathered invaders.

House sparrow

Passer domesticus

A common visitor to birdfeeders and city parks, house sparrows have adapted to living close to people. They were originally brought to New York from Europe in 1850, and by 1910 had spread west to California. There are now noticeable differences within the North American population: northern individuals are larger, while those from southwestern arid areas are paler. House sparrows form loose flocks, with larger numbers gathering where food is plentiful. They spend much time on the ground, hopping along while watching for predators such as cats. It is not uncommon for them to build nests during winter, to serve as communal roosts. The bills of cock birds turn black at the start of the nesting season in spring. Several males often court a single female in what is known as a "sparrows' wedding."

Identification: Rufous-brown at the back of the head, with gray above. A black stripe runs across the eyes and a broad black bib extends down over the chest. Ear coverts and underparts are grayish, with a whiter area under the tail. Hens are browner overall with a pale stripe prominent behind each eye.

Distribution: Southern Canada, across the U.S.A., into Central and South America.
Habitat: Urban and more rural areas.
Food: Seeds and invertebrates.
Size: 6in (15cm), wingspan 9.5in (24cm).
Nest: Under roofs and in tree hollows.
Eggs: 3–6, whitish with darker markings.

Common starling

European starling *Sturnus vulgaris*

The common European starling is another New World invader, introduced in 1890 when a small flock of 60 starlings brought from England was set free in New York's Central Park. A further 40 were released there the following year, making the millions of starlings now present in the whole of North America direct descendants of this initial group of 100 birds. (The release came about as part of an unfulfilled plan to introduce all the birds described in the works of British playwright William Shakespeare to North America.) Small groups of starlings are often to be seen feeding in backyards, although occasionally much larger groups comprised of hundreds of birds may visit an area. In flight, European starlings are adept at avoiding predators such as hawks by weaving back and forth in close formation, to confuse a would-be attacker. Their undemanding breeding habits and belligerent nature mean that these starlings will commandeer nest holes from native species for their own use.

Distribution: Occurs widely throughout North America, just ranging south into Mexico.
Habitat: Near houses and buildings.
Food: Invertebrates, berries, birdfeeder fare.
Size: 8.5in (22cm), wingspan 15–17in (38–43cm).
Nest: Tree hole or birdhouse.
Eggs: 2–9, white to pale blue or green.

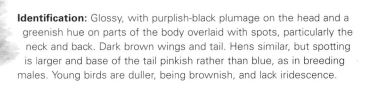

Identification: Glossy, with purplish-black plumage on the head and a greenish hue on parts of the body overlaid with spots, particularly the neck and back. Dark brown wings and tail. Hens similar, but spotting is larger and base of the tail pinkish rather than blue, as in breeding males. Young birds are duller, being brownish, and lack iridescence.

WRENS

These diminutive, rather stumpy birds are often found in residential areas, especially the aptly named house wren, which has one of the widest distributions of all birds in America, occurring virtually throughout the entire region. Other wrens have more localized distributions, benefiting from birdfeeder offerings to sustain themselves during the cold winter months.

House wren

Troglodytes aedon

The house wren appears to be a rather nondescript bird, but its lively, jerky movements make it instantly recognizable, even from just a brief glimpse. These wrens often frequent backyards, usually being seen among dense vegetation since they are instinctively reluctant to leave cover for long. Although wrens are small in size, they can be determined and belligerent birds, especially in defense of a chosen nest site such as a woodpecker hole in a tree, and are quite able to force the creator of the chamber to go elsewhere. They will also take occupancy of a birdhouse, particularly when sited in an area of a backyard where they feel secure. A pair will collect a jumble of vegetation such as moss and small twigs to line the interior, as well as adding feathers to make a soft pad for their eggs. House wrens are prolific breeders, frequently producing two broods of chicks during the season.

Identification: Brown upperparts, with black barring evident on the wings and tail. Underparts lighter brown, with whitish throat area. Generally indistinct pale eyebrow stripes. Narrow, relatively short bill. Sexes are alike. Young birds have a rufous rump and are a darker shade of buff on the underparts.

Distribution: Present across much of North America except the far north, extending down through Mexico and right across South America.
Habitat: Vegetation in parks and backyards.
Food: Invertebrates.
Size: 5in (12cm), wingspan 7in (18cm).
Nest: Pile of twigs and sticks.
Eggs: 5–9, white with brown spotting.

Carolina wren

Thryothorus ludovicianus

Carolina wrens are relatively easy birds to identify, due partly to their extensive white facial markings. They move with the same jerky movements as other wrens, frequenting bushes and similar dense areas of vegetation through which they can move inconspicuously. Carolina wrens are also quite noisy birds, with a song that is surprisingly loud for a bird of their size. It is uttered throughout the year, rather than just at the start of the breeding season, and sounds in part like the word "wheateater," repeated constantly. Unfortunately, young Carolina wrens often have an instinctive tendency to push northward from their southern homelands. Although in mild years they will find sufficient food to withstand the winter cold, widescale mortality occurs in these northern areas when the ground is blanketed with snow for long periods, almost wiping out the species. In due course, however, their numbers build up again, until the cycle is repeated again at some future stage.

Identification: Chestnut-brown upperparts, with black barring on the wings and tail, and white bands running across the wings. Distinctive white eye stripes, edged with black above and bordered by chestnut below. Black and white speckling on the sides of the face. Throat is white, underparts buff. Sexes are alike.

Distribution: Throughout eastern U.S.A., notably in North and South Carolina.
Habitat: Shrubbery.
Food: Invertebrates feature prominently in the diet of this species, with some seeds.
Size: 5.5in (14cm), wingspan 7.5in (19cm).
Nest: Cup of vegetation.
Eggs: 4–8, whitish with brown spotting.

TITMICE AND CHICKADEES

These small birds are most likely to be seen in backyards during the winter months, when the absence of leaves on many trees makes them more conspicuous. They often visit bird tables and feeders during colder weather too. Members of this group are very resourceful, clearly displaying their aerobatic skills as they dart about and hang upside down to feed.

Tufted titmouse

Baelophus bicolor

Distribution: Eastern North America, from southern Ontario south to the Gulf of Mexico, although not present in southern Florida. Range expanding in areas of Canada.
Habitat: Light, deciduous woodland.
Food: Invertebrates in summer; seeds during winter.
Size: 6in (15cm), wingspan 8–10in (20–24.5cm).
Nest: Small tree holes and nest boxes.
Eggs: 3–8, creamy white with brown spots.

This is the largest member of the tit family occurring in America. It is quite conspicuous through its range, thanks in part to its noisy nature. The vocal range of male tufted titmice is especially varied, and individuals are able to sing more than 15 different song patterns. Hens also sing, but not to the same extent and mainly during spring and early summer. The range of these titmice has increased northward, largely because bird-table offerings guarantee them food throughout the year. In the south, they have been recorded as hybridizing with black-crested titmice (*B. atricristatus*) in central parts of Texas. The resulting offspring have grayish crests and a pale orange band above the bill. In spite of their small size, these titmice are determined visitors to bird tables, driving off much larger species. They can be equally fierce in defending their nests.

Identification: Characteristic black band immediately above the bill, with gray crest and crown. Cheeks and underparts are whitish, with pale reddish-orange flanks. Sexes alike. Young birds are duller overall, with less contrast in their plumage.

Above: The nest cup of a titmouse, lined with soft material.

Carolina chickadee

Parus carolinensis

This species is very closely related to the black-capped chickadee (*P. atricapillus*), which occurs further north, and it is not unknown for the birds to hybridize where they overlap. Studies of their song patterns have revealed that the Carolina chickadee has a four-note call, whereas the black-capped type has a two-note whistle. Although pairs have their own territories during the summer, Carolina chickadees form larger groups in the winter months. During cold weather, they spend much longer periods roosting in tree hollows to conserve their body heat, sometimes remaining there for up to 15 hours per day. This is also the time of year when chickadees are most likely to be seen visiting bird tables in search of food.

Identification: Black area extends to back of the head, with black under the bill broadening across the throat. White on the sides of the face. Underparts are whitish with a slightly orange cast. Wings and tail are primarily grayish-olive. Sexes are alike.

Distribution: Northeastern U.S.A. south to Texas and northern Florida.
Habitat: Light, broad-leaved woodland.
Food: Invertebrates and seeds.
Size: 5in (12cm), wingspan 7.5in (19cm).
Nest: In small holes in trees, also uses nest boxes.
Eggs: 3–9, white with reddish-brown spots.

CITY SONGBIRDS

Many of these birds are a common sight in cities and backyards, thanks to their adaptable nature.
They often undertake seasonal movements southward to warmer climates in search of more favorable
feeding opportunities over the winter period. Their return is keenly anticipated, however, as an indicator
of the arrival of spring. Pairs will then breed perhaps twice before returning south again.

Distribution: From southern Ontario, Canada south through the U.S.A. to the Gulf of Mexico, and down to Belize.
Habitat: Edges of woodland, parks, and backyards.
Food: Seeds and invertebrates.
Size: 9in (23cm), wingspan 10–12in (24–30cm).
Nest: Cup-shaped, made of vegetation.
Eggs: 3-4, whitish or grayish white, with darker spots and blotches.

Virginian cardinal

Northern cardinal *Cardinalis cardinalis*

The range of these cardinals continues to increase both in northern and western areas, especially since the first breeding record from Canada, which dates back to 1901. This expansion probably results from bird-table offerings. The stout, conical bill of these birds is adapted to crushing seeds, although Virginian cardinals will also hunt invertebrates, particularly when they have chicks in the nest.

Identification: Predominantly red, with a pointed crest. A black mask surrounds the bill extending back to the eyes and down onto the throat. Wings, back and tail are of a slightly duller shade. Hen is predominantly brown, with a slight reddish suffusion over the wings and tail. The bill in adults of both sexes is bright red, whereas that of young birds is blackish, enabling them to be distinguished from adult hens.

Scarlet tanager

Piranga olivacea

Distribution: Migrates north to southeastern Canada and eastern U.S.A., overwinters in Central and South America, east of the Andes.
Habitat: Light forest and woodland.
Food: Mainly invertebrates.
Size: 7in (17cm), wingspan 11.5in (29cm).
Nest: Cup-shaped, made of stems and roots.
Eggs: 2–5, whitish to greenish blue with dark markings.

These tanagers undertake long flights each year to and from their breeding grounds. Individuals sometimes venture further afield, and are observed in more northerly and westerly areas than usual, even reaching Alaska on rare occasions. A pair of scarlet tanagers rears only one brood during the summer before returning south. These birds catch invertebrates in the undergrowth and also in flight. More unusually, scarlet tanagers rub live ants onto their plumage. This behavior, known as "anting," results in formic acid being released by the ants among the feathers, which in turn drives out parasites, such as lice, from the plumage. The bright coloration of these birds is linked in part to their diet.

Identification: Mainly yellowish-olive, with underparts being more yellowish than upperparts. Cock distinguishable from the hen by having black rather than brownish wings and tail. In breeding plumage, the male has characteristic vivid scarlet plumage. Young cock birds in their first year have more orange rather than scarlet plumage.

UNDERSTANDING FISH

The world of fish is more complex than many people imagine. Compared with birds, mammals, and other creatures that we are accustomed to seeing around us, few people are able to observe aquatic life to quite the same extent. However, fish are as interesting and varied as any other group of animals on Earth.

Although bounded by water, fish have lives that in many ways parallel those of animals that live on land. Like all creatures, they are driven by basic instincts—the need to find food, to avoid predators, and to reproduce. These requirements have driven the evolution of a range of body shapes and colors.

Fish are the world's most numerous vertebrates, both in terms of species and living beings. To date, some 28,000 different species have been identified and named—more than all of the amphibians, reptiles, birds, and mammals in the world put together.

Given that 70 percent of the Earth's surface is covered by water, it is perhaps not surprising that there is such a vast and mind-boggling variety of fish and aquatic creatures that live within it. A remarkably large proportion of this enormous category of wildlife spends its life in fresh water. Being more easily accessible to us than their ocean-going relatives, freshwater fish have been more closely studied and are better understood. Even so, new species continue to be discovered every year.

The following pages highlight the fascinating variety of fish and creatures that dwell within North American fresh waters and oceans, with detailed discussions on evolution, anatomy, behavior, reproduction, senses, diet, and habitats.

Left: A kelp bass swimming through the kelp off Catalina Island, south of the Californian coastline in the Pacific Ocean.

EVOLUTION

The story of life began in the sea. Fish are the most ancient vertebrates on Earth, and developed much earlier than land creatures. All other vertebrates—amphibians, reptiles, birds, and mammals, including our own species—can trace their ancestry back to fish.

When the first amphibians pulled themselves out of the water onto land, the world's seas and freshwater habitats were already bursting with fish. All three of the major fish groups—jawless, cartilaginous, and bony fish—had evolved long before this momentous event happened.

Fish themselves had evolved from more primitive animals known as "cephalochordates." These weird-looking creatures represent a link between invertebrates and vertebrates, and are given a subphylum of their own in animal classification. Before the first fish appeared, cephalochordates were the most complex creatures on the planet. They lacked the bones that would later define fish and other vertebrates, but they had many of the other characteristics that we now associate with these creatures.

Above: The whale shark (Rhincodon typus) *is a plankton feeder and the world's largest living fish. Like all sharks, it has a skeleton of cartilage rather than bone.*

Below: The fossilized remains of Pterichthyodes, *an armored placoderm fish that swam in the planet's oceans around 370 million years ago.*

Below: Dunkleosteus *was the largest of all the placoderms—some specimens grew as long as a bus. A fearsome predator, it included other fish in its diet.*

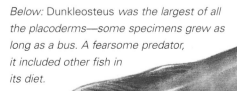

Like vertebrates, the cephalochordates had a spinal cord and V-shaped bundles of muscles along their flanks—features that had never existed in any animals before them. Cephalochordates did not need to move much to find food, but when under attack they were capable of a sudden burst of speed. They used bundled muscles to sweep their flattened tails from side to side, which would drive them through the water, like fish today.

A few cephalochordates still exist today. One group, the lancelets, look very similar to the creatures that gave rise to the first ancient fish. Lancelets are filter feeders that survive by sifting plankton from the water, and it is thought that the cephalochordate ancestors of fish lived in a similar way.

Well protected

With such a streamlined design, the next stage in fish evolution seems almost a backward step. The first true fish were covered in heavy body armor, which limited their ability to swim much at all. Rather than darting through the water, these creatures were much more plodding and deliberate in the way that they moved. Unlike most modern fish, they lacked fins, but they had retained the cephalochordates' flattened, flexible tail, albeit covered with thick, protective scales. When they did lift themselves up from the bottom and swim along slowly, it was by sweeping their tails from side to side as their ancestors had done.

These early armored fish were the first animals on Earth to have bones. While the cephalochordates had a flexible quill-like structure to protect their spinal cord, these first fish had true vertebrae. Other bony elements in their body structure included a simple skull, which surrounded the brain. To begin with, however, there were still no jaws or teeth. The earliest armored fish, which lived in the seas around 450 million years ago, were like underwater vacuum cleaners, feeding on detritus that they sucked up from the bottom.

Perhaps surprisingly, considering their abundance today, fish were not an instant success. For the first 40 million years after they appeared, they remained relatively rare, making up only a small proportion of all the creatures that lived in the world's oceans and freshwater habitats. The restricting factor was almost certainly the fact that they still lacked jaws. This limited their options when it came to feeding—the jawless fish that survive today are all either detritus feeders, scavengers, or parasites on other fish.

As the eons passed, the jawless fish did diversify a little in shape but they never grew very large. Few of them reached more than 8in (20cm) long. These fish must have been targets for the large invertebrate predators that existed at that time, since they all retained their body armor.

Vertebrates get bite

Around 400 million years ago, a new group of fish appeared, the "placoderms." Outwardly they looked very similar to the armored fish that had gone before them, but they differed in one important respect—they had jaws. The evolution of jaws gave the opportunity for these fish to expand and diversify. Now they were able to hunt. Although the placoderms only existed for around 40 million years, in that time they came to dominate all of the world's aquatic habitats. A few of them grew into absolute monsters, unlike anything that had been seen on the planet before. Among the last of the placoderms was a particularly famous giant: *Dunkleosteus* (*see* opposite page), a huge predator that grew up to 33ft (10m) long. Although its jaws lacked true teeth, they had fearsome shearing edges, which could slice through the body of almost any prey with ease.

A tale with no end

Evolution is a process that continues today. In the future, the world will see new species of fish appear and then become extinct, just as they have in the past.

Many of the fish that are living on Earth today evolved fairly recently—often in response to geographical changes. The cichlids of Africa's Rift Valley lakes, for example, sprang up in the past 12 million years, after the lakes themselves had become cut off from the sea. A few ancestral species, which made their way up the rivers that flowed from the lakes, found them largely uninhabited. These pioneering fish then quickly evolved into new species to fill the many vacant niches, resulting in the great variety of cichlids that live in the lakes today.

Above: All of the cichlids pictured here are from Lake Tanganyika. This is a young humphead (Cyphotilapia frontosa).

Above: The pearly shelldweller (Lamprologus meleagris) lays its eggs in empty snail shells.

Below: A male yellowtail slender cichlid (Cyprichromis leptosoma). The female is much less colorful.

Below: The convict julie (Julidochromis regani), or sardine cichlid, is a popular aquarium fish.

Living in the waters alongside the placoderms were schools of smaller fish from another group, known as the "acanthodians." These creatures looked much more like most of the fish we know today. They had scaly, rather than armored, bodies and they also had proper fins. These were supported by long spines and could be raised or lowered at will. More importantly, the acanthodians had teeth. Unlike the majority of fish that had gone before them, they swam in open water, rather than spending most of their lives on the bottom. They are the earliest known fish to have possessed the lateral line sensory organ that is able to detect slight disturbances in the surrounding water.

Scientists are divided over the exact position of the acanthodians in the evolutionary scheme of things. Some believe that they were the direct ancestors of the bony fish, which today make up the vast majority of fish species. Others place them in the evolutionary line leading to the cartilaginous fish, which include modern sharks and rays.

Certainly, both bony fish and cartilaginous fish appeared soon after the first acanthodians. Although the acanthodians had all died out by the end of the Permian period, 245 million years ago, these other fish lived on. Bony fish were the more successful in terms of numbers, but it was the cartilaginous fish that would become the dominant predators, evolving species that would become the largest fish on Earth, no doubt a factor in their success. Today, of course, they include the sharks and rays—groups that are widespread in the oceans but less common in fresh water.

CLASSIFICATION

We tend to think of fish as a homogeneous mass, a huge group of animals that share characteristics that separate them from other vertebrates. However, when scientists look at fish, they see them in terms of four very different groups.

Fish comprise four vertebrate classes: Actinopterygii (ray-finned fish), Chondrichthyes (cartilaginous fish, such as sharks), Cephalaspidomorphi (lampreys and lamperns), and Pteraspidomorphi (hagfish). Each of the other four main vertebrate groups —amphibians, reptiles, birds and mammals—has a class of its own. In other words, scientists consider ray-finned fish and cartilaginous fish to be as different from one another as reptiles are from birds.

Ray-finned fish

The vast majority of freshwater fish belong to the class Actinopterygii, as, indeed, do most marine fish species. These fish are defined by the characteristic in their common name— all of their fins are supported by rays, which are not unlike fingers. This enables them to be opened or folded at will. In addition, the fins of most ray-finned fish have a joint where they meet the body, allowing them to be spread outward or held tight against

Above: The pygmy sunfish (Belonesox belizanus) is a ray-finned bony fish, and belongs to the cichlid family.

the sides. Having such flexible fins is a great advantage and has served these fish well. As well as improving maneuverability in the water, it allows them to turn their fins to different functions. Some ray-finned fish, for example, use their fins for display.

Most of the world's ray-finned fish, and indeed most North American fish, belong to the infraclass Teleostei (an infraclass is subordinate to a subclass but superior to an order or a superorder). Better known as the bony fish, this group contains the bulk of the fish species most of us will encounter in our lives. They are not only the most common fish but also the ones most likely to end up on our plates. Cod, haddock, tuna, salmon and trout are all teleosts.

The infraclass Teleostei is split into 13 superorders, 8 of which contain freshwater species. The largest of the superorders is Acanthopterygii, which includes all of the perchlike fish. Many members of this superorder are marine, such as the mackerel, mullet, and seahorse. However, there is also a huge number of freshwater families. Those with North American members include the sticklebacks and the true perches.

Above: Common names can be confusing. The pike topminnow (Belonesox belizanus) is a member of the superorder Atherinomorpha. True pike are grouped with other Protacanthopterygii.

Another large superorder of teleosts is Clupeomorpha. Most of the families in this group are marine: those with American members include Clupeidae, which includes the herrings, sardines and shads. As these examples might suggest, clupeomorph fish are important food fish for humans. Many North American people make their livelihoods from catching or selling species from this group.

Freshwater clupeomorph fish are much less numerous, and most of those species that do exist spend at least some of their life in the sea. This fact is also true of most eels, which make up the teleost superorder Elopomorpha. There is only one true eel species in North America, the American eel (*Anguilla rostrata*). This species lives in fresh water but swims to the ocean in order to spawn.

Other teleost superorders are widespread, but only some of them have species that live in or around Great Britain. The second largest (after Acanthopterygii), and perhaps most significant to us, is the superorder Ostariophysi. This contains all of the world's catfish, including the wels (*Silurus glanis*), as well as all of the so called carp-like fish. This latter group contains many of North America's

*Above: The common dogfish (*Scyliorhinus canicula*) is a type of small shark. Like all sharks it has a skeleton made of cartilage and belongs to the class Chondrichthyes.*

freshwater fish species. Carp-like fish include chub, dace, roach, and minnows, as well as carp themselves. The other major freshwater superorder in North America is Protacanthopterygii. It contains all of the world's trout and salmon, and the predatory pikes.

Of the entirely marine teleost superorders with North American representatives, perhaps the most familiar is Paracanthopterygii. This superorder contains the family Gadidae, which includes cod, haddock, and plaice. It also contains the anglerfish, deep sea hunters that lure their prey toward them, and are themselves caught by humans for sale in restaurants as "monkfish."

Cartilaginous fish

While bony fish make up the vast majority of North American species, our largest fish come from another group, Chondrichthyes. Members of this class of animals are more commonly known as "cartilaginous fish." This name refers to the fact that their skeletons are made of cartilage rather

than bone. Cartilaginous fish include all of the world's sharks and rays. The vast majority of its members are marine, and every one of the American species is found in sea water. North America's cartilaginous fish range from rays such as the common skate (*Raja batis*) and small sharks like the common dogfish (*Scyliorhinus canicula*), sold in restaurants as "rock salmon," to true giants like the basking shark (*Cetorhinus maximus*), the second biggest fish in the whole world.

Jawless fish

The other two classes of fish are the most primitive and ancient, in evolutionary terms. Although they have been on Earth longer than either bony or cartilaginous fish, they have far fewer living members. The two classes are often lumped together under the umbrella of the common name, "jawless fish." This name refers to the fact that they lack true jaws. Instead they have a circular, almost sucker-like mouth, often surrounded by numerous small, sharp teeth. North America's jawless fishes include the river lamprey (*Lampetra fluviatilis*) and brook lamprey (*Lampetra planeri*), and the hagfish, which are marine species.

Below: Lampreys belong to the class Cephalaspidomorphi, one of two classes of jawless fish. As this picture shows, while they might lack jaws, they often have formidable teeth.

ANATOMY

Many people are unsure exactly how fish are defined. Confusingly, some animals are called fish but are not fish at all—starfish and cuttlefish are just two examples—so it is useful to know what physical features set fish apart from other animals.

Fish are defined by certain physical characteristics. First and foremost, they are vertebrates—animals with backbones. Other vertebrates include mammals, reptiles, amphibians, and birds. Fish differ from these animals in having fins rather than legs, and gills that they use to extract oxygen from the water. Some mammals, such as dolphins and whales, look like fish and are often confused with them. However, unlike dolphins and whales, fish can breathe underwater and are not forced to return to the surface

Below: Freshwater tilapia (Oreochromis), *caught for food and packed in ice. For many people, this is the only way fish are seen.*

every so often to fill their lungs with air. (Some fish gulp air to supplement the oxygen obtained from the water through their gills, but none have true lungs.)

Fins and scales

One external feature all fish have in common is fins. These originally evolved for locomotion, to drive fish along and help them control their position in the water. In some species, however, they have since taken on additional roles. Some fish use the supporting spines of their fins for defense, for example. Many more use their fins like flags for display.

Most fish have seven fins: four paired and three single fins. The paired fins are the pectoral fins, which emerge on either side of the body just behind the head, and the pelvic fins, which emerge from the underside a little farther back. Directly behind the pelvic fins is the single anal fin. Made famous by the film *Jaws*, the dorsal fin is probably the best known fin on a fish. As its name suggests, it emerges from the back. The seventh fin is the

Breathing apparatus

All fish have gills, which they use to remove oxygen from water. Gills are similar to lungs in that they have a very large surface area and many tiny capillaries for absorbing oxygen into the blood.

Below: In beluga and starred sturgeon (Huso huso *and* Acipenser stellatus), *the gill slits, through which oxygen-rich water passes, can be clearly seen.*

caudal fin, sometimes known as the tail fin. It is usually split into two lobes, although it may have a rounded or straight rear edge. Generally, fish with crescent-shaped or strongly forked caudal fins tend to be fast swimmers. Those fish with rounded or straight rear fins are slower and normally live in still or very slow-moving waters.

The body plan of bony fish

This is a generalized anatomy of a bony fish. A vast range of body shapes and fin arrangements exist.

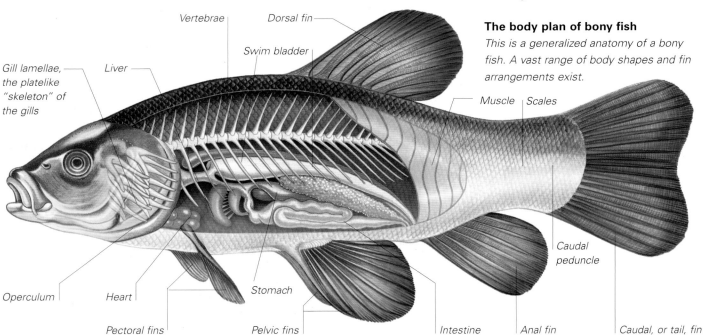

Vertebrae | Dorsal fin

Swim bladder

Gill lamellae, the platelike "skeleton" of the gills | Liver

Muscle | Scales

Caudal peduncle

Operculum | Heart

Pectoral fins | Stomach | Pelvic fins | Intestine | Anal fin | Caudal, or tail, fin

Fish and fin shapes

Above: Large dorsal fin of Leopard sailfin pleco catfish (Glyptoperichthys gibbiceps).

Below: The beautiful fins of the Red melon discus (Symphysodon aequifasciata).

Above: Long, feathery fins of the Siamese fighting fish (Betta splendens).

Below: A blackear shark catfish (Pangasius larnaudii) *has a triangular dorsal fin.*

Above: The Common chub (Leuciscus cephalus) *has a small dorsal fin.*

Below: Electric eel (Electrophorus electricus) *has a fin that extends to the tail.*

While seven fins is the norm, it is far from the rule. Some fish have a small eighth fin—called the adipose—between their dorsal fin and caudal fin. Others lack some of the fins or have evolved in such a way that their fins have merged together. Eels are a good example. Although they have paired pectoral fins, they lack pelvic fins, and their dorsal, anal, and caudal fins have grown together into a single long strip.

The vast majority of fish swim by using their caudal fin. This is swept from side to side, unlike the tail flukes of a dolphin or whale, which move up and down. A few fish, such as rays, move by means of their pelvic fins, but in most fish, these are used to help change direction or are sculled to maintain the fish's position in the water. The dorsal fin and anal fin help to keep fish stable and upright as they swim along. These are the fins most often elaborated for display.

All fish have fins and the majority have scales. The scales of sharks and rays (cartilaginous fish) are hard and toothlike. They jut from the skin, giving it a rough texture. Most bony fish have smoother scales, which grow from the outer layer of the skin. These scales have either rounded or comb-shaped rear edges and are only loosely attached. A few fish, such as the armored catfish, have bony plates (scutes) in place of scales. These offer extra protection from predators.

Internal organs

The bulk of a fish's body is made up of muscle. These slabs of flesh are the fillets we cook and eat. Beneath the muscle the internal organs are not dissimilar to our own. The main difference is the lack of lungs and the presence of a swim bladder. This is an impermeable sac filled with gas, used by fish to control their buoyancy. The amount of gas it holds is increased or reduced, by introducing oxygen from the blood vessels surrounding it, or by absorbing oxygen back into the blood. This feature is unique to bony fish and has been lost by a few bottom-dwelling groups, such as the gobies. Sharks, rays, and the jawless lampreys lack this organ completely and sink to the bottom as soon as they stop swimming.

Anatomically speaking, freshwater fish do not differ all that much from their cousins in the sea. Many families have both marine and freshwater representatives. There are even some species that travel between the sea and fresh water. However, fish that are able to do this are rare. Fish have skin that is slightly permeable, and in fresh water their bodies are constantly soaking up water, due to the level of dissolved salts in their blood being higher than in their surroundings. To avoid expanding and bursting, freshwater fish have to continually excrete water through their urine and gills—up to ten times their body weight in a single day. Marine fish have the opposite problem. In the sea, they lose water from their bodies through their skins to the surroundings, since dissolved salt levels here are higher than in their blood. To survive, marine fish have to continually drink and excrete excess salt.

One peculiarity to some freshwater fish is the presence of the labyrinth organ, which is absent from all marine fish. It is located near the gills and is made up of rosette-shaped plates full of blood vessels. The vessels let fish absorb oxygen from gulped air.

MOVEMENT

When it comes to moving around, the physical properties of water can be a mixed blessing.
The density of water is about 800 times that of air, meaning that it offers plenty of support.
However, pushing through it requires a lot of energy—swimming is hard work!

Fish swim using symmetrical blocks of muscles arranged in a repeating pattern along either side of the body. This pattern of repetition, known as "metamerism," was inherited from the common ancestor of all bony, cartilaginous, and jawless fish, and is more obvious in some species than in others. Because a fish's body is supported by the noncompressible backbone, contraction of the muscles on either side causes it to flex. If the muscles on opposite sides of the trunk contract alternately, the body performs a side-to-side wiggle, pushing against the surrounding water, and thus, propelling the fish forward. The addition of median fins (the dorsal caudal and anal fins) increases thrust to the animal's movement and also adds stability.

Types of swimming

In long-bodied fish, such as eels, swimming involves the side-to-side undulations of the whole body, a form of swimming known as "anguillaform." The undulations are greatest toward the tail end, which generates considerable turbulence, making this an energetically expensive means of moving from place to place. Turbulence is reduced by a tapering body shape and the addition of a tail fin. The fin also increases the surface area available to generate propulsion.

Modes of swimming

The carangiform mode (shown right) is a powerful method of swimming adopted by many fish, including jacks, salmon, and snappers. These fish swim using their trunk muscles, but most of the movement is in the rear half of the body, while the head remains steady (1). The tail undulates in one direction, then snaps back (2), propelling the fish forward. The tail then undulates toward the opposite side, to repeat the process.

A modified and less powerful version of carangiform swimming is often described as "oscillatory." This is where contractions of the trunk muscle cause the body to flick from side to side (3), passing through an S-shaped wave (4).

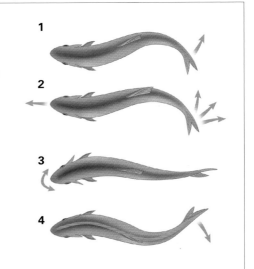

The most energy-efficient mode of swimming is that adopted by members of the family Carangidae, a group that includes jacks, pompanos, and their kin. With these marine and brackish-water fish, side-to-side movements are restricted to the rear end of the fish only, and a large tail fin serves to reduce turbulence and increase efficiency. When this type of swimming technique is adopted, the head remains still, helping to stabilize the fish's vision and maintain a steady direction.

A few fish use just their fins for propulsion. Examples of fish that use this swimming technique include the opah, or moonfish (*Lampris regius*), which sculls with its pectoral fins, or the batfish, which uses its pectoral and pelvic

Above: The rainbow runner (Elagatis bipinnulata), found in warm and tropical seas, swims in the carangiform style.

fins to pull itself along the sea floor. Seahorses and oarfish swim with the body held vertically in the water, so that the dorsal fin is at the back— wavelike ripples running along the dorsal fringe and fanning movements of the pectoral fins are enough to propel the fish very slowly forward.

Buoyancy

The lifting force exerted by water on an object less dense than itself is known as "buoyancy." Objects that are less dense than water are positively buoyant, and they float or rise toward

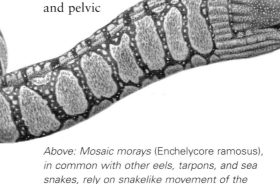

Above: Mosaic morays (Enchelycore ramosus), in common with other eels, tarpons, and sea snakes, rely on snakelike movement of the whole body to propel themselves forward.

the surface. Objects that weigh more than their equivalent volume of water are negatively buoyant. They will sink.

The body of a fish contains several types of dense tissue, such as muscle and bone, that are negatively buoyant. For species that make a living close to the sea floor, this is an advantage—they are able to save energy simply by letting gravity take effect, and many will spend long periods resting on the bottom. They are able to raise themselves up into the water when necessary by expending energy and swimming. For fish that live in very deep water, where food is scarce, the ability to save energy is a crucial survival adaptation.

The swim bladder

However, space is limited on the ocean floor, especially compared with the vastness of the open ocean, and so there can be advantages to life in mid-water. Most pelagic bony fish have a specialized buoyancy organ, the swim bladder, which helps reduce the energy required to maintain a constant depth.

The swim bladder is a large, gas-filled chamber whose volume can be adjusted so that the fish achieves neutral buoyancy and so can "hang" stationary in mid water. Gas can pass in and out of the bladder via a direct connection with the outside (by the esophagus), or it can be removed by absorption into the bloodstream through a permeable area of the wall lining. Alternatively, the bladder can be inflated by secretion of gas from a

Above: A peacock flounder (Bothus lunatus) *rests on coral. This flounder favors reefs as a habitat, although it is often difficult to see as it may be partially buried in sand.*

Below: The batfish (Ephippidae) *moves from place to place using its pelvic and pectoral fins to effectively "crawl" along the ocean floor.*

Above: Fast-swimming schools, such as these needlefish (Platybelone argalus), *may swim in a diamond formation, taking advantage of the slipstream created by other individuals.*

Below: Seahorses, such as this long-snouted species (Hippocampus reidi), *use their dorsal fins to propel their body forward through the water. The tail is used to "moor" when at rest.*

gland, known as the *rete mirabilis*, associated with a specialized network of capillaries in animals.

One of the chief limitations of the system is that the volume of the bladder cannot be adjusted instantaneously. Thus, if the fish is brought suddenly to the surface—for example, on the end of a line—the abrupt decrease in

pressure causes the gas in the bladder to expand very rapidly, crushing other organs and sometimes rupturing the bladder itself. Once a swim bladder has overexpanded, the fish is so buoyant that it becomes unable to return to its preferred depth.

A few types of bony fish have given up on the swim bladder. For example, mackerel rely on speed and agility to hunt as well as to evade predators, and this means that sudden changes in pressure are part of their daily lives. Their oily muscles are positively buoyant, and this goes some way to compensating for the lack of a swim bladder, but even so, they must swim continuously in order to hold their position. They have also dispensed with any kind of pump to deliver water to the gills, relying solely on the flow of water generated by swimming.

Left: The bulge of the swim bladder can be seen in this map pufferfish (Arothon mappa).

SENSES

Fish, like all other creatures, rely completely on their senses to survive. Without them, they would be unable to detect danger or find food. Certain senses are more important to some fish than others. It all depends on where they live, what they eat, and when they are most active.

The senses that fish rely on are touch, smell and hearing. A fish's ability to sense what is around it includes an electrical sense—for a few species— or a line of receptors designed to pick up tiny movements in the water.

Touch

All fish possess the sense of touch. This sense is most developed in species that are nocturnal or live in murky water. The sense of touch is often enhanced by fleshy, whiskerlike projections known as barbels. These invariably grow from the head and are usually concentrated around the mouth. Several types of fish bear barbels, but they are most common and exaggerated among the catfish. Most of the members of this group are bottom feeders and many are nocturnal, so they use their barbels to locate prey. Catfish have become so successful at this mode of existence that they now dominate the murky bottoms of ponds, lakes, and rivers in many parts of the world—having quickly established themselves in most of the places where they have been introduced.

The electrical sense

Touch is the sense that we would naturally associate with navigation and locating objects in the dark. Some fish,

How the lateral line works
The lateral line is used to detect pressure changes in the water. Fish use it to detect the movement of others and to orient themselves in currents.

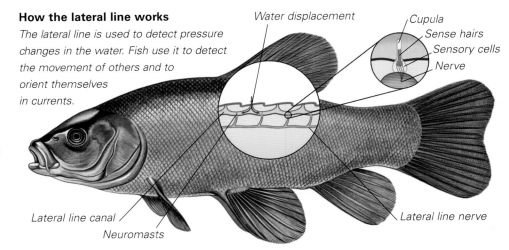

Water displacement — Cupula — Sense hairs — Sensory cells — Nerve

Lateral line canal / Neuromasts

Lateral line nerve

however, have extra senses that work in tandem with touch, or even replace it. One such sense is the electrical sense which is found in sharks and rays, as well as in some bony fish. This can be used to detect the muscular activity of other animals, even when they are buried beneath mud or sand. Rays use it to find prey hidden in the sediment. Other fish with this sense find it just as useful for detecting and avoiding predators in the darkness.

The electrical sense is unique to fish. A few species are able to use it to navigate and detect inanimate objects, as well as living ones. Fish can effectively "see" objects in the water around it, as any objects entering the electric field distort it and can be

Below: As its name suggests, the electric eel (Electrophorus electricus) *uses electricity both to sense prey and to stun it.*

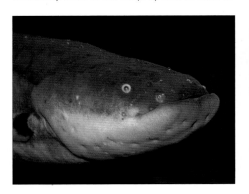

Below: The nocturnal redtailed catfish (Phractocephalus hemioliopterus) *uses its chin barbels to navigate the bottom.*

detected by the fish. Its electrical sense gives the fish a good idea of the shape and size as well as the distance away of the detected object.

The lateral line

Other fish have a more basic system for detecting things around them, based on the lateral line. This line is a series of tiny receptors, which usually run from the rear edge of the gill covers to the base of the tail. Each of these receptors contains microscopic, hairlike projections, much like those in the human inner ear. These are surrounded by a jellylike substance and are usually set at the bottom of a short canal or pit in the fish's skin. The lateral line picks up small movements in the water, so it can detect the presence of living things that might be out of view. It cannot detect inert objects, however, nor gauge the distance of moving objects from a fish.

The lateral line plays an important role in helping fish to sense the world around them. It is particularly useful for schooling fish, allowing individual fish to immediately judge and react to the movements of fish adjacent to them. This both helps avoid collisions and enables the synchronized movement displayed by fish shoals.

All fish use the lateral line to detect

movements in the water around them. Fish living in streams, rivers, and other areas of flowing water also use it to orient themselves so that they normally face into the current. This allows them to hold their position in the water and prevents them from being washed downstream.

A few species use the lateral line to detect prey. Killifish, which feed on insects and other invertebrates that fall into the water, use it to sense the ripples made by prey struggling on the surface. Blind cavefish have large concentrations of the receptors normally found in the lateral line located on their heads. These fish, living in absolute darkness, rely entirely on these mechanical receptors to detect and home in on prey.

Vision
The highly developed mechanical receptor system in blind cavefish is an evolutionary response to their inability to see. The ancestors of most cavefish had perfectly good vision and some species that have only evolved fairly recently still show the remnants of eyes. Vision is an important sense for most

---

Compensating for blindness
Eyes are useless in the pitch black of caves, and most cavefish have lost them completely. In their place, these fish have evolved an extreme sensitivity to movements in the water. The fronts of their heads are covered with the sensors normally confined to the lateral lines of fish. Cavefish use these sensors to find prey but cannot use them to navigate. Inanimate objects in their surroundings are sensed by touch.

Below: Like most cavefish, this species from Oman (Garra barreimiae barreimiae) has lost all trace of skin pigmentation.

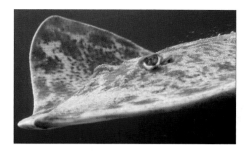

Above: Rays have eyes like turrets on the tops of their heads. They use their eyes mainly to alert them to potential danger, as they find their prey with touch and their electrical sense.

Below: Striped eel catfish (Plotosus lineatus) have barbels but combine their sense of touch with vision to find food.

fish, even those that are nocturnal or live in murky waters. In subterranean caves, darkness is complete, but in most other habitats there is always some light, even at night. Although bottom-living fish may rely on touch or other senses to find food, vision can warn them of danger. A shadow passing overhead is enough to alert most fish.

Vision is most vital for fish that live near the surface or in shallow waters. These species tend to rely on sight more than any other sense. For active predators in particular, the ability to see is indispensable. It is hard to imagine fish such as pike living long without eyes: for these precision hunters, accurate targeting and the ability to follow the movements of prey make the difference between catching it and going hungry. Plant-eating fish also rely on vision to locate food, as do most species that feed on invertebrates.

Smell and hearing
Being land-living creatures, we tend to think of smell as a sense that only works in air. However, fish can smell

---

Above: Salmon such as these chum salmon (Oncorhynchus keta) use their sense of smell to help them find their way back to their home rivers from the sea to build their nests and breed.

Below: Goldfish (Carassius auratus) are among the few fish known to use hearing to find food.

just as we can—the only difference is that they smell by detecting organic matter and other particles in water. It is known that some species use their sense of smell to help them find food. Sharks are famous for their ability to detect minute quantities of blood in the water. Piranhas have a similar ability. It is also possible that many freshwater fish use smell to help them find their way around. It is known that salmon use it to help them locate their home rivers when returning from the sea to breed. Every river has a unique signature odor that builds up as the water passes over rocks, sand, or mud on the bottom. This odor is imprinted in the brains of young salmon, and when they near the coast as adults, they sense it and follow it to the mouth of the river in which the salmon hatched.

Hearing in fish is poorly understood, but this sense is not well developed in most fish. A few species, however, can hear quite well—for example, the goldfish, which probably uses hearing to help find food.

BEHAVIOR

Compared with some creatures, such as mammals, the behavior of individual fish can appear quite simple. Certainly the imperatives that drive fish are few, and boil down to the need to eat, the need to avoid being eaten, and the need to reproduce. Of all these, finding food is the most pressing.

Fish, like all animals, must eat to live. For most, however, surviving is also a constant battle to avoid becoming meals themselves. It is these two imperatives that basically govern the behavior of all marine and freshwater fish.

Staying alive

One of the most common behavioral responses to the threat of predation is shoaling. By gathering in groups, fish make it harder for predators to pick them off. The majority of shoaling fish belong to species that live in open water, a place where it is virtually impossible to hide. These fish use the bodies of others for cover. A predator following one individual will often see it disappear into the mass and become distracted by the sudden appearance of

others. Additionally, many shoaling fish are colored so that their outlines seem to merge together. This makes it much harder for predators to target individuals. The other advantage of living in shoals is that they act as early warning systems. With so many pairs of eyes gathered together, predators are much more likely to be spotted before they are close enough to attack. For fish, there really is safety in numbers.

Not all fish try to avoid being eaten by shoaling. Many bottom-living fish rely on camouflage to avoid being seen in the first place. This tactic generally works as long as the fish in question keep still. Another common way of staying out of sight is to become nocturnal. Many freshwater fish hide beneath rocks or in underwater crevices by day and only emerge at

Fish that breathe air

A few types of freshwater fish gulp air to supplement their oxygen intake. Most of these species inhabit stagnant pools, swamps, or other habitats where the levels of dissolved oxygen are low. Gulping air also has another advantage—it allows some fish to cross land and find new homes. This ability is particularly useful in areas that are subject to drought, where pools often dry up or become overcrowded as they shrink under the heat of the sun.

Below: By gulping air, the tarpon (Megalops atlanticus) is able to live in oxygen-poor water, such as swamps.

night to feed. This tactic is particularly effective as a defense against visual predators such as birds. Of course, this makes these fish much harder for humans to spot too. As a result, most people are unaware of the wide variety of fish living in their local rivers and streams.

Finding food

Fish have evolved to feed on a wide range of organic matter, from detritus and plankton to other fish. Most fish spend a large part of their lives gathering food. Detritus feeders have to rummage through a lot of mud to find enough edible matter to live on. For fish that eat invertebrates, the most time-consuming part of feeding is finding their small prey. Plankton feeders are surrounded by their food—the tiny animals and algae that live in the water—but gathering and filtering

Above: Like other schooling clupeids, Pilchards (Sardina pilchardus) move in schools of similarly sized and aged fish.

Below: A plaice (Pleuronectes platessa) relies on its incredible camouflage and ability to lie perfectly still on the sea bed for defense against predators.

Above: Pike (Esox lucius) stalk their prey from behind reeds. They stay incredibly still, then launch their ambush at speed.

Below: Here a parasitic sea lamprey (Petromyzon marinus) can be seen sucking the blood from a salmon as the host fish leaps upstream to spawn.

out enough of these to make a meal takes time. Plant-eating fish, like plankton eaters, have little trouble finding food but need to eat a lot of it, as plants and algae are relatively low in nutrients. The only fish that spend relatively short periods feeding or finding food are the larger predators. That said, many of these spend long periods lying in wait for prey.

Breeding behavior

The behavior of fish within species is fairly uncomplicated and predictable, but across the group as a whole it is surprisingly varied. Nowhere is this more true than in the breeding behavior of freshwater fish.

The vast majority of ocean fish scatter their eggs and sperm together in open water and then leave the fertilized eggs to develop and hatch on their own. This type of breeding behavior is also seen in some freshwater fish, particularly shoaling species that live in lakes and other large areas of open water, but many others put a great deal more effort into the process of reproduction.

Many freshwater fish build nests. These vary from simple scrapes in the sand or gravel, such as the redds made by salmon and trout, to far more complex constructions. Three-spined sticklebacks, for instance (*Gasterosteus aculeatus*) form tube-shaped nests from algae. These are built by the males, which entice females in to lay. As soon as the eggs have been laid and fertilized, the males guard them closely until they hatch. The males also fan the eggs to keep them well-supplied with oxygen.

Below: An eel feeds on a worm in a river. Young eels swim upstream until they eventually reach the sea, where they spawn.

Above: After returning from the sea, sockeye salmon (Oncorhynchus nerka) *breed in fresh water.*

Below: A female sockeye salmon uses her fins to excavate her nest, or redd.

Other freshwater fish use natural crevices or gaps beneath rocks as nests in which to lay their eggs. Again, the eggs are often guarded and fanned until hatching. Nest-building fish that do not guard their eggs tend to hide them by covering them with sediment.

Perhaps the most unusual of all nests are the bubble nests built by some species of freshwater fish. These are formed from bubbles of oral mucus, which float at the surface like rafts. Females lay their eggs, which are buoyant, on the undersides of these rafts; they are then guarded by the male (or occasionally by both parents).

A few freshwater fish have dispensed with nests altogether and instead brood their eggs and their young in their mouths. This behavior is most common among cichlids. The advantages in terms of protecting developing offspring from predators are obvious, but the disadvantage is that, while brooding, these fish are unable to eat.

In the ocean, seahorses and pipefish take care of their eggs. Once the eggs have been laid, they are attached to a brood pad on the male's body. The male then carries them around until they hatch.

Not all fish lay eggs—a few species give birth to live young. Like mouth brooding, this strategy improves the chances of the young surviving to adulthood. Live young are much larger than eggs, however, so fewer can be produced in a season.

Many fish migrate in order to breed. This is particularly true of species that live in rivers. Breeding migrations tend to be upstream, with eggs being laid nearer the headwaters. As the eggs hatch and the young grow, they gradually move downriver, until they are themselves big enough to breed. This separation between young and mature fish ensures that there is little competition between adults and fry for food, and also avoids cannibalization.

Some fish spend part of their lives in fresh water and other parts in the sea. Salmon migrate between salt and fresh water, entering rivers and swimming upstream to lay their eggs.

FEEDING

Feeding is an essential part of day-to-day life for most fish species. Food webs can be enormously complex and feeding strategies vary greatly, with one thing assured—no species is exempt from the possibility of one day becoming food for other predatory or scavenging animals.

For fish, the endless search for food is expressed in a variety of ways; some are predators, others are prey, while some are herbivores or filter feeders.

The digestive process in fish begins in the mouth, the size and positioning of which is variable between species. Fish that engulf large prey or are active hunters usually have a mouth that opens at the front, bottom feeders have an underslung mouth, and those that pluck small prey from the surface or lie on the bottom to attack prey passing above have a mouth directed upward.

The mouth and jaws of some species are highly modified. The tiny tubular mouth of the pipefish family (Syngnathidae) opens at the tip of a

Cleaning stations

Several groups of bony fish have become specialized "cleaners." They are adapted to feed only on the small external parasites that attach themselves to the bodies of other fish. A heavy load of parasites can place a severe strain on the body of a host, so the ministrations of cleaner fish can be highly beneficial. In fact, many large fish, even voracious predators, will wait in line for this marine valet service. Cleaners and their "clients" develop an extraordinary level of mutual trust—the cleaners venturing close to jaws than could snap them up in an instant, and the client waiting patiently while the cleaner nibbles away at gills and other vulnerable body parts.

Below: An Argus grouper (Cephalopholis argus) *being cleaned by a much smaller cleaner wrasse* (Labroides *species*).

narrow snout, working like a pipette to suck up small items of food from small crevices. At the other end of the spectrum, the gulper eel (*Eurypharynx pelecanoides*) engulfs small prey along with large volumes of water. Most fish that hunt larger prey have smaller but more powerful jaws, typically lined with sharp teeth.

These teeth might be excellent for snagging prey and preventing its escape, but they are not much use for cutting it up—thus the scariest-looking fish often swallow their prey whole. Often teeth of this sort flex toward the back of the throat to ease the inward passage of prey and prevent it from escaping. Teeth used for slicing and dicing, like those of sharks, which bite large prey into chunks, need to be more rigid and robust.

Herbivores

A vegetarian diet is rare among fish. Virtually all species eat other animals, especially during the early stages of life, when a large intake of protein is required. However, some species do become essentially herbivorous later on

Above: The basking shark (Cetorhinus maximus) *is the second-largest fish in the world after the whale shark. It feeds by swimming through clouds of plankton and sifting them out of the water with its sieve-like gill rakers.*

in life. Where insects or other invertebrates are scarce, adult carp (*Cyprinus carpio*) can survive entirely on a diet of plant matter, for instance. Among sea fish, a vegetarian diet is more common in the tropics, where warm water and long hours of bright sunlight permit plentiful growth of marine plant material.

Filter feeding

Bony fish have four pairs of gills located within the pharynx, or "throat." In filter feeding species, the bony arches that support the gills also bear long, slender rakers—rigid structures that project inward, forming a sort of sieve through which water passing in via the mouth and out through the gill slits is strained. The size of food taken varies with the species, from algae to baby fish, squid, and shrimps.

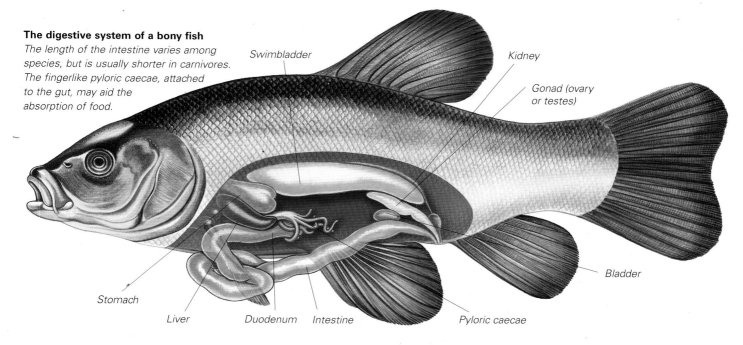

The digestive system of a bony fish
The length of the intestine varies among species, but is usually shorter in carnivores. The fingerlike pyloric caecae, attached to the gut, may aid the absorption of food.

Swimbladder

Kidney

Gonad (ovary or testes)

Bladder

Stomach

Liver

Duodenum

Intestine

Pyloric caecae

Predators

Most fish are hunters. Zooplankton and communities of small, bottom-dwelling invertebrates, including worms, molluscs, and crustaceans, are an important source of food, as are fish fry. Hunting techniques among predatory fish vary from opportunistic snapping at any small passing animals to lie-in-wait ambush techniques.

Many ambush predators are very well camouflaged—the disguises of stonefish (order Scorpaeniformes) can fool the sharpest eyes. The ambush is taken a step further by species of anglerfish (order Lophiiformes), which not only exhibit perfect camouflage, but also draw prey near with a food-like lure dangling from their head as if from a fishing line.

Ambush predators often have a relatively large mouth—when opened, prey is carried in with the inrushing water. Other forms of weaponry, such as stings or electric shocks, may also be used by fish for defense against predators larger than themselves.

Parasites

There are numerous interesting twists on the predatory theme in the fish world. A number of fish are themselves parasitic—they live in close association with their prey, feeding off them without damaging them. The key to being a successful parasite is to avoid

killing the host—once dead, it is of limited use, but kept alive it may provide a source of sustenance for life. Some parasites are better adapted to this than others. For example, the carapid cucumberfish lives within the body of a sea cucumber, feeding off the tissues of the respiratory and reproductive systems, which keep

Above: The dogfish can use its dorsal spines to pierce and poison a predator.

Below: Carp are onmivorous, and scour the bed for fungi, plants, crustaceans, and worms.

regenerating, providing an endless source of food. Not all parasites commit to physically living on a single host—many simply swim to their victim, take a single bite and swim away. Often they improve their chances of getting close enough by impersonating harmless or benign species, especially cleaners (*see* box opposite).

Above: The pipefish can probe into crevices and suck up food with its tubular mouth.

Below: The fangtooth targets squid and other types of fish with its huge, sharp teeth.

REPRODUCTION

*Individual fish share their habitats with many others, and all must find a way to maximize their
own success and survival among the competitors, predators, and potential mates. Most breeds of fish
are egg layers, but a few species give birth to live young.*

Reproduction in fish is diverse, with gender differences often less defined than in mammals, and with unique features such as semelparity (*see* opposite) also affecting the way that they breed.

Bony fish employ a large variety of breeding strategies. Often zoologists talk of oviparity (egg laying) versus viviparity (live bearing). Female oviparous fish produce eggs, which they release into the water, where they are fertilized by sperm from the male. In most cases, the numbers of eggs involved are extremely large. Viviparity is far less common, and only about one in every 30 families of fish have true live-bearing species in which mating occurs and embryos develop inside the female, nourished by way of a connection to the mother.

Between these two apparently distinct strategies there is a large gray area, known as "ovoviviparity," that leads to some degree of confusion. Ovoviviparity is where a female fish produces eggs that are fertilized and hatch internally, so that the mother gives birth to live young at any stage from early larvae to fully formed, sexually mature offspring.

Parental types
As well as physiological differences in reproductive biology, fish also exhibit a striking variety of behaviors and strategies, designed to maximize their chances of successful breeding. These can be grouped into three main types, or guilds, based on how the parent fish treat their offspring. These types are non-guarders, guarders, and bearers.

Non-guarders are oviparous. They produce eggs and sperm, either in a single large spawning or several smaller sessions, and leave nature to take its course. In some cases, the eggs are released in open water as part of a mass spawning, while in others they are shed above a specially selected substratum—for example, gravel or weed. In both cases, the chances of any single fertilized egg developing to adulthood is tiny, so non-guarders tend to produce eggs in vast numbers.

The eggs of species that show some substratum selectivity may have a slightly improved chance of survival, and may thus be produced in slightly smaller numbers than those that are simply released to the mercy of the prevailing current.

Guarders are also oviparous, but they tend to produce fewer eggs and therefore take rather more care of them, sticking around and defending the eggs, which are typically laid in a nest or adhesive mass, to be guarded externally. Sticklebacks are one group of freshwater species that exhibit this breeding strategy.

Above: A male bullhead (Cotis gobis) *watches over its eggs, which are anchored to a nest.*

Bearers may be oviparous, viviparous or ovoviviparous, but in all examples the offspring are carried with one of the parents as they develop—either as eggs or as larvae. In oviparous bearers, the female lays eggs, but they are then gathered up into the mouth of one of the parents, who holds them there until they hatch.

Males and females
Among mammals, the differences between sexes usually seem clear cut. The distinction is often less definitive in fish, and hermaphroditism—where both male and female sex organs develop within the same individual—is common.

In most of these instances, fish are sequential hermaphrodites—meaning they start life as one gender and then at a later stage switch to the other.

Below: The male yellowhead jawfish (Opistognathus aurifrons), *an oviparous bearer, broods hundreds of eggs in its mouth.*

Below: Free-swimming larvae mingle with eggs that have not yet hatched in this school of planktonic life.

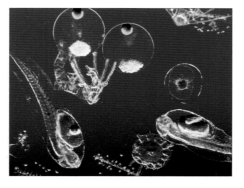

Schooling

A "school" is the term used for a group of similar-sized fish that move in a coordinated manner, always swimming in the same direction and reacting almost as one. There is no leader. Members of a school use sight and the lateral line sense to stay together.

There are several benefits to be gained from schooling behavior. First, there is never any difficulty finding a mate. Second, the members of a school may help each other to find food. Finally, and perhaps most important of all is the principle of "safety in numbers"—the greater the numbers, the better the chance of members surviving an attack from predators, who may find it difficult to target and pick off individuals.

Of course, the system is not perfect—larger schools are conspicuous, and some hunters specialize in herding fish together into a dense bait ball that can be taken whole. But in general, as long as the school remains larger than the average predator's appetite, the benefits outweigh the risks.

Below: Very large schools may present predators with a formidable moving "wall."

respond physiologically to environmental conditions—the temperature, day length and lunar cycles, for example.

Some fish breed at any time of year. These tend to be species of the warm tropics, where conditions remain relatively constant year round, and so no season is particularly favorable. The same is true of deep-sea habitats, which are beyond the influence of surface temperatures and day length. It is thought that many deep-sea species are year-round breeders, though details of this are rarely understood in full.

Larvae protection strategies

Fish larvae are highly vulnerable to predation, but most have developed at least some adaptations that help reduce the risk of being eaten.

Some larvae, for example, are almost transparent, making them hard to see. Many have large spines or filaments that make them difficult for other small animals to swallow, while others grow exceptionally fast in order to minimize the time they spend at risk from predators of a certain size. Very often, schools of larvae live in different locations or at different depths to adults of their own species, thus reducing the risk of cannibalism when the latter feeds on small organisms.

Below: The characteristic flat, oval shape of this flounder is easy to identify in the advanced larval state.

For example, some gobies start out as males and later change into females. This makes physiological sense because sperm are relatively cheap and easy to produce, even for small fish, whereas eggs require much more investment, something that is more readily afforded by large individuals.

But there can also be a sound ecological advantage to working the other way around—many wrasses and sea basses (families Labridae and Serranidae) begin life as females and become males only when they have grown sufficiently large to maintain control of a territory or a harem. Synchronous hermaphrodism, where a fish produces both female and male gametes that can function at the same time, is less common, but in species such as tripodfish this may allow individuals to self-fertilize.

Semelparity

For some fish, breeding is a once-in-a-lifetime event. These species are called semelparous, and they include eels, roughies and some salmonids, adults of which invest all their available body resources in producing large numbers of high-quality eggs to ensure a good chance of survival for their young. Spawning leaves the adults drastically weakened and with quite literally nothing more to live for.

Seasonality

Most fish species of temperate seas and freshwater habitats are seasonal breeders—in other words, they come into breeding condition at much the same time each year. Seasonality is regulated by hormones—chemicals released into the blood by glands, such as the hypothalamus and pituitary—which allow the fish to

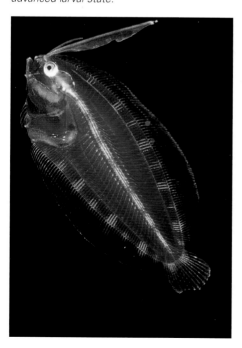

ENVIRONMENTS

Fish are the most widespread and numerous vertebrates on Earth. Their watery realm covers around two-thirds of our planet. The vast majority of the world's fish live in the sea, the biggest of all natural habitats, but the freshwater world is home to a more specialized group of creatures.

New species of fish are being discovered and described all the time, both from marine and freshwater habitats. While the majority of fish live in the oceans, there are almost as many species in fresh water. Of the 28,000 known species of fish in the world today, 11,950 are confined to fresh water. Many of these species are unique to the rivers or lakes they live in.

Each body of fresh water is effectively an island, surrounded by land and cut off from other lakes and rivers. Just like islands, many of the creatures they are home to live in that area and nowhere else.

Ocean fish, in contrast, have fewer boundaries. With an average depth of just over two miles (three kilometers), the sea is a habitat in three dimensions, and fish living in it exist throughout the water column. In addition to that, every part of the ocean is linked to the rest. Unlike freshwater species, marine fish are not physically separated from one another; a species

Below: The creatures that inhabit shallow waters of the world's oceans are very different to those that live in the depths.

that occupies a particular niche on one side of an ocean is very likely to be found in a similar niche on the other side of the ocean.

This means that there are very few truly rare fish found in the oceans. Many freshwater fish, on the other hand, are much more vulnerable, simply because the ranges they inhabit are so comparatively small.

Although there are two main environments for fish—marine and fresh water—within these there are several different variations of watery habitats, to which fish have adapted, to benefit from and survive within.

Marine habitats

By their very nature, marine habitats tend not to exist in isolation as they are largely continuous. Seas and oceans often blend with each other in such a way that it can be difficult to say where one ends and the next begins. That said, many marine fish are only found in particular parts of the ocean. Some species live in the well-lit upper layers of the open ocean, for example, while others are found only in the deeper, darker waters.

Above: While some sea creatures spend their lives swimming in the sea, others, like this hermit crab, are found on the seabed.

Just as fish may be adapted for life in open water, so they may also be specialized for life on the bottom. In shallow waters the nature of the seabed may dictate their appearance. Rays and flatfish that live on sandy areas of the sea floor are often colored and patterned to match that sand. Similarly, fish that live over mud or shingle may be colored and patterned accordingly.

Marine habitats tend to be most varied near the coast. Here the seabed rises up toward the surface and may even break through it at low tide. The combination of abundant sunlight and a solid substrate allows seaweeds and other marine algae to grow. These, in turn, provide food and hiding places for invertebrates and fish. In tropical seas, corals often take the place of algae. There are coral reefs off the coast of Florida, although there are fewer than those of warmer waters.

Freshwater habitats

Although all fish have certain features in common, as a group they are incredibly varied. This great diversity reflects their many different lifestyles. Some are bottom feeders, others find

Above: Slow-moving rivers are inhabited by a wide variety of aquatic life.

Above: Fast-moving waters will be full of oxygen, but may lack food.

their food in the water column, while others hunt and forage at the surface.

Sea water is pretty homogeneous wherever it is found on the planet. The main variables in marine habitats are water temperature and light. In freshwater habitats there is also a great amount of variation in water quality and flow. For instance, mountain streams run quickly, and are clear and full of oxygen. On the other hand, they are often relatively sparse in terms of food. Swamps, by contrast, are full of organic matter, meaning that food is rarely hard to find. However, the water is stagnant, and dissolved oxygen levels are low.

Freshwater fish vary immensely in color and shape. Even within species, individuals may look quite different, depending on their age, sex, and habitat. Color may be used to attract a mate, but it can also help fish to hide. Like their marine cousins, many freshwater species are camouflaged to blend in with their surroundings. Bottom feeders often perfectly match the substrates (or bottom level) where they feed—for example, those living in rocky streams tend to be cryptically patterned in various shades of brown, making them very hard to spot when they are not moving. Fish that feed in clear, open water, such as those found in lakes, are more often silvery to reflect any light that falls on them. This has the effect of helping them to disappear in the blue.

Shape, as well as color, may be used to help camouflage fish. However, shape is more often a reflection of the type of life a fish leads: for example, how it is equipped to feed. Bottom feeders tend to have rather flat, wide bodies, with mouths that are positioned quite low down on the head. Open-water feeders, on the other hand, have their mouths positioned at the front of the head.

Of course, the freshwater world is not inhabited by fish alone. Fish share their environment with amphibians such as frogs, toads and newts, and mammals such as otters—not to mention insects, plants, and birds. The co-existence of these different types of creatures has, naturally, influenced the evolutionary process: many creatures have developed specific habits and physical characteristics that reflect their place in the food chain.

A hidden wealth of wildlife

North America has a great variety of aquatic creatures, and just below the surface of the rockpools, rivers, lakes, and oceans is an astonishing array of life, and below this there is even more.

Below: Freshwater fish share their habitats with mammals such as the otter.

FRESHWATER CONSERVATION

Many people perceive freshwater habitats as naturally formed bodies of water, yet humans have also created "new" homes in the form of canals and reservoirs. Although not built as sanctuaries for freshwater animals, creatures do thrive in them. Sadly, proximity to humanity brings hazards to freshwater life.

The vast majority of towns and cities are built along rivers, which now often pass right through their centers. Back when these urban areas were first founded, hundreds, or even thousands of years ago, rivers were the main means of transporting goods. They were natural highways that cut through the wilderness that separated human settlements.

Today, many rivers have lost much of their traffic. The spread of road and train networks means we are much less reliant on them than we once were. Nevertheless, those rivers continue to flow and within them there is often a wealth of wildlife living unseen by the people walking along their banks or over the bridges that cross them.

New homes

Other freshwater habitats have been physically built by humans. Networks of canals, for instance, were created by people to transport resources to places rivers did not reach. Like rivers, these waterways often pass through

Below: Large waterfalls like this are natural barriers to most fish, separating populations and in some places, even species.

cities and towns. Indeed, some North American cities are peppered with canals. Although today many canals have fallen into disrepair, they provide quiet havens for wild creatures among the urban bricks and concrete.

In the developed world, most of us take it for granted that we can turn on a faucet and get fresh running water at any hour of the day or night. This water, however, has to be collected and stored before it can be treated and then distributed to people's homes. In many parts of the world, man-made reservoirs are now more common than natural lakes. Fed by rivers, these large bodies of water have become homes for a wide variety of fish and other aquatic creatures, as well as water birds and other freshwater life. Some reservoirs are stocked with fish brought in from elsewhere for angling. Although artificial, many of these reservoirs have become important habitats in their own right.

On a much smaller scale, many people have created their own freshwater habitats in the form of backyard ponds. Isolated from streams and rivers, these are rarely important homes for native fish, but they do provide a lifeline for other forms of

Above: As well as being ugly to look at, the litter and the resulting pollution of this swamp habitat threatens the populations of fish and other creatures that live in it.

aquatic life. Amphibians such as frogs and newts use them as places to breed, and many insects lay their eggs in them and spend their lives in them as larvae. Ponds serve another important function by bringing wildlife closer to people. For many children, they are a first introduction to freshwater life.

Wild waters

The majority of freshwater habitats are neither man-made nor found in towns or cities. They are natural parts of the landscape, and most have been here much longer than humankind has existed. The paths taken by natural waterways, such as rivers and streams, may have changed a little over time, but in essence, these water courses, and the bodies of fresh water they feed, are permanent features, millions of years old. The major habitat types are lakes, rivers, swamps, ponds, and streams, and their capacity to nurture different forms of aquatic life is considered on the pages that follow. A little like the inhabitants of terrestrial

islands, which have evolved to live in somewhat confined, specialized environments, freshwater species are vulnerable to changes in their habitat. While their homes remain unaltered, they are safe, but in many parts of the world, human activity is having a serious impact on freshwater life.

Man-made problems

The most serious threat to freshwater life in most places is pollution. Pollution is the addition of substances to the water that do not naturally occur there. Sources of pollution include industrial waste, untreated sewage, and surface runoff containing pesticides or fertilizers used in farming. Effects on freshwater life depend on the contaminants involved.

Sewage and fertilizers affect water quality by increasing its load of nutrients, such as nitrates and phosphates. Although this does not have an immediate impact on fish or other aquatic life, it can cause aquatic algae to bloom and clog up waterways. Numbers of bacteria and protozoan organisms also rise. As they do so, they use up dissolved oxygen, causing fish and other creatures to slowly suffocate.

Chemical pollutants, such as pesticides and contaminants from industrial waste, kill more directly. Pesticides sprayed on crops may be washed into rivers by rain, just as fertilizers often are. Industrial waste may be dumped or continually flow into the water. In most developed nations, the environmental cost of such pollution is recognized, and laws have been enacted to prevent it. Elsewhere in the world, however, such waste continues to be flushed straight into rivers and other water courses, as does sewage.

Acid rain is another serious problem for freshwater habitats in some parts of the world. This is caused by the burning of fossil fuels, particularly the burning of coal in power stations. The chemicals in the smoke produced include nitrogen oxide and sulfur

Above: Even natural habitats may offer limited prospects for aquatic life. Narrow woodland streams in temperate regions, for example, offer fewer feeding opportunities than a slow-moving river rich in algae.

dioxide. When these react with the tiny droplets of water in clouds, they form nitric and sulfuric acid, which then falls with the rain. Acid rain has proved a particularly difficult problem to eradicate, mainly because the places where it is produced are rarely badly affected by it. It is other places downwind that suffer. For instance, many of the lakes in Scandinavia are largely devoid of life because of pollution originating in Great Britain and other parts of western Europe.

While pollution is the greatest threat to freshwater life in most areas, human activity has caused, and continues to cause, other problems. Although the building of dams provides us with both power and a reliable source of water, it can also have a serious impact on migratory fish. Species that travel upstream to breed can find their paths blocked, and river-dwelling species may have their populations effectively split in two. This may result in a decrease in numbers for both categories of fish.

Left: Dams provide us with electricity and water from the reservoirs they create. However, they act as barriers to river fish, meaning that the range of some species has become much more restricted.

MARINE CONSERVATION

Humans have always depended on the sea to provide food, as a means of travel and exploration, and as a source of scientific insight. However, all this exploitation of our oceans' resources comes at a price, one that threatens to land us all in very deep water.

Man's insatiable appetite for food and resources has placed enormous stress on marine ecosystems. Many species have been hunted or harvested to the brink of extinction, and some have already disappeared.

One of the most shocking examples of this was the hunting of Steller's sea cow (*Hydrodamalis gigas*)—a relative of the dugongs and manatees that was hunted to extinction just 27 years after its discovery in 1741. Other large marine mammals were almost lost—and some may still disappear despite efforts to conserve them—blue whales, fin whales, right whales, and sei whales are all listed as endangered by the IUCN (*see* panel, opposite).

One of the best documented cases of overfishing concerns cod. Hundreds of years ago, these fish were so common in some parts of the northwest Atlantic that they could be scooped out with a basket. Even 120 years ago, biologists believed it would be impossible for them ever to be fished out. But improved fishing technology changed all that and allowed trawlers to pursue ever dwindling stocks with greater intensity.

The western Atlantic cod fishery reached crisis point in 1992, when the Canadian government was forced to

Below: These living stromatolites, rocklike organisms, are the oldest form of life on Earth. They are only found in two sites—the Gulf of California and Shark Bay, Western Australia.

establish a total moratorium on fishing for cod. The ban remains in place, since stocks have still not returned to levels where cod fishing could be sustained. Recovery remains doubtful.

Pollution

The seas have been used as a dumping ground for waste for centuries. With human civilization now consuming more raw materials than at any time in history, the volume and variety of waste is greater then ever. Wastes that end up in the sea include heavy metals, pesticides, and persistent toxic and even radioactive chemicals originating from agriculture and industrial sources.

However, not all pollution involves man-made chemicals. Any substance put into the oceans in inappropriate quantities can be damaging. Silt, for example, is a fine sediment that occurs naturally in rivers and is ultimately washed out to sea. But in areas where deforestation leads to excessive erosion, the silt load can be immense, choking all life close to the river estuary. Oil is another natural substance, but released into the sea, it can cause severe damage not only to the environment, but to all species that rely on the water.

Above: The emissions from power stations and heavy industry continue to pollute land and water and to cause world-wide global warming

When oil breaks up, the chemicals it contains can still cause problems—for example, polynuclear aromatic hydrocarbons (PAHs) lead to abnormalities in fish and marine life.

Other toxic chemical pollutants include mercury, which accumulates in the bodies of animals that consume contaminated food. In this way, it becomes more concentrated the higher up the food chain it travels. Dioxins from paper-making and agrochemicals cause mutations in living cells and are known carcinogens. Polychlorinated biphenyls (PCBs), which were released in large quantities up until the 1980s, lead to reproductive problems in many animals. Tributyl tin (TBT), widely used in paints designed to prevent barnacles and other fouling organisms settling on ships' hulls, was found to be the cause of deformities in many shellfish, often masculinizing females. Other chemicals that frequently enter the water system have similar gender-bending effects on fish and other aquatic organisms.

Above: Cage traps are easily entered but hard to escape. Since they do not damage the catch, they may be used by the aquarium trade.

Light and sound are also a form of pollution, and both have been shown to disrupt the behavior of marine animals. Several recent mass strandings of whales have been attributed to military operations involving loud underwater explosions.

Global warming

Climate change and global warming driven by the greenhouse effect are often cited as the most serious problems facing today's world. Rising sea levels and increasingly stormy, unpredictable weather patterns will undoubtedly cause problems for animals living on land, especially on the coasts. But what about those living in the sea? Climate change is already taking a toll in all our oceans. Even slight increases in average temperatures can lead to sensitive animals, such as corals, dying off across wide areas. The phenomenon known as coral bleaching has already hit parts of all the world's major reef systems.

Other likely effects of warming include changes in some of the major ocean currents, which may mean whole seas changing their temperature or nutrient profile. Local species not able to adapt will then face extinction.

The fossil evidence of millions of years shows that life in the oceans has suffered enormous setbacks before. Life has continued, one way or another. But the environmental decisions being made now may determine how long our oceans retain the assemblages of species we are familiar with today.

Conservation

The story of man's relationship with the sea and the animals that live in it is not all one of exploitation and

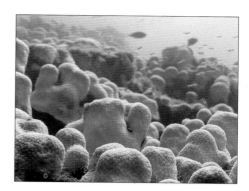

Above: These corals died when the seawater became too warm. The process, known as "bleaching," is an increasing problem.

destruction. In recent years, the conservation movement has made significant advances that go some way to redressing the balance.

In response to international concerns over the state of the world's oceans, the United Nations has designated a number of natural World Heritage Sites with a marine element, and various nations around the world have given areas of coast or ocean protected status as marine National Parks or reserves. Several global conservation charities invest heavily in marine projects, and there are literally hundreds of charities and nongovernmental organizations devoted exclusively to the protection of the seas and marine animals.

In 1986, the International Whaling Commission established a global ban on commercial whaling, although Japan has exploited a loophole allowing them to kill a certain number of whales "for scientific purposes," and Norway has resumed hunting minke whales in contravention of the ban.

Another international agreement, the Convention on International Trade in Endangered Species of Wild Flora and Fauna (CITES), was signed in 1973. It now has 169 signatory nations. International agreements are also in place to protect migrating animals (the Convention on Migratory Species), stocks of fish, and other marine animals. Even though these systems involve an enormous amount of bureaucracy, their attempts to moderate exploitation must be seen as a step in the right direction.

Marine life in peril

The International Union for Conservation of Nature and Natural Resources (IUCN) Red List profiles species considered to be at risk of extinction. Species on the list have been assessed by experts and are placed into categories that reflect the severity of the threat they face. Species included within the categories Vulnerable, Endangered, and Critically Endangered include 429 mostly marine crustaceans, nearly 1,000 mollusks (marine, freshwater, and terrestrial), 66 sharks and rays, 731 bony fish (freshwater and marine), and 14 cetaceans.

Other groups are less represented on the list, but this does not mean they are not at risk. The inaccessible nature of many marine habitats means that many species could dwindle and disappear without recognition.

Below: The IUCN lists the hawksbill turtle (Eretmochelys imbricata) as Critically Endangered. Many drown in fishing nets.

Below: The shell of a drowned hawksbill is cleaned for display as part of a school campaign addressing threats to local fauna.

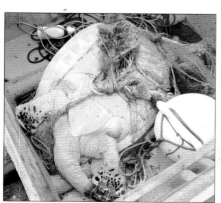

DIRECTORY OF OCEANIC SPECIES

The following pages provide a wealth of fascinating information on hundreds of marine animals, from the common starfish to circumglobal species such as killer whales and swordfish, and of course, some of the 25,000 known species of bony fish that dominate the fauna of North American oceans.

Although the popular perception of the marine realm concerns life in the oceans and seas, a number of the shallow-water creatures included here have adapted to an existence in brackish estuaries, or occupy intertidal zones devoid of water for part of the day. These habitats are quite accessible and their communities are well studied. Their deep-water counterparts, a large proportion of which have long evaded human observation, offer much more scant data. The concise profiles presented here are accurate in light of the information currently available, but in some cases are based necessarily upon a degree of carefully considered conjecture.

The directory is organized into three major categories, based loosely on habitat type. Beginning with the inhabitants of seashores and estuaries, it moves on to the shallow waters approximating to continental shelf and reef systems. It then concludes with the most remote parts of the larger bodies of water on Earth—the open ocean and deep sea.

Left: Spotted eagle-rays (Aetobatus narinari) *swimming over coral reef, with divers in the background.*

CRABS

True crabs are familiar animals of seashores and estuaries, and they make up a widespread and fascinating group of crustaceans. Horseshoe crabs are not true crabs, despite their common name. These ancient, shallow-water arthropods are the sole survivors of a group of invertebrates that flourished millions of years ago.

Mud fiddler crab

Uca pugnax

Identification: Carapace squarish with an H-shaped depression in the middle. Eyes born on long, thin, prominent stalks. Males have one claw hugely enlarged and covered in granules. Other walking legs banded. Females and young crabs have claws of equal size. Color of carapace brown to yellowish; claws yellowish to white.

Fiddler crabs are so called because males have an enlarged claw they use to protect their burrows, and which they wave to attract females when mating. This claw may account for 65 percent of the crab's body weight. Males also engage in ritualized arm waving when confronting rivals, although serious injury is rare. The smaller of the two claws is used to collect and sift mud and other material when looking for decaying plant and animal matter to eat. Fiddler crab burrows may be 12in (30cm) deep, and provide a safe haven from predators and a site for mating. At low tide, fiddlers leave their burrows to look for food, quickly returning to them—or to any other convenient burrow—if any danger should threaten.

Distribution: Mid-Atlantic U.S. coast.
Habitat: Muddy and sandy estuaries and shores.
Food: Detritus and algae.
Size: 1in (2.5cm).
Breeding: Reproduces sexually; fertilization of eggs is external.

Right: Aerial view of the mud fiddler crab, illustrating the disproportionally large claw.

Horseshoe crab

Limulus polyphemus

The horseshoe crabs in the class Merostoma are primitive marine arthropods, whose ancestors arose in the Silurian Period, more than 400 million years ago. In fact, the horseshoe crabs, or king crabs as they are also known, are more closely related to the extinct trilobites and to modern spiders and ticks than they are to true crabs and crustaceans. The body is covered by a protective, hinged carapace, and a long caudal spine extends from the back. The caudal spine can be used to right the animal if it is accidentally turned over. Under the carapace are the chelicerae and five pairs of walking legs. The horseshoe crab burrows in sand and mud, although it can swim.

Worms and other invertebrate food are crushed by the pincerlike chelicerae on either side of the mouth. During mating, these crabs congregate in the intertidal zone, where the female lays her eggs in holes in the sand. The horseshoe crab can live for about 20 years.

Identification: Horseshoe-shaped carapace broad, domed, and hinged; back of carapace bears spines. Long, tapering caudal spine. One pair each of pedipalps (mouth appendages) and chelicerae (modified fangs). Five pairs of walking legs. Color of carapace dark-brown.

Distribution: Eastern U.S. coastline from Maine to Gulf of Mexico.
Habitat: Sandy and muddy substrates down to 98ft (30m) or more.
Food: Worms, mollusks, crustaceans.
Size: 24in (60cm).
Breeding: Reproduces sexually; females lay between 2,000 and 20,000 eggs.

STARFISH

With no front or back and able to change direction without turning, starfish are most unusual creatures. These echinoderms are immediately recognizable from their shape, which basically consists of a body drawn out to form distinct arms, or rays. There are usually five or six arms present, although some species have considerably more—perhaps as many as 20. The mouth is found on the underside.

Common starfish

Asterias rubens

Distribution: North Atlantic.
Habitat: Among rocks and in mussel and oyster beds on lower shore.
Food: Crustaceans, mollusks, worms; predator as well as scavenger.
Size: 19.7in (50cm) across, though usually smaller.
Breeding: Eggs are fertilized externally and develop into planktonic larvae.

Identification: Robust body drawn out into five arms; body highest in the middle, tapering to ends of arms. Body covered with spines and bears tiny, pincerlike structures (pedicellariae) that help remove parasites. Underside of body bears rows of tube feet; arms grooved on underside. Color is yellow-brown above, paler on the underside.

One of the most familiar images of the seaside, the common starfish has a body covered in small spines and drawn out into five broad arms, or rays. Like other starfish, it moves by means of tube feet—small, fluid-filled structures on the underside of the arms that expand and contract, pulling the animal along. The tube feet may also be used to grip prey when feeding. The common starfish is predatory, tracking down its food mainly by smell. Once it finds a suitable prey item, such as a bivalve mollusk, it engulfs it with its arms, everts its stomach over the prey, or into the shell in the case of many mollusks, and digests it before absorbing the contents. The common starfish is found among rocks and in mussel beds, often in large congregations.

Common sunstar

Crossaster papposus

Distribution: Northeastern Atlantic; Pacific seaboard of U.S.A. down to Gulf of Maine; population also found at Budget Sound, Alaska.
Habitat: Among rocks, on sand, and in mussel and oyster beds in shallow water at about 33–130ft (10–40m).
Food: Echinoderms, mollusks, sea pens.
Size: 10in (25cm) across.
Breeding: Eggs are fertilized externally and develop into planktonic larvae.

This highly distinctive and attractive starfish, sometimes called the rose sea star, is immediately recognizable by its large, round disk and its array of between 8 and 16 arms, or rays, each of which is shorter than the width of the disk itself. The body of this species is further characterized by the very prominent spines that cover the disk and the arms. The common sunstar is found in sheltered locations, often in the company of other echinoderms, such as brittlestars. It feeds by everting its stomach onto its prey and digesting it. Among its food items are other, smaller starfish, such as cushion stars. The common sunstar is itself preyed on by other starfish, such as Morning Sun Star.

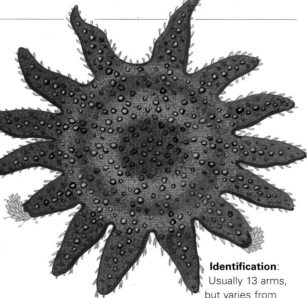

Identification: Usually 13 arms, but varies from 8 to 16; each arm about half the width of the disk. Body covered in conspicuous spines. Color varies from purple, brownish-red, yellow, or red above; yellowish-white below. Patterning also variable—combinations of colors or a single color with a concentric white ring.

GROUND SHARKS

The seven families of sharks of the order Carcharhiniformes are collectively known as ground sharks, and vary widely in size, shape, and behavior. All the sharks of this family have a nictitating membrane, or third eyelid, capable of being drawn across the eyeball. These animals are found in temperate, subtropical, and tropical oceans, and the range of some species even includes fresh water.

Bull shark

Carcharhinus leucas

Big, powerful, and aggressive, the bull shark's tolerance of both sea and fresh water means it is found in rivers as far apart as the Zambezi in Africa and the Mississippi. It has even been found 2,600 miles (4,200km) up the River Amazon. Although implicated in a number of marine attacks on humans, assaults in fresh water are comparatively rare. In marine environments, bull sharks are found swimming close to the shore, where they feed on almost anything they can catch. Inland, the shark's food list may include sizeable mammals, such as dogs and antelopes that stray into the water, and even hippos. In the Ganges, corpses consigned to the river in funerals have also been consumed. In the Nile, bull sharks are themselves preyed upon by crocodiles.

Distribution: All tropical and subtropical regions; also tropical rivers inland.
Habitat: Along coastlines and estuaries; also found in rivers and lakes.
Food: Almost anything edible, such as fish, turtles, birds, squid, crustaceans, dolphins, and other mammals, including land mammals when populations range upriver.
Size: 11.5ft (3.5m).
Breeding: Ovoviviparous; bears 1–13 young.

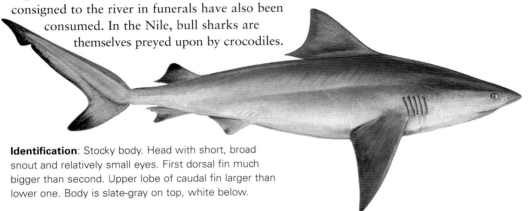

Identification: Stocky body. Head with short, broad snout and relatively small eyes. First dorsal fin much bigger than second. Upper lobe of caudal fin larger than lower one. Body is slate-gray on top, white below.

California horn shark

Heterodontus francisci

Identification: Tapering body. Large, blunt, piglike head with prominent ridge originating in front of each eye; eyes set high on head. Mouth has fine pointed teeth at front and flatter teeth at back. Stout spine in front of each dorsal fin. Large pectoral fins. Body color grayish brown with dark spots (although spots may be absent).

This small, solitary shark bears a resemblance to the Port Jackson shark, although it has a different form of body patterning. The California horn shark usually lies hidden in caves or under rocky ledges and other safe spots by day, emerging at night to hunt for food on the seabed and among kelp. Food consists of fish and invertebrates, such as crabs and squid. California horn sharks are found in water down to about 36ft (11m) deep, and although they can swim freely, they are usually seen moving sluggishly along the bottom using their powerful pectoral fins. These sharks are egg layers, and the auger-shaped egg case has two filaments at one end. These are used to help anchor the egg case in place among rocks, where it hatches out about seven to nine months later.

Distribution: Eastern Pacific Ocean, mainly southern California; also Peru.
Habitat: Rocky, sandy, and muddy bottoms and kelp beds down to around 35ft (11m).
Food: Crabs, squid, worms, sea urchins, anemones, fish.
Size: 4ft (1.2m).
Breeding: Oviparous; spiral egg cases laid.

EELS AND ELOPIFORMS

Eels are slender-bodied fish with long dorsal and anal fins, but no pelvic fins. They occur worldwide, except in polar seas. The tarpon, ladyfish and bonefish are members of the order Elopiformes. They are related to eels and have slender bodies and forked tails. All produce eggs which hatch into thin, transparent planktonic larvae called leptocephali.

California moray eel

Gymnothorax mordax

There are about 200 species of moray eels found in the world's tropical and warm-temperate oceans. Some have highly colorful body markings and prominent nasal appendages. All morays are predatory fish, with an often well-deserved reputation for aggressive behavior if disturbed. Indeed, there are instances of moray eels chasing divers out of the water and then lunging at them from the surf. This species hunts at night, sometimes lurking in rocky crevices waiting to ambush prey, but also seeking it out using a well-developed sense of smell. The eel constantly opens and closes its mouth to ensure a constant supply of oxygenated water is forced over its gills. The red rock shrimp (*Lysmata californica*) is often found sharing the lair of the California moray eel. The shrimp keeps the eel free of parasites and dead skin, and in return, the eel provides its "cleaner" with protection and possibly scraps of food.

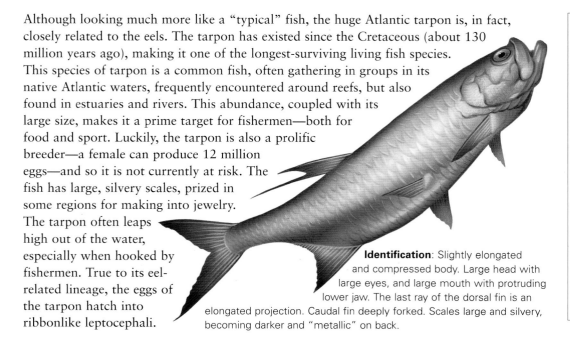

Identification: Muscular, snakelike body lacking scales. Head small with numerous sharp, pointed teeth. Body lacks pectoral fins. Dorsal and anal fins long, fused at tail with caudal fin. Color light or dark brown or green, often mottled.

Distribution: Eastern Pacific Ocean from Baja California northward; also Galapagos Is.
Habitat: In crevices on rocky reefs at 3–65ft (1–20m).
Food: Octopuses, crabs, urchins, fish.
Size: 5ft (1.5m).
Breeding: Oviparous; external fertilization; eggs hatch into planktonic leptocephali.

Tarpon

Megalops atlanticus

Although looking much more like a "typical" fish, the huge Atlantic tarpon is, in fact, closely related to the eels. The tarpon has existed since the Cretaceous (about 130 million years ago), making it one of the longest-surviving living fish species. This species of tarpon is a common fish, often gathering in groups in its native Atlantic waters, frequently encountered around reefs, but also found in estuaries and rivers. This abundance, coupled with its large size, makes it a prime target for fishermen—both for food and sport. Luckily, the tarpon is also a prolific breeder—a female can produce 12 million eggs—and so it is not currently at risk. The fish has large, silvery scales, prized in some regions for making into jewelry. The tarpon often leaps high out of the water, especially when hooked by fishermen. True to its eel-related lineage, the eggs of the tarpon hatch into ribbonlike leptocephali.

Identification: Slightly elongated and compressed body. Large head with large eyes, and large mouth with protruding lower jaw. The last ray of the dorsal fin is an elongated projection. Caudal fin deeply forked. Scales large and silvery, becoming darker and "metallic" on back.

Distribution: Eastern Atlantic from Senegal to Angola; western Atlantic from North Carolina, U.S.A., to northern Brazil.
Habitat: Over reefs, in estuaries, and in rivers.
Food: Fish, mollusks.
Size: 7.8ft (2.4m).
Breeding: Oviparous; spawns in shallow water; eggs hatch into planktonic leptocephali.

DOLPHINS AND WHALES

These widely distributed, powerful marine mammals are social animals, highly adapted for an aquatic life. The body is streamlined and is totally lacking hair, the limbs are modified to form flippers, and a broad tail is used for swimming. They are found all over the world in rivers, inshore waters, and the open ocean. The young are born at sea.

Common dolphin

Delphinus delphis

With its markings, long beak, and pointed flippers, the common dolphin has been the inspiration of artists and sculptors. It is an intelligent animal with a well-developed, hierarchical social structure, often occurring in schools several hundred strong. It is frequently encountered cavorting around boats. The common dolphin's behavior includes many instances of individuals coming to the aid of injured companions. Dolphins are air-breathing mammals, but can dive for five minutes or more at depths down to several hundred yards as they search for fish and squid, which they often find using a sophisticated system of echolocation.

Identification: Body slender and torpedo shaped. Slender, sickle-shaped dorsal fin. Long, slender beak and distinct forehead. Body color variable: brownish-black or black upper parts; chest and belly cream-white; tan or yellowish hourglass pattern on flanks; black stripe from lower jaw to front of flipper and from beak to eye; flippers black, gray, or white.

Distribution: Warm and temperate waters of Atlantic, Pacific, and probably Indian oceans.
Habitat: Coastal and offshore waters.
Food: Fish, squid.
Size: 7.2ft (2.2m).
Breeding: One calf; calving period once every 2 years.

Killer whale

Orcinus orca

This is the largest member of the dolphin family Delphinidae, a robust animal with a rounded head and no beak. The huge, triangular dorsal fin of an adult male is 6.5ft (2m) high, but is smaller and more curved in females and juveniles. The killer whale can travel at speeds of up to 40mph (65kmh)—the fastest of all sea mammals—and can track prey by echolocation. Its body markings help it to remain concealed in the shallow, turbid waters in which it often stalks. Killer whales sometimes cooperate when hunting. This species is known to live for up to 100 years.

Identification: Body robust but streamlined. Rounded head with no beak. Mouth with about 50 teeth. Large, paddle-shaped flippers. Dorsal fin tall and erect in males; smaller and sickle-shaped in females and juveniles. Body color black on sides and back; white under head and chest extending up to flanks; white patch above and behind the eye.

Distribution: All oceans.
Habitat: Coastal and offshore waters.
Food: Fish, squid, marine mammals, such as seals, porpoises, walruses.
Size: Male 23ft (7m) or more; female slightly smaller.
Breeding: One calf; calving period every 3–5 years.

TRUE SEALS

Seals are marine mammals that are adapted to live in the sea, although they all spend some part of their life ashore, moving around clumsily on their flippers when on land. True seals are distinguished from the similar-looking sea lions, because they lack external ear pinnae, or structure, and their hind flippers cannot be brought forward in front of the body.

Leopard seal

Hydrurga leptonyx

Sleek, powerful, and streamlined, the leopard seal is built for hunting a range of marine animals from penguins to krill—although it will also take carrion. It usually waits to take penguins underwater as they move off the ice. It is one of the largest species of seal, with an almost reptilianlike head armed with massive jaws and large teeth. The leopard seal is known to be aggressive toward small boats and their occupants when approached too closely. Females give birth to young on the pack ice, but the males are not present at the time. The coats of young leopard seals are similar to those of adults. This species is known to live for 26 years or more.

Identification: Sleek and elongate seal. Neck well defined. Wide-gaping mouth with large canines and large, post-canine teeth. Long foreflippers. Coat color silver to gray above, lighter below, with a mixture of light and dark spots.

Distribution: Polar and subpolar waters of Southern Hemisphere. **Habitat**: At the edge of the pack ice, on Antarctica, and around some islands. **Food**: Penguins, krill, seals, carrion. **Size**: Females 10.8ft (3.3m); males slightly smaller. **Breeding**: Little known of behavior; pups born September–January.

Common/harbor seal

Phoca vitulina

The common seal is a nonmigratory, usually solitary species with a wide distribution. There are five subspecies known, ranging from one found in the northeastern Atlantic Ocean to one that lives in the northwestern Pacific Ocean. The common seal frequently hauls out to sleep and bask on sheltered tidal rocky and sandy sites, and sometimes travels up rivers and is seen in lakes. It feeds mostly during the day, and can dive for up to 30 minutes in search of squid and other food, although dives are usually only of five minutes or so in duration. Pre-mating behavior includes males and females blowing bubbles and biting each other's necks.

Identification: Body rounded and relatively short, with large head proportionately. The face somewhat doglike in appearance. The flippers are short. The coat color is highly variable, ranging from gray-white, brown, or black overlaid with rings, blotches, or spots in adults.

Distribution: Northern Atlantic and Pacific Oceans. **Habitat**: Temperate and subarctic coastal waters. **Food**: Crustaceans, squid, fish. **Size**: Males 6ft (1.8m); females slightly smaller. **Breeding**: Mating takes place in the water; typically one pup born per year.

SEA LIONS, WALRUS, AND SEA COWS

Sea lions are distinguished from true seals by having external ear pinnae, and because they can bring their hind flippers underneath the body. The walrus, the only member of its family, is a huge, tusked mammal found in the Arctic. The sea cows are slow-moving, plant-eating aquatic mammals, such as dugongs and manatees, that exist entirely in the water.

California sea lion

Zalophus californianus

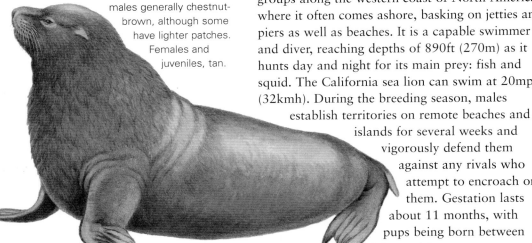

Identification: Streamlined body with well-developed flippers. Head doglike; external ears. Males have horny crest on head creating domed effect. Color of coat: males generally chestnut-brown, although some have lighter patches. Females and juveniles, tan.

This sea mammal, once common in circuses, is still a popular attraction at many marine theme parks and zoos. It is a sociable animal, living in groups along the western coast of North America, where it often comes ashore, basking on jetties and piers as well as beaches. It is a capable swimmer and diver, reaching depths of 890ft (270m) as it hunts day and night for its main prey: fish and squid. The California sea lion can swim at 20mph (32kmh). During the breeding season, males establish territories on remote beaches and islands for several weeks and vigorously defend them against any rivals who attempt to encroach on them. Gestation lasts about 11 months, with pups being born between May and June.

Distribution: Pacific Ocean, from Baja California to Alaska; also Galapagos Islands.
Habitat: Breeds on coasts and islands.
Food: Fish, squid.
Size: Males 8ft (2.4m); females 6ft (1.8m).
Breeding: One pup, nursed for 5 or 6 months or up to 1 year. Pups and their mothers communicate in rookeries through vocalizations.

Northern fur seal

Callorhinus ursinus

The northern fur seal spends most of its life at sea, usually feeding at night, and rarely comes ashore except to breed. A northern fur seal pup may spend up to 22 months at sea before returning to land. At breeding time, nearly three-quarters of the species' total population (about 1 million individuals) congregate on the Pribilof Islands of St. George and St. Paul in the Bering Sea. After the pup is born, it is left for days at a time while the mother goes back to sea to hunt. When she returns, she is able to locate her offspring by its unique call. Although no longer hunted in huge numbers, the northern fur seal is still caught in some places. It also becomes ensnared in trawl nets that have been set for fish.

Identification: Moderately built seal; males have stockier neck, shoulders, and chest than females. Muzzle short and downcurved. Flippers long, wide, and tapering. Fur on foreflippers extends only to "wrist." Coat color: males gray, black, reddish, or brown with yellow or gray frosting on mane; females silver-gray with cream or tan chest; pups born blackish with lighter chin and muzzle.

Distribution: North Pacific Ocean: Bering Sea to waters of northern Japan and southern California.
Habitat: Breeds on islands in range.
Food: Mainly squid, fish.
Size: Males 7ft (2.1m); females 5ft (1.5m).
Breeding: One small, black pup produced in June.

Walrus

Odobenus rosmarus

Distribution: Bering and Chukchi Seas in Arctic Ocean.
Habitat: Pack ice, rocky islands, open water.
Food: Mollusks, crustaceans, fish, worms; occasionally seals.
Size: Males 10.5ft (3.2m); females 8.9ft (2.7m). Tusks up to 21.6in (55cm) in males.
Breeding: Females give birth to young every other year; one well-developed pup produced.

The gregarious walrus is an impressive creature, immediately recognizable by the pair of prominent tusks—larger in males—that extend downward from the mouth. The tusks have many uses. They are employed in defense, as tools to smash holes in the ice, as ice picks to help haul the animal out of the water, but primarily they are used to signal social position in the hierarchy. Those with the biggest tusks are the most dominant animals and can secure the most advantageous sites for mating. If challenged by another individual, however, a walrus' tusks can become fearsome stabbing weapons. Cumbersome on land, the walrus is an agile and strong swimmer. It feeds on a variety of mainly bottom-dwelling bivalve mollusks, which it senses with the "moustache" of bristles around its mouth, and then digs out with its horny lips.

Identification: Massively built with short neck and squarish head. Flat, wide snout bears stiff, sensory bristles. Upper canines modified to form two tusks. Color of skin brown to tawny, darker on chest and abdomen. Skin becomes pinker when exposed to sun.

Steller sea lion (*Eumetopias jubatus*): 9ft (2.8m)
This species, the largest of the family Otariidae, or eared seals, overlaps its range with the California sea lion, but its larger size and lighter body color help distinguish it. The Steller sea lion inhabits the North Pacific Ocean. After breeding, individuals disperse far and wide, sometimes traveling thousands of miles. The species is an opportunistic feeder, hunting near the shore and over the continental shelf for fish and mollusks, and, occasionally, seals.

Australian sea lion (*Neophoca cinerea*): 8ft (2.4m)
This sea lion has a large head, tapering muzzle, and small external ears. It breeds on sandy beaches on islands off the coast of western and southern Australia. A nonmigratory species, it lives close to its breeding site in fairly large colonies, feeding on fish, squid, and penguins. It is much less awkward out of water than many sea lion species, and may occur inland when rough weather forces it from the sea.

Dugong (*Dugong dugon*): 13ft (4m)
Also known as the sea cow, the dugong bears a close resemblance to the manatees, although it can be told apart by its crescent-shaped tail fluke. The dugong can be found in the southwest Pacific Ocean, Indian Ocean, and Red Sea—also in coastal shallows, where it grazes on sea grasses.

West Indian manatee

Trichechus manatus

This large, docile aquatic mammal is found in coastal areas and rivers. Together with three other species, including the dugong, it comprises the order Sirenia. Early mariners thought these creatures were mermaids—hence the name "sirenians" (sirens of the sea). Among mammals that never leave the water, sirenians are the only ones that exploit plants as their chief food source. The West Indian manatee only has foreflippers, the rear part of the body terminating in a broad, rounded tail fluke. It feeds by foraging for plants. The animal's eyesight is poor, but both its hearing and sense of touch are good. The manatee is a sociable animal, living in small groups. When not feeding it usually lies on the seabed, coming to the surface to take in air through its large nostrils. Newborn calves stay with their mothers for up to 18 months. In captivity, the species has been known to live for more than 60 years.

Distribution: U.S. coasts: mainly Florida, also west to Texas and north to Virginia. From coastal Central America to Brazil, South America.
Habitat: Shallow coastal waters, estuaries, rivers.
Food: Water hyacinths, sea grasses.
Size: Up to 14ft (4.3m).
Breeding: One calf produced every 2–5 years.

Identification: Heavy bodied with short neck and blunt, oblong head. Broad snout bears sensory bristles (vibrissae) on upper lip, and nostrils are set far back. Foreflippers long with rudimentary nails. Tail fluke broad and rounded. Body color gray-brown; hairless.

JELLYFISH

These cnidarians consist of a bell-shaped, jellylike structure enclosing internal organs. Suspended from the bell are the animal's tentacles, covered in stinging cells. Most jellyfish undergo a life cycle involving a free-swimming medusa stage and a sessile polyp stage. In scyphozoan jellies, often referred to as "true jellyfish," the former is the dominant stage—and the state in which they are most likely to be seen.

Moon jelly

Aurelia aurita

Among the world's most common true jellyfish species, the moon jelly (or common jellyfish) often occurs in large numbers, drifting together on currents and tides. Each animal is a disk of jelly with a central mouth on the underside surrounded by four short arms. Inside the body is a branching system of channels—the jellyfish version of a digestive and vascular system—which distributes nutrients and oxygen around the body. There is no brain or central nervous system, just a loose network of nerves that coordinates responses to stimuli, such as light and the "scent" of chemicals in the water. The moon jelly feeds mainly on particles that accumulate around the edges of the bell among the short tentacles. Moon jellies have only a very mild sting.

Identification: Saucer-shaped bell fringed with short, fine tentacles. Four frilly edged arms hanging down from bell. Four pinkish or purple, horseshoe-shaped reproductive organs visible inside the body among radiating channels of branched gut.

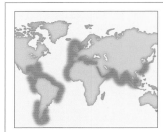

Distribution: Tropical and temperate oceans and seas.
Habitat: Surface waters, most commonly in coastal areas; may enter estuaries.
Food: Small particles of organic debris and plankton.
Size: Up to 20in (50cm) across.
Breeding: Alternating sexual and asexual generations: medusae produce eggs and sperm. Fertilized egg develops into a larva, then a sessile polyp, which buds off more sexually reproducing medusae.

Stalked jellyfish

Haliclystus auricula

Unlike most jellyfish, in which the medusa stage is a graceful, free-swimming organism floating in the ocean currents, a few species spend this part of their life cycle firmly anchored in one place. One such jellyfish is the stalked, or sessile, jellyfish. It attaches itself to seagrasses, seaweeds such as *Fucus* species, or firmer supports, such as rocks, by means of an adhesive stalk. The trumpet-shaped bell is drawn out into eight lobes, each one bearing a cluster of small, clublike tentacles that the creature uses to catch plankton and other small marine animals. There are also kidney-shaped anchors found between the tentacles. Although the stalked jellyfish is fairly common throughout its range, it is not a large creature and so is often overlooked, particularly when it is not fully extended.

Identification: Bell is a trumpetlike or flowerlike cup extended into eight lobes, each one bearing clublike tentacles. Attaches to substrate by an adhesive stalk. Color variable: mainly translucent shades of green, brown, orange, or red.

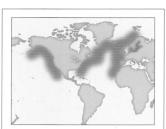

Distribution: North Pacific to California; North Atlantic; Baltic Sea.
Habitat: Attached to seaweeds or rocks in rockpools and shallow water.
Food: Small marine animals.
Size: Bell about 1in (2.5cm) across; stalk about 0.6in (1.5cm) high.
Breeding: Alternating sexual and asexual generations: medusae produce eggs and sperm.

CEPHALOPOD MOLLUSKS

Cephalopods are mainly active creatures with well-developed senses. They have cylindrical or saclike bodies, and most species have no external shell—although some have a small internal shell. The foot is modified to form a ring of suckered tentacles surrounding the mouth, which itself has a parrotlike beak. Octopuses can swim by jet propulsion, forcing water rapidly from a siphon.

Common octopus

Octopus vulgaris

Identification: Saclike body lacking a shell; warty upper surface. Eight arms, each bearing two rows of muscular suckers; arms relatively long. Color variable: greenish or gray-brown, according to mood.

This eight-legged cephalopod is one of the most widespread of all marine animals. Highly territorial, it lurks in holes and under ledges waiting for its prey, which is captured at night with long, suckered arms. New research suggests that it "stockpiles" supplies of bivalves and other sedentary food items near its lair, and sometimes it camouflages its lair with stones and shells. The octopus can change shape to squeeze into tiny gaps, and change color according to its mood and surroundings. The common octopus has highly developed sense organs. In laboratories, it has been shown to have the ability to learn simple tasks and undertake problem solving.

Distribution: Found worldwide in most temperate and tropical oceans and adjoining seas.
Habitat: In crevices of rocks close to the shore and in shallow water down to 650ft (200m).
Food: Crustaceans, mollusks, and other marine animals.
Size: Up to 3.25ft (1m) long.
Breeding: Internal fertilization; up to 500,000 eggs laid on substrate in shallow water and protected by female.

Paper nautilus

Argonauta argo

Distribution: Worldwide in tropical and subtropical oceans.
Habitat: Swimming in surface water as well as creeping on the bottom. Rarely found near shores.
Food: Plankton and other small organisms.
Size: Female up to 8in (20cm); male 0.4in (1cm). Shell up to 12in (30cm).
Breeding: Internal fertilization; eggs carried by the female, protected within her shell until they hatch.

Despite its common name, *Argonauta* is not a nautiloid, but is a member of the order Octopoda. The female is about 20 times larger than the male. Her body is partly encased in a thin, coiled shell, which she holds tightly using two modified arms with flattened ends. During reproduction, the male inserts his sperm into the female's pouch with a modified arm, called a "hectocotylus." The fertilized eggs are protected inside the shell as they develop. Due to its fairly small size and pelagic habits, the paper nautilus is rarely seen by seashore visitors, although it is not especially rare. The shell, sometimes washed ashore—usually without its attendant female—is prized by collectors.

Identification: Female has saclike body bearing eight arms, two of which are modified and have spatulate ends for gripping the shell. Shell is coiled, laterally compressed, and has a narrow keel and numerous sharp nodules. Male is much smaller and lacks shell. Color and pattern of animal variable: from silver-white to gray, red, or blue. Shell white.

MACKEREL SHARKS

Mackerel sharks comprise about 16 species of varied appearance and lifestyle. Among the seven families in the order are some of the best known of all sharks, including the great white and the mako. However, there are also some rarely seen species, such as the goblin shark and the megamouth. As a group, mackerel sharks are found in most of the world's oceans at depths ranging from shallow water to deep water.

Great white shark

Carcharodon carcharias

The great white, the largest predatory shark, has a reputation as a ruthless killer. Attacks on humans may occur because the shark mistakes swimmers for its natural food of seals or turtles. When a great white attacks, it usually lunges up from below, delivering a lightning-fast bite before pulling back. Once the prey has been rendered helpless, it returns to shear off chunks with its triangular, serrated teeth. Smaller prey may be taken whole. After a large meal, the shark may not feed again for several weeks. Wide-ranging and usually solitary, the great white breeds at about 10 to 12 years, producing live young after a gestation of about 12 months.

Identification: Torpedolike body with pointed, conical snout. Mouth bears large 3in (7.5cm) serrated teeth in both jaws. Well-developed lateral keels on caudal peduncle. Upper part of body blue-gray or brownish, lower part white. Large caudal (tail), dorsal, and pectoral fins; pectoral fins with blackish tips on underside.

Distribution: Temperate and tropical oceans worldwide.
Habitat: One of the more coastal mackerel sharks, but also found in open water to depths of 4,260ft (1,300m).
Food: Fish, turtles, seabirds, seals, sea lions, dolphins.
Size: Up to 20ft (6m).
Breeding: Two to ten young; livebearer.

Basking shark

Cetorhinus maximus

This giant, the second-largest species of shark, gets its common name from its habit of cruising leisurely at the surface of the water in summer as if sunbathing, although it may also swim at depths of about 650ft (200m). Basking sharks may be found alone, in pairs, or in groups. Despite its size, the basking shark feeds solely on tiny plankton, which it filters from the water using comblike structures on its gill arches. To help it obtain sufficient food, the basking shark swims along at about 3mph (5kmh) with its huge mouth wide open, taking in thousands of gallons of water per hour.

Identification: Huge, with pointed snout and cavernous mouth. Gill slits very large and prominent. Large caudal fin with longer upper lobe. Small teeth, but these are used for mating, not feeding. Body variably colored blackish, brown, or blue on back, becoming pale toward belly. Fins prized for making shark-fin soup.

Distribution: Temperate oceans worldwide. Common along Pacific coasts of U.S. during winter months.
Habitat: Highly migratory species. Found inshore in surface waters, but possibly also deeper water.
Food: Plankton.
Size: 33ft (10m), but occasionally up to 50ft (15m).
Breeding: Little known about breeding behavior; it may produce up to six young in a litter; livebearer.

REQUIEM SHARKS

*All of these sharks belong to the family Carcharinidae, often known as Requiem sharks, which is one
of the seven families of ground sharks that, altogether, amass more than 200 members. Taxonomists
sometimes group hammerheads in a separate family, Sphyrinidae. The great hammerhead and the tiger
shark are among the best known and most voracious sharks to be found anywhere in the world's oceans.*

Great hammerhead shark

Sphyrna mokarran

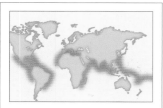

Distribution: Circumtropical
in coastal warm temperate
and tropical waters between
latitudes 40°N and 37°S.
Habitat: From shallow
coastal areas to far offshore
at depths of 985ft (300m),
usually less than 260ft (80m).
Food: Marine invertebrates,
bony fish, sharks, and rays.
Size: 20ft (6m).
Breeding: From 6 to 42
young; livebearer.

The largest of the eight or nine species of hammerheads
(family Sphyrinidae), this shark, like all hammerheads, has
extended lateral lobes on either side of the head forming the
so-called "hammer." However, in other species, the lobes
may be more scalloped, winglike, or shovel-shaped. Ranging
from inshore reefs to depths of about 980ft (300m), the
great hammerhead hunts a variety of animals including rays
and sea snakes, feeding mainly at dusk. It migrates to
cooler waters at the poles during the summer months.
Unlike most other sharks, mating often takes place
near the surface. After about an 11-month gestation,
young are born in the Northern
Hemisphere.

Identification: Muscular body
with prominent first dorsal fin;
pectoral and pelvic fins relatively
small; caudal fin with long upper
lobe bearing notch. Head with
conspicuous lateral lobes; eyes
and nostrils on lobes. In all
species, eyes and nostrils located
at the ends of hammer; this may
give them a wider sensory field
for locating prey. Hammer also
acts as a bow-plane, improving
maneuverability. Body brown,
gray, or olive above, fading
to white below.

Tiger shark

Galeocerdo cuvier

Distribution: Circumglobal
in temperate and tropical
oceans and seas. Common
around Australian coasts.
Habitat: Coastal waters,
including estuaries, and over
continental shelf down to
about 460ft (140m), but
sometimes deeper.
Food: Very varied: scavenger
as well as predator of range
of creatures including fish,
crustaceans, mollusks,
seabirds, marine reptiles,
and mammals.
Size: Up to 20ft (6m).
Breeding: 11–82 young;
livebearer.

This species gets its common name from the tigerlike body
markings. One of the largest and most aggressive of all
sharks, the tiger shark is renowned for its varied tastes in
food. A powerful and fast swimmer when attacking its prey,
it will swallow almost anything that will fit into its mouth,
including sea lions, sea snakes, turtles, other sharks, and
seabirds. It has also been known to swallow items of more
dubious nutritional value, such as car license plates and
tires. It has also been implicated in attacks on human
swimmers. Tolerant of both marine and brackish conditions,
the tiger shark sometimes enters river estuaries
and is known to attack land mammals that
come to the water to drink.

Identification: Fast-swimming,
aggressive shark. Body tapers
toward tail. First dorsal fin much
longer than second dorsal fin.
Upper lobe of caudal fin long with
subterminal notch. Head with
large eyes and a broad, blunt
snout. Wide mouth bears rows of
large, serrated teeth. Body color
grayish with black spots and
vertical bars (reminiscent of a
tiger), more prominent in young
individuals, pale below.

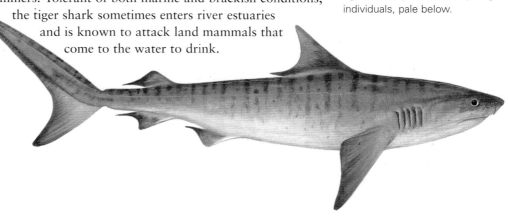

SAWFISH AND ELECTRIC RAYS

Sawfish and rays are grouped, along with sharks and chimaeras, in the class Chondrichthyes.
The sawfish have elongated rostrums bearing rows of lateral teeth, and resemble saw sharks. The electric
rays have flattened bodies and broad, winglike pectoral fins. They can produce pulses of electricity
to stun prey and ward off predators.

Small-tooth sawfish

Pristis pectinata

The largest of the six or so species of sawfish, the small-tooth sawfish is found around reefs at depths down to about 33ft (10m), although it often occurs in brackish or even freshwater conditions. It may sometimes venture into deeper water to reach offshore islands. Like other sawfish, the snout is extended to form a long rostrum bearing sharp, horizontal teeth, which it uses to rake up the sea bed, searching for hidden prey, or to ward off predators. Once prey—such as open-water or bottom-living fish—has been found, the sawfish disables it with sideways swipes of its rostrum. Valued not only as a food fish, it is also prized for other parts of its body, such as its oil (used in medicine) and its rostrum. Overfishing and habitat destruction have seen the species eradicated from much of its range.

Identification: Body long and flattened with winglike pectoral fins. Two large dorsal fins. Flattened head with long rostrum bearing 24–32 teeth on each side. Eyes large. Large spiracle behind each eye. Body color brownish-gray above, underside white.

Distribution: Western Atlantic: North Carolina, U.S.A. to Brazil; Eastern Atlantic: Gibralter to Namibia; Indo-Pacific: Red Sea and East Africa to Indonesia, parts of Southeast Asia, and northern Australia.
Habitat: Near to coasts; enters estuaries and rivers.
Food: Small fish, invertebrates.
Size: 18ft (5.5m); sometimes up to 25ft (7.6m).
Breeding: About 15–20 young; livebearer.

Atlantic torpedo ray

Torpedo nobiliana

Distribution: Subtropical and temperate waters of the Atlantic Ocean.
Habitat: Pelagic but also on sandy sea beds and reefs at 6.5–2,600ft (2–800m).
Food: Mainly small fish.
Size: 6ft (1.8m).
Breeding: About 60 young; livebearer.

One of the largest members of the family Torpedinidae, the Atlantic torpedo ray is one of 50 or more species of rays that can produce an electric current using specially modified muscle cells. In some species, including the Atlantic torpedo, the strength of the shock delivered can be up to 220 volts. Electric rays use the electricity both as a form of defense and to capture prey. Fish are the main food of Atlantic torpedos, and prey is usually caught as the ray delivers a stunning shock while wrapping its pectoral fins around it. The ray then maneuvers the victim into the mouth. Using this method, the ray can catch even fast-moving fish. Juveniles are usually found on the bottom, but adults often swim in open water.

Identification: Most of body flattened and disklike. Two dorsal fins. Paddle-shaped caudal fin. Snout short. Large spiracle behind each eye. Body color blackish to chocolate-brown above, white below.

GUITARFISH AND STINGRAYS

The guitarfish are so called because their body shape resembles the musical instrument. These flattened cartilaginous fish favor tropical coastal waters. In these fish, the pectoral fin is fused to the head to give a more or less disk-shaped body. Stingrays have venomous spines at the base of the tail, which are used primarily for defense. Stingrays have been known to grow up to 35ft (10.7m) long.

Atlantic guitarfish

Rhinobatos lentiginosus

Somewhat between a ray and a shark in overall shape, the 40 or so species of guitarfish get their common name from their distinctive body shape. The body is long, like that of a typical shark, with well-developed dorsal fins, but it is rounded at the front with broad pectoral fins, and the gill slits are on the underside, like those of a ray. Guitarfish swim by moving their caudal fins from side to side, in the same fashion as sharks. The Atlantic guitarfish is one of the smaller species in the family Rhinobatidae. It often buries itself in the sand or mud and is sometimes found in brackish or even fresh water. The Atlantic guitarfish feeds on bottom-dwelling fish, mollusks, and crustaceans. It often uses its snout, or rostrum, to hold the prey down before eating it. Fertilization is internal, with live young being born. This species is of little commercial fishing interest.

Identification: Body flattened and guitar shaped. Two well-developed dorsal fins. Pectoral fins fused to head. Elongated snout. Eyes on top of head. Conspicuous spiracles behind eyes. Paddlelike tail. Body color brown, gray, or olive above, usually with white speckles, yellowish-white below.

Distribution: Western Atlantic range extends from North Carolina, U.S.A., to Yucatan, Mexico.
Habitat: Mainly tropical coastal areas near sea bed down to about 100ft (30m); also in estuaries and fresh water.
Food: Fish, mollusks, shrimp, other invertebrates.
Size: 30in (76cm).
Breeding: About six young; livebearer.

Spotted eagle ray

Aetobatus narinari

Distribution: Wide-ranging in tropical and temperate Atlantic, Pacific, and Indian Oceans, and Red Sea.
Habitat: Sandy coastal regions and reefs, but also found in estuaries and open water.
Food: Clams, oysters, shrimp, octopuses, squid, sea urchins, fish.
Size: 8.2ft (2.5m) excluding tail; may reach 16ft (5m) in total with tail.
Breeding: Up to four pups; livebearer.

The spotted eagle ray's common name is due to its large size and also because of its swimming movements, which resemble those of a flying eagle. Beautifully marked with white spots on a black, gray, or brown background above, and with contrasting white below, the diamond-shaped spotted eagle ray is an active swimmer, often forming into large schools as it migrates across the oceans. This large ray is also found close to the bottom in shallow water, where it digs into the substrate for food, such as clams and other mollusks, using its curious flat, duck-billed snout. At the base of the long, whiplike tail, it has a battery of highly potent stinging spines. These are used in defense to deter or injure would-be predators. The spotted eagle ray can also leap out of the water when pursued. This species is no less dangerous if caught and hauled aboard a boat; the lashing fish can deliver painful, occasionally fatal, stings to humans.

Identification: Body disk flattened and diamond-shaped. Eyes on side of head. Large spiracles. Broad, bill-shaped snout.

CHARR AND SALMON

The Salmoniformes are characterized by having a fatty adipose fin on the back between the dorsal fin and tail. Many species in this group make long-distance migrations between the sea and their breeding grounds in rivers. Charr fish are close relatives to salmon and trout, and are important commercially. Charr that weigh as much as 20 pounds (9 kilograms) have been recorded.

Arctic charr

Salvelinus alpinus

Identification: Form typically troutlike, with rounded, streamlined body. Slightly pointed snout and large mouth with teeth in both jaws. Adipose fin present. Caudal fin slightly forked. Color highly variable according to habitat, size, and time of year: often brown or greenish on back, flanks silvery with pinkish or red spots; underside paler. Spawning adults usually have bright orange-red ventral surface and pelvic, pectoral, and anal fins.

The arctic charr is found mainly in cold, northern waters. There are both landlocked, freshwater varieties and others that migrate between freshwater habitats—where they spawn—and the sea. The species is an opportunist feeder, taking food from small crustaceans to members of its own species. Spawning takes place between September and October, with the preferred site being shallow, gravelly bottoms. The female builds a nest by turning on her side and using her caudal fin to clear away an area, known as a redd, in which to lay her eggs. After a period of courtship, eggs are laid in the redd and fertilized by the male. Where charr are migratory, the young first venture to the sea after a period of between two and six years.

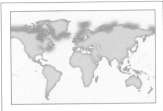

Distribution: North Atlantic, including northern Norway, southern Greenland, and Iceland. Also northwestern Canada and U.S.A.; Beaufort Sea.
Habitat: Deep runs of rivers and lakes, and—in migratory individuals—brackish waters and shallow seas.
Food: Small crustaceans and fish, including other charr.
Size: Usually about 17.7in (45cm), but may be bigger.
Breeding: Nest builder; eggs shed in gravel beds of rivers, and fertilized externally

Atlantic salmon

Salmo salar

This is one of the most famous of all fish, partly because it is a valuable food species—so much so that it is now raised in fish farms—but also because of its spectacular spawning migrations. After some years feeding in rich ocean waters, adult wild salmon navigate their way back to the rivers where they spent their early lives, and swim upstream to reach spawning sites in shallow, gravelly streams. This involves adapting from salt to fresh water, and up rapids and waterfalls against the current. They use so much energy in the process that many die after spawning, but some migrate back to sea and return to spawn again.

Identification: Large, streamlined fish with a relatively small head, an adipose fin, and a shallowly forked tail. Breeding males develop a hooked lower jaw (kype). Adults fresh from the sea are silver-sided with greenish-blue backs, heads, and fins; white below. They become darker and browner as spawning nears, with black and red spots. Young salmon in fresh water are dark, with a line of dark blotches and red spots on flanks.

Distribution: North Atlantic from Canada and Greenland to Iceland, northern Europe and Scandinavia, and Barents Sea. Also adjoining rivers.
Habitat: Rivers when young and when spawning; mainly coastal waters at sea.
Food: Crustaceans, insect larvae when young in fresh water; small fish and shrimp when at sea. Spawning salmon do not feed.
Size: 4ft (1.2m).
Breeding: Nest builder; eggs shed in gravel beds of rivers, and fertilized externally.

HADDOCK AND COALFISH

The fish described here are some of the best known relatives of the Gadiforms, or common codfish. Both the haddock and coalfish are heavily exploited by commercial fishing fleets, causing concern among conservationists. Haddock dwell close to the seabed in deep waters ranging from 131ft (40m) to 436ft (133m), and have even been recorded at depths of 984ft (300m).

Haddock
Melanogrammus aeglefinus

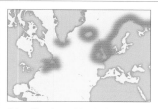

Distribution: North Atlantic from eastern Canada and New England to southern Greenland, Iceland, northern Europe, Scandinavia, and the Barents Sea.
Habitat: Close to the seabed on continental shelf, mainly at depths of 130–980ft (40–300m).
Food: Bottom-dwelling invertebrates and small fish such as sand eels.
Size: 30in (75cm).
Breeding: Eggs shed are fertilized externally and hatch into planktonic larvae.

Identification: A large-eyed fish with three dorsal fins—the first triangular, with long anterior rays—and two anal fins. It has a very short barbel beneath its short lower jaw. Dark greenish brown on the back, grayish silver on the sides and white below, it has a conspicuous, thumbprint-like black blotch between the pectoral fin and the arched lateral line.

One of the most heavily exploited of food fish, becoming scarce as a result, the haddock is a close relative of the cod (*Gadus morhua*) that feeds on the bottom in the relatively shallow waters of the continental shelves. In the north of its range, it feeds inshore in the summer, migrating to deeper water in the winter, but farther south it does the opposite. Although adult fish feed on the bottom, their eggs are buoyant, floating near the surface. The young then feed in the plankton, often swimming with large, drifting jellyfish whose trailing tentacles provide some protection from predators. When they reach about 2in (5cm), the young haddock move down to the seabed to feed on worms, crabs, mollusks, brittlestars, and small fish.

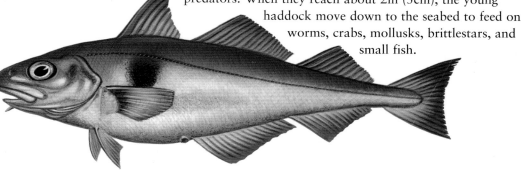

Coalfish
Pollachius virens

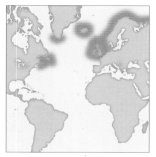

Distribution: North Atlantic from eastern Canada and New England to southern Greenland, Iceland, northern Europe, Scandinavia, and the Barents Sea.
Habitat: Schools near the surface and in midwater to depths of 656ft (200m).
Food: Marine crustaceans and fish.
Size: 4.25ft (1.3m).
Breeding: Eggs shed are fertilized externally; the larvae drift in plankton.

Also known as the saithe or pollock, and not to be confused with the similar pollack (*Pollachius pollachius*), the coalfish lives in large schools in continental shelf seas. These waters are richer in food resources than the deep oceans, owing to the nutrients scoured up from the relatively shallow seabed, so even surface-dwelling fish favor them. Mature coalfish feed mainly on smaller schooling fish, frequenting coastal waters in the spring and summer, and returning to deeper waters in the winter. They spawn from January to April, and their eggs and larvae drift into the coastal shallows, where the young fish feed on planktonic crustaceans and small fish for two years before moving into deeper water.

Identification: A typical cod, deep in the belly but tapering toward the tail, with large eyes, a small chin barbel when young that disappears with age, three dorsal fins, and two anal fins. Brownish-green back, with silvery sides and belly and a cream-colored or lighter gray lateral line.

SILVERSIDES AND NEEDLEFISH

These fish belong to two closely related orders. Silversides such as grunion are atheriniforms, while the elongated, sharp, and pointed snouts of needlefish and halfbeaked fish are typical of those families within the order Beloniformes.

California grunion

Leuresthes tenuis

This small, herringlike fish is famous for its spawning behavior. Instead of shedding its eggs into the water, where they are likely to be eaten, it spawns at night on sandy beaches, just after the higher-than-normal spring tides that occur at the full and new moon. Large numbers of grunion swim in with the waves until they are virtually stranded, and each female works her tail end into the wet sand to deposit her eggs. The male coils around the female to fertilize her eggs, then both fish slip back into the sea. The timing ensures that the eggs remain above water level for about two weeks until they are washed out by the next high spring tide. By this time, they are ready to hatch, and the larval grunion emerge within two or three minutes and are swept out to sea.

Identification: A slender, sinuous fish with large eyes, pectoral fins set well forward, two small dorsal fins, an anal fin with an elongated base, and a forked tail fin. It has a bluish-green back, silvery sides and belly, and a blue-tinged silvery band bordered with violet along each flank.

Distribution: Coastal eastern Pacific Ocean, from Monterey Bay, California, U.S.A. to northern Baja California, Mexico.
Habitat: Coastal waters and bays at depths of no more than 60ft (18m).
Food: Plankton.
Size: 8in (20cm).
Breeding: Eggs are deposited on beaches below the highest tide line, and fertilized externally.

Hound needlefish

Tylosurus crocodilus

Widespread in the tropical oceans of the world, this is one of more than 50 similar species of needlefish. It gets its common name from its elongated, cylindrical form and extremely sharp snout, and is notorious for the way that it leaps from the water when agitated or alarmed, perhaps by predators, or when attracted toward lights at night. The fish flies through the air like a spear, and people have been impaled by flying needlefish—some being seriously injured or even killed. It also has a habit of skittering across the ocean surface at high speed to escape predators or to move out of the way of boats, using its rapidly vibrating tail something like an outboard motor—a technique that is reminiscent of the takeoff runs of the closely related flying fish. It is a predator of other fish, swimming very rapidly in pursuit of its quarry, although young needlefish feed on plankton.

Identification: A very elongated, cylindrical fish with a sharp, needlelike snout lined with many sharp teeth. This is the only species of needlefish in which the teeth protrude outward in juveniles, although they are straighter in adult fish. The dorsal and anal fins are set well back on the body, long-rayed at the front and with short-rayed extensions toward the tail fin, which is deeply forked. Body is dark blue above and white below, with silvery sides.

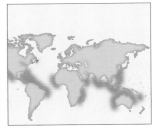

Distribution: Tropical Indo-Pacific Ocean from the Red Sea and South Africa to Polynesia and Japan; also Indonesia and northern Australia; tropical Atlantic range from New Jersey, U.S.A. and Brazil to West Africa.
Habitat: Coral reefs and associated lagoons, to depths of 40ft (13m).
Food: Smaller fish.
Size: 5ft (1.5m).
Breeding: Eggs shed in the water are fertilized externally, and attach to corals and other objects.

DORIES AND SCORPIONFISH

Dories, a well-known commercial food fish, are dominant in the order Zeiformes. They have narrow, deep bodies and large mouths with distensible jaws. Scorpionfish, such as lionfish and gurnards, are an attractive, though often venomous, family of scorpaeniforms.

John dory

Zeus faber

Identification: Very deep, narrow body; high-set eyes and protrusile jaws. Two dorsal fins, the first with 9–11 strong spines with extended rays; two anal fins. Generally gray with yellow and brown stripes and blotches; yellow-ringed black spot on each flank.

The very distinctive-looking John dory appears to be bulky when viewed from the side, but its body is flattened like a plate. When viewed from the front, it presents an extremely narrow profile, and it may rely on this to make itself seem less threatening and less visible as it slowly approaches its prey, such as herrings, anchovies, sardines, and the occasional invertebrate. When it gets close enough, it rapidly shoots out its protrusile jaws to engulf the animal, sucking it in with a current of water. The John dory spawns inshore in the spring—or earlier in the year where the waters are warmer; the young take four years to mature.

Distribution: Widespread in shallow temperate seas, including the eastern North Atlantic Ocean, the Mediterranean and Black Seas, the western North Pacific Ocean around Japan and Korea, and the western South Pacific Ocean around Australia and New Zealand.
Habitat: Inshore waters close to the seabed, at depths of 16–1,310ft (5–400m).
Food: Schooling fish, plus occasional crustaceans, octopus, and cuttlefish.
Size: 25.5in (65cm).
Breeding: Eggs are shed into the water where they are fertilized externally.

Flying gurnard

Dactylopterus volitans

Despite the winglike proportions of its enlarged pectoral fins, the flying gurnard cannot actually fly. It spends most of its time exploring the seabed, creeping over soft sediments with its pectoral fins expanded so that it resembles a foraging ray. It uses the detached front lobes of these fins like legs, both to propel itself and probe for prey, such as buried bivalve mollusks or small crabs. In the process, it flushes small mobile animals into open water, and the gurnard is often shadowed by opportunist predatory fish that snap up any escapees.

Identification: A large-eyed fish with a big, blunt, armored head and a long backward-pointing spine on each cheek. Two dorsal fins, the first with two free spines at the front. Greatly enlarged, fanlike pelvic fins, with the front six rays separated to form a mobile lobe. Mainly orange-red with some blue spots on the back; paler below. Pelvic fins mainly brown, with lighter and darker spots.

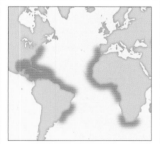

Distribution: Subtropical and tropical Atlantic Ocean, from the U.S.A. to Argentina, and from France to the Azores. Also found in brackish estuarine waters.
Habitat: Sandy or muddy seabeds, often near reefs, in shallow water to depths of 330ft (100m).
Food: Crabs, shrimp, clams, and small bottom-living fish.
Size: 15in (38cm).
Breeding: Eggs are shed into the water where they are fertilized externally.

PERCHLIKE FISH

The sheer breadth of this order of ray-finned fish has already been noted.
Among the large-bodied, mostly warm-water and tropical perciforms shown here are representatives
from significant food fish groups, such as the giant sea bass from the Serranidae family
and the common sea bream from the Letherinidae family.

Snook

Centropomus undecimalis

The big, silvery common snook is widespread in the warm waters of the Caribbean region and adjacent Atlantic, and the most abundant species in its family, Centropomidae. It occurs in shallow coastal areas of salty and brackish water, usually at depths less than 65ft (20m), where it preys on smaller fish and crustaceans such as shrimp and crabs. It has few predators apart from human sport fishers, for whom it is a prize catch. It spawns in salt water near river estuaries between May and September, and the young larvae then move upriver to live in freshwater tributaries.

Identification: A streamlined, humpbacked fish with a sharp snout, protruding lower jaw, and sloping forehead. It has two dorsal fins—the first spiny—a forked tail fin, and a prominent black lateral line. It is dull gray in color above with a yellow or green tinge, and silvery on the sides and belly. In some populations of fish, many of the fins are yellow.

Distribution: Western central Atlantic, Gulf of Mexico and Caribbean, from the Carolinas south to Rio de Janeiro, Brazil.
Habitat: Coastal waters, lagoons, and mangrove-lined estuaries, penetrating into brackish and fresh water.
Food: Fish and crustaceans, such as shrimp.
Size: 5ft (1.4m).
Breeding: Eggs shed in salt water, where they are fertilized externally. Larvae migrate to brackish and fresh waters.

Royal gramma

Gramma loreto

Identification: Small, with a long-based dorsal fin and elongated pectoral fins. It is bluish-purple at the front, fading through pink to yellow at the back. Oblique black stripe through eye; black spot at front of dorsal fin.

This small, brightly colored, rainbow-patterned reef fish lives in caves and crevices among the coral, often hanging upside down from the roof of a cavity with just its head protruding. Like many reef fish, the royal gramma changes sex as it ages, starting out as a female and becoming a male. It is territorial, and when a territory-holding male dies, a female will change sex in order to take over the role. Breeding males lure females to spawn by preparing nursery sites in small crevices and then lining them with pieces of seaweed and coral. When the eggs are laid, both sexes defend them until hatching, about seven days later.

Distribution: Caribbean and western central Atlantic Ocean from Bermuda to Venezuela.
Habitat: Crevices in coral reefs.
Food: Small planktonic crustaceans, such as copepods; also picks skin parasites off other fish, such as snappers.
Size: 3in (8cm).
Breeding: Eggs shed into a crevice, where they are fertilized by the male and tended by both parents.

Giant sea bass

Stereolepis gigas

Distribution: Eastern Pacific from California to Mexico.
Habitat: Rocky reefs with kelp beds, in depths of about 16–150ft (5–46m).
Food: Mainly bottom-dwelling fish, squid, octopuses, lobsters, and crabs.
Size: 8.2ft (2.5m).
Breeding: Eggs are fertilized externally and float to the surface of the water, where they hatch within 1–2 days. Larvae are planktonic.

Now extremely scarce throughout its restricted range, the giant sea bass is a bottom-feeding predator that targets slow-moving rays, flatfish, crabs, and cephalopods. Cruising through the rocky reefs that are its favored habitat, it approaches its prey and rapidly opens its huge mouth to create a suction current, drawing the victim in. As an adult, its only natural enemies are large sharks, but it has been intensively exploited as a commercial and sport fish. As a slow-breeding species, it has been unable to make good the losses. Its bottom-feeding habits also make it vulnerable to pollution, since the seabed off California is badly contaminated with toxic chemicals.

Identification: A very large, stout-bodied fish with a big head and a huge mouth, an arched back, and a spiny, long-based first dorsal fin. Bright orange with black spots when juvenile, it turns bronze-purple and then gray or black with age. Adults can change color rapidly, from jet black to light gray, and hide or display black spots at will.

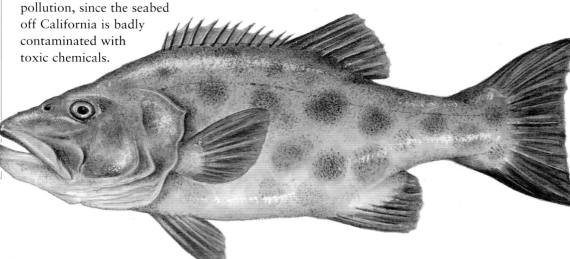

Common sea bream

Pagrus pagrus

Usually found on or near rocky reefs and wrecks, the common sea bream is a bottom-feeding fish that preys mainly on crabs, brittlestars, mollusks, and small fish. Despite its name, it is now much less common than it once was, having been overexploited by commercial fisheries. Larger, older fish are now rare, and since this is a species that changes sex with age—from female to male—the selective removal of larger fish seriously unbalances the sex ratio. However, like many warm-water fish, the common sea bream tends to accumulate toxins in its body, through eating filter-feeding animals that have themselves ingested mildly toxic microorganisms. The risk of becoming a victim of such poisoning, known as "ciguatera poisoning," may make humans regard the species less favorably as a food source, and improve its chances of survival.

Identification: A deep-bodied, laterally compressed fish with a large, blunt head, big eyes, a spiny dorsal fin, and a forked tail. Silvery red with reddish dorsal, pectoral, and tail fins, and faint yellow spots on each scale, giving a yellow-striped effect.

Distribution: Eastern Atlantic: Strait of Gibraltar to Madeira and the Canary Is; also Mediterranean and northward to the British Isles. Western Atlantic: New York state and northern Gulf of Mexico to Argentina.
Habitat: Rocky or sandy seabeds to a depth of about 820ft (250m).
Food: Crustaceans, echinoderms, mollusks, and fish.
Size: 35in (90cm).
Breeding: Eggs are fertilized in the water.

WHALES

Whales are air-breathing mammals totally adapted to a life spent entirely in an aquatic environment—even the young are born in the water. These animals swim by using powerful up-and-down movements of their horizontal tail flukes. These are most often social animals living in groups from a few individuals up to many hundreds.

Beluga

Delphinapterus leucas

Often known as the white whale because of its gleaming white skin when adult, the beluga is a northern species favoring coastal waters, and in the winter, the edge of the floating pack ice. It is gregarious, usually traveling in groups of ten or more. Groups are either all males or all females and their darker-skinned young. All-male herds of more than 100 are known. Belugas feed mainly on fish, such as herring, cod, and salmon, but also dive to the seabed for crabs and mollusks. They communicate with whistles, squeaks, and belching sounds, and have an echolocation system that is probably used when feeding. Like many whales they are threatened by hunting, and in some areas, pollution.

Identification: A relatively small whale with a stocky frame, a bulbous forehead, and a mobile face. It has gleaming white skin when mature, but is darker skinned when young. The dorsal fin has been replaced by a dorsal ridge, which is more prominent in males. The males are some 50 percent heavier than the females.

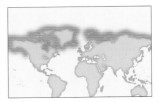

Distribution: Arctic Ocean and adjoining seas, including the Sea of Okhotsk, Bering Sea, Gulf of Alaska, and Hudson Bay, plus a small population in the Gulf of St. Lawrence, Canada.
Habitat: Fjords, estuaries, and shallows in the summer; near ice edge in the winter.
Food: Fish and squid, plus crabs, octopuses, and other bottom-living invertebrates.
Size: 13ft (4m).
Breeding: One calf born after a 12-month gestation; birth interval 2–3 years.

Narwhal

Monodon monoceros

Related to the beluga (*Delphinapterus leucas*) described above, the narwhal is famous for the single, long "unicorn" tusk of the adult male. This is a modified tooth, which grows to a length of 6.5ft (2m) or more, and has a pronounced left-hand spiral. The function of the tusk is not certain: it is extremely well supplied with nerve endings that make it sensitive to water temperature and pressure, but it is not clear why this sensitivity is not shared by females. Since narwhals are social animals, usually seen in small groups that sometimes associate in larger herds, the tusk may act as an indicator of male status—like the antlers of deer. Both sexes take the same prey, often feeding at depth on bottom-living invertebrates as well as fish taken in open water.

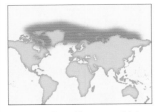

Distribution: Ranges widely throughout the Arctic Ocean, from northeastern Canada and Greenland to northwestern Siberia.
Habitat: Mainly deep water near pack ice, following the ice edge as it advances and retreats with the seasons.
Food: Mainly fish, squid, and shrimp.
Size: 14.75ft (4.5m).
Breeding: A single calf (rarely twins) born after a 15-month gestation; birth interval 2–3 years.

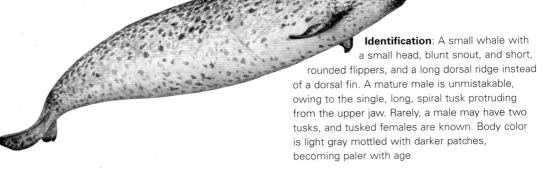

Identification: A small whale with a small head, blunt snout, and short, rounded flippers, and a long dorsal ridge instead of a dorsal fin. A mature male is unmistakable, owing to the single, long, spiral tusk protruding from the upper jaw. Rarely, a male may have two tusks, and tusked females are known. Body color is light gray mottled with darker patches, becoming paler with age.

Humpback whale

Megaptera novaeangliae

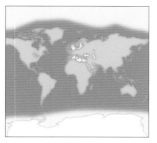

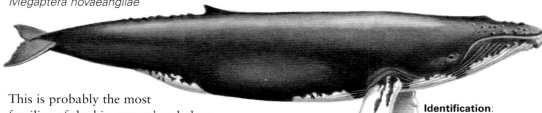

Distribution: All oceans, but seasonally resident in cold polar waters in the summer, and warm subtropical or tropical waters in winter.
Habitat: Feeds and breeds in relatively shallow waters, but crosses deep oceans on migration.
Food: Schooling fish and krill.
Size: 46ft (14m).
Breeding: Single calf born every 2 years or so, in warm-water wintering areas.

This is probably the most familiar of the big rorqual or baleen whales, thanks to its spectacular acrobatic displays. Despite its immense weight, it may leap right out of the water, falling back with a huge splash: a behavior known as breaching. Both sexes also slap their tail flukes and flippers on the water, and males communicate with a complex repertoire of whale "songs." They are social animals, traveling and feeding in small groups that often form part of larger aggregations. They have a cooperative feeding technique that involves swimming around and below fish or krill while releasing a rising curtain of bubbles to concentrate the school. Each whale then lunges upward to scoop up a vast volume of prey and water. It expels the water through the sievelike baleen plates lining its mouth.

Identification: A large whale with a pronounced hump in front of its dorsal fin, a stout body, and very long flippers—the longest of any whale. There are rounded knobs on top of the large head, beneath the jaw, and on the front edges of the flippers. These are often encrusted with barnacles. Some 12–36 grooves extend from the chin to the belly. Body color is basically black, with a variable pattern of white patches below and on the flippers and tail flukes.

Southern right whale (*Eubalaena australis*): 56ft (17m)
Found only in the waters around Antarctica, between 30 and 50 degrees south, this large whale was considered the "right" whale to catch by whalers. It has a very big head, no dorsal fin, and no throat grooves, and is basically brown to black in color with white horny growths on its head. It feeds on planktonic crustaceans such as copepods and krill.

Gray whale (*Eschrichtius robustus*): 46ft (14m)
This north Pacific Ocean whale has a very coastal distribution, since it feeds by sieving small animals from the bottom sediments, usually in water that is less than 164ft (50m) in depth. The whale feeds in Arctic waters during the summer months, migrating to the subtropics for the winter season. It has a relatively small head, and its gray skin is encrusted with variable paler patches of barnacles.

Bryde's whale (*Balaenoptera edeni*): 39ft (12m)
Identifiable by the three ridges located on top of its head, prominent sickle-shaped dorsal fin, dark-gray back, and pale-colored throat, Bryde's whale occurs worldwide in warm tropical or subtropical oceans. It is an opportunistic feeder, taking mainly schooling fish and crustaceans by straining water through the baleen plates lining its mouth.

Long-finned pilot whale

Globicephala melas

The pilot whales are basically big dolphins, and this species has the same habit of living in large groups, or "pods," of between 10 and 50, and occasionally 100 or more. It is essentially oceanic, roaming nomadically in search of schools of squid, or failing that, fish. Its preference for the deep ocean means that it is poorly adapted for shallow coastal waters, and it is prone to becoming stranded on tidal shores. Its social bonds are so strong that one disoriented whale is followed by others, and mass strandings are common. The long-finned pilot whale also has a long history of exploitation in the North Atlantic, particularly in the Faeroes, where a traditional hunting practice involves driving whole pods ashore to be killed. Some 1,200 pilot whales are killed in this way each year.

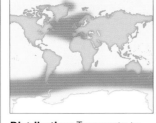

Distribution: Temperate to sub-polar waters of the North Atlantic Ocean, entering the western Mediterranean Sea, and the southern Pacific, Atlantic, and Indian Oceans.
Habitat: Mainly the deep oceans, but may stray into shallower coastal waters in search of food.
Food: Mainly squid, plus schooling fish.
Size: 16.4ft (5m).
Breeding: A single calf is born after a gestation of 15–16 months. Birth interval 3–4 years.

Identification: A medium-size whale with a very bulbous head, especially in males. It has long, backswept flippers and a round, slightly hooked dorsal fin. It is black or dark gray with a white diagonal stripe behind the eye, and grayish areas on the belly and chin.

CEPHALOPOD MOLLUSKS

The cephalopods rank among the most highly evolved and intelligent invertebrates. Several species of squid have adapted to life in the open ocean, and some live at extreme depths. Biologists are only just beginning to learn the secrets of these mysterious deep-sea mollusks, some of which have famously evaded human observation for decades, existing only in legend.

Nautilus

Nautilus pompilius

Identification: The shell is an expanding spiral, with brown bands above, but pure white below. The opening of the shell is shielded by a tough hood. Two prominent eyes and a cluster of small tentacles protrude from the large living chamber.

The genus *Nautilus* is all that remains of a once great order of mollusks. They are the closest living relatives of another vast but wholly extinct group, the ammonites. Nautili are considered very primitive—they have retained a large external shell and their movements are slow—more like that of snails than of other cephalopods. The shell contains a series of sealed chambers—the body of the animal occupies the largest of these, which is also the most recently made. The others contain gas for buoyancy, as well as the gas-producing organ. The nautilus propels itself by weak jet propulsion or crawls over the sea floor using its tentacles. It spends the day in deep water but rises to shallower areas at night. Food is collected by the tentacles around the mouth. Nautili are long-lived by cephalopod standards, but breed slowly—females produce a dozen or so large eggs in a year, which hatch into nautili 0.75in (2cm) across.

Distribution: Tropical areas of Indian and Pacific Oceans.
Habitat: Deep water close to reefs down to 2,600ft (800m).
Food: Small fish, crustaceans, and dead animals.
Size: Up to 10in (25cm).
Breeding: Internal fertilization; large eggs develop directly into miniature versions of the adult, reaching maturity in 5–10 years.

Vampire squid

Vampyroteuthis infernalis

Identification: Gelatinous body with spiny arms connected by a web and two oval fins resembling flapping ears. Has very large eyes.

The scientific name of this species is rather unflattering. It means "Vampire squid from hell"—a little melodramatic considering the animal is no larger than a human hand. The vampire squid is a small, nimble, swimming deep-water squid. The eyes are large—relative to the animal's size, perhaps the largest in the animal kingdom. The arms bear rows of sharp spines with which the squid grasps its prey. The arms are connected by an extensive web. The second pair of arms are retractile, and can be extended to several times the length of the body. There are numerous light-producing organs all along the arms and the tips. It can secrete clouds of glowing fluid, which may be used to confuse predators in much the same way as other squids use ink.

Distribution: Tropical and temperate oceans worldwide.
Habitat: Typically found at depths of 2,000–4,000ft (600–1,200m).
Food: Copepods, prawns, and cnidarians.
Size: 5in (13cm).
Breeding: Internally fertilized eggs, up to 0.16in (4mm) across, are released into the water, where they drift within small, free-floating masses.

KRILL AND SHRIMP

The class Malacostraca includes some of the world's most abundant species, and some of the most exploited. Apart from being a great natural spectacle, swarms of krill and shrimp are a vital resource for larger animals and increasingly a target of commercial fisheries. Research is underway in various oceanic locations to verify the impact of overfishing on numbers and breeding.

Deep water opossum shrimp

Gnathophausia ingens

Identification: Usually distinguished by its large size and bright red color, *Gnathophausia* is a primitive opossum shrimp, in which only the first pair of appendages on the thorax are modified into mouthparts. The other thoracic legs and abdominal appendages are used for swimming.

The order Mysidacea includes about 800 small, shrimplike crustaceans named for the pouch marsupium in which females brood their larvae—which is a little like the pouch of marsupial mammals such as opossums. By the time the young emerge from the pouch, they have developed into miniature versions of their parents. The group also includes the extremely delicate-looking fairy shrimp. Opossum shrimp live in large swarms, usually close to the sea floor. They are eaten by many kinds of fish, and many species seek sanctuary among stinging anemones, moving carefully between the stinging tentacles. Deep-sea species such as *Gnathophausia* produce bioluminescence when disturbed, presumably in an attempt to confuse potential predators. They feed mainly on plankton and other organic material filtered from the water using their bristly thoracic legs.

Distribution: Likely to be present in all oceans.
Habitat: Benthic, from near surface to deep water.
Food: Mainly algae and detritus drifting down through the water.
Size: 0.04–13.75in (0.1–35cm).
Breeding: Eggs fertilized and develop into larvae within the female's brood pouch.

Pelagic red crab

Pleuroncodes planipes

Distribution: Pacific Ocean.
Habitat: Benthic most of the year, rising to surface waters of open ocean to breed.
Food: Plankton.
Size: 0.75–3in (2–8cm).
Breeding: Females brood developing eggs attached to their abdomen; larvae develop through several molt stages.

The red crab belongs to a group of crustaceans known as squat lobsters. The body appears short because of the small carapace and a characteristic posture in which the abdomen and tail are tucked up under the body. Of the five pairs of walking legs, the first are very large and bear robust claws. There are no specialized swimming appendages, but red crabs still swim, using powerful flicks of the abdomen. For most of the year, they live and feed on the seabed, but in the spring, they swim to the surface to molt and breed. They form aggregations numbering millions or even billions of animals, and provide a food resource for both gray and blue whales, loggerhead turtles, and predatory fish such as tuna. From time to time—especially in El Niño years—red crab swarms are washed ashore.

Identification: Small, lobsterlike crustacean with bright-red body. First pair of walking legs bear long claws. All legs have bristles to help gather small food items from the water.

SHARKS

The gentle whale shark spends most of its time in the open ocean, along with several much smaller and more aggressive sharks, which make a living through speed, ferocity, and superbly acute senses. The rarely-sighted megamouth is not especially large, fast, or fierce—but it is exceptional in other ways.

Whale shark

Rhincodon typus

This, the world's largest living fish, is only just beginning to be understood. Until recently, it was known mainly from shallow seas, as a seasonal visitor to reefs and coasts. But for several months a year it disappeared. Studies have revealed it to be migratory and able to descend to great depths in search of food. Like other large marine organisms, it is a filter feeder, specializing in plankton and small fish. Where food is plentiful, whale sharks may temporarily gather in groups of up to 100 or more. They are hunted mainly for their fins. Left undisturbed, they can live for more than 100 years.

Identification: Vast, bulbous-bodied shark with square snout and large mouth. The body has several longitudinal ridges, is dark gray to brown above, white below, and marked with a pattern of white spots and horizontal stripes on back and flanks. Of its two dorsal fins, the second is very small; the pectoral fins are triangular, the pelvic and anal fins small. Its tail is large with a longer upper lobe.

Distribution: Tropical and warm temperate oceans worldwide.
Habitat: From coastal reefs to deep, open ocean, down to 3,300ft (1,000m) or more.
Food: Plankton and small fish.
Size: Up to 66ft (20m).
Breeding: Ovoviviparous, with large litters of up to 300 pups.

Blue shark

Prionace glauca

Identification: Long, narrow body with asymmetrical caudal fin. Dorsal fin is not particularly large, but pectoral fins are very long. Eyes appear large on conical, flattened head. Body is strikingly countershaded—dark blue on the back, bright blue on the flanks, and paler in color underneath.

Also known as the blue whaler because of its frequent association with dead whales, the blue shark is a species whose future may be under threat due to increased commercial exploitation—more than 10 million are killed annually for food. Blue sharks are curious and opportunistic, and readily investigate any possible source of food, including divers and shipwreck victims, thus earning a reputation as one of the more dangerous shark species. However, more usual food sources include squid and small fish, such as herring—schooling species are especially favored in the open ocean, where feeding opportunities can be few and far between. Female blue sharks can produce a great many young. One female was recorded carrying 134 embryos, though it is unlikely all would have survived to birth.

Distribution: Tropical and temperate oceans and seas worldwide.
Habitat: Open water to 1,150ft (350m) deep.
Food: Smaller fish and invertebrates, including octopuses and squid; may also scavenge carcasses of larger animals.
Size: Up to 13ft (4m). There have been unconfirmed reports of larger individuals being sighted.
Breeding: Ovoviviparous, 4–80 pups born per litter; there is no parental care.

Oceanic white tip shark

Carcharhinus longimanus

Distribution: Tropical and subtropical waters of all oceans.
Habitat: Surface waters of open ocean down to about 500ft (150m).
Food: Mainly bony fish, but this opportunistic feeder will eat virtually anything.
Size: Up to 13ft (4m).
Breeding: Ovoviviparous; litters of 1–15 pups.

The oceanic white tip is a solitary wanderer and an opportunistic feeder. It spends most its time cruising the warm surface waters of open oceans, with its acute senses alert to the possibility of food. Temporary aggregations may form around plentiful food resources, and the species is often involved in feeding frenzies. It is intensely curious and will eat almost anything, including medium to large fish, especially tuna and dorados, as well as other sharks, rays, squid, turtles, seabirds, and even human garbage. It will also eat humans, and it is often among the first of the large scavengers to gather at the scene of a disaster at sea. However, attacks close to shore are less likely. It is often accompanied by remoras, a species of fish that it seems not to eat.

Identification: A stout shark with a very large dorsal fin. The rest of the body is brownish-gray above and pale-colored below. Pectoral fins are long and tapering; tail fin lobes are asymmetric. All but the smallest fins are tipped with white. Often seen in association with remoras, which may hitch a ride by attaching themselves to the shark's body.

Silky shark (*Carcharhinus falcifomis*): up to 11.5ft (3.5m)
This is a long, slender, deep-water specialist found in subtropical and tropical waters as deep as 13,100ft (4,000m), but equally at home in surface waters, where it is regarded as dangerous to humans. In fact, the opposite is much more often the case, since this is one of the most intensively fished shark species, and is exploited for its meat, hide, fins, and liver oil.

Night shark (*Carcharhinus signatus*): up to 9ft (2.8m)
A slender brown shark with a long, pointed snout. Night sharks lurk in waters off Atlantic continental shelves, often in schools. They are nocturnal and eat small fish and squid. They pose no threat to humans.

Spinner shark (*Carcharhinus brevipinna*): up to 10ft (3m)
This gray-colored shark of the tropical and subtropical Atlantic, Indian, and Indo-Pacific Oceans has a very pointed snout and a highly asymmetric tail with a greatly elongated upper lobe. It is named for its feeding behavior, which involves a spectacular open-mouthed vertical ascent—complete with rapid spinning motion—through schools of fish. This is conducted at such speed that the shark may leap clear of the water.

Megamouth shark

Megachasma pelagios

This bizarre-looking species is known only from 27 confirmed sightings and just six landed specimens, the first of which was taken off Hawaii in 1976. Named for its enormous jaws, which can be protruded forward, the megamouth sounds intimidating, but the jaws are lined with very tiny hooked teeth and the species is at least a partial filter feeder, taking nothing larger than shrimp, jellyfish, and small pelagic fish. It migrates vertically on a daily basis, rising to surface waters at dusk along with the planktonic animals it feeds on. When the jaws are protruded, a bright white band of tissue is exposed between the upper lip and jaw. This is highly conspicuous, even in gloomy water, and may play some role in feeding or in individual recognition.

Distribution: Tropical waters of Pacific and Atlantic Oceans.
Habitat: Pelagic in open ocean, from surface waters possibly down to 3,300ft (1,000m).
Food: Larger planktonic animals, small fish, and jellyfish.
Size: Up to 18ft (5.5m).
Breeding: Ovoviviparous.

Identification: Large, rounded head and large mouth. Dark bluish-gray above, paler below. One large and one small dorsal fin; pectoral fins very large, as is the asymmetrical tail, fins usually tipped with white.

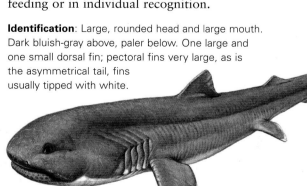

LANTERN FISH, OPAH, AND RIBBONFISH

The small order Myctophiformes contains about 250 species of lantern fish and blackchins, most of which are small and deep-dwelling, thus relatively little is known about them. The other species shown here all belong to the more diverse order Lampridiformes, which includes some of the most remarkable-looking and elusive fish in the seas.

Blue lantern fish

Tarletonbeania crenularis

Identification: The mouth of the blue lantern fish is large, extending back past the eye. The body is countershaded—dark metallic blue on the back, fading to silvery white on the underside. Even when not emitting light, the light organs on the belly and flanks can be seen as small, round spots (pimples).

Adult blue lantern fish spend their daylight hours at depth, rising much closer to the surface at night when they feed on plankton-dwelling crustaceans. Large eyes help the lantern fish to see in the gloom of deep water and in the dim light of moonlit surface waters. They are eaten by larger predatory fish, such as albacore. Different species of lantern fish are distinguished largely by the pattern of the light-producing photophores found on their lower body. In the blue lantern fish, these photophores are arranged in sparse clusters and rows. Unlike their parents, larval lantern fish cannot afford to expend the energy required to retreat to deep water and so remain in surface waters for several weeks, feeding on smaller plankton, such as algae, and fish and invertebrate larvae.

Distribution: Temperate and subarctic areas of the northern and eastern Pacific Ocean—off the coasts of North America, Russia, and Japan.
Habitat: Deep mid-water down to 2,300ft (700m).
Food: Crustaceans.
Size: Up to 5in (13cm).
Breeding: Oviparous; external fertilization; spawning occurs in winter and spring; no parental care.

Opah

Lampris guttatus

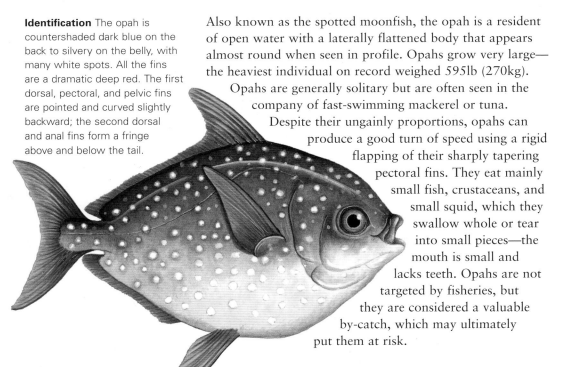

Identification The opah is countershaded dark blue on the back to silvery on the belly, with many white spots. All the fins are a dramatic deep red. The first dorsal, pectoral, and pelvic fins are pointed and curved slightly backward; the second dorsal and anal fins form a fringe above and below the tail.

Also known as the spotted moonfish, the opah is a resident of open water with a laterally flattened body that appears almost round when seen in profile. Opahs grow very large—the heaviest individual on record weighed 595lb (270kg). Opahs are generally solitary but are often seen in the company of fast-swimming mackerel or tuna. Despite their ungainly proportions, opahs can produce a good turn of speed using a rigid flapping of their sharply tapering pectoral fins. They eat mainly small fish, crustaceans, and small squid, which they swallow whole or tear into small pieces—the mouth is small and lacks teeth. Opahs are not targeted by fisheries, but they are considered a valuable by-catch, which may ultimately put them at risk.

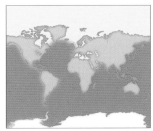

Distribution: Tropical and temperate Atlantic, Pacific, and Indian Oceans, and some adjoining seas.
Habitat: Mid-water at 150–1,600ft (50–500m).
Food: Smaller fish, crustaceans, and squid.
Size: Up to 6.6ft (2m).
Breeding: Oviparous; spawning occurs in spring.

Blackchin (*Scopelengys tristis*): up to 8in (20cm)
A small, drab-looking relative of the lantern fish, lacking light organs and metallic coloring. Blackchins are plankton eaters found throughout the tropics, and appear to spend their entire adult lives in water more than 1,300ft (400m) deep.

Dealfish (*Trachipterus arctica*): up to 10ft (3m)
One of several deep-sea ribbonfish species, the dealfish has a long, laterally flattened body that tapers steadily from head to tail. Confined to Arctic and north Atlantic waters, it eats smaller fish and squid and has a very slow reproductive cycle—taking 14 years to reach sexual maturity.

Scalloped ribbonfish (*Zu cristatus*):
up to 4ft (1.2m)
This tropical ribbonfish has an abruptly tapering body, is laterally flattened but it is less planklike than its larger relatives, the dealfish and oarfish. Juveniles have an undulating, scalloped edge to the belly. The first rays of the dorsal fin and the pelvic fins form long streamers.

Sailfin (*Velifer hypselopterus*):
up to 15.75in (40cm)
A disk-shaped, laterally flattened fish with large, ragged-looking dorsal and anal fins. Thought to be rather rare, the species is restricted to tropical waters of the Indo-Pacific Ocean.

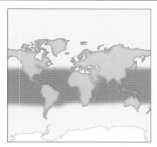

Oarfish

Regalecus glesne

The oarfish may well be the longest species of fish—specimens up to 55.8ft (17m) long have been reported, though the largest reliable record is of a specimen 36ft (11m) long. This extraordinary creature is thought to be the inspiration for many myths of sea monsters—even the Loch Ness monster. Oarfish are most often encountered washed up on land—sightings of live individuals are rare. Two recent accounts suggest that the fish maintains a vertical position in the water, propelling itself slowly with rippling movements of the dorsal fin, which runs the entire length of the body. The long, ribbonlike pelvic fins, meanwhile, are held out to the sides as stabilizers. Oarfish have no teeth and instead of scales their skin is covered with a fine coating of guanine, the material that gives all fish their silvery color.

Distribution: Recorded in Atlantic Ocean and Mediterranean Sea, also in Indo-Pacific waters and eastern Pacific Ocean.
Habitat: Mid-water of open oceans at 60–3,300ft (20–1,000m).
Food: Pelagic crustaceans, small fish, and squid.
Size: May exceed 36ft (11m) in length.
Breeding: Oviparous; larvae known from surface waters.

Identification: Enormously long body is laterally flattened, silvery in color with dark, bluish-gray markings. The fins are crimson. The first dozen or so rays of the long fringing dorsal fin form a spectacular crest. Each of the pelvic fins comprises a single soft ray.

Tube-eye

Stylephorus chordatus

Distribution: All tropical oceans worldwide.
Habitat: Deep water.
Food: Small planktonic animals, mainly copepods.
Size: 12in (30cm).
Breeding: Not known.

A fish of deep tropical oceans, the tube-eye has upward-pointing goggle eyes and a long, silver body that tapers to the tail. The lower lobe of the tail fin is elongated to form a whiplike extension. Like the oarfish (above), the species has a dorsal fin running the length of the body, and it swims vertically in the water. It migrates from the deep ocean to surface waters in order to feed each evening, and it uses powerful suction to draw small crustaceans, such as copepods, into its small mouth. The buccal cavity (mouth chamber) can expand like a balloon to 40 times its resting volume to generate the necessary suction. Plankton is filtered from the water as it drains out through the gill slits. The details of its life history and breeding are virtually unknown.

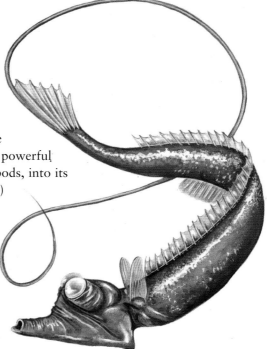

Identification: Long, tapering body ends in very long, whiplike tail fin, the rays of which are up to twice as long as the rest of the body. Large eyes are telescopic. The snout is tubular and the mouth is small.

ANGLERS AND TETRAODONTIFORMS

The grotesque-looking anglerfish, many of which have evolved dorsal apparatus to "lure" bait, are often used to illustrate the weird and wonderful life of the deep oceans, though many species actually live in shallow water. The order Tetraodontiformes is famous for another reason—it includes the world's largest bony fish, the magnificent oceanic sunfish.

Sargassum fish

Histrio histrio

Identification: The body is in variable shades of brown with various flaps and frills to mimic the fronds of weed among which it usually lives. The dorsal fin ray is modified into a stout fishing lure to tempt prey close enough to ambush.

This unusual anglerfish is a shallow-water, open-ocean specialist. It is usually associated with the floating seaweed *Sargassum*, but will also make use of other flotsam. The pelvic fins are specialized and able to grasp, something like hands. The Sargassum fish is a relatively weak swimmer, but uses its fins to hold onto fronds of weed to avoid being swept away. Its camouflage makes it difficult to see among the weeds. Breeding starts with courtship, with the male closely following the female. She then makes abrupt darts to the surface to spawn. The eggs are embedded in a jelly that expands on contact with seawater, creating a floating raft. The eggs may drift far from shelter, and young fish are vulnerable.

Distribution: Ranges widely in Indian Ocean and Indo-Pacific; also found in western and southern Pacific and Atlantic.
Habitat: Surface waters in drifts of *Sargassum* seaweed.
Food: Smaller fish and crustaceans (shrimp).
Size: 8in (20cm).
Breeding: Eggs fertilized externally, develop in floating mass with no parental care.

Giant sea devil

Ceratias holboelli

This is the original sea devil—the first and largest deep-sea angler to be described. Prey, in the form of smaller fish, is attracted by the sea devil twitching a fishing lure (the esca), formed from the modified first spine of the dorsal fin (the ilicium), and is then engulfed by the angler's huge mouth. Needlelike teeth ensure there is no escape. The other dorsal fin rays form distinctive knobbly protuberances, called "caruncles," along the back. These fish are slow swimmers. Female sea devils produce eggs that float in rafts of jelly and hatch into tiny larvae that live as plankton. Males remain very small, and when mature, seek out the larger mature females, which release chemical signals to guide suitors in the dark water.

When it finds a female, the male latches onto her body with sharp teeth and in time becomes permanently fused. He extracts what little nourishment he needs directly from her blood supply, through a placentalike intermeshing of blood vessels, and produces sperm to fertilize her eggs.

Distribution: Tropical, subtropical, and temperate oceans worldwide.
Habitat: Mostly deep water to 6,562ft (2,000m).
Food: Smaller fish.
Size: Females up to 4ft (1.2m) long; males from 0.4–6.3in (1–16cm).
Breeding: Males form parasitic attachments to females. Eggs fertilized externally, develop in floating mass with no parental care.

Identification: Adult female has a bulbous body that tapers to the tail. Mouth is huge and opens upward. Dorsal fin is modified into a fishing lure and caruncles.

Toothed sea devil (*Neoceratias spinifer*)
2.4–2.8in (6–7cm)
This mini-monster of the western central Pacific is the only known member of its family. Unusual among anglers in lacking a lure, it relies on a nightmarish array of moveable teeth mounted on the outer jaws.

Deep sea angler (*Linophryne macrodon*):
females 3.5in (9cm); males 0.8in (2cm)
Females of this eastern central Pacific species have the most elaborate appendages of any angler species. They also bear a large barbel dangling from the lower jaw. Both lure and barbel are bioluminescent.

Whipnose (*Gigantactis elsmani*):
females 15in (38cm)
The fly fishermen of deep-sea anglers, the large upper jaw bears a highly elongated ilicium, or fishing rod, with a fleshy, tentacled lure at the tip. Recorded in various deep-water Pacific habitats, but full range still unknown.

Deep sea coffinfish (*Bathychaunax melanostomus*): up to 4in (10cm)
This Indian Ocean species belongs to a family of anglers known as sea toads. Its bulbous body and narrow tail are covered with small spines. Lure rests in a groove on the head when not in use.

Spotted oceanic triggerfish

Canthidermis maculatus

Triggerfish are named for the shape of the first dorsal fin, which can be locked in an upright position, presumably as an antipredation measure that makes the fish difficult to swallow. This species is characterized by a mainly blue or purple body, with some countershading. Unlike most other triggerfish, which are associated with reefs and coastal waters, the oceanic trigger is something of a nomad. It relies on the shelter of floating debris, such as detached fronds of weed, logs, or pieces of floating wreckage and debris. This cover is essential—without it, the trigger is exposed to predation. It eats other, smaller fish it finds there, but is especially intolerant of other triggers. It will dash at intruders aggressively, driving them away from its territory.

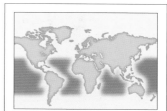

Distribution: Tropical and subtropical oceans worldwide.
Habitat: Surface dweller down to about 330ft (100m), associated with flotsam.
Food: Smaller fish and pelagic invertebrates.
Size: 20in (50cm).
Breeding: External fertilization, no parental care.

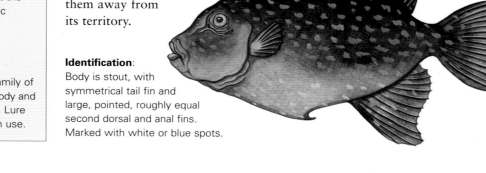

Identification:
Body is stout, with symmetrical tail fin and large, pointed, roughly equal second dorsal and anal fins. Marked with white or blue spots.

Giant oceanic sunfish

Mola mola

Distribution: Tropical to temperate waters of Pacific, Atlantic, and Indian Oceans.
Habitat: Open ocean, close to surface, but may dive to 1,600ft (500m) or more.
Food: Jellyfish, fish, mollusks, crustaceans, and echinoderms.
Size: 11ft (3.3m) long.
Breeding: Produces hundreds of millions of tiny eggs that are fertilized externally; these drift in the oceans with no parental care.

This is the world's largest bony fish, weighing anything up to 5,070lb (2,300kg). The vast, disk-shaped body is laterally compressed and stabilized by tall dorsal and anal fins. The name refers not to the fish's shape, but to its habit of "sunbathing" while floating on its side near the surface. There is no tail; instead the body ends with a rounded rudder (the clavus) formed from the last few rays of the dorsal and anal fins. The skin is scaleless and tough. The sunfish has well-developed teeth, which are fused to form a kind of beak. The jaws are powerful enough to bite through shell and bone, but the mouth is small and the sunfish is not a fast swimmer, so it preys mostly on slow-moving or drifting animals. Mature females produce an astonishing number of tiny eggs, which drift the oceans—the chances of any one being fertilized and surviving infancy are small.

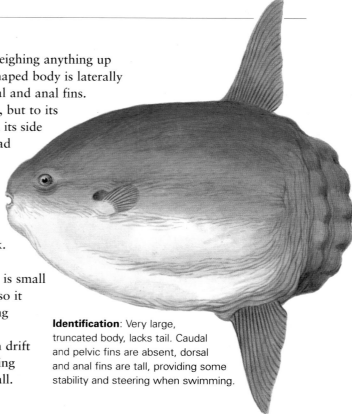

Identification: Very large, truncated body, lacks tail. Caudal and pelvic fins are absent, dorsal and anal fins are tall, providing some stability and steering when swimming.

JACKS, REMORAS, AND RELATIVES

These members of the large order Percifomes reflect just some of the diversity within this vast group. They all possess spiny fin rays, pelvic fins located well forward at the throat, and thin, bonelike scales with a serrated edge. Most are fast-swimming predators, but a few are positively sluggish and some even resort to hitching rides on other fish.

Yellowtail amberjack

Seriola lalandi

Yellowtail amberjacks are a familiar sight on reefs and in coastal waters, but they also live in open ocean—juveniles, in particular, often live in schools far out to sea, having been carried with ocean currents as larvae. Large adults are more often solitary. All jacks are efficient swimmers—the carangiform mode of swimming, where the head stays still and the tail sweeps from side to side, is named after this family. The tall, forked tail fin offers powerful thrust without excessive turbulence. Amberjacks are predators of smaller fish species and invertebrates, which are ambushed and caught with a burst of speed.

Identification: Long, torpedo-shaped body with large, forked tail. Body is dark blue above and white below; tail fin is yellow or dark with yellow trailing edge. Single dorsal and anal fins are small with a triangular leading portion and an elongate fin base reaching nearly to the tail.

Distribution: Tropical and warm-temperate waters worldwide.
Habitat: Coasts, reefs, and open ocean, usually close to sea floor, from shallows to 2,700ft (825m).
Food: Small fish, cephalopods, and crustaceans.
Size: 8.2ft (2.5m).
Breeding: Oviparous; no parental care.

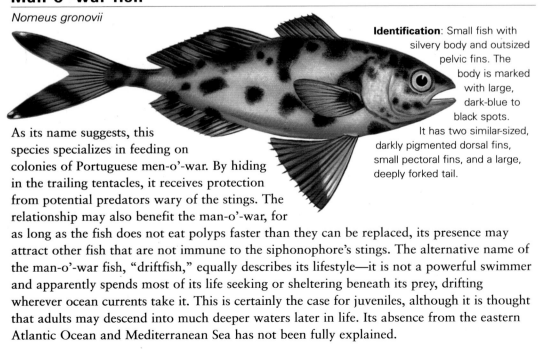

Man-o'-war fish

Nomeus gronovii

Identification: Small fish with silvery body and outsized pelvic fins. The body is marked with large, dark-blue to black spots. It has two similar-sized, darkly pigmented dorsal fins, small pectoral fins, and a large, deeply forked tail.

As its name suggests, this species specializes in feeding on colonies of Portuguese men-o'-war. By hiding in the trailing tentacles, it receives protection from potential predators wary of the stings. The relationship may also benefit the man-o'-war, for as long as the fish does not eat polyps faster than they can be replaced, its presence may attract other fish that are not immune to the siphonophore's stings. The alternative name of the man-o'-war fish, "driftfish," equally describes its lifestyle—it is not a powerful swimmer and apparently spends most of its life seeking or sheltering beneath its prey, drifting wherever ocean currents take it. This is certainly the case for juveniles, although it is thought that adults may descend into much deeper waters later in life. Its absence from the eastern Atlantic Ocean and Mediterranean Sea has not been fully explained.

Distribution: Tropical and subtropical waters of Indian, Pacific, and western Atlantic Oceans.
Habitat: Juveniles and sub-adults, surface waters from coastal areas to far offshore; adults may live near seabed.
Food: Jellyfish and siphonophores.
Size: 15.4in (39cm).
Breeding: Oviparous; details not known

Pilotfish (*Naucrates ductor*): up to 28in (70cm)
The pilotfish (above) is a bold-patterned relative of the jacks. Its body is a dark-blue color or black with seven or eight broad, evenly spaced, white vertical bands. It lives in the surface waters of tropical and subtropical seas worldwide, and it is associated with floating objects, such as seaweed and jellyfish.

Halfmoon fish (*Medialuna californiensis*): up to 19in (48cm)
A Pacific chub, from the perciform family Kyphosidae, the halfmoon is found around coasts and rocky reefs. Farther out to sea, it habitually associates with floating kelp or sargassum weed, or other flotsam. It is a popular food fish and is caught both commercially and for sport.

Horse mackerel (*Trachurus trachurus*): up to 28in (70cm)
A widespread pelagic (a fish favoring the open ocean) carangid, the horse mackerel is a medium-size, schooling fish of the Atlantic and western Pacific Oceans. The body is a greenish-gray color above and silvery below, and it has large keeled (ridged) scales on the flanks. It is fished commercially in the eastern Atlantic Ocean and the North Sea.

Remora

Remora remora

Remoras can live a free-swimming existence, but their particular speciality is hitching a ride by attaching themselves to the body of larger fish, especially sharks and rays. They will also travel attached to turtles, cetaceans, and even inanimate objects, such as ship hulls or diving gear. The attachment is made by a modification of the dorsal fin, which forms a large suction disk just behind the head. The disk is made up of stout, flexible membranes that can be raised and lowered to generate suction. The remora "pays its fare" by picking off any parasites clinging to the host's skin—mainly copepods. It may also detach from the host in order to pursue free-living prey. Remoras are not parasites and appear to be tolerated by their hosts.

Distribution: Tropical, subtropical, and warm-temperate oceans and seas worldwide.
Habitat: Reef and pelagic zones as passengers of larger animals.
Food: Parasitic crustaceans and small, free-living planktonic invertebrates.
Size: 33.5in (85cm).
Breeding: Details not known.

Identification: Elongate body, large, slightly forked tail fin. Pectoral fins are rounded, second dorsal fin is a low triangle. First dorsal fin is modified into an oval-shaped suction disk on head. Color variable from dark gray or brown to off-white.

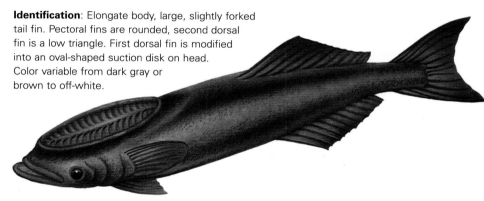

Dorado dolphinfish

Coryphaena hippurus

Distribution: Tropical and subtropical waters of Atlantic, Indian, and Pacific Oceans.
Habitat: Open ocean, and coastal areas, occasionally brackish water; surface waters down to 280ft (85m).
Food: Small fish and zooplankton.
Size: 6.6ft (2m).
Breeding: Oviparous; breeds several times a year in its 5-year lifespan, associating in pairs to spawn.

This large, boldly colored fish is known from coastal and open oceans. It lives in schools and frequently shelters under pieces of flotsam. Dorados or mahimahi are a prized food fish, often sold simply as "dolphin," to the confusion of nonlocals. Dorados are themselves active predators—as larvae and juveniles, they feed mainly on small crustaceans, graduating to fish as they grow larger. As adults, they will tackle almost anything of suitable size. They are quick swimmers, able to make darting pursuits even of other swift species, such as flying fish. They themselves fall prey to other speed specialists, such as tuna and billfish.

Identification: Body tapers from a large head and upper body to a large, forked tail. Downturned mouth. A single dorsal fin runs the length of the body, pectorals and pelvics large, anal fin long and low. Males have conspicuous bony head crest. Body is vibrantly colored: green, blue, and yellow on back and flanks, white and yellow underside. Fins are blue and green.

TUNAS, MACKEREL, AND BARRACUDAS

With their torpedo-shaped, muscle-packed bodies, these perciforms are built for speed and endurance.
They are among the most voracious hunters in the seas, but also among the most hunted—their meaty,
oily flesh makes them enormously popular, and they support large fishing industries. Overfishing, plus
the increasing levels of pollutants being accumulated in the flesh, are arousing serious concern.

Northern bluefin tuna

Thunnus thynnus

This is probably the largest of all the tuna species. The largest known individual was 15ft (4.58m) in length and weighed 1,508lb (684kg). This size is achieved through an insatiable appetite for smaller fish and invertebrates, which the bluefin hunts day and night outside the breeding season. Bluefins live in schools often containing a mix of species, but all members of the school will be of similar size to avoid accidental cannibalism. These "warm-blooded" fish migrate north in the summer and spend the winter in the tropics, where they breed. Their huge swimming muscles make them exceptionally meaty. There is real concern that the species is being overfished.

Identification: Large, torpedo-shaped fish, two dorsal fins followed by series of finlets on tailstock. Pectoral and pelvic fins short, anal and second dorsal fin highly falcate (sicklelike), caudal fin a stiff, symmetrical crescent with darkly pigmented lobes. Body countershaded—bluish-gray above, silvery below.

Distribution: Northern Atlantic, Mediterranean, and Black Sea. Sub-population off coast of South Africa. American range extends from Canada to Brazil.
Habitat: Oceanic, usually in surface waters, occasionally down to 9,800ft (3,000m); visits coastal waters.
Food: Smaller fish and pelagic invertebrates; will also take benthic animals and kelp close to shore.
Size: 14.7ft (4.5m).
Breeding: Oviparous, spawning up to 10 million floating eggs a year.

Albacore

Thunnus alalunga

Identification: Body rotund but highly streamlined with pointed snout and tapering tailstock. Eyes are large. Two dorsal fins and dorsal and ventral rows of finlets. Pectoral and anal fins are small; dark-blue caudal fins form a shallow crescent-shaped tail with pointed tips. Pectoral fins are very long. Body steely blue above, silvery white below.

These fish move around their distributional range in schools, performing extensive migrations in search of food or to spawn in tropical waters in the summer. They often congregate at thermoclines—depths where the water changes temperature, where upwelling currents bring nutrients up from below and prey is more abundant. Large albacore tend to live deeper than small ones. Albacore have a strong schooling instinct and often form mixed schools with other types of tuna. As with other tunas, overfishing is a concern. The flesh is considered to be excellent and is sold as high-quality canned tuna. Also worrying from a consumer's perspective is the tendency of the species to accumulate high levels of mercury in the flesh.

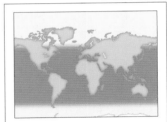

Distribution: All tropical and temperate oceans and seas including Mediterranean. Very common off Australian coast.
Habitat: Pelagic in open ocean, mainly in surface waters to 1,968ft (600m).
Food: Smaller fish.
Size: 4.6ft (1.4m).
Breeding: Oviparous; spawn in tropical waters during the summer.

Wahoo (*Acanthocybium solandri*):
up to 8.2ft (2.5m)
A close relative of tunas and mackerel, the wahoo (above) is a long, narrow-bodied predatory fish known from the surface waters of warm, tropical, and subtropical oceans and seas worldwide. It can be solitary or schooling, and is fished commercially and for sport.

Skipjack tuna (*Katsuwonus pelamis*):
up to 3.5ft (1.08m)
A small, cosmopolitan species of tuna. Skipjacks live in schools, and hunt smaller fish and pelagic invertebrates. They are important prey for larger tunas and sharks. Skipjack tuna account for the majority of tuna consumed by humans.

Bonito (*Sarda chiliensis*): up to 3.25ft (1m)
A pelagic schooling tunafish of tropical and temperate oceans, the bonito is also an important commercial and game species.

Spanish mackerel (*Scomberomorus maculata*):
up to 36in (90cm)
A streamlined, silvery mackerel of Atlantic and Pacific surface waters. Spanish mackerel form huge schools that are targeted by highly commercial fisheries. Like other scombrids, they are fast swimmers and prey on smaller fish and zooplankton.

Atlantic mackerel

Scomber scombrus

Schools of this species tend to remain in deep water in the winter, but in the summer, feed close to the surface, traveling in search of suitable prey. Plankton, crustaceans, and fish larvae make up the bulk of the diet, but the mackerel is also well adapted for pursuing small fish such as sand eels. Mackerel lack a swim bladder, and rely on lightweight oily musculature as well as continual, fast swimming to stop them from sinking. Their gills are ventilated by the force of water passing into the open mouth rather than by any kind of pump, so if they stop swimming, they die. The species is highly commercial and supports large fishing industries.

Identification: Slender, near cylindrical body with pointed snout and tapering tailstock. Tiny scales; body is silvery green to white on belly, marked with vertical or slightly oblique black bands on back and flanks. All fins are small, tailstock bears tiny finlets, caudal fin forms a pointed crescent.

Distribution: Parts of northern Atlantic, also Mediterranean and Black Sea. Western Atlantic range is from Labrador to Cape Lookout, Oregon.
Habitat: Oceanic, in surface waters to 650ft (200m).
Food: Zooplankton and small fish.
Size: 23.6in (60cm).
Breeding: Oviparous; larvae feed actively and attain lengths of 10in (25cm) in first year.
Status: Common and widespread, but heavy exploitation may lead to declines; not listed by IUCN.

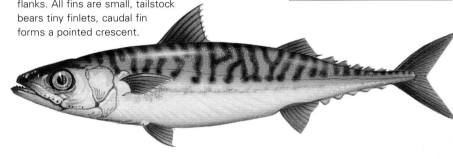

Great barracuda

Sphyraena barracuda

Unlike most tunas and mackerel, the great barracuda is a largely solitary species, though juveniles may form small schools and adults will gather at rich food resources. Barracudas are opportunistic or ambush predators of other fish, capable of short bursts of rapid acceleration. Their sharp teeth easily snag prey, and the jaws are powerful enough to bite fish in half that are too large to be swallowed whole. They are curious of divers and swimmers, but despite a bad reputation, pose little serious danger. Attacks on humans do occur, but these usually consist of a single lunge, and although painful, a barracuda bite is unlikely to be fatal. The species is fished for sport and sometimes for eating, although it is frequently contaminated with dangerous levels of toxins.

Identification: A long, slender, cylindrical body with a long, pointed head and large eyes. Very sharp teeth. Lower jaw extends further than upper jaw. Body is silvery green, marked on upper flanks with dark bands and also black blotches of variable size and shape. Dorsal and anal fins can be raised and lowered to aid steering.

Distribution: Tropical and subtropical waters of oceans and seas worldwide.
Habitat: Surface waters down to 330ft (100m); most often recorded near shore, but performs extensive migrations into open ocean.
Food: Fish.
Size: 6.6ft (2m).
Breeding: Oviparous; spawns offshore in deep water during the spring.

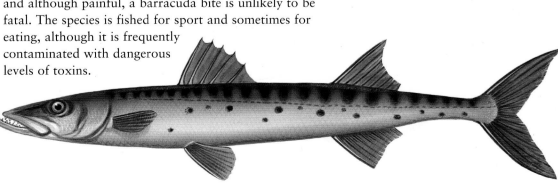

BILLFISH

These spectacular members of the order Perciformes rank among the most glamorous of marine fish—their speed and athleticism is legendary and their dramatic fins and coloration make them the ultimate trophy for many game fishermen. All billfish possess a bony, swordlike extension of the upper jaw, which is used to strike down prey.

Blue marlin

Makaira nigricans

The largest and most spectacular of the billfish, the blue marlin is well adapted for sustained, high-speed swimming. Its extremely muscular body is superbly streamlined, and its powerful tail generates enormous thrust, allowing it to swim fast and tirelessly. The pelvic and pectoral fins fold into grooves in the body to enhance streamlining. The species is also highly acrobatic, sometimes leaping a yard or more clear of the water surface. These qualities make is a very popular gamefish. It also makes good eating and is heavily fished in many parts of its range. Marlin are generally solitary and hunt by day in surface waters. Certain populations appear to show a marked preference for open, deep water. Swipes of the bill are used to stun prey. Marlin sometimes work cooperatively when hunting and in the excitement, some of the colors on the body appear to "light up" as the pigment cells glow under nervous stimulation.

Distribution: Range shown here is pantropical in Atlantic, Indian, and Pacific Oceans. However, there is some debate as to whether Pacific and Indian dwellers constitute a separate species, *M. mazara*.
Habitat: Pelagic; open ocean down to 660ft (200m).
Food: Smaller fish, cephalopods.
Size: 16.4ft (5m).
Breeding: Oviparous; no parental care.

Identification: Cylindrical body tapers from the back of the head to the tail. First dorsal fin is long and tall, second much smaller; pelvic and pectoral fins are small. Tail fins form a slender crescent; bill is less than a quarter of body length and stout. Dark blue or black dorsal area; below lateral line is silvery-white with 15 vertical stripes on each flank, each bearing pale blue spots.

Swordfish

Xiphias gladius

The scientific name *gladius* means "sword," as in gladiator. The bill of the swordfish is flat with sharp edges, and is used as a deadly weapon, to kill and slice prey into pieces small enough to swallow. Swordfish tackle a wide variety of prey, mostly other fish, but also pelagic invertebrates. They travel long distances, overwintering and spawning in warm waters in springtime, then heading for cooler waters to take advantage of seasonally abundant prey over the summer. Juveniles have a fully developed sword that is 0.4in (1cm) long, and begin hunting immediately. Females grow slightly faster than males and reach a larger size. Swordfish is a tasty food fish; however, the species' position at the top of the food chain means it has a tendency to accumulate dangerously high levels of certain marine pollutants, especially mercury, so frequent consumption is not recommended.

Distribution: Tropical and temperate oceans and seas worldwide.
Habitat: Pelagic in mid-water at 650–2,600ft (200–800m).
Food: Fish, cephalopods, crustaceans.
Size: 15ft (4.55m).
Breeding: Oviparous; spawns in spring, and larvae develop rapidly.

Identification: Body tapers from head to tail, which bears long caudal fins forming a crescent. Pelvic fins are absent, pectorals are long and low slung. Single dorsal fin is tall, and single anal fin is small—both are falcate. Head is large with large eyes, and the upper jaw is modified into a long, bladelike bill.

DEEP-SEA WHALES

These giant whales include the largest members of the animal kingdom. Most undertake vast migratory journeys in a lifetime, and some may live for more than 100 years. They may communicate with others of their species across hundreds of miles via "songs." The slow reproduction rate means that populations are unable to recover rapidly from the impact of past commercial exploitation.

Sperm whale

Physeter macrocephalus

The largest of the toothed whales and the largest predatory animal on Earth, sperm whales tackle prey up to 33ft (10m) long. They are also the deepest-diving mammals, able to descend an estimated 10,000ft (3,000m). Sperm whales mature slowly—calves begin taking solid food at 2 years, but may continue to supplement this with milk for 10 years or so. This slow reproductive rate makes them vulnerable to overexploitation, and they suffered heavy losses before hunting was banned in the 1980s. The oil inside the head, known as spermaceti, was used as a high-quality lubricant. In life, the spermaceti is thought to control buoyancy and focus sound. Also of value are the teeth, used in scrimshaw, and ambergris—a gray substance voided from the gut and used in perfume making.

Identification: Massive head, which contains spermaceti organ, is one-third body length. Teeth present only on lower jaw, which is very narrow. Skin of body is often wrinkled. Dorsal fin is very small and set well back, followed by several small bumps. Pectoral fins are short and broad; tail flukes are very wide.

Distribution: All oceans except ice-bound polar waters, although may be seen close to pack ice.
Habitat: Deep water; dives to 10,000ft. (3,000m)
Food: Giant squid and other deep-water cephalopods.
Size: Up to 60ft (18.3m).
Breeding: Single calf born every 4–6 years after a gestation period of 15–18 months; calf weaned at 2 years. May live for more than 70 years.

Bowhead whale

Balaena mysticetus

Identification: Very large, deep-bodied whale with a massive head, and enormous, highly arching jaws that support 600 or more strips or plates of baleen up to 13ft (4m) in length. There is a ridge on top of the head, in front of the blowholes. Dorsal fin is absent, pectorals are broad and triangular, and tail flukes form a notched triangle. Males vocalize a haunting and highly varied song in the spring, in order to attract females.

This giant of Arctic waters spends its life close to the edge of the sea ice. It can travel considerable distances under ice, and if necessary, can ram air holes in ice almost 6.6ft (2m) thick. There is evidence that this species uses echolocation to help it navigate around ice floes and icebergs. Vocalizations, or "songs," are common. The massive head and bowed jaw support hundreds of strips, or plates, of a horny material known as baleen. These plates act as strainers, filtering planktonic life from the water as the whale swims. The discovery of nineteenth-century harpoon tips in individuals alive at the end of the last century suggests the species is very long-lived.

Distribution: Circumpolar waters of the North Atlantic, North Pacific, and Arctic Oceans.
Habitat: Deep water, close to pack ice.
Food: Mainly krill and copepods, as well as other planktonic invertebrates.
Size: Up to 65ft (19.8m).
Breeding: Single calf born every 3–4 years; weaned from about 12 months, but may stay with mother several more years. May live for over 200 years.

DIRECTORY OF FRESHWATER SPECIES

The freshwater world is dominated by rivers. These ribbons of life cut through the landscape and feed lakes, swamps, and virtually all other freshwater habitats. Some continents are known as much by their great rivers as by their countries. The names of these waterways alone are enough to evoke the feeling of the regions they flow through, even if those are places we have never been to or seen. Some continents are dominated by just one or a few great rivers. South America, for instance, has the Amazon, and much of Africa is drained by the Niger, Congo, and Nile. Other continents, however, have many of these arteries. In North America, they include the Mississippi, Colorado, and Columbia, to name just a few.

Just as rivers are the dominant freshwater habitats, so fish are the dominant vertebrates within them. Fish have evolved a great variety of shapes and forms to take advantage of the diversity that freshwater habitats offer. Some fish have become highly streamlined, high-speed hunters, while others have evolved perfect camouflage and spend much of their time almost stationary. Where waters are murky, many fish have become adept at finding their way around using touch and other senses. Physical conditions have dictated the directions in which these creatures have evolved. Although some fish are generalists, many have become so perfectly adapted for living in particular types of freshwater habitats—or even in particular regions within those habitats—that they are rarely found anywhere else.

Left: Zebra danio (Danio rerio) *school within a shallow, densely vegetated habitat. The creatures common in this type of freshwater environment are often camouflaged with stripes to blend in with the dappled light and plant roots.*

LAMPREYS AND STURGEONS

Lampreys and sturgeons include some of the most primitive of all freshwater fish. Lampreys predate even the sharks and rays in evolutionary terms. They have large eyes, one nostril on the top of the head, seven gills on each side, and no pectoral fins. Sturgeons are primitive bony fish, with skeletons made partly from cartilage, partly from bone. Their flesh is edible and their roe is used to produce caviar.

American brook lamprey

Lampetra appendix

Lampreys are primitive fish comprising the last living relatives of some of the first fish to appear on Earth. Unlike other fish, they lack jaws and instead have sucker-shaped mouths surrounded by rings of teeth. Many lampreys are predatory or parasitic, clinging to the sides of other fish and using their teeth to slice out divots of flesh. The American brook lamprey, however, is different. Larvae feed by burrowing into sand and silt and filtering tiny organisms, often in slow-water areas of the streams where they live. The adults do not feed at all, and only live long enough to spawn before dying.

Identification: A long, eel-like body with two distinct dorsal fins and a black stripe at the base of them. The oral disk is narrower than the rest of the head. Teeth are blunt rather than sharp and pointed, as they are in predatory or parasitic species.

Distribution: Atlantic river basins south of St. Lawrence River, Quebec. Also Great Lakes and Mississippi River basin.
Habitat: Gravel or sandy riffles and runs of clear water streams.
Food: Protozoans, algae, and other microorganisms.
Size: Up to 13.75in (35cm).
Breeding: Gravelly areas. Female lays eggs in saucer-shaped nest, built by the male using his mouth.

White sturgeon

Acipenser transmontanus

One of the biggest freshwater fish in the world—and North America's biggest—the white sturgeon has been known to reach 20ft (6.1m) in length, and weigh as much as 1,389lbs (630kg), almost three-quarters of a ton. Because of its great size, this fish is hard to miss but it is also very rare. As a top predator, it is naturally less common than many smaller species, but pressure from anglers, combined with the construction of dams in some of the rivers where it lives and spawns, have caused it to decline in parts of its range. River pollution is also thought to have had an impact on the species.

Identification: Unmistakably a member of the sturgeon family (Acipenseridae). Gray or brownish above, with a pale belly. This species is distinguished by having four barbels very close to the snout tip. The barbels are usually closer to the snout tip than they are to the mouth. The snouts of young fish are quite sharp but become more blunt with age.

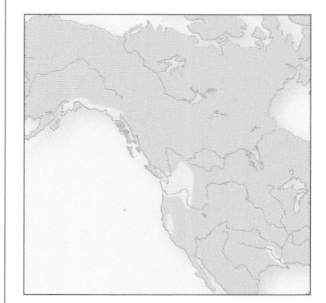

Distribution: Pacific coast, coastal rivers from Alaska to central California. Introduced into lower Colorado River.
Habitat: Estuaries of large rivers. Colorado River population is landlocked.
Food: Opportunistic—wide range of fish and aquatic invertebrates.
Size: Up to 20ft (6.1m).
Breeding: Adults migrate upstream to breed. Eggs and sperm released into open water during times of peak river flow.

Lake sturgeon

Acipenser fulvescens

This fish resembles the white sturgeon, but is smaller in size and occupies a different habitat range. Like all sturgeons, it has rows of bony plates (scutes) running down its back, belly, and the sides of its body. These scutes protect the fish against predators, particularly when they are young, since they make the fish unpalatable. Adult lake sturgeon migrate to the pebbly shores of lakes to breed, where one female may lay as many as 3 million eggs in a single season. Despite being smaller than the white sturgeon, this fish can still reach 6ft (1.8m) long and weigh 198lb (90kg) on average, and much larger individuals have been recorded over the years.

Identification: The body is olive-brown to gray above and white below. The barbels are farther back than in white sturgeon, lying almost beneath the nostrils. The scutes on the back and sides are the same color as the skin.

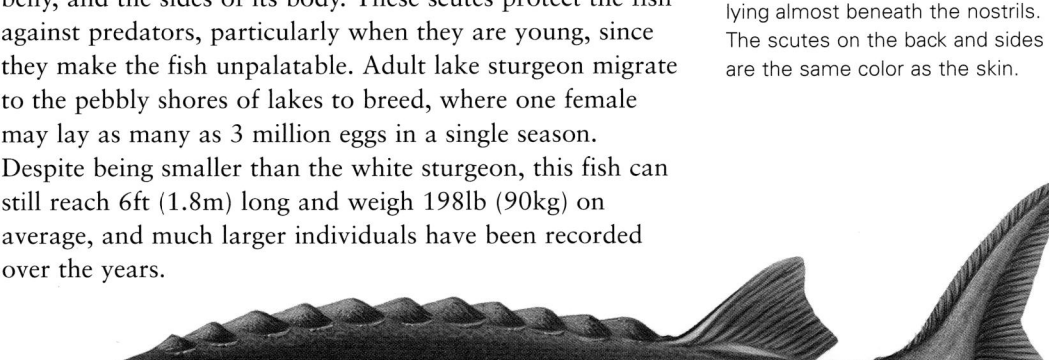

Distribution: Lakes, Atlantic-draining rivers from Hudson Bay through Mississippi drainages to Alabama. Recorded in Great Lakes and large lakes in New York State and Vermont.
Habitat: Gravel bottoms of large, clear rivers and lakes.
Food: Smaller fish and aquatic invertebrates.
Size: Up to 9ft (2.7m).
Breeding: Pebbly areas with no mud. No nests—sperm and eggs released into water.

Pacific lamprey (*Lampetra tridentata*): up to 30in (76cm)
As its name suggests, this parasitic lamprey spends most of its life in the Pacific Ocean. However, it also enters the clear coastal rivers and streams of North America's Pacific seaboard to breed. It resembles the American brook lamprey, but it has sharper teeth and an oral disk that is wider than the rest of its head. It is the only North American species of lamprey that is known to spawn more than once in its lifetime.

Chestnut lamprey (*Ichthyomyzon castaneus*): up to 15in (38cm)
This freshwater lamprey is most easily recognized by its color, which also gives it its name, being yellow or tan above and white to light olive-yellow below. Also a parasitic species, it lives in Atlantic-draining rivers and streams, and in lakes along their courses, including the Great Lakes.

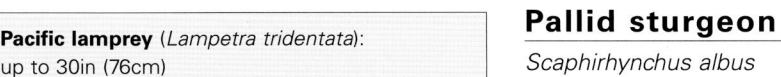

Shortnose sturgeon (*Acipenser brevirostrum*): up to 3.6ft (1.1m)
The common name of this species (*above*) highlights its distinguishing feature, the one by which it is most easily separated from its relatives. It inhabits the estuaries and bays of the Atlantic coast from New Brunswick to Florida, traveling up coastal rivers to spawn. It is listed as Vulnerable and is protected by law throughout its range.

Pallid sturgeon

Scaphirhynchus albus

This sturgeon is found in large, silty rivers with swift currents. It was only identified as a separate species in 1905 and is now listed as Endangered by the IUCN. The pallid sturgeon is a larger relative of the similar-looking and more common shovelnose sturgeon (*Scaphirhynchus platorynchus*), which also lives in the Mississippi River basin. It has a flattened, shovel-shaped snout that it uses to stir up the sediment to find its prey. It is one of the largest fish found in this river basin, weighing as much as 80lb (36kg). In contrast, the shovelnose sturgeon rarely exceeds 5lb (2.25kg). Like all sturgeons, it is a long-lived fish, with individuals often exceeding 50 years in age.

Distribution: Main channels of Missouri River and lower Mississippi River.
Habitat: Deep river channels, usually in fast-flowing, turbid water over sand or gravel.
Food: Other fish and aquatic invertebrates.
Size: Up to 6ft (1.85m).
Breeding: Over gravel or other hard surfaces. Eggs take 5–8 days to hatch. Adults may go for as long as 10 years between spawnings, although most breed every year or two.

Identification: There are four fleshy lobes on the lower lip and the belly is completely scaleless. The snout is long and flattened. The bases of the outer barbels are usually positioned farther down the snout than those of the inner barbels.

SALMON AND TROUT

Salmon and trout are among the most important of North America's freshwater fish, providing a livelihood for fishermen and food for a wide range of animals. Salmon have a special cultural meaning for many Northern Pacific coastal dwellers—some tribes have a ceremony to honor their annual return—and the grizzly bears drawn to rivers during the salmon migration are one of the world's great wildlife spectacles.

Sockeye salmon

Oncorhynchus nerka

Adult sockeye salmon can be seen crowding the western seaboard's rivers every fall as they scramble upstream to spawn. Females dig nests in the gravelly riverbed for eggs and sperm, cover them up, and then move upstream to dig more. Once they have spawned, the adults die; their rotting bodies add valuable nutrients to the waters where their eggs will later hatch. The rivers where eggs are laid tend to have lakes in their watershed. After hatching, the young make their way down to these lakes, where they spend the first few years of their lives before migrating to the sea. Some develop into adults in these lakes and never leave. They are known as "kokanee."

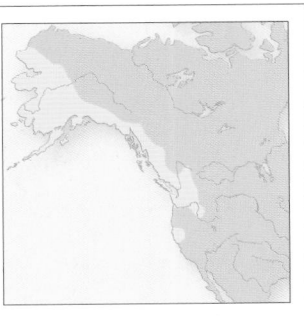

Distribution: Arctic and Pacific rivers; associated lakes from Alaska to the Sacramento River, California. More common in northern part of its range.
Habitat: Lakes and the open ocean.
Food: Plankton sieved from water with gill rakers. Also small invertebrates.
Size: Up to 33in (84cm).
Breeding: Female creates 3–5 nests in riverbed, attended by male.

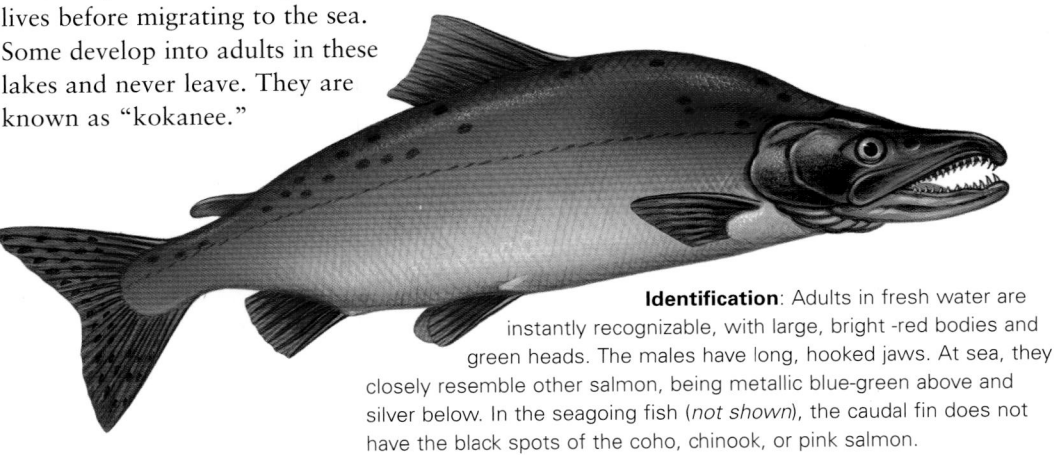

Identification: Adults in fresh water are instantly recognizable, with large, bright-red bodies and green heads. The males have long, hooked jaws. At sea, they closely resemble other salmon, being metallic blue-green above and silver below. In the seagoing fish (*not shown*), the caudal fin does not have the black spots of the coho, chinook, or pink salmon.

Coho salmon

Oncorhynchus kisutch

This species occupies a similar range to the sockeye salmon and is superficially similar, apart from its coloration. Like the sockeye, the coho salmon spends most of its adult life in the ocean and returns to rivers along North America's Pacific coast to spawn. At this time, both sexes develop hooked jaws, but these are more noticeable in the males. Their bodies also change color when they leave the sea. Most fish leave when they are three years old, searching for the rivers where they hatched. A few precocious males, known as "jacks," will return to spawn when they are just two years old.

Identification: Similar to the chinook, but smaller. Cohos also have whitish gums on the lower jaw and small spots on the upper lobe of the caudal fin. At sea, the body is metallic blue above and silver below (hence their alternative name—silver salmon). When leaving to breed, the body changes to darker shades of green and brown. Breeding males have bright-red sides, and those of the females are pinkish.

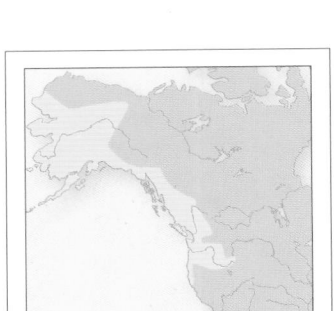

Distribution: Arctic and Pacific rivers, estuaries from Alaska to Monterey Bay, California.
Habitat: The open ocean, clear rivers, and streams.
Food: Plankton, crustaceans, and freshwater insects.
Size: Up to 38.5in (98cm).
Breeding: Female lays eggs in several nests ('redds'), which hatch after 6–7 weeks. Maturing young migrate to the sea.

Chinook salmon

Oncorhynchus tshawytscha

This splendid fish, also commonly known as the king salmon, is the biggest North American salmon of all. Adults often exceed 40lb (18kg) in weight, and individuals as large as 126lb (57kg) have been recorded. The name *chinook* originated among the indigenous Americans of Alaska and Siberia, where it is also found. Unlike most other salmon, chinooks migrate upstream to spawn at various times of the year. Even within a single river, there may be as many as four distinct spawning migrations, or runs. Most chinooks remain at sea for between one and six years before returning to spawn and then dying. Some "jacks" (*see* coho salmon, *opposite*) live for just a few months in salt water before making their way back upstream to breed.

Distribution: Arctic and Pacific drainages from Alaska to California's Ventura River. Introduced to Great Lakes.
Habitat: Rivers and lakes.
Food: Young: aquatic insects, invertebrates; adults: other fish.
Size: Up to 4.8ft (1.47m).
Breeding: Female builds single redd with 4–5 "nesting pockets," then guards eggs until death (up to a month).

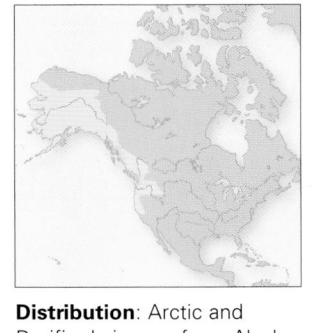

Identification: Most easily told apart by its size. Breeding adults lack the pale gums of coho salmon and have large, irregular black spots on both lobes of the caudal fin.

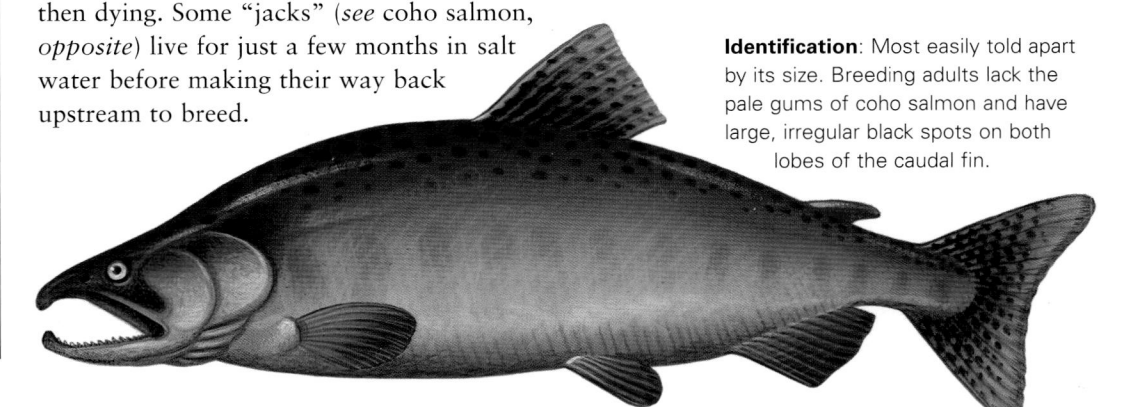

Pink salmon (*Oncorhynchus gorbuscha*): up to 30in (76cm)
Both sexes of this salmon have pink sides, which gives the species its name. Large, mostly oval black spots can be found on its back and both lobes of the caudal fin, and its underside is almost white. Breeding males have humped backs and long, hooked jaws. It is native to Pacific rivers and introduced to the Great Lakes. It also occurs in Asian rivers and the western Pacific, as far south as the Sea of Japan.

Chum salmon (*Oncorhynchus keta*): up to 3.3ft (1m)
Like other Pacific salmon, the chum salmon spends most of its life at sea. Schools migrate up rivers to spawn from winter to early spring. Unlike other Pacific salmon, breeding males have relatively short, hooked jaws and resemble female coho salmon. Chum salmon are sometimes called dog salmon or keta.

Gila trout (*Oncorhynchus gilae*): up to 12.5in (32cm)
This species (*above*) resembles the cutthroat trout, but its "cutthroat" mark is yellow not red. It is named for the Gila river system in Arizona and New Mexico, its native home. It prefers clear mountain headwaters and lakes, and is protected as a threatened species.

Cutthroat trout

Oncorhynchus clarki

This species, familiar to anglers across much of the western United States, is native to Pacific rivers, but it has also been widely introduced elsewhere. Historically, it occurred as 14 distinct subspecies, but these have been blurred as introductions have caused them to mix through interbreeding. In most of its range, the cutthroat trout is migratory, spending almost all of its adult life at sea and swimming upstream only to breed in fresh water. But some populations never leave the rivers in which they were spawned. The species varies widely both in size and coloration. In some places, it rarely exceeds 6in (15cm) in length, but in others, it may reach almost 3.25ft (1m).

Identification: The defining feature is the red "cutthroat" mark across the neck. Most individuals are heavily spotted.

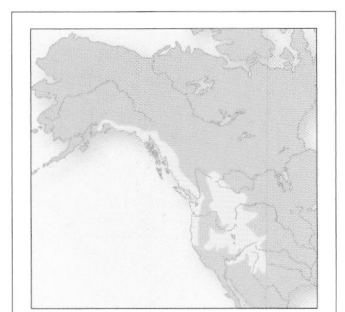

Distribution: Pacific rivers from Alaska to Eel River, California. Also Rocky Mountains. Widely introduced elsewhere.
Habitat: Rivers.
Food: Freshwater insects, other invertebrates, and small fish.
Size: Up to 39in (99cm).
Breeding: Adults migrate from the sea into rivers to spawn. Female lays up to 1,700 eggs in shallow nest. Eggs hatch within 7 weeks.

CATFISH AND BULLHEADS

All of the fish on these pages belong to the same genus, Ameiurus. Catfish are named for their long barbels—appendages that look and function very much like a cat's whiskers, amplifying the sense of touch. North American bullheads are actually catfish and are not related to the true bullheads of Europe and Asia, which are more closely related to sculpins.

White catfish

Ameiurus catus

Identification: The common name of this species is misleading. The underside is white or pale yellow, but most of the body is blue-gray to blue-black. The caudal fin is moderately forked and the pectoral spine has relatively large, sawlike teeth on its rear side.

This catfish is native to the southeastern corner of the United States, from Florida to the Hudson River. A popular game and food fish, it has been widely introduced elsewhere in the country and has also become established in several reservoirs in Puerto Rico. It is a typical member of its family, with long barbels around its head for detecting prey and finding its way around in murky water. It generally reaches around 3–5lb (1.35–2.25kg) in weight but can grow much bigger. The largest white catfish ever recorded tipped the scales at 22lb (10kg). Unlike most catfish, which tend to be largely nocturnal, this fish often feeds by day. It is extremely adaptable and will live happily in almost any freshwater habitat into which it is introduced.

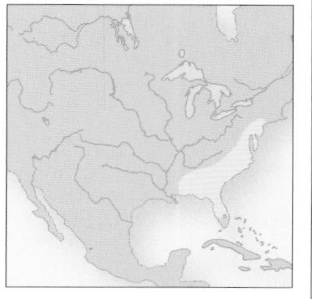

Distribution: Native to Florida and eastern seaboard states as far north as New York. Widely introduced elsewhere.
Habitat: Muddy pools, backwaters, lakes, and reservoirs. Also found in open channels of some large rivers.
Food: Smaller fish and aquatic invertebrates.
Size: Up to 24in (62cm).
Breeding: Both partners build large nest. Males guard eggs and young while they are still small.

Black bullhead

Ameiurus melas

Despite its common name of "bullhead," this species is in fact a close relative of the white catfish. Its native range includes the U.S. Plains States, between the Appalachian and Rocky Mountains, although it has been introduced into many other places as well. The black bullhead is also known as the polliwog or the chucklehead cat. It is relatively short-lived, usually dying before it reaches six years old. Adults rarely weigh much more than 2.2lb (1kg), although some have been known to reach 8.8lb (4kg). In many parts of the world, black bullheads are sold as aquarium fish. Although they make interesting pets, they are voracious predators and should be kept on their own.

Identification: As with the white catfish, the common name is misleading. The body is usually dark olive, brown, or yellow-brown. The chin barbels, however, are dusky or black. The anal fin is relatively short and rounded, and the caudal fin is slightly notched.

Distribution: Native to the Great Plains of the U.S.A. Also introduced to British Columbia, Alberta, Mexico, California, Arizona, and Nevada.
Habitat: Muddy pools, oxbow lakes, and backwaters.
Food: Plant and animal matter, including carrion.
Size: Up to 24in (62cm).
Breeding: Both partners build a nest in the mud on the bottom and guard eggs until they hatch. Areas with some cover preferred for nesting. Eggs hatch after 4–6 days.

Flat bullhead (*Ameiurus platycephalus*): up to 11.5in (29cm)
This rare fish lives in lakes, ponds, reservoirs, and river pools. It has a flat head, which, combined with a large blotch at the base of its dorsal fin, helps distinguish it from the similar-looking brown bullhead. Found in Georgia, North and South Carolina, and Virginia.

Yellow bullhead (*Ameiurus natalis*): up to 18.5in (47cm)
This species closely resembles the black bullhead, but it has yellow rather than dark-colored barbels. It also has large, sawlike teeth on the back of its pectoral spine. This fish prefers sluggish creeks and rivers and is relatively common. Its native range stretches from New York state to northern Mexico and it has been widely introduced elsewhere.

Brown bullhead (*Ameiurus nebulosus*): up to 19.75in (50cm)
The mottled sides of this species (*above*) are almost unique—only the flat bullhead has similar patterning. This fish is a nest-builder that guards its tadpole-like young. It is widely distributed throughout eastern North America, occurring from Florida to far north Quebec. It can tolerate pollution better than most other fish and so has remained common throughout most of its range.

Spotted bullhead

Ameiurus serracanthus

Compared with the white catfish and the black bullhead, the spotted bullhead is small. Most adults grow to just 7in (18cm) long. Unlike its larger relatives, this species prefers relatively clear, fast-flowing waters, inhabiting rivers and streams with rocky or sandy bottoms. The spotted catfish can be quite beautifully patterned, making it popular with aquarium enthusiasts. In the wild, it is rare wherever it is found, although it is not considered vulnerable or endangered. It feeds mainly on freshwater snails, eating many more of these than any other types of prey. This has earned it another common name—the snail cat.

Identification: The light, round spots of this catfish, combined with its small size, make it difficult to confuse with any other species. The fins have black edges and the pectoral spine has 15–20 large, sawlike teeth on its rear side.

Distribution: Northern Florida drainages, southern Georgia, and southeastern Alabama.
Habitat: Deep sand or rock-bottomed pools of swift rivers and streams.
Food: Mostly aquatic snails but also other invertebrates.
Size: Up to 11in (28cm).
Breeding: Little known about habits, although breeding is thought to begin early spring.

Snail bullhead

Ameiurus brunneus

Distribution: Atlantic slope drainages from the Dan River in Virginia, to the Altamaha River in Georgia. Also found in St. John's River in Florida.
Habitat: Clear, fast-flowing streams and rivers.
Food: Aquatic invertebrates and some plant matter.
Size: Up to 11.5in (29cm).
Breeding: Little known, although small fry appear in streams in mid spring.

Slightly larger than the spotted bullhead but very similar in its general body form, the snail bullhead originates from the far southeastern United States. Although its range is not vast, it is common almost throughout that area. Like other members of its genus, it does not shoal and is usually found singly, except when breeding. It prefers rocky runs and swift-flowing pools in clear streams and small rivers. Like the spotted bullhead, it is sometimes kept as an aquarium species and feeds mainly on snails. Although it is a relatively abundant fish, it has been little studied, and there is still a lot to learn about its general biology and life history.

Identification: A flat head with a blunt, almost square-ended snout when seen in profile. Most of the fish is yellow-green to olive in color, although the fins have narrow black edges. The anal fin is short and rounded in outline. Some populations, such as the one in the St. John's River, are strongly mottled.

SUCKERS

Suckers are among North America's most common freshwater fish, yet few Americans have ever seen one or even heard of them. Well-camouflaged and lying still or in deep water during the day, they are difficult enough for wild fish-eating birds and mammals to find, let alone humans. Many species look very similar, so the best guide to identification is location, since their ranges mostly tend to be separate.

Flannelmouth sucker

Catostomus latipinnis

This is one of the more common fish of the Colorado River and its tributaries. Even so, it has declined in numbers since the start of the last century due to alterations in its habitat. The Colorado River has been dammed at several points to provide water and power for desert cities such as Phoenix and Las Vegas, and now it is only during high-water periods that it flows right to the sea. The flannelmouth once migrated up and down this river to take advantage of seasonal abundances of food, but can no longer do so to the same extent. It overlaps part of its range with the razorback sucker, with which it sometimes hybridizes. This species can reach a weight of 2.25lb (1kg).

Identification: In most populations, the caudal peduncle—the area where the tail joins to the rest of the body—is narrow and pencil-shaped. A prominent snout, ventral mouth, and well-developed lips, the lower lip with large, fleshy lobes. The caudal and dorsal fins are both relatively large. Color varies from green to blue-gray above, and is paler below.

Distribution: Colorado River basin, from southwestern Wyoming to southern Arizona.
Habitat: Rocky pools and runs of the main river channel and its larger tributaries. Less often in creeks and streams.
Food: Insect larvae and other aquatic invertebrates.
Size: Up to 22in (56cm).
Breeding: Thought to spawn in open water, like most of its relatives.

Bridgelip sucker

Catostomus columbianus

Identification: Varies in color from green to blue-black above and white to yellow below. Males develop an orange band along their sides and extra scales on the rear of their bodies as the breeding season approaches.

A typical member of its family, it is difficult even for experts to distinguish this species. The bridgelip sucker originates from the northwestern U.S.A. and British Columbia. Its Latin name gives a clue to its stronghold—the Columbia River basin. This fish lacks the indentations at the corners of the mouth that separate the lips in other, closely-related species, hence the name "bridgelip." It spawns during late spring, soon after the winter ice that covers many of the smaller rivers has broken up.

Distribution: Columbia River and its tributaries. Also found in Fraser River in British Columbia.
Habitat: Lakes and the backwaters and edges of rivers with sandy or muddy beds.
Food: Aquatic invertebrates and algae.
Size: Up to 12in (30cm).
Breeding: Females shed small yellow eggs into open water, where they are fertilized by attendant males.

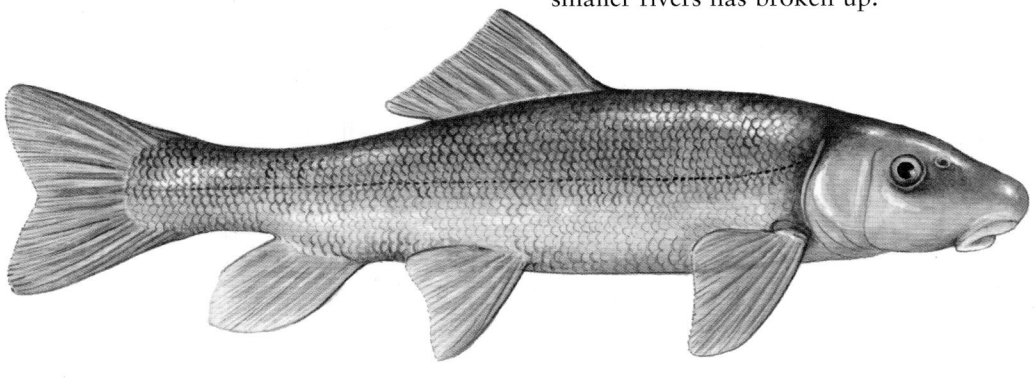

Mountain sucker

Catostomus platyrhynchus

Distribution: From the Saskatchewan River, Canada, southward on both sides of the Rocky Mountains to the Colorado River and its tributary streams in California.
Habitat: Clear, swift mountain streams, rivers.
Food: Mostly algae, sometimes small invertebrates.
Size: Up to 9.75in (25cm).
Breeding: Moves upstream to smaller streams to spawn in open water above gravel.

This is one of the most widespread of all suckers, occurring throughout most of western North America, from the Canadian Arctic as far south as the Colorado River. As its name suggests, it is primarily a species of cool mountain streams, being most abundant in the Rockies, although it is sometimes found at lower altitudes. The mountain sucker is unusual because it feeds mainly on algae, scraping it from boulders and smaller rocks. Insect larvae and other aquatic invertebrates are also taken when the opportunity arises, but these do not form such an important part of the diet as they do for other suckers. Due partly to the high altitudes at which it lives, this sucker is a late breeder, spawning between June and August.

Identification: The body is gray to moss green above, usually with a dark stripe on the side, which turns red in breeding males. The upper and lower lips are separated by deep indentations at the corners of the mouth. The fins are clear to pale red.

Longnose sucker (*Catostomus catostomus*): up to 25in (64cm)
This has an unusually long snout, similar in relative length to that of the razorback sucker, but flatter. It is the most widespread sucker in North America, found throughout most of the northern U.S.A., almost all of Canada, and Alaska. A fish of clear, cold deep lakes and their tributary rivers and streams, it also occurs in Siberia.

White sucker (*Catostomus commersoni*): up to 25in (64cm)
This fish is often confused with the similar-looking longnose sucker, with which it shares part of its range. Like the longnose, this species is often found in the headwaters of lakes, though it is more common in small, cold-water streams and rivers. It is most easily told apart from the longnose by the fact that its snout is rounded, rather than flattened toward its tip.

Bluehead sucker (*Catostomus discobolus*): up to 16in (41cm)
With its bluish head, which is very bright in some individuals, the bluehead (*above*) is one of the more colorful suckers, a group that is generally patterned for camouflage rather than display. It occurs in the Snake and upper Colorado Rivers in shallow, fast-flowing water. The blue of the head becomes darker and more intense in the adults as they age.

Desert sucker

Catostomus clarki

If the mountain sucker is a fish of steep topography and icy waters, then the desert sucker is its natural opposite. The rocky rivers this fish inhabits flow through some of the flattest, most scorched landscapes of North America. In common with many other suckers, it stays out of sight during the day to avoid predators. When the sun is up, it lurks in the relative safety of deep pools, hidden from most fish-eating birds. It feeds at night, swimming up into the shallow riffles which are the home of most of its insect prey. The desert sucker is found throughout the hot and arid regions of the southwestern U.S.A. and northern Mexico.

Identification: Varies in color from silver-tan to dark green above and from silver to yellow below. The upper and lower lips are separated at the corners of the mouth by deep indentations. Caught fish can be told apart from their close relatives by the fact that they have between 27 and 43 gill rakers beneath the gill covers.

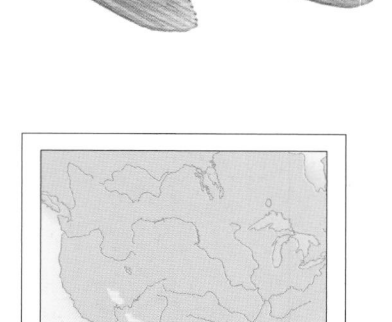

Distribution: Common across most of range. Lower Colorado River drainages (downstream of Grand Canyon). Also found in Virgin, Bill Williams, and Gila River systems.
Habitat: Small to medium-size rivers with rocky or sandy bottoms.
Food: Insect larvae and other aquatic invertebrates.
Size: Up to 13in (33cm).
Breeding: Likely to be open-water spawner, in common with most of its relatives.

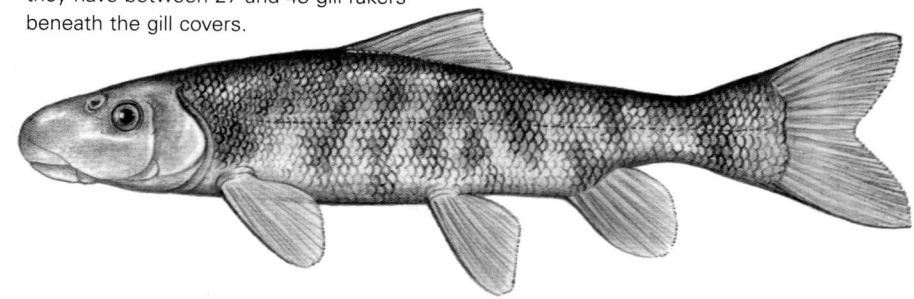

BASSES

Although they are all known as basses, the fish on these pages belong to two different families. The striped bass, yellow bass, and white bass are all members of the family Moronidae, better known as the temperate basses, which also have representatives in Europe and northern Africa. The other bass species belong to the Centrarchidae, a family of fish found exclusively in North America.

Striped bass

Morone saxatilis

This is the United States' most important game fish, drawing anglers from all over the country to the lakes and rivers where it is found. It is the largest of the temperate basses, and crucial to the economy of several coastal fishing towns in the southern and eastern states. Although it can spend its whole life in fresh water, it is naturally a fish of bays, estuaries, and shallow coastal seas, and only enters rivers to spawn. The striped bass is a large, powerful fish with tasty flesh—the perfect combination for anglers. Individuals can weigh as much as 125lb (57kg) and may live up to 30 years, providing they manage to avoid being caught.

Identification: Six to nine dark gray horizontal stripes on each side of the body. The rear of the tongue has one or two patches of teeth. The body is dark olive to blue-gray above and silvery-white on the sides. The pelvic fin and the edge of the anal fin are white on large adults.

Distribution: Atlantic and Gulf slope drainages from St. Lawrence River in New Brunswick to Louisiana. Introduced to some Pacific rivers and landlocked lakes.
Habitat: Coastal waters and large rivers.
Food: Young: invertebrates; adults: fish.
Size: Up to 6.6ft (2m).
Breeding: Travels upriver in March. Eggs semibuoyant, float downstream in water column, then hatch.

Yellow bass

Morone mississippiensis

Identification: The body is olive-gray above, with silver-yellow sides, displaying five to seven horizontal black stripes. These stripes are offset and broken on the lower half of the fish. The fins are clear to blue-gray in color. The tongue is devoid of teeth.

If the striped bass is a giant, the yellow bass might be considered something of a dwarf. This fish typically weighs around 0.5lb (0.25kg), and although it can grow larger, never reaches anything like the size of its seagoing cousin. As a result, it is not actively sought by anglers, although it is often caught, being fairly common across most of its range. It tends to be found in schools, although sometimes it may be seen swimming alone. The yellow bass is an exclusively freshwater fish. A species of slow-moving or still, often turbid, waters, it feeds primarily on insect larvae, worms, and crayfish, although larger individuals may capture small fish. Yellow bass sometimes school with the similar-sized white bass (*see* box opposite).

Distribution: Natural range is Lake Michigan and Mississippi River basins. Widely introduced elsewhere.
Habitat: Lakes, ponds, and pools in rivers.
Food: Aquatic invertebrates and small fish.
Size: Up to 18in (46cm).
Breeding: Schools enter small streams to spawn over gravel. Eggs are left to develop unguarded.

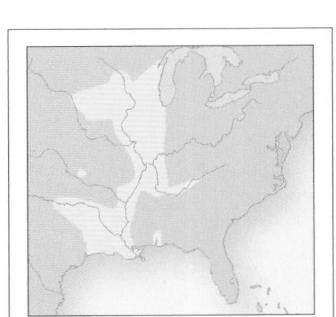

Largemouth bass

Micropterus salmoides

This fish, also known as the Billy bass, is another favorite with U.S. anglers. In the quiet, clear waters it inhabits, it is often the top predator, giving it a certain cachet as a sports fish. It can grow substantially—the largest recorded weighed just over 25lb (11.3kg). It is also long-lived, reaching as much as 23 years in the wild. The male largemouth is a careful parent. As the breeding season begins in the spring, he builds a crude nest on the bottom and entices a female to lay her eggs in it. If he is successful, he fertilizes them, then guards them until they hatch. The tiny fry then school around their father for the first month of their lives.

Identification: As its name suggests, this fish has a very large mouth. There are two dorsal fins, which are almost completely separate from one another. The body is silver to brassy green above, although it often looks brown in the water. A broad black stripe, which is often broken, runs along each side as far as the snout.

Distribution: Native to the eastern half of the United States, but widely introduced elsewhere. Now common in many parts of the country.
Habitat: Clear ponds, lakes, swamps, and pools of rivers with abundant vegetation.
Food: Young: aquatic invertebrates; adults: fish.
Size: Up to 38in (97cm).
Breeding: Male builds nest on bottom in shallow water, guards eggs (typically 3,000) and young.

White bass (*Morone chrysops*): up to 17.75in (45cm)
This popular game fish feeds at dawn and dusk. Large schools can be seen driving prey to the surface, which leap from the water as they try to escape. The white bass inhabits lakes, ponds, and pools in rivers. Its native range covers a broad band stretching from Mexico to southern Canada across the U.S.A. east of the Rockies.

Rock bass (*Ambloplites rupestris*): up to 17in (43cm)
This fish (*above*) is the largest member of its genus, weighing up to 3lb (1.4kg). It is popular with anglers and is sold commercially as a food fish. It is found in vegetated areas of lakes, rivers, and streams across the eastern U.S.A. and southeastern Canada. In parts of Canada, it is known as the red-eye, red-eye bass, or goggle eye. Elsewhere it goes by the name rock perch.

Spotted bass (*Micropterus punctulatus*): up to 24in (61cm)
This fish occupies a similar native range to the largemouth bass, but generally speaking, this is a species of clear rivers, and it is found in areas of stronger current than the largemouth. It can also be told apart from its relative by the rows of small, black spots on its lower side.

Shadow bass

Ambloplites ariommus

The shadow bass and its close relative the rock bass are unusual among freshwater fish in being able to change color to match their background. This makes them very successful predators, but also makes them difficult to spot in the wild. The shadow bass prefers clear, vegetated lake margins and pools in rivers. It spends much of its time sitting still on the bottom, waiting for smaller fish to swim into reach. When they do, it reacts with surprising speed, darting out to swallow them up. It can weigh up to 1.75lb (0.8kg) but is usually smaller. Common throughout parts of Florida, Georgia, Alabama, Mississippi, and Louisiana, there are also isolated populations in Arkansas and southern Missouri.

Identification: A compressed body and relatively large eyes. Its ability to change color can make identification difficult, but most fish have irregular marbling of gray or brown on their sides. There are usually between 15 and 18 rows of scales across the breast, between one pectoral fin and the other.

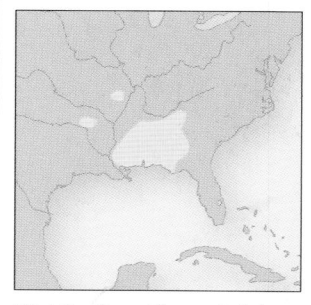

Distribution: Rivers draining into Gulf of Mexico, from Apalachicola river basin of Georgia to lower Mississippi basin in Louisiana.
Habitat: Vegetated pools of streams and rivers over gravel, sand, or mud.
Food: Aquatic invertebrates and small fish.
Size: Up to 8.75in (22cm).
Breeding: Males build nests and guard eggs and young. Nests may sometimes be built close together in colonies.

SUNFISH

Freshwater sunfish evolved in North America and are native to this continent alone. Within North America, most species have been widely introduced to new regions and habitats by anglers. Some, such as the pumpkinseed, have also been taken abroad and now live wild in Europe and Africa. Freshwater sunfish are members of the perch family, and are completely unrelated to the oceanic sunfish, Mola mola.

Pumpkinseed

Lepomis gibbosus

Identification: The pumpkinseed has a bright red or orange spot on its gill cover. The pectoral fin is long and pointed. The cheeks and gill covers have distinctive wavy blue stripes running over them. The mouth is small with the upper jaw not reaching back as far as the pupil of the eye.

This sunfish is native to the northeastern United States and the far southeast of Canada, and has been widely introduced elsewhere in North America. It is a fish of clear water with abundant vegetation. Its range overlaps with the rock bass, largemouth bass, and bluegill. The male builds nests for breeding, nearly always in shallow water near the shore. Females are enticed to lay in the nest, and as soon as one has done so and her eggs have been fertilized, the male begins fanning them. He guards them fiercely until hatching and watches over the young fry until they leave the nest after about 11 days. He then refurbishes his nest and prepares to spawn again with the same, or occasionally a different, female.

Distribution: Native to Atlantic drainages from South Carolina to New Brunswick, but widely introduced elsewhere in North America.
Habitat: Vegetated ponds, lakes, and pools in rivers.
Food: Aquatic invertebrates and small fish.
Size: Up to 16in (40cm).
Breeding: Male builds nest and guards eggs and young. Pumpkinseeds usually spawn more than once during a single season.

Longear sunfish

Lepomis megalotis

Identification: The body of the adult fish is dark red above and bright orange underneath, with blue spots and marbling. As with the pumpkinseed, there are wavy blue stripes on the cheeks and gill covers. The ear flap is unusually long, and usually bordered by a thin blue line.

This sunfish shares part of its range with the pumpkinseed, but is generally a more southerly species. Like its cousin, it is a nest builder, with the males guarding both the eggs and young. However, it usually nests in colonies rather than alone. In recent years, it has started to become popular with aquarium enthusiasts. As well as being striking to look at, it is widely regarded as being the easiest sunfish to keep. In the wild, it prefers shallow, well-vegetated areas of slow-moving upland streams. It feeds on a wide range of small prey, including fish fry, and occasionally eats algae. There is significant variation in the appearance of this fish across its range, and it is thought that there may be as many as six different subspecies, although these have yet to be properly defined and classified.

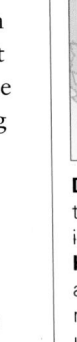

Distribution: Great Lakes to far northeastern Mexico; introduced to other regions.
Habitat: Pools of streams and small to medium-size rivers over rock or sand, usually near to vegetation.
Food: Aquatic invertebrates and small fish.
Size: Up to 9.5in (24cm).
Breeding: Males usually nest in colonies and guard both the eggs and young.

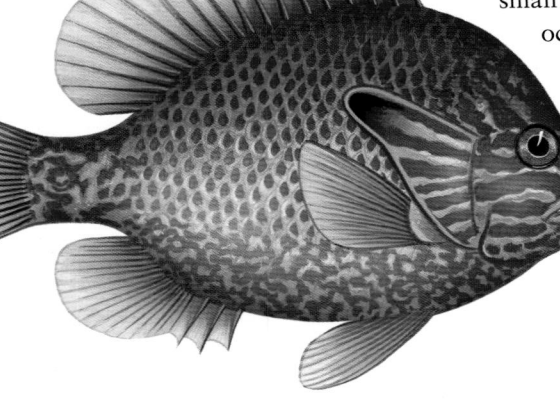

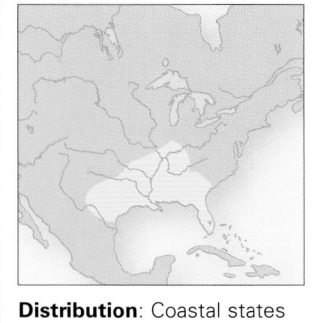

Distribution: Coastal states of the U.S.A., from far south of North Carolina to central Texas. Also in Arkansas, Missouri, Iowa, Illinois, Kentucky, and Tennessee.
Habitat: Swamps, heavily vegetated ponds and lakes, weedy pools in streams, and small to medium-size rivers.
Food: Insect larvae and other aquatic invertebrates.
Size: Up to 8in (20cm).
Breeding: The nest-building male guards eggs and young.

Spotted sunfish

Lepomis punctatus

A fish of the southeastern United States, the spotted sunfish usually inhabits swamps and heavily vegetated ponds, lakes, and pools, but is also found in brackish streams near the coast, being more tolerant of salt water than other species of sunfish. It feeds mainly on insect larvae, which it picks from submerged logs and vegetation. This habit has earned it the alternative common name of "stumpknocker." Like other sunfish, most of the males build nests, which they defend aggressively from other males. Some, however, act as nest parasites, diving in and attempting to fertilize the eggs of a female as she lays in the nest of another male. Male spotted sunfish make a grunting sound when courting females and trying to induce them to lay.

Identification: This forms two subspecies: *Lepomis punctatus punctatus* has a relatively pale body with many black specks on its head and body. *L. punctatus miniatus* (*below*) has no black specks but does have rows of red and yellow spots on its sides. In both, the pectoral fin is short and rounded.

Bluegill (*Lepomis macrochirus*): Up to 16in (41cm)
This fish is native to the eastern United States, southeastern Canada, and northeastern Mexico, and has been introduced throughout the U.S.A., northern Mexico, and parts of Canada. It lives in shallow waters, spawns in colonies, and is a prolific breeder. It has a large black spot at the rear of its dorsal fin, a long, pointed pectoral fin, and an extremely compressed body.

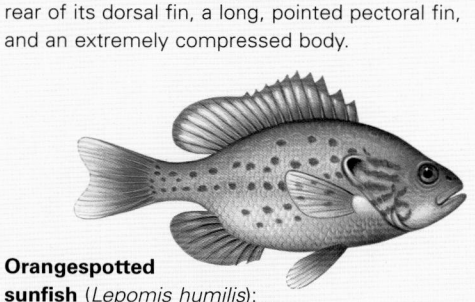

Orangespotted sunfish (*Lepomis humilis*): Up to 6in (15cm)
The native range of this sunfish (*above*) covers most of the central U.S.A. It lives in quiet pools of streams and rivers, often in turbid water. Smaller than most other sunfish, it feeds almost entirely on invertebrate prey. Its silver-green sides are speckled with spots. These are bright orange on males and red-brown on females.

Redear sunfish (*Lepomis microlophus*): Up to 10in (25cm)
The redear spawns in deeper water than most other species and so is less often caught or seen. As its name suggests, it has a bright red or orange spot on the back of its ear flap. Native to the southeastern U.S.A., it has been introduced as far as New Mexico and Michigan.

Green sunfish

Lepomis cyanellus

A real survivor, the green sunfish is able to tolerate much lower levels of oxygen in the water than most other fish and survives in temporary pools during droughts where many other species suffocate and die. It is also quick to breed when conditions change, usually making it the first fish to repopulate such intermittent watercourses. Males construct nests, often colonially, in which females lay their eggs. These nests are usually situated in shallow water near sheltering rocks, logs, or clumps of vegetation. Like spotted sunfish, the males often make grunting sounds when courting potential mates. Green sunfish may breed several times in a single year.

Identification: The body appears slender but is quite thick. The mouth is large, with the upper jaw extending to beneath the pupil of the eye. There is a large, black spot at the rear of both the second dorsal and the anal fin. These and the caudal fin have orange or yellow edges.

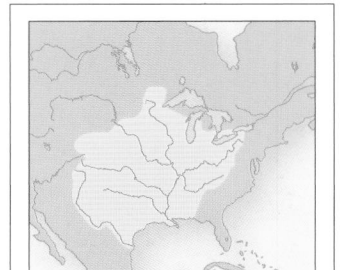

Distribution: Central U.S.A.; also far south of Ontario and northern Mexico.
Habitat: Lakes, ponds, and quiet pools of sluggish streams.
Food: Aquatic invertebrates, small fish, and algae.
Size: Up to 12in (31cm).
Breeding: Male builds nest in shallow water (usually in colonies), fans eggs, and then guards young.

STUDFISH AND KILLIFISH

Four of the species on these pages belong to the same genus as the topminnows. Although they share many physical characteristics, they differ in their behavior, tending to feed in the water column or nearer the bottom. All of the fish featured here are small and provide food for a great many larger, predatory animals.

Northern studfish

Fundulus catenatus

Despite his small size, the male northern studfish is an unusually aggressive fish. At the start of springtime, he establishes a territory in shallow water over gravel, and for months he defends this vigorously from other males. Spawning occurs in these territories from April until August. Although the male does not tend the eggs, by guarding his territory, he does inadvertently protect them from predators. The species has two main populations (*see box*), but smaller communities also exist in southwestern Mississippi and in southwestern Arkansas. Adult fish are bottom feeders, seeking out insect larvae and water snails. Younger fish hunt near the surface and often leap to grab mayflies and other insects flying above the water. Feeding activity tends to peak in the morning and late in the afternoon. By night, the fish is largely inactive.

Identification: The body is light yellow-brown above with silver-blue sides, and rows of small brown or red-brown spots. There is a gold band across the back just in front of the dorsal fin. During the breeding season, the sides of the male turn vivid blue, and he develops red spots on his head and fins.

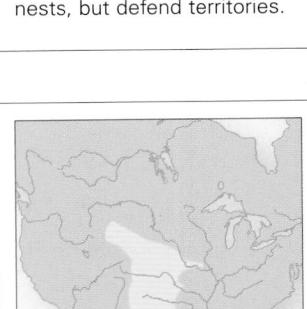

Distribution: Two populations. 1:Tennessee, parts of Kentucky, northern Alabama, and northern Mississippi; 2: southern Missouri and northern Arkansas.
Habitat: Streams and small to medium-size rivers, in margins, pools, and backwaters.
Food: Young: flying insects; adults: aquatic invertebrates.
Size: Up to 7in (18cm).
Breeding: Males do not build nests, but defend territories.

Plains killifish

Fundulus zebrinus

Identification: Both sexes have white or yellow bellies and are tan to olive in color above. The sides are silver-white with between 12 and 26 gray-green bars on each. During the breeding season, the male develops bright orange to red coloration on the paired, anal, and dorsal fins.

This fish lives in habitats where few other fish can survive. It is very tolerant of both high salt levels and very alkaline water, and has a breeding system that enables it to survive through even the toughest droughts. Once fertilized, the eggs of the plains killifish develop and hatch out in two to six weeks. However, should the pools in which they were laid dry out in that time, they are able to lie dormant for an almost indefinite period. When the rains return and refill the pools, they continue to develop and quickly hatch. The adults are unfussy feeders, consuming almost anything edible that is small enough to enter their mouths. They spend much of their time buried in sand, on the bottoms of the streams, rivers, and pools, with only their mouths and eyes visible. The exact reason for this behavior is unclear but has probably evolved either to help them avoid predators or to capture prey.

Distribution: Native to Great Plains, down to Gulf of Mexico in southwestern Texas. Probably introduced into upper Missouri River basin and Colorado River basin in Utah and Arizona.
Habitat: Headwaters, streams, and pools in small to medium-size rivers.
Food: Aquatic invertebrates, plant matter, algae, detritus.
Size: Up to 4in (10cm).
Breeding: When conditions are favorable. Eggs scattered, left unguarded.

LIVEBEARERS

All of the fish on these pages give birth to live young. Males fertilize the females internally by means of a structure known as the gonopodium, which is formed from modified elements of the anal fin. Livebearers are particularly successful wherever they are introduced, having evolved a system that cuts out the problem of egg predation suffered by most other fish species.

Sailfin molly

Poecilia latipinna

Distribution: Atlantic and Gulf coasts from far south of North Carolina to northern Mexico. Widely introduced elsewhere.
Habitat: Ponds, lakes, quiet pools, and backwaters of streams.
Food: Algae, occasionally aquatic invertebrates.
Size: Up to 6in (15cm).
Breeding: Fertilization is internal, gestation takes 3–4 weeks. Female gives birth to broods of 10–140 live young.

Identification: The huge, sail-like dorsal fin of the male makes it hard to confuse with any other species. This fin has black wavy lines on its lower half, black spots on its upper half, and is edged with orange. The head is small and the fleshy base of the tail unusually deep. The sides of the body are olive with iridescent yellow flecks and five rows of dark brown spots.

With its unusual habits, hardy nature, and strikingly large dorsal fin, the sailfin molly is a great favorite of aquarists around the world. Over the years, several different color morphs have been bred in captivity and these have increased its popularity as a pet fish. The sailfin molly is native to the southern United States and is particularly common in Florida. It has also been introduced into parts of the western U.S.A. and Hawaii. Introductions in California seem to have contributed to the decline of the endangered desert pupfish there. The sailfin molly is an adaptable fish able to survive in a wide range of habitats. It lives in marshes, streams, ponds, estuaries, and even roadside ditches. It is also found in coastal marine waters in the Gulf of Mexico.

Mosquitofish

Gambusia affinis

Distribution: Southeastern U.S.A. Widely introduced in many other parts of the world where malaria remains prevalent.
Habitat: Standing, slow-flowing fresh or brackish water.
Food: Mosquito larvae and other aquatic invertebrates.
Size: Up to 2.5in (6.5cm).
Breeding: Fertilization is internal. Between 12 and 100 young born per brood and females may produce up to four broods a year.

Identification: The dorsal and caudal fins each have between one and three rows of black spots. There is a black teardrop below each eye. There are no obvious dark spots or stripes on the sides, as there are in most of the other, closely related *Gambusia* species. The body is yellow-brown to olive-gray above with a dark stripe along the back as far as the dorsal fin.

Named for the insect larvae and pupae that make up the bulk of its diet, the mosquitofish is possibly the most widely distributed freshwater fish in the world. It is native to the southern United States east of the Rockies, but has been introduced to tropical and temperate countries around the globe in attempts to suppress populations of *Anopheles* mosquitoes, which transmit malaria. It is also widely kept in home aquariums and is sometimes sold as a live food fish for larger, carnivorous species. The mosquitofish is an extremely hardy species, able to tolerate high salinities, high temperatures, and low levels of oxygen. It is quick to mature, sometimes breeding within three months of hatching, and has spread rapidly in most places where it has been introduced. As with all *Gambusia* species, fry are left to fend for themselves immediately after birth.

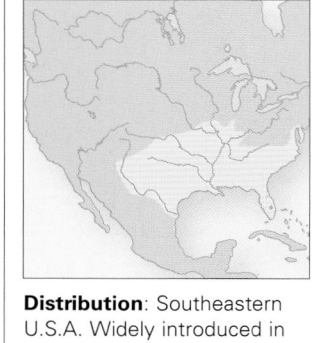

DARTERS

In total, there are 113 members of the genus Etheostoma, *commonly known as darters, and all of them are found only in North America. Most of these differ so subtly in appearance that they can only be told apart by experts, and then often only by looking at their skeletons and internal organs. Although some darters are widespread, most inhabit restricted ranges, and some are endangered.*

River darter

Percina shumardi

Identification: Predominantly dusky olive in color, with between 8 and 15 black bars running down each of its sides. The first dorsal fin has a small black spot at the front and a large black spot near the back. There is a black teardrop below each eye and a small black spot at the base of the caudal fin. The snout is fairly blunt.

The Latin name of this fish was given in 1859 after the man who discovered it. Dr. G. C. Shumard was a surgeon traveling with the U.S. Pacific Railroad Survey. At the time, it was common practice for the surgeon on an expedition to double up as the resident naturalist, and Shumard spent much of his time documenting the many new plants and creatures he saw. The river darter could not have been easy to spot. With its dappled olive and black body, it is well camouflaged against the rocks and gravel of rivers. It spends much of its time on the bottom, propped up by its pectoral fins or hiding behind rocks. It is only when it moves that it really becomes visible and when it does, it does so quickly, as its name suggests.

Distribution: Hudson Bay, Mississippi River, and southern Great Lakes drainages. Also found in drainage basin of San Antonio Bay.
Habitat: Rocky riffles of rivers.
Food: Insect larvae and other aquatic invertebrates.
Size: Up to 3in (7.8cm).
Breeding: Spawning begins in January in Texas but later, farther north. Eggs scattered and develop unguarded.

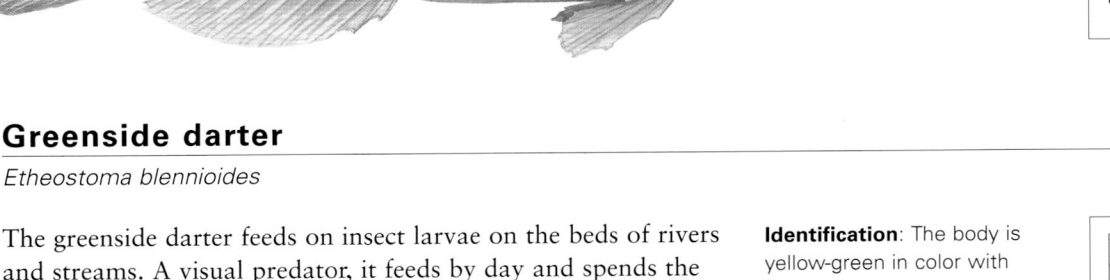

Greenside darter

Etheostoma blennioides

The greenside darter feeds on insect larvae on the beds of rivers and streams. A visual predator, it feeds by day and spends the hours of darkness in hiding, using large rocks or logs as shelter from nocturnal predators. Like other darters, it lacks a swim bladder, and this helps it to maintain its position on the bottom. If it spots a predator by day, it tends to freeze, relying on its coloration to help it blend into the background. It only swims away if the offending creature comes too close; otherwise it stays stock still until the danger has passed. This fish is most common in areas where the rocks on the bottom are covered with filamentous green algae. Although this algae is not fed on by the fish themselves, it shelters most of the invertebrates they eat.

Identification: The body is yellow-green in color with six or seven square, dark green saddles. There are between five and eight green bars on each side, sometimes forming W or U shapes. The skin of the snout is fused to that of the rear edge of the upper lip. The dorsal fins of the male are green, and those of the female are dusky or clear. The bases of these fins are red in both sexes.

Distribution: Eastern and central United States, but virtually absent from the Atlantic Plain.
Habitat: The shores of large lakes and rocky riffles in streams and small to medium-size rivers.
Food: Insect larvae and other aquatic invertebrates.
Size: Up to 6.75in (17cm).
Breeding: Males defend small territories among algae-covered rocks and gravel. Eggs develop unguarded.

SCULPINS

Most of the world's sculpins live in marine habitats, but a few have evolved to spend their lives in fresh water. Freshwater sculpins are confined to North America, northern Asia, and Europe. Sculpins are among the most difficult of North American fish to tell apart. All have similarly shaped bodies and they vary only very subtly in coloration.

Mottled sculpin

Cottus bairdi

Identification: The body is robust and the head quite large. The two dorsal fins are joined together at the base. There are two or three black or dark brown bars on each side beneath the second dorsal fin. In color, this fish is brown above with darker brown or black mottling on its back and sides. The first dorsal fin has large black spots at the front and the rear.

This is a beautifully camouflaged fish. Lying still on the bottom of a river or stream, it blends in so perfectly that it can be impossible to see, even when you are looking straight at it. As if this camouflage was not enough, the mottled sculpin commonly hides beneath large rocks and may only be seen when disturbed after one of these has been turned over. These fish breed in the spring, which can mean anytime from March to June. Adult males set up their breeding sites in cavities beneath large rocks and wait for females to approach. When a female does come into range, the male swims out to meet her, shaking his head and opening his gill covers as a display to entice her in.

Distribution: Widespread, occurring in two distinct populations separated by the Great Plains.
Habitat: Streams and small rivers over gravel or rubble; also the rocky shores of some lakes.
Food: Aquatic invertebrates, fish eggs, and small fish.
Size: Up to 6in (15cm).
Breeding: Males defend nest cavities beneath rocks. They fan and guard the eggs until they hatch.

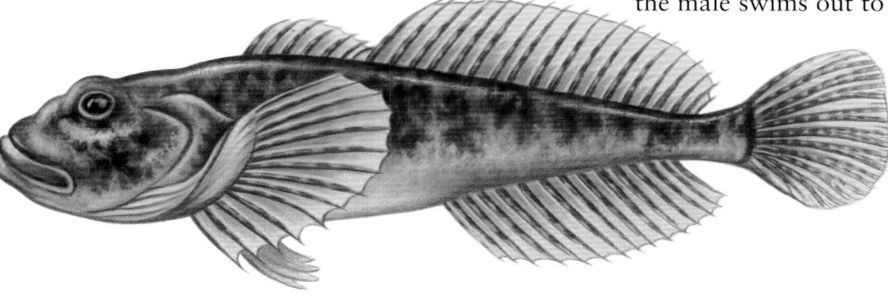

Marbled sculpin

Cottus klamathensis

Identification: The body is fairly deep for a sculpin. The first dorsal fin has a black spot near its rear edge and is joined at the base to the second dorsal fin. The back and sides are pale brown with black mottling, and the underside is white or yellow. The fin rays have a marbled pattern of light and dark spots, hence the common name of this fish.

This sculpin lives in the border region between California and Oregon. It inhabits mainly soft-bottomed streams with abundant vegetation, but only in places where there are boulders, cobbles, or other large rocks. Like the mottled sculpin, it is beautifully camouflaged, but its coloration is designed to help it blend in with sand and gravel rather than rocks. It feeds on insect larvae and rarely swims more than an inch or so above the bottom. Breeding occurs during February and March. The males defend burrows beneath cobbles and display to entice females to lay eggs inside them. Females lay their eggs in a small mass that sticks to the underside of the rock. The largest males are the most successful, sometimes attracting several different females to lay in their nest burrows.

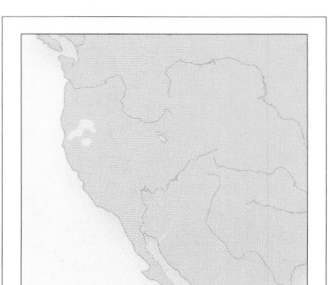

Distribution: Klamath River drainages and parts of Pit River system in Oregon and California.
Habitat: Soft-bottomed runs of clear streams and small rivers.
Food: Aquatic invertebrates and occasionally, fish eggs.
Size: Up to 3.5in (9cm).
Breeding: Males defend nesting burrows. They fan and guard the eggs until they hatch. Several different females may lay eggs in the same nest burrow.

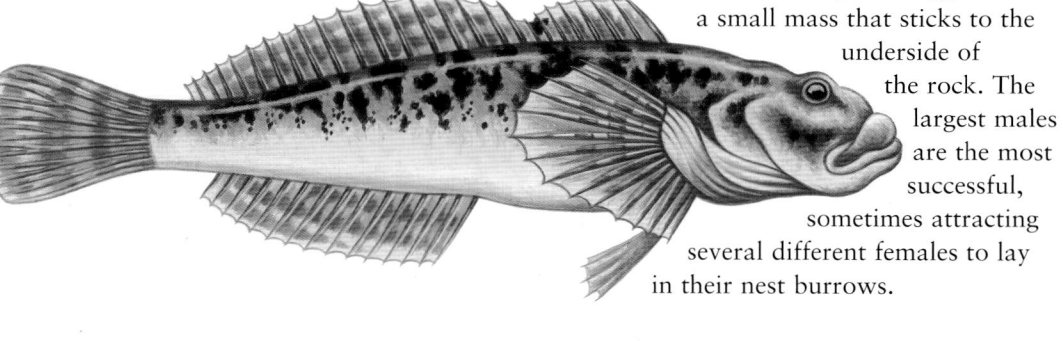

AQUATIC SALAMANDERS

North America is home to several aquatic salamander species. Although these creatures are amphibians, they look and behave much like fish. As adults, aquatic salamanders breathe using gills, a feature that sets them apart from most other amphibians, which have lungs. They include small fish among their prey, but are in turn sometimes preyed upon by larger fish species.

Hellbender

Cryptobranchus alleganiensis

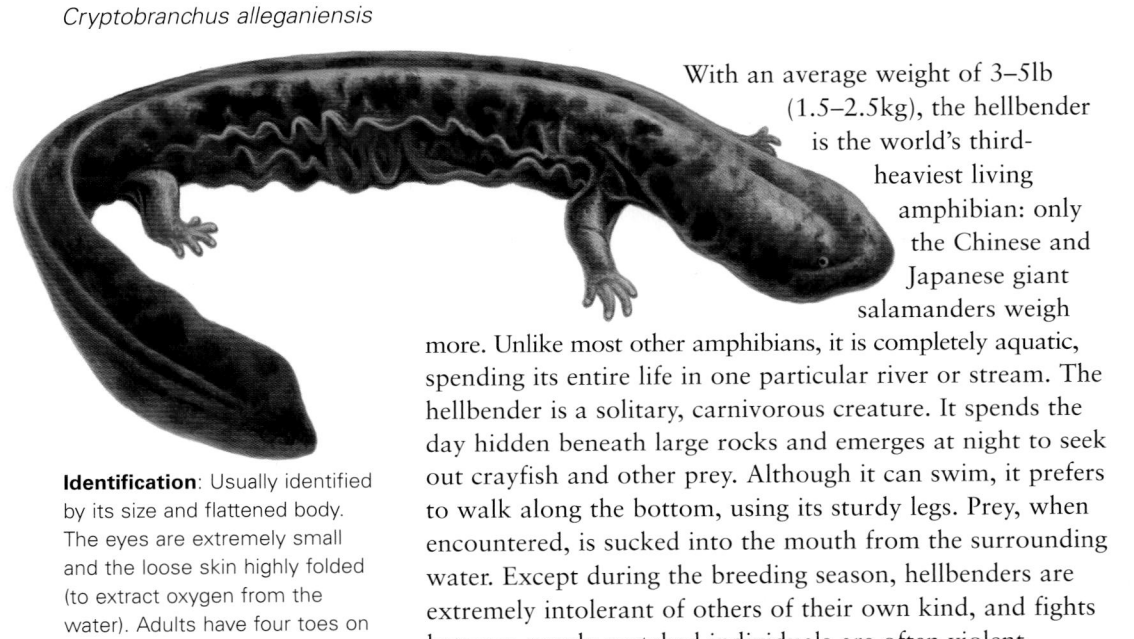

With an average weight of 3–5lb (1.5–2.5kg), the hellbender is the world's third-heaviest living amphibian: only the Chinese and Japanese giant salamanders weigh more. Unlike most other amphibians, it is completely aquatic, spending its entire life in one particular river or stream. The hellbender is a solitary, carnivorous creature. It spends the day hidden beneath large rocks and emerges at night to seek out crayfish and other prey. Although it can swim, it prefers to walk along the bottom, using its sturdy legs. Prey, when encountered, is sucked into the mouth from the surrounding water. Except during the breeding season, hellbenders are extremely intolerant of others of their own kind, and fights between evenly matched individuals are often violent. The hellbender is the only member of its genus.

Identification: Usually identified by its size and flattened body. The eyes are extremely small and the loose skin highly folded (to extract oxygen from the water). Adults have four toes on the front feet and five on the rear. The young have external gills.

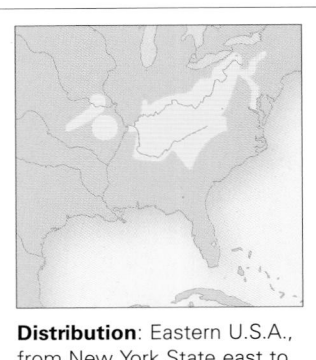

Distribution: Eastern U.S.A., from New York State east to Missouri and Arkansas.
Habitat: Clear, fast-flowing streams and rivers, usually with rocky bottoms.
Food: Crayfish and worms. Occasionally small fish and smaller members of its own species.
Size: Up to 28.5in (72.5cm).
Breeding: Males excavate nests beneath flat rocks and defend eggs, laid in strings, until they hatch.

Mudpuppy

Necturus maculosus

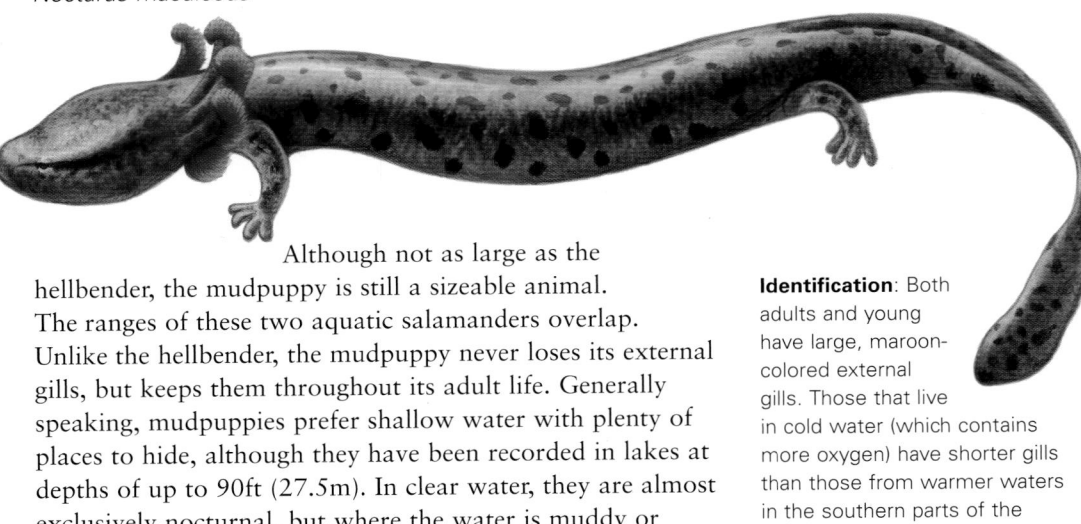

Although not as large as the hellbender, the mudpuppy is still a sizeable animal. The ranges of these two aquatic salamanders overlap. Unlike the hellbender, the mudpuppy never loses its external gills, but keeps them throughout its adult life. Generally speaking, mudpuppies prefer shallow water with plenty of places to hide, although they have been recorded in lakes at depths of up to 90ft (27.5m). In clear water, they are almost exclusively nocturnal, but where the water is muddy or choked with weeds, they may sometimes be active by day. They mate in the fall or winter, and the females lay their eggs the following spring, attaching them to the undersides of large rocks. Unusually for amphibians, fertilization is internal.

Identification: Both adults and young have large, maroon-colored external gills. Those that live in cold water (which contains more oxygen) have shorter gills than those from warmer waters in the southern parts of the range. The tail is flattened, with fins on the upper and lower edges for swimming. There are four toes on each of the limbs, front and rear.

Distribution: Southern Quebec to southeast Manitoba, and south to Missouri and Georgia.
Habitat: Lakes, ponds, rivers, and streams.
Food: Aquatic invertebrates and small fish.
Size: Up to 13in (33cm).
Breeding: Females lay between 50 and 100 eggs in the spring. The mothers stay with their eggs and guard them until they hatch. This may take from 4 to 8 weeks.

REPTILES

Several reptiles live alongside North America's freshwater fish. Some of these reptiles prey on them and others compete with them for food. The most commonly seen freshwater reptiles are turtles, most of which eat fish when the opportunity arises. In fact, because of their habit of basking out of the water to warm up their bodies, reptiles are often much easier to spot than fish.

Painted turtle

Chrysemys picta

The painted turtle is the most common and widely distributed turtle in North America, occurring in lakes, ponds, rivers, and swamps from southern Canada to northern Mexico. It prefers quiet and relatively shallow waters over thick mud. Young turtles are carnivorous but as they grow older, they eat more and more plant material. Painted turtles spend a lot of time basking in the sun and seem to favor particular sites. Sometimes as many as 50 may be seen crowded onto a single log. In most parts of their range, they bask from sunrise until around nine or ten in the morning, then begin foraging. They rest during the middle of the day and then often forage again from late afternoon until the early evening. In the winter, these turtles become inactive, burying themselves in the mud at the bottom and absorbing oxygen through their skin.

Identification: One of North America's smaller turtles. The carapace is smooth and flattened, and ranges from green to black in color. Some populations have red markings on the carapace. The skin ranges from black to olive and has red and yellow stripes on the legs, tail, and neck. The head has yellow stripes only. Both sexes have visible tails.

Distribution: Occurs across North America, from the Atlantic to the Pacific coast.
Habitat: Shallow, slow-moving, or still fresh water.
Food: Aquatic invertebrates, fish, plant matter, and carrion.
Size: Carapace up to 10in (25cm) long.
Breeding: From May until July. Female digs nest in soil at the water's edge, lays eggs, then covers them up and leaves them to develop unguarded.

Common musk turtle

Sternotherus odoratus

This is another common North American turtle, although it is restricted to the eastern half of the continent. The common musk turtle inhabits shallow, quiet areas of lakes, ponds, and rivers. It forages for food on the bottom and is unusual in that it uses its legs to walk along the bottom rather than swimming. Like the painted turtle, it is an omnivore, feeding on a wide range of water plants and eating whatever animals it can catch. It also feeds on carrion. This turtle is perhaps best known for its unusual and unpleasant defense system. If it finds itself under attack, it releases a foul-smelling liquid from its musk glands. This habit has earned it another common name, the "stinkpot turtle." The males, in particular, are very aggressive and will not hesitate to bite.

Identification: The carapace is highly domed and has a distinct keel running along its length. It is black or brown in color. The skin ranges from dark olive to black. Two yellow lines run along the side of the head, one from the top of the eye and the other from the edge of the mouth, joining up at the base of the neck.

Distribution: Southern Ontario and Quebec, Canada, southward to Florida and Texas.
Habitat: Shallow still or slow-moving fresh water.
Food: Aquatic invertebrates, small fish, plant matter, and carrion.
Size: Carapace up to 5in (13cm) long.
Breeding: Females dig nests at the water's edge, sometimes communally. The eggs develop unguarded, and hatch after 75–80 days.

INDEX

PICTURE ACKNOWLEDGEMENTS

The publisher would like to thank the following for granting permission to use their photographs in this book.
Key: t= top; m=middle; b=bottom; l=left; r=right

Photographs
The following photograph was taken by Amy-Jane Beer and supplied courtesy of Origin Natural Science: 192bl.

Alamy; 174b, 175t, 175b, 181tl, 182ml, 182mr, 182bl, 182br, 184t, 185ml, 185mr, 185bl, 186tl, 188tr

Ardea; 104br, 105b, 108tr, 109br, 112t, 112bl, 113t, 113b, 115t, 115b, 116b, 117t, 117m, 119, 120b, 121tr

Image Quest Marine; 172t, 172b, 173t, 173b, 174 all, 175all, 177all, 178l, 178r (panel), 179all, 180mr: Masha Ushioda; 181bl: Carlos Villoch; 183all, 184all, 185t, 185b, 186 (panel): Hal Beral/V&W; 187bl: Carlos Villoch; 187br: Peter Herring; 188t: Jez Tryner; 188bl: James D. Watt; 188br: Peter Parks; 189tr: Roger Steene; 189br: Peter Parks; and 194–5: Carlos Villoch.

Istock; 2, 6tr, 6bl, 7tl, 7tr, 7b, 10, 22bl, 29br, 37tl, 37tr, 37bl, 106tm, 108tr, 113t, 122, 170, 188b, 189tl, 189tr, 189b, 192t, 194, endpaper

marinecreatures.com; Rowan Byrne, 181tl, 181tr, 181ml, 181mr, 187tl, 187tr, 189 (panel) and 193 (all).

NHPA; 22tr, 23tl, 23tm, 30tr 30b, 31b, 32t, 32b, 33tl, 34t, 36t, 36b

Oxford Scientific; 101, 106t, 107tl, 107ml, 109bl, 111tr, 111b, 114t, 117b, 120t, 121tl, 121b

Illustrators: Mike Atkinson, Peter Barret, Penny Brown, Peter Bull, Vanessa Card, Jim Channell, Felicity Rose Cole, Julius Csotonyi, Anthony Duke, John Francis, Stuart Jackson-Carter, Paul Jones, Martin Knowelden, Jonathan Latimer, Stephen Lings, Richard Orr, Denys Ovenden, Andrew Robinson, Mike Saunders, Sarah Smith and Studio Galante.